MEDIEVAL WARFARE

A HISTORY

MEDIEVAL WARFARE

A HISTORY

Edited by
MAURICE KEEN

OXFORD
UNIVERSITY PRESS

OXFORD
UNIVERSITY PRESS

Great Clarendon Street, Oxford OX2 6DP
Oxford University Press is a department of the University of Oxford.
It furthers the University's objective of excellence in research, scholarship, and education by publishing worldwide in

Oxford New York

Athens Auckland Bangkok Bogotá Buenos Aires Calcutta
Cape Town Chennai Dar es Salaam Delhi Florence Hong Kong Istanbul
Karachi Kuala Lumpur Madrid Melbourne Mexico City Mumbai
Nairobi Paris São Paulo Singapore Taipei Tokyo Toronto Warsaw

and associated companies in Berlin Ibadan

Oxford is a registered trade mark of Oxford University Press
in the UK and certain other countries

Published in the United States
by Oxford University Press Inc., New York

First published 1999

British Library Cataloguing in Publication Data

Data available

Library of Congress Cataloging in Publication Data

Data available

ISBN-0-19-820639-9

1 3 5 7 9 10 8 6 4 2

Typeset by Jayvee, Trivandrum, India
Printed in Great Britain
on acid-free paper by
Bookcraft Ltd.
Midsomer Norton,
Somerset

Frontispiece: battle scenes from the Courtrai Chest, carved in the early fourteenth century to commemorate the victory of the Flemings over the French at Courtrai, 11 July 1302 (see pp 113–14, 137–42). The chest was found in the early twentieth century at a farmhouse at Stanton St John, Oxfordshire, the property of New College, Oxford, and is now in the Warden's Lodgings there: its previous history is unknown.

EDITOR'S PREFACE

WARFARE was a formative influence on the civilization and the social structures of the European middle ages. Its history in that period is in consequence of high significance alike for those who are interested in the middle ages for themselves and for their legacy, and for those whose interest is in war and its place in the story of human development. The twelve of us who have collaborated in the writing of this book have sought to bear both these parties in mind. We have also borne much in mind the richness of the material that can illustrate visually the importance of warfare to lives and minds in the medieval age: castles which still stand; artefacts and archaeological remains; tombs and monumental brasses depicting warriors in their armour; vignettes of battle and campaign in illuminated manuscripts. Our book has been conceived and planned not just as a history, but as an illustrated history.

The book is divided into two parts, the first chronological, the second thematic. In the first part a series of chapters explores the impact of wars and fighting over time, from the Carolingian period down to the end of the Hundred Years War. There follow in the second part thematic discussions of specific aspects of warfare and its conduct: castles and sieges; war-horses and armour; mercenaries; war at sea; and the fortunes of the civilian in wartime.

In the process of putting the book together a great many obligations have been incurred, which must be gratefully acknowledged. We are all of us indebted to the successive editors at the Oxford University Press who watched over our work, Tony Morris, Anne Gelling, Anna Illingworth, and Dorothy McLean. We owe a major debt of gratitude to Sandra Assersohn, for her wise and patient help in the quest for apposite illustrations; and to Frank Pert who compiled the index. Each of us has besides debts of personal gratitude to friends and colleagues who read our contributions in draft and offered their advice and criticism. My own debt as editor is above all to my fellow contributors, who have worked together with such courtesy and despatch, from the book's conception to its completion. We all hope the results may prove worth the generosity of those who have done so much to help us.

MAURICE KEEN

CONTENTS

LIST OF MAPS AND FIGURES

LIST OF CONTRIBUTORS

Christopher Allmand	Emeritus Professor of Medieval History, University of Liverpool
Andrew Ayton	Senior Lecturer in History, University of Hull
Howard B. Clarke	Statutory Lecturer in Medieval History, University College, Dublin
Peter Edbury	Reader in History, University of Wales, Cardiff
Felipe Fernández-Armesto	Member of the Modern History Faculty, Oxford
John Gillingham	Emeritus Professor of History, London School of Economics
Norman Housley	Professor of History, University of Leicester
Richard L. C. Jones	Research Officer, Sussex Archaeological Society
Maurice Keen	Tutorial Fellow in Medieval History, Balliol College, Oxford
Michael Mallett	Professor of History, University of Warwick
Timothy Reuter	Professor of Medieval History, University of Southampton
Clifford J. Rogers	Assistant Professor of History, United States Military Academy, West Point

1 INTRODUCTION: WARFARE AND THE MIDDLE AGES

MAURICE KEEN

THE philosophical tradition of what we call the Western world had its origins in ancient Greece, its jurisprudential tradition in classical Rome. Christianity, the religion of the West, was nursed towards its future spiritual world status in the shelter of Roman imperial domination. Yet the political map of Europe, the heartland of Western civilization, bears little relation to that of the classical Hellenistic and Roman world. Its outlines were shaped not in classical times, but in the middle ages, largely in the course of warfare. That warfare, brutal, chaotic, and at times seemingly universal, is historically important not only for its significance in defining the boundaries and regions of the European future. Fighting in the medieval period, in the course of regional defence against incursions of non-Christian peoples with no background or connection with the former Roman world, and in the course of wars of expansion into territories occupied by other peoples, both Christian and non-Christian, and their absorption, played a vital role in the preservation for the future West of its cultural inheritance from antiquity. It also furthered the development of technologies that the antique world had never known.

Because the notion of sovereign governments with an exclusive right to war-making was in the early middle ages effectively absent and only developed slowly during their course, medieval wars came in all shapes and sizes. To Honoré Bouvet, writing on war in the later fourteenth century, the spectrum seemed so wide that he placed at the one extreme its cosmic level—'I ask in what place war was first found, and I disclose to you it was in Heaven, when our Lord God drove out the wicked angels'— and at the other the confrontation of two individuals in judicial duel by wager of battle. In between, he and his master John of Legnano placed a whole series of levels of human wars, graded according to the authority required to licence them and the circumstances which would render participation in them legitimate. For the historian, it is easy to think of alternative approaches to categorization to this that Bouvet offered to his contemporaries: indeed the problem is that there are almost too many possibilities to choose from.

The middle ages witnessed great defensive wars, or series of wars, to resist invasions, by Vikings and Magyars for instance in the ninth and tenth centuries, or, later, against the Ottoman Turks in Eastern Europe. There were wars of expansion, the Norman conquests of England and Southern Italy, for example, and the German conquests of former Slav territories east of the Elbe. There were also, of course, the crusades. Under that head must be reckoned not only the crusades to Palestine, but the wars for the reconquest of Spain from the Moors and for the attempted conquest of once Byzantine lands in Greece, the Balkans, and Asia Minor. Crusades, indeed, offer a good illustration of the difficulties of tidy categorization. Because the popes, in the course of their long struggle with the emperors for universal authority in Christendom, came often to give the status of crusader (with its formal privileges and indulgences) to those who would serve them against their imperial rivals (as also to those prepared to fight other excommunicates, heretics, or schismatics within the Christian homeland), crusading war can blend easily into the history of the major internal confrontations of Europe, which did so much to shape its future political map.

In looking at these confrontations, the kind of approach to categorization adopted by Bouvet, with its emphasis on the authority required to make war lawful and on the legitimacy of participation, does become useful. Looking at it in his way, one can place at one extreme what I have called the great confrontations, wars waged on the authority of popes, kings, and princes. Notable among these were the struggles between popes and emperors of the period 1077–1122 (the Wars of Investiture) and of the Hohenstaufen period (between 1164 and 1250): the series of wars (which grew out of them) that we call the War of the Sicilian Vespers, and their subsequent ramifications (1282–1302, and beyond): the great Hundred Years War of England and France (1337–1453). At the other end of the scale stand endless petty confrontations, often amounting to no more than family feuds between aggressive local lords or castellans, but potentially not much less devastating than great wars for the welfare of local people. In between there were wars between protagonists at every level of domination, between rival lords at comital, ducal, or princely level in competition for land and inheritances, and between rival cities; and between protagonists at different levels of dominance, of leagues of barons against kings (as in England in King John's time and in the time of Simon de Montfort, and later in the Wars of the Roses), of leagues of cities against their overlords (as of the Lombard League against the Emperor Frederick I), and endless individual baronial rebellions against overlords who they claimed had oppressed them or had infringed their rights. The resort to violence was a ready one in the middle ages, at every level of authority.

The difficulty with this sort of classification is that it can be very difficult to keep the categories apart. In medieval political conditions, greater struggles and lesser rivalries very easily blended into one another, though without, in most cases, one fully absorbing the other. This was a consequence of underlying conditions and the limitations of even the most effective and authoritative of medieval power structures. Between the time of Charlemagne and the later middle ages, virtually no royal, princely, or papal government had the resources in terms of money, manpower, and supply to sustain on its own continuous, large-scale hostilities over an extended period. The solution to the problem was obvious, to find allies whose interests might induce them to join in whatever cause was at stake at their own expense and for their own advantage. Such a struggle as the Wars of Investiture between the popes and the German Salian Emperors Henry IV and Henry V had an almost infinite capacity to draw other parties and their quarrels into its orbit; Saxon and princely rebels against Salian kingship, Norman adventurers in South Italy seeking superior sanction for their conquests, Patarene anti-clericals at odds in Milan with episcopal authority. The later, Hohenstaufen chapter of the papal-imperial rivalry illustrates the same point in a different but comparable way. The party labels Guelf and Ghibelline which loom so large in the story of the wars of Italy in the thirteenth and fourteenth centuries originally denoted theoretically the allies and supporters of the church and the pope (Guelfs) and of the emperor (Ghibellines). In fact from the start they were collective labels for the rival lords, rival city governments, and rival family factions which the two great protagonists succeeded in enlisting to the aid of their respective causes because they were at each other's throats anyway. Long after the main struggle had been decided against the Empire in the later thirteenth century, Guelfs and Ghibellines continued to league together and to fight one another under the same old labels. Wars tended constantly to spread outwards from their epicentres as well as inward towards them. This made it very hard to delimit and control their scale, impact, and duration, let alone to define their 'level' in terms of categorization.

War is thus central to the narrative political story of the middle ages. It is also central to their cultural history. Indeed, their martial secular culture may arguably be claimed to be, along with their Christian ideology, one of the two chief defining features of their civilization. The middle ages are often recalled as the Age of Faith: they are often also recalled as the Age of Chivalry, or as the Feudal Age.

In a famous triad, the thirteenth-century author of the *Chanson des Saisnes* (the 'Song of the Saxon Wars') declared that there were three 'matters' of which every man should know something: the matter of Britain, the matter of France, and the matter of Rome the Great. The matter of Britain meant the stories of King Arthur, and of the adventures of his knights in battles and tournaments. The matter of France meant the stories of Charlemagne and his paladins, and their part in wars against Saracens and in the internecine struggles of the Carolingian nobility. The matter of Rome the Great meant the history of Greece and Rome, of the wars of Alexander and Caesar and, most emphatically, the Trojan war. These three matters did indeed become the most staple themes of secular aristocratic literary creation from the twelfth century on. Lays and romances based on them inevitably focused around warfare, around accounts of wars, battles, tournaments, and single combats (in the medieval versions of the classical stories, their antique heroes appear as knights in contemporary armour, with fine war horses and heraldic blazon on their shields). Literature thus became a powerful influence in reinforcing and fostering for the secular aristocracy a martial value system whose bellicosity should not be underestimated. Along with courage, loyalty, and liberality, it set a very high price on physical strength, good horsemanship, and dexterity with weapons, and on impetuous ferocity in combat. This value system was what we call the code of chivalry, and these military virtues and skills were the defining features of its cult of honour.

Alongside this literary triad of the author of the *Chanson des Saisnes* may be set another triad, the traditional medieval division of Christian society into three orders or estates. These were, first, the clergy, whose business was with prayer and with pastoral ministration to society's spiritual needs; secondly, the warriors, whose business it was with their swords to uphold justice, protect the weak, and to defend church and homeland; and, third, the labourers, by whose toil the land was tilled and whose work provided for the material needs both of themselves and of the two other, more socially elevated estates. First clearly articulated by King Alfred in his translation of Boethius, this conception of society in terms of three functionally related estates achieved over time such wide currency as to seem almost a truism: 'you know that there be three estates of men', the poet Gower wrote in the fourteenth century. It was of course at best an ideal formulation which never accurately reflected the facts of life and of social gradation. The specific justification that it offered for the warrior's calling as a Christian vocation with a vital social function was however profoundly influential. It underpinned the secular aristocracy's self-image as a hereditary martial estate and gave a firm ideological grounding to its claims to status and privilege.

It is natural and appropriate to associate this threefold vision of society and its view of the warrior's place in it, with what historians call feudalism. True, the military model of feudalism, which has been widely used in order to explain relations in the upper echelons of medieval society in terms of a hierarchic structure of contracts, based on grants of land by superior lords to lesser men in return for military service, is now looked at askance by many scholars. Nonetheless it remains true that in the relations between a great (or even not so great) lord and his subordinates, whether as his bodyguards or household servants or tenants or kinsmen, or as in later medieval England as retainers, military service throughout the middle ages was consistently presented as a specially prized and dignified form of service. Whether we call them feudal or not, notions of lordship and clientage to which military service was central permeated medieval conceptions of social relationships at the aristocratic, landowning level, and to a considerable degree, at other levels as well.

An acceptance, in some measure at least, of the aristocrat's right of resort to military violence was the natural obverse to this perception of obligations. That is what lies behind the tone of moral confidence with which nobles tenaciously resisted (for instance in France in the time of Louis IX) attempts to curb their customary seigneurial right to pursue their own claims by private wars on their own motion (in what is sometimes called 'feudal' war), notwithstanding the adverse social consequences which could so obviously stem from the privilege. The dignity associated with the warrior's functional status could serve as a reminder of his ethical and social duties: it could also promote more wars.

Both feudalism and chivalry—or something rather like them—were features of medieval civilization in its *longue durée*. There are variations in their specific modes of manifestation over time and from region to region, but they or something like them are always there. One reason for this was the very slow rate of technological advance in the art of warfare during the middle ages. There were developments, and important ones at that: the extended use of stone in fortification (especially in castle building): new techniques for manufacturing better armour for both fighting men and horses: new sophistications in the design of crossbows and longbows. Yet there was nothing that altered radically and rapidly what John Keegan has called 'the face of battle'—until the coming of gunpowder artillery and of new techniques in ship design and navigation at the end of the medieval period. The cultural perception of the warrior aristocrat and of the code of behaviour and social standing appropriate to the military calling did not shift very markedly or very fast, largely because the conditions of the martial context of battle, to which a warrior was expected to respond, shifted only very slowly.

A second reason for the longevity of the chivalrous ideal and of feudal factors (or comparable ones) is more complex, and requires more careful consideration. In the twelfth century there was a real breakthrough, not in the art of war but in bureaucracy and the techniques of literate administration. The exponential growth in governmental records of all sorts from that point on bears impressive witness to its impact. This breakthrough opened new vistas of possibility for central governmental supervision down to local level (provided the 'centre' was not too remote geographically). Static administrative headquarters, such as Paris and Westminster, acquired a new importance. Princely rulers, with the aid of their professional clerical servants, gained a new capacity to supervise legal processes and local conflicts of interest, and above all to tax (and to borrow, offering anticipated revenue as collateral) on a greatly extended scale. This should have had a very important effect on the capacity of such rulers to plan, organize, and direct large-scale military operations, and indeed it did. Yet in the context of warfare that effect was in many respects secondary, especially once the scene changed from the planning table to the operational field. The impact on traditional martial attitudes and behaviour in belligerent conditions was in consequence less sharp than one might expect it to have been, and only began to be fully apparent after a considerable time lapse, arguably not until well into the fifteenth century.

One positive and more immediate effect of the new administrative potential of government was that rulers such as the kings of France and of England in the thirteenth, fourteenth, and fifteenth centuries found themselves able to gather large armies from a wider recruiting base than had their immediate predecessors, and to entertain higher and better defined territorial and dynastic ambitions for the outcome of successful war. They also found it possible, through literate publicity, organized preaching, and other brands of stage management, to reach out for a more conscious and patriotic collective response to their war-making from their subjects, and thus to justify more imperative fiscal demands. These were among the most important factors which, in the later middle ages, were visibly accelerating the definition on the map of the future power structures of Europe.

Greatly improved and professionalized though administrative services became, they nonetheless still had their limits. War is and always has been a highly cost-intensive business. For a very long time—in effect till the end of the middle ages—the new fiscal and monetary resources into which rulers were now able to tap, while adequate to pay for military service during actual campaigns, were not sufficient to enable them to maintain standing, permanent forces on any really significant scale, let alone to train them. They could of course employ mercenaries, whose captains came ready equipped with standing forces and technical military skill. Demand here helped to create supply: but mercenaries did not come cheap, and there were other problems, notably what to do with them when a campaign was concluded. In order to raise armies late medieval rulers had in consequence still to rely primarily, as their predecessors had done, on their greater subjects, who had the wealth to equip themselves and their followers, an established social charisma, and a nexus of connections among kinsmen, vassals, tenants, and servants which made them ideal recruiting agents. Untrained in the formal sense, these lords and magnates, along with their followers, and like their ancestors before them, were men who had been brought up physically to martial exercises, to horsemanship, hunting, and jousting, and civilly to a sense of social obligation with very strong martial resonances. In the field, the service of such men and their followers was a very adequate substitute for a professional army. What assured their availability, however, even now that they were usually paid or promised pay for a campaign's duration, was not that they had 'taken the king's shilling', but their traditional sense of their standing in society and its functional obligations. In these conditions, it was positively in a ruler's interest to cultivate rather than to castigate their traditional outlook, to present himself as the companion and generous patron of his martial, aristocratic subjects, to heed their sensibilities and maintain their privileges. Otherwise he risked losing control of his war machine. Small wonder then that it was only very slowly and partially that the new administrative capacities of government began to have a significant effect on feudal and chivalrous manners of living, and on the accompanying mental attitudes that had been formed and forged in earlier times.

Thus for a long time it seemed necessary, from a ruler's point of view, to accept the price that was attached to this condition of things, alternatives to which were in any case perceived only dimly, if at all. That price was the ongoing risk that the martial energies and resources of a ruler's greater subjects continued to be all too easily channelled into causes other than his, into crusades, into confrontations with fellow magnates, into private territorial adventures—and rebellion. That is a chief reason why the middle ages, to their close, were so dominated by wars at so many levels.

But time passes. Lessons of experience sank in, and perceptions of new potentialities sharpened. At the end of the middle ages rulers were getting richer and were learning more about how to flex their governmental and administrative muscle. One symptom of this was the more strenuous and better directed effort made to control the right of their great noblemen to make war other than by their leave: another (partly as a means to that first objective) was that we find them (or some of them, the Kings of France and Spain in particular) beginning to establish large-scale military forces on a standing, paid basis. Chronologically, this opening of the story of professional, national standing armies coincides with the time in which technological advances in gunnery and navigation were beginning to have significant impact—and when a good many historians recognize the passing of the age of chivalry. Around 1500, shifts in conditions which had been from a military point of view defining features of the medieval period were beginning to accelerate. That is why this book ends there.

The fact that warfare and the warrior ethos were so central to the secular history of the middle ages, political, social, and cultural, has shaped the planning of this book. It is divided into two parts. The aim of the contributors to Part I has been to bring out, stage by stage and age by age, something of the societal experience of war, and of the impact of its demands on human resources and human endurance. Contributors of the first four chapters of Part II have sought to trace thematically the most important developments in the art of warfare: in fortification and siegecraft, in the role and equipment of the armoured cavalryman, in the employment of mercenary forces. The penultimate chapter examines the gradual emergence of an articulate approach to the non-combatant; and the final one considers some of the factors that were changing the face of battle at the close of the middle ages.

Limitations of space have meant that we have not been able to give separate attention to as many themes and topics as we would have wished. Ideally, this book would include individual chapters on, for instance, medieval opinions about the just war, on feudal relations and changing perceptions of their military significance, on chivalry and the tournament, on rights to loot and ransoms, and on taxation for war purposes. We have done our best to incorporate some treatment of these and other matters into the framework of various chapters, but inevitably there has been some skimping on topics that we recognize as important.

One omission imposed by lack of space is the absence of any in-depth treatment of the Byzantine face of medieval warfare. To have attempted to do justice to it would have meant placing in context a whole series of great wars, in the Balkans, Asia Minor, Syria, and beyond, which have no direct connection with the warfare discussed in this volume. It would have meant, too, outlining a structure of military organization radically different from that of the contemporary Western European world—a structure moreover that under force of circumstances was altered over time almost beyond recognition. So the telling of that story will have to wait for the publication of the forthcoming illustrated history of Byzantium from Oxford.

Nevertheless one very broad and general point seems worth making here. The Byzantine story is in many ways the reverse of that which this volume seeks to trace. At the beginning of the period here covered the Byzantine Empire was a major territorial power, served by a sophisticated bureaucracy and with an effective system of tax collection. Its army was a powerful military machine, with an established provincial command structure, readily mobilizable for large-scale campaigns. In his *Precepts*, the great tenth-century soldier Emperor Nicephorus Phocas was able to outline for the army principles of recruitment and training, to detail the arms and equipment needed by respectively light and heavy cavalry, infantry, javeliners, and archers, and to discuss with assurance tactics and strategy. Yet the eleventh century would see the erosion of imperial authority through the growing independence of the great, semi-feudal landowners of the provinces, and the loss of control of the Anatolian hinterland as a result of Seljuk incursions, and, at its end, a new threat developing from the West. In the twelfth century, relations with the crusading West deteriorated steadily, and in 1204 the army of the Fourth Crusade stormed and seized Constantinople. Though the Byzantines did succeed in recovering their capital city in 1261, theirs was thereafter an empire in name only. They failed to regain Greece, and their last strongholds in Asia Minor were soon lost to the Ottomans. At the end there was still an administrative bureaucracy in Constantinople but there was no longer a recruiting base for an army. Well before the time that the emergent Western monarchies began to show signs of an ability to curb effectively aristocratic martial independence, Byzantium had lost control of its provinces to regional great nobles, and in the Balkans to warlike invaders, Slav, Bulgar, and Serb. In the end all went down before the Turk, whom the Westerners succeeded ultimately in halting, a little within the line of the Danube.

To both these contrasted histories, Western and Eastern, Latin and Greek, warfare and its outcomes provide an essential connecting theme. It is now time to turn to look in more detail at the Western side of the story, with which this book is principally concerned, beginning in the time of Charlemagne, whose eighth-century Frankish empire resembled that of contemporary Byzantium perhaps only in that both were essentially military powers.

PART I

PHASES OF MEDIEVAL WARFARE

2 CAROLINGIAN AND OTTONIAN WARFARE

TIMOTHY REUTER

WARFARE was perhaps the most dominant concern of the political elites of the eighth, ninth, and tenth centuries. Other medieval social orders have been described as 'a society organized for war': Carolingian and Ottonian societies were largely organized *by* war. The political community, when it came together, was often called 'the army' even when it was not functioning as one. And usually it did come together in order to function as one. Massive coercive force was repeatedly deployed against subordinate peoples on the frontiers, with considerable success. It was also deployed, with less consistent success, against invading predators—Northmen (Vikings) along the Atlantic and North Sea coastlines from the early ninth century, Muslims along the Mediterranean coastline from the last years of the eighth century, Magyars from the Danube valley from the last years of the ninth century. And of course it was deployed against rivals within the Frankish world, by both rulers and magnates. Its deployment required substantial investment in organization (taxation and other forms of funding, transport, command structures), physical resources (food, water, equipment), and manpower (conscripted and 'voluntary'). Increasingly also investment in defensive fortifications was required. Success in warfare brought prestige, authority, and power beyond the immediate results of the campaigning itself; failure similarly risked a crisis in the legitimacy and stability of political authority.

The significance of warfare becomes obvious as soon as we examine the course of late Frankish and post-Frankish history. The eighth century saw an almost unchecked sequence of Frankish military successes under the leadership of what was to become the Carolingian family, acting first as mayors of the palace under the titular rulership of the last members of the Merovingian dynasty, from 751 onwards as kings, then finally, after Charles the Great's coronation by the pope in 800, as emperors, with a Roman resonance to their title and dominion. Looking back from the early ninth century, the Carolingians saw their own rise as dating from the battle of Tetry in 687, when Pippin II and the eastern Franks had defeated the western Franks. Much of the military activity of the period up to the death of Charles Martel in 741 was devoted to internal consolidation: eliminating the 'tyrants' within the kingdom, as Charles the Great's biographer Einhard put it. But there were other campaigns: campaigns to re-establish authority over the formerly dependent peoples in Alamannia and Bavaria; a major war of conquest taking Frankish control down through Burgundy and the Rhône valley to the Mediterranean coast; successful battles against Islamic invading forces in 732/3 and in 737 which ended the possibility of Islamic expansion beyond the Pyrenees.

The two generations which followed saw the final subjugation of Alamannia and Bavaria as well as of the remainder of southern France, the conquest of the Lombard kingdom of Italy in a lightning campaign in 774, and the conquest and Christianization of the Saxons in a series of campaigns between 772 and 785, 792–3, and 798–803. In the 790s, the major potential rival to Frankish hegemony in Continental Europe, the Balkan empire of the Avars, was crushed in a few brief campaigns, and the wealth accumulated by the Avars in more than two centuries of plundering raids and tribute-taking was carted off to Francia, where Charlemagne distributed it to churches and to his military following.

By the early ninth century, the Franks and their rulers had largely run out of opponents against whom they could profitably campaign. The maximum extent of earlier Frankish domination in the late sixth and early seventh century had been re-established and put on a quite different footing. The Celtic and Slav peripheries along the Breton and east Frankish frontiers offered only meagre opportunities. Neither the Danes to the north of Saxony, nor the Byzantine outposts and Lombard principalities to the south of central Italy, nor the emergent Muslim powers in Spain were attractive targets: wealth was there, but not for the taking. The Franks never campaigned in the Danish peninsula, nor, after the first decade of the ninth century, against the Byzantines in Italy. The territorial gains made by the Franks in what was to become Catalonia were made, after Louis the Pious's campaigns in 801–2 and 810, by local forces rather than by the Frankish kings themselves.

Yet the apparatus of military power built up in the course of eighth-century expansion still needed maintaining. Increasingly, the Frankish elite turned in on itself. Between 830 and the end of the century, a substantial proportion of

THE WARS OF CHARLEMAGNE, 770–814

all campaigns fought by Frankish forces were fought against other Frankish forces. In the early 830s and early 840s two extensive civil wars turned on the succession to Louis the Pious, Charlemagne's son and successor: these culminated in the partition of the Frankish empire into three at the treaty of Verdun (843); Charles the Bald, Louis's youngest son, became king of west Francia (what would become France); Louis became king of the eastern Franks (what would become Germany), and Lothar, the eldest, ruler of a corridor of lands stretching between these two kingdoms down to Italy, the 'middle kingdom'. Further partitions followed, and further disputes: the attempts in 857–8, 876, and 879–80 by the rulers of east or west Francia to take control of the other's kingdom; the series of campaigns between 861 and 880 to decide the distribution of the middle kingdom; and the fighting between 888 and 895–6 to settle the nature and extent of the hegemony to be exercised by Arnulf, king of east Francia, over the remaining Frankish kingdoms.

Increasingly also, the Franks and their rulers were themselves threatened militarily. It was probably news of their own successes and the wealth they had accumulated which attracted predators: attacks by Islamic pirates on the Mediterranean coastline of the Frankish empire are recorded from the late

WARFARE IN THE EAST FRANKISH LANDS, 930–970

eighth century, becoming frequent from the middle of the ninth century, especially on the southern French coast and in southern Italy. At about the same time, slightly after their first recorded appearances in the British Isles, Viking incursions began along the Channel and Atlantic coasts. These too increased sharply from the 840s onwards, with brief remissions in the 870s and 890s. Finally, two decades later, the east Frankish lands began to suffer from the incursions of the Magyars, a horsed confederation originating from the Russian steppes with a formidable capacity for swift movement and effective deployment of archery and cavalry, for scattering to ravage over a wide area and for reconcentrating their forces with unexpected speed when opposed.

The patterns established in the later ninth century—warfare against invaders or rivals—continued to hold good in the tenth century in the western and southern parts of the Carolingian empire, west Francia, and Italy. Raids on west Francia declined, without ever entirely ceasing; warfare against rivals increased to compensate, and, in an anticipation of the world of the high middle ages, moved down a level from wars between kings to wars between princes and magnates. In Italy Carolingian-style disputes over kingship continued until the mid-960s, and predatory Muslim raiding along the coast and in the south was a problem for even longer.

In east Francia, however, events took a rather different turn. Under the leadership of the Liudolfing frontier dukes of Saxony, the kingdom was reshaped and reforged in the first half of the tenth century. In some ways this remaking resembled that carried out by the early Carolingian leaders in Francia two centuries earlier, and it too culminated in an imperial coronation, that of Otto I in 962. Carolingian success against Islamic invaders was mirrored by Ottonian success against Magyar horsemen, at Riade (933) and on the Lechfeld, south of Augsburg (955). But there were also significant differences. Carolingian imperialism had brought about major disturbances in the patterns of landholding and power within the Frankish lands. The Liudolfing/Ottonian reconstruction was a more peaceful affair; there were few battles and campaigns, not many magnates lost power. Ottonian hegemony was based on the acknowledgement of military success by the political community of tenth-century east Francia, not on the reshaping of that community.

Although the Ottonians campaigned successfully beyond their frontiers, as the Carolingians had done in their heyday, the campaigns of expansion on the eastern frontier were in general much more local affairs. Charles the Great had been able to raise large armies from most of his kingdom to campaign against the Saxons, and even in the era of Carolingian decline a Charles III or an Arnulf could still mount large-scale campaigns against the Vikings with forces drawn from a number of regions. By contrast, the campaigning on the eastern frontier in the tenth and early eleventh century was much less large-scale. Very occasionally, as in some of the campaigns against the Magyars (notably those leading to the Magyar defeats at Riade and on the Lechfeld), or in some of the campaigns on the north-eastern frontier under Otto III and Henry II, rulers drew on forces from most or the whole of their kingdom, but many expeditions were local, Saxon affairs; even the rulers themselves did not always participate. Large-scale forces were assembled for the asserting of hegemony within the former Frankish world; for the Ottonian invasions of west Francia in 946 and 978, and for the Italian expeditions from 950 onwards.

It is easy enough to give a summary account of the importance of war in this period, but as soon as we start to go beyond this we find that there are great gaps in our knowledge and understanding. Perhaps the most striking are those in our knowledge of the practical conduct of war itself. There is no shortage of warfare in the narrative sources for the period. The major works of semi-official Carolingian historical writing—the continuators of Fredegar in the eighth century, the authors of the *Royal Frankish Annals* and their continuators in ninth-century east and west Francia—as well as many more 'private' accounts, like the so-called *Annals of Xanten* and *Annals of Saint-Vaast*, give much attention to campaigning. The great tenth- and early eleventh-century histories devote much of their pages to warfare: Regino of Prüm, looking back on Carolingian decline since Fontenoy from his early tenth-century Lotharingian exile; Widukind of Corvey, charting the course of the Saxons' rise to empire; Liudprand of Cremona, an Italian follower of Otto I to whom we owe much of our knowledge of Italian warfare between the late ninth and the mid-tenth century; Flodoard and Richer of Rheims, describing west Frankish warfare in the tenth century, the one in a dry bare-bones narrative, the other with Sallustian brilliance; Thietmar of Merseburg, an east Saxon bishop who had campaign experience and came from a great warrior family.

Yet the 'face of battle', in John Keegan's memorable phrase, generally eludes us when we read these works. Even the very rare eyewitness accounts do not help. On 25 June 841 the followers of Louis and Charles, rulers in east and west Francia, fought a major battle at Fontenoy against the followers of Lothar, emperor and ruler of Italy, which was to determine the outcome of the succession crisis created by the death of Louis the Pious in 840. One of the participants, Nithard, like the leaders a descendant of Charles the Great, has left a description of the battle:

After the negotiations had failed, Charles and Louis rose in the dawn light and occupied a hill close to Lothar's camp; there they awaited his arrival at the second hour of daylight according to the oath their representatives had sworn, with about a third of their forces. When both sides were present, they joined battle at the stream of the Burgundiones with hard fighting. Louis and Lothar fought hard at the place called Brittas, where Lothar, being overcome, turned tail. The part of the army which Charles had led to the place called Fagit in the common tongue fled; the part which had thrown itself against Adelhard and the others and to which I gave not a little assistance with God's help, also fought hard; each side seemed at times to have the upper hand, but in the end all on Lothar's side fled.

The most striking thing about this narrative is its brevity. Nithard, who was to die in battle not long after he wrote these words, was an experienced warrior, but he evidently did not see the actual practice of war as something which needed lengthy description. The excerpt just translated takes up less than an eighth of the chapter in which Nithard describes the Fontenoy campaign; most of it is devoted to showing how Lothar delayed battle by spinning out negotiations until his ally Pippin had had time to join forces with him.

Warfare may have been the dominant concern of early medieval elites, but neither those who practised it, like Nithard, nor those who merely recorded it (often at some distance of either space or time or both) normally felt the need to articulate its meaning and the working assumptions with which they approached it. It was a practical, not a theoretical art. It is not only the direct experience of war itself which eludes us; contemporaries' assumptions about strategy and tactics were hardly ever articulated in forms which have come down to us. Occasionally we get a comment which shows that they could and did reflect on the practice of warfare. An account in the revised version of the *Royal Frankish Annals* of a battle between Franks and Saxons in 782 criticizes the defeated Franks for advancing at a gallop as if they were pursuing a defeated enemy rather than in line at a measured pace; Regino of Prüm describes a battle against the Northmen in Brittany in 890, in which the initially victorious Duke Vidicheil ignored the basic principle that one should not push a defeated enemy too far, to be annihilated when his opponents turned at bay and counter-attacked.

Yet such moments of explicit reflection are rare. Military treatises, like those which have survived in some numbers from ninth- and tenth-century Byzantium, are absent from the West in this period. The classical treatises of antiquity, by Vegetius and Frontinus, were indeed known and copied: Hrabanus Maurus, a mid-ninth-century archbishop of Mainz, produced a revised version of Vegetius' treatise with additions intended to adapt it to Frankish warfare; Bishop Frechulf of Lisieux produced a copy for the library of Charles the Bald. But the impulse behind this was perhaps as much antiquarian as practical: neither work circulated extensively in manuscript in the Carolingian

Opposing forces of cavalry meet in battle. The pictorial strategy is unclear: have the forces on the right been penetrated by their opponents, or are they turning and fleeing? All warriors here use lances (brandished overhead, not couched, as they have no stirrups), though the siege from the same artist (*see p. 29*) shows the use of long-swords on horseback.

Facing: together with mailed byrnies (*see p. 22*) it was expensive layered long-swords like this which gave Frankish military forces their technological edge. Such swords, often with an inscription (probably the manufacturer's, not the owner's, as here) on the blade, have survived in small numbers from the ninth and tenth centuries in church treasuries and in larger numbers as casual finds.

period. The literature of antiquity served as a source of phrases and vocabulary rather than ideas for ninth- and tenth-century writers: Livy's account of early Roman history was plundered at will by the authors of the *Royal Frankish Annals* for their descriptions of campaigns. This absence of reflection creates two opposing dangers for the historian. The first is mistakenly to deduce from the fact that contemporaries did not record their thoughts on warfare that they had none, which gives us the notion of Carolingian and Ottonian armies as an undisciplined rabble. The second is to assume that we can fill out the silences in the record of their thinking with the timeless principles of warfare enunciated by the great modern military theorists from Clausewitz onwards, which gives us Carolingian and Ottonian campaigns as yet another illustration of staff college manuals.

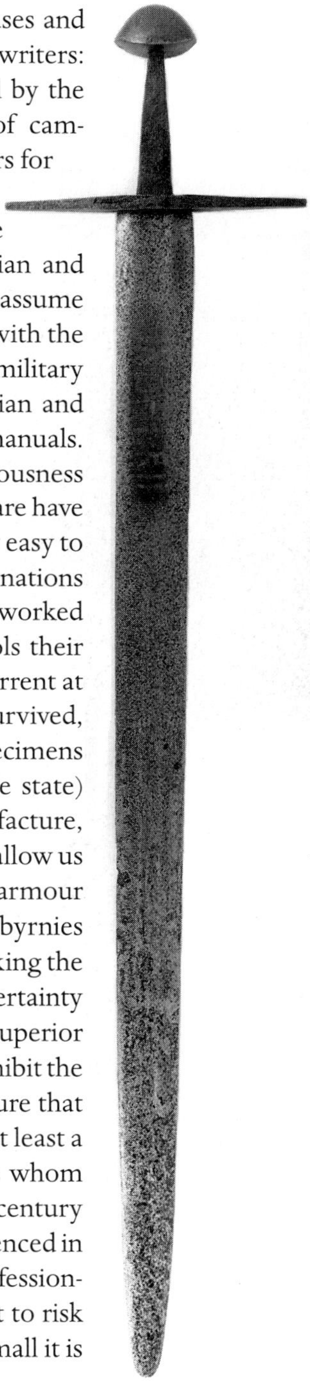

The gaps in our knowledge are not confined to the consciousness which lies behind action. Though the material remains of warfare have survived quite extensively from this period, they are not usually easy to date or interpret with confidence. A few manuscript illuminations show warriors and their arms, but since the artists frequently worked from earlier exemplars and the traditions of their own schools their work cannot always be taken as depicting the state of affairs current at the time they were working. Some arms and armour have survived, most notably swords and helmets, but since high-quality specimens (which are the most likely to have survived in a recognizable state) might be used and reused for a long period after their manufacture, they rarely come with the archaeological context which might allow us to interpret them more securely. We can list the weapons and armour in most frequent use—long-sword, short axe, bows, helmets, byrnies (leather jackets with armour plating, probably in this period taking the form of scales rather than of ring-mail), without having much certainty about how widespread their use was. We know, though, that superior military technology was vital. Carolingian rulers sought to prohibit the export of byrnies in particular, while themselves trying to ensure that members of their armies met basic standards of equipment—at least a bow, not merely a wooden stave. The 'unarmed' commoners whom Viking armies occasionally met and slaughtered in the ninth century have sometimes been taken by historians to have been inexperienced in fighting; but it is at least as likely that they were simply not professionally equipped. As late as 990 a Slav prince could be advised not to risk battle against an invading Saxon force because 'although it is small it is composed of excellent warriors, and all in iron'.

A good illustration of a mounted Frankish warrior from an early ninth-century psalter. It is the defensive armour which made warriors like this the equivalent of the tank in the ninth and tenth centuries: bossed shield and helmet, possibly leg-coverings, and a *brunia* or byrnie, a leather jacket with 'fish-scale' metal plates for protection against arrows and cutting weapons.

Much has not survived; we know virtually nothing about the physical appearance of Frankish shipping and Frankish siege machinery, for example, but we know that both existed, and indeed the expansion of the eighth century owed much to the Franks' ability to move heavy equipment against their opponents over long distances and deploy it effectively. The most spectacular example of military engineering was the failed attempt in 793 by Charles the Great to link Main and Danube with a canal, whose remains are still visible today. Fortified sites are better preserved, though here too there are problems. There are often disparities between what we know from written sources and the sites which survive on the ground and can be dated with confidence to within our period; and survival (or at least identified survival) is much more common in some areas than others: a number of English *burhs* survive in identifiable form from the campaigns of Alfred and his descendants against the Northmen, for example, but the archaeological record on the Continent is much less satisfactory. Thus, though we know that fortified bridges were very important in checking Viking incursions into west Francia in the 860s and 870s, there is little to show on the ground for these. King Henry I of east Francia is said to have instituted a series of large-scale fortifications, with groups of settler-warriors responsible for their upkeep and defence, as part of his strategy for ending the threat from Magyar raiders in the period 924–933. But although this sounds very like the West Saxon *burhs*, there are no equivalents of Wallingford in east Saxony or elsewhere in the east Frankish kingdom and indeed there is no site which all agree to have been one of Henry's fortifications.

It is therefore not easy to visualize warfare in this period, either from written descriptions or from its material remains. There is rather more evidence for its organization. This is particularly true of the Carolingian era. Here rulers like Charlemagne not only sought to ensure the preservation of older 'tribal' law-codes in writing, they also—especially in the period between about 780 and about 830, and in west Francia and Italy beyond that almost to the end of the ninth century—issued so-called 'capitularies', mixtures of admonitions, instructions, and regulations, many of which refer to such things as military obligation or the regulation of arms exports. From these, from scattered references in other sources to money taxes (especially *heribannum*, 'army-tax') and services (provision of carts and other transport; bridge- and fortress-work) imposed on the dependent population, and from the narrative sources, we can get a picture of Carolingian warfare in its heyday. Campaigns were prepared for at assemblies, often in late spring or early summer, at which rulers won

Bowmen played a significant role in Frankish warfare, though unlike Magyars Frankish archers usually fought on foot. Written references suggest that bowmen were of lesser standing than mounted warriors, but this early ninth-century psalter shows the same body armour found on the mounted warrior, and a cloak and brooch denoting high social status.

agreement and support for them. Carolingians could campaign at any time of the year, but the preferred period was August to October, after the new harvest and before the onset of winter. Campaigning took the form of assembling massive forces, which for the most important campaigns might be divided, perhaps as much because of the difficulties of feeding large bodies of troops as for any strategic considerations. These were deployed slowly and thoroughly in short campaigns, whose main aim was to lay waste opponents' strongholds and economic resources rather than crush opponents in battle. Such armies were vulnerable to guerilla attacks (as for example at Roncevaux in 778, where the Frankish rearguard was annihilated in a Basque ambush), or to bad weather, or to diseases amongst the horses or cattle they needed for transport. They were also inflexible: opponents capable of much faster movement (Magyars and Saracens), or movement over difficult terrain (Vikings) were hard for them to deal with.

Already by the later ninth century this kind of warfare was no longer the norm (except along stretches of the eastern frontier of the east Frankish kingdom), and by the Ottonian period the picture has become much less clear. Capitularies and other forms of legislation and regulation had by this time disappeared throughout the regions of the former Frankish empire. Taxes such as the *heribannum* continued to exist in name, but probably no longer had any serious connection with raising or supporting armies. Occasional survivals of documentary evidence have thus had to bear more weight than they probably can. For example, much discussion of Ottonian warfare has turned round the *indiculus loricatorum* ('list of armed warriors'), a document listing the military contingents to be provided from east Francia for a campaign in Italy. Internal evidence shows that it must have been used in connection with Otto II's Italian campaign of 980–3, but it is still unclear whether it refers to the initial contingent raised for his expedition or to reinforcements summoned later. Most of our information about tenth-century warfare comes from incidental details in narrative accounts.

Yet pessimism can be taken too far. However difficult it is to answer many of the traditional questions of military history, we still have enough evidence left to tackle the most fundamental ones: how armies were raised, and what purpose warfare served. How were armies raised? This is not easy to answer, and the numerous (and widely varying) solutions which have been offered in the course of a century and a half of the professional study of medieval history in many ways cloud the picture more than they paint it. Rather than take the reader through a lengthy account of the historiography, it seems more helpful to begin by discussing the different possible categories and the different types of warfare, for defence against incursions had quite different requirements from the armies raised to attack internal enemies or campaign beyond frontiers. From the point of view of a ruler, we can identify four main categories of fighting-men in this period: bodyguards and other household warriors; magnates (who might themselves bring other magnates and would certainly have had their own bodyguards and household warriors); conscript forces; and auxiliaries from outside the kingdom.

Like late Anglo-Saxon rulers, Carolingian and Ottonian rulers undoubtedly had a personal bodyguard which could also function at need as a rapid response force, a *scara* (meaning a squadron or troop; compare the modern German *Schar*). Such warriors are much less visible in the sources than were the housecarls of eleventh-century England, but they were certainly there: Carolingian rulers gave them gifts on regular occasions, and they were no less important in the tenth century. It was Otto I's bodyguards who foiled an attack on his life at the Easter celebrations of 941, and a Slav bodyguard who saved Otto II's life after the disastrous outcome of the battle of Cotrone against the Sicilian Muslims. There was certainly a tendency to use 'foreigners' for such purposes, as seen elsewhere in Europe at this time: the Anglo-Saxon rulers' housecarls, the Varangian guard of the eleventh-century Byzantine rulers (mainly Franks and Scandinavians), or the elite troops of the tenth-century Caliphs of Cordoba (mainly Slavs imported from the Frankish eastern frontier as slaves) are all examples of the technique. The well-born or the lucky might graduate from such permanent military duties to modest wealth in the form of an estate.

The personal bodyguards of rulers probably differed in size rather than composition from those of the magnates who turned out in Carolingian and Ottonian armies, though these will have drawn less on foreigners and more on their own followers, perhaps also on outlaws and possibly slaves, for such contingents. 'Magnates' is a catch-all term: it includes great secular officials like counts, great ecclesiastics like bishops and the abbots of royal abbeys (although prelates were not supposed to fight in person, they were expected to lead contingents of troops). It also includes wealthy nobles who did not hold secular or ecclesiastical office. Such men undoubtedly acted as leaders, as Nithard's account of Fontenoy shows, and where narrative accounts mention casualties it is men of this type that they name. Their importance for the cohesion of armies cannot be overestimated; the numerical contribution they and their own followings made to armies is, as we shall see, more difficult to assess.

Conscript forces are referred to more frequently in the first half of our period (down to the mid-ninth century) than in the second. There was a clear obligation on all free men to turn out and fight in case of invasion. Many historians have also thought that there was a general obligation in the Frankish world on all free men to fight on campaigns beyond the frontiers. It cannot be shown definitively that there was no such obligation, but it does seem unlikely, for a number of reasons. First, campaigning, especially in the eighth and again in the mid-tenth century, was often an annual affair. It is hard to see how this could have been a general obligation unless there was some kind of selection mechanism; had there not been, small freeholders would have been bankrupted by less than a generation of annual campaigning. Indeed, if such an obligation did exist there must have been a selection mechanism in any case, since even quite moderate assumptions about the total population of the Frankish empire and the proportion of free men of weapon-bearing age within that population suggest that a complete call-up on such a basis would have produced an army of at least 100,000, an absurdly high figure. We do indeed begin to hear about selection mechanisms in the early years of the ninth century, but that was at a point at which warfare had become very largely defensive. Second, it is difficult to see how 'ordinary freemen' could have achieved the degree of professional fighting ability which would have made it useful for rulers to call on their services on a large scale: even in the eighth century, warfare was a matter of quality (siege specialists and well-armed warriors) more than of quantity.

Auxiliary forces made a significant contribution to many Carolingian and Ottonian campaigns. Recently subjugated or tributary peoples on the Frankish periphery—Frisians, Saxons, Carinthians, Bavarians—acted as auxiliaries in Frankish armies, much as their counterparts in imperial Roman armies had done, and with the same general characteristics: fast moving, lightly armed irregular troops. As late as the battle on the Lechfeld, both Magyar and east Frankish forces had Slav auxiliaries with them, and Henry II campaigned against the Christian dukes of Poland with support from the pagan Slav Liutizi, who marched under their own heathen banners, much to the scandal of Saxon churchmen like Brun of Querfurt and Thietmar of Merseburg. In general, though, this form of troop-raising seems to have become less important in the course of our period, though it survived on the European periphery rather longer: as late as 1063 the Welsh promised to serve Edward the Confessor 'by land and by sea'.

A rather different kind of auxiliary force from that provided by subject peoples along the borders was the use of peoples who normally acted as predatory invaders as allies or mercenaries (the word is used here in a loose sense; we are not usually told much if anything about the means of payment). Almost the earliest appearance of Magyars in Western sources, for example, was their participation in Arnulf's campaign of 892 against the Moravians, and they were used in this way in the complex politics of the Italian kingdom in the early tenth century on a number of occasions. Long before that, disaffected Franks had occasionally allied themselves with Viking bands, as for example did Charles the Bald's son Pippin in the 860s or Hugo of Lotharingia with the Northmen leader Gottfried in 883–5.

Gottfried himself was an example of a third kind of auxiliary: the predatory invader given land and a frontier command in the hope that he would provide an effective defence against other invaders of the same kind. Most examples of this type are of Viking leaders: Gottfried himself, and Herold and Roric, who were given frontier commands in Frisia by Louis the Pious and Lothar I, and of course most famously of all Rollo, whose invasion of northern France in the early tenth century was legitimized by the west Frankish ruler Charles the Simple at Saint-Claire-sur-Epte in 911 and whose descendants (though they long maintained Scandinavian links and alliances) created the duchy of Normandy out of this initial frontier command. Like the use of subject peoples, this was a technique which became less common in the course of the tenth century, though the early dukes of Poland took on some of the appearance of marcher counts on the Saxon frontier.

It is easier to analyse these different components of military forces qualitatively than it is to do so quantitatively. Narrative sources normally simply tell us that an army was raised; they do not say how, or what it consisted of. Sometimes (in the east Frankish / German kingdom usually) they mention the ethnic components of armies ('an army of Franks and Saxons' or 'of Bavarians and Slavs'), but this probably tells us more about how armies were organized once raised than it does about how they were raised in the first place. Many historians have thought nevertheless that there are good grounds for supposing that Carolingian and Ottonian armies were made up of warriors in the second category of those just analysed: magnates and their followings. They have in many cases further argued that these magnates served rulers (and were served in their turn by their own followings) because of a legal duty to do so arising out of a double relationship: followers commended themselves (became the 'men' of) leaders, who in turn rewarded them with gifts of land to be held as long as they served and were faithful. In a word, Carolingian and Ottonian armies were 'feudal'. To offer such a view of the world, however, is to simplify a much more complex picture. It is far from clear that magnates served (and were served in their turn) because of legally defined obligations arising out of a single relationship. Indeed, it may not be particularly helpful to conceive such obligations in terms of lawful expectations on either side: the ability of rulers (whether kings or at regional level dukes and counts) to command support was much more a matter of charisma, military reputation, and ability to reward service than of claiming what all sides acknowledged was due. In any case, for most campaigns in this period the truth is that we simply do not know who made up the armies and in what proportions.

The question of how large armies were or could be, whatever their composition, has also much exercised historians, and has proved no easier to answer definitively. The numbers given not infrequently by narrative sources are generally agreed to be unreliable: suspiciously often, they are round numbers, frequently multiples of 600 like 30,000 or 6,000, and such figures were probably not intended to be taken literally but rather to signify considerable size. They may be more reliable as guides to the relative strengths of forces, but even this is uncertain. An alternative is to work from estimates of the possible numbers of troops who might be called upon, but this too has led to widely divergent results. Whereas the French medievalist Ferdinand Lot suggested a maximum size of 5,000 for armies of the Carolingian period, the German Karl-Ferdinand Werner argued a generation later for a maximum of 15,000–20,000, drawn from a reservoir at least twice that size. Whatever one thinks of these estimates, they provide a theoretical maximum rather than an average likely to have been encountered in practice.

One possible clue lies in the numbers of casualties. We have a list of those who fell in Saxony in a battle against an invading band of Northmen in 880: two dukes, two bishops, and eighteen royal vassals. We are not told that the army was annihilated (though it was evidently a crushing defeat); nevertheless, it hardly seems likely on these figures that the total strength of the Saxon army exceeded a few hundred. The casualties reported for the battle of Firenzuola in Italy in 921 again amount to a mere fifty. Even Fontenoy, where there was everything to play for and the two sides will each have put much of their strength into the field, does not seem to have brought about extensive casualties, even though the disaster remained in Frankish memories for generations and Regino of Prüm saw it as the point at which so many irreplaceable Frankish warriors were killed that from that point on the power of the Franks began to decline.

On the whole it seems most likely that armies did not normally exceed two thousand fighting men, the figure implied, incidentally, by the *indiculus loricatorum*, though possibly some of the largest campaigns, with divided armies, may have been conducted with larger forces. Armies of this size would, of course, have been much larger in total because of the accompanying servants

Facing: this highly stylized depiction of a siege gives a good idea of a troop of Frankish mounted warriors in action, using lances, a longsword of the Ingelri type (*see above*) and unusually, the bow. The troop-leader bears a pennant as distinguishing-mark and rallying-point.

and specialists. Even if we take into account the existence of royal roads with royal estates which could permit the provisioning of armies en route, it still seems doubtful that armies much larger than 2,000–3,000 could have survived for any length of time before inflicting starvation both on themselves and on the surrounding countryside, not at least unless they were accompanied by carts with food for the men and fodder for the animals, and by cattle and sheep on the hoof; here a point must quite soon have been reached at which the whole operation would have ground to a halt under its own weight. Even the largest towns of northern Europe probably did not exceed a population of 15,000–20,000 in this period, and most were far smaller, yet even these fixed and predictable locations needed a highly developed infrastructure to survive.

It is even more difficult to decide on the relative proportions of cavalry and infantry in Carolingian and Ottonian armies than to determine their overall size. It is clear that small army groups (*scarae*) could move very fast and probably were mounted, and it is also clear that the Franks attached much importance to the ability to ride: young aristocrats spent much time learning to do so. By the time of the battle of the Dyle in 891, at which Arnulf defeated a force of Vikings by ordering his followers to advance slowly on foot, it appears that Frankish forces were unaccustomed to fighting dismounted. But there were special circumstances of terrain and fortification here, and there are good reasons for thinking that the role of cavalry, especially heavily armed cavalry, in this period has probably been overestimated. Neither in siege warfare, nor in the steam-roller-like campaigns of devastation on the frontiers, was there normally much place for such forces. Fighting from horseback was reserved for the much rarer moments of actual battle; campaigning on horseback was probably as much a matter of social status and prestige as of military necessity.

On the whole, historians have concentrated much more on the how than on the why of warfare in this period, probably because they have taken its practice for granted rather than because they have preferred to abstain from enquiry in the face of the lack of direct evidence mentioned at the opening of this chapter. Yet the reasons for warfare are not self-evident, even when invasion threatened. Invaders did not have to be fought; they could be (and were) bought off, and although the Northmen did not hold themselves much bound by such payments, the Magyars, so far as we can tell, kept strictly to the terms of paid truces. In any case, although the histories of west Francia in the later ninth century and of east Francia in the early tenth century might suggest otherwise, a great deal of warfare in this period was not directed against threats from outside the system, as we have seen. Campaigns were mostly fought either against settled opponents beyond the frontier or against rivals within, whether we are talking about the level of the kingdom, the principality, or the local region.

There would appear to have been two main reasons for conducting warfare: to acquire wealth and to translate claimed authority into real power. The two were seldom mutually incompatible, and could be happily pursued side by side, but they need to be examined separately. The pursuit of wealth was inherent in a world in which warfare was not yet the crippling expense that it was to become for all European governments from the twelfth century onwards and at the same time offered opportunities for rapid enrichment nowhere else to be found, certainly not in the more peaceful activities of government or estate management. To make war was to plunder; to threaten to make war was to force your opponents to plunder themselves by paying you tribute (or Danegeld and ransoms when Carolingian and Ottonian elites were on the receiving end of these tactics). Even from opponents with little by way of treasures of real value, slaves might still be taken. It has been plausibly conjectured that the revival of Carolingian-style imperialism under the east Frankish rulers Henry I and Otto I was fuelled by profits from the slave-trade with Islamic Spain: the very word 'slave', which starts to displace the classical *servus* around this time, is cognate with Slav. At the very least, warriors on campaign could earn their own keep rather than eating their heads off at home.

Alongside the acquisition of movable wealth lay the use of force to compel others to acknowledge authority. Carolingian and Ottonian narrative sources often imply that campaigns against frontier peoples, whether Slav, Breton, or Beneventan, were responses to disobedience or disrespect of a kind which needed no further specifying: clearly such things as withholding tribute payments or border raiding would qualify, but sometimes one has the impression that the 'disrespectful' actions which provoked Carolingian or Ottonian response were more ambiguous than this. The ponderous nature of 'official' war-making was well suited to disciplinary purposes: Frankish and Saxon armies faced down militarily inferior opponents, daring them to risk battle while destroying their infrastructure, much like the forces of the Raj on the north-west frontier and in Afghanistan. Acknowledging authority took the form not only of paying tribute and other symbolic forms of submission but also of fighting: subject peoples, as we have seen, played a significant part in ninth- and tenth-century warfare.

Within the political community the methods used might be slightly more tempered, but only slightly. Henry I consolidated his position within east Francia by concluding agreements of 'friendship' with the other dukes of the kingdom, but it was the application of military force which made such

Siege, Liber Maccabaeorum. Manuscripts of biblical books provide most of the rare depictions of warfare in the ninth and tenth centuries. Illustrated manuscripts of Macchabees are rare, but the work itself was an important source of literary imagery for those who wrote about war. The siege depicted here shows the attackers using cavalry and archery but not siege-machines.

agreements acceptable. His west Frankish contemporaries were rarely able to summon up enough force to give conviction to the demands they made of people whom they thought subject to their authority, hence the narrative of political indecision and confusion offered by Flodoard. When what was at stake was who was to exercise authority, the game was played with rather different rules. Ravaging might alienate support; what was most important was to give the impression of such overwhelming military power that your opponent's support simply melted away, as Bernard of Italy's did in 817 against Louis the Pious and Charles the Bald's did in 858 against Louis the German (though not for long). If this could not be achieved, either by a show of force or by soliciting and seducing the opposing following, then battle was the most likely outcome, and it might be a very bloody one. There were a handful of really crushing defeats of Frankish forces by invading predators (especially Vikings and Magyars) in this period, but the list of battles with major losses, at least before about 950, is largely made up from the encounters in the course of disputed kingships, starting with the battles of the 830s, then Fontenoy (841), Andernach (876), Firenzuola (921), Soissons (923), Birten and Andernach (939).

Success in warfare against internal opponents consolidated power and authority; but success externally consolidated reputation as nothing else could do in this period; even the saintly were described in military metaphors (which go back beyond this period but were used more and more frequently during it) as battling against the forces of evil. The legend of Charlemagne the warrior was not created by the romances of the high middle ages; it was already being formed in the ninth century. Swords with magical inscriptions proclaimed the decline since his time; treasured anecdotes showed him embodying warrior virtues even after power, fame, and affluence might have been expected to soften him. Later in the ninth century, the deeds of prominent military leaders like Robert the Strong, the ancestor of the later French Capetian kings, or the east Frankish warleader Henry were celebrated by contemporary narrators, and their deaths mourned; their fame transmitted itself to their descendants. Successful non-royal war-leaders of the early tenth century—Arnulf of Bavaria, Otto of Saxony, Alan of Brittany—came near to establishing kingship on the strength of military success. The victories of Henry I and Otto I over the Magyars were the making of the Ottonians and their dynasty, and the justification for Otto's imperial coronation. Militarily successful rulers were the leaders of God's people; they were, to use an image frequently invoked in the ninth and tenth centuries, the new *Maccabees.

Comparisons of this kind bring us once again to contemporaries' attitudes

* Leaders of the Jewish resistance to the Seleucids, 2nd century BC.

to warfare. If its practice was unarticulated by warriors and commanders, though not necessarily incoherent, its morality and justification were explicitly addressed by ecclesiastics, though the results were not coherent. It was clerics who depicted successful warriors as Maccabees, and urged kings at their coronations to defend the church and the defenceless against not only pagans but also 'bad Christians'. But it was also clerics who insisted with increasing frequency that they themselves should not participate in warfare (though many of them did: there is a long list of ninth- and tenth-century bishops and abbots killed and wounded in battle). Their counsels to the laity were divided. On the one hand, they continued to argue that killing in warfare was a sin, for which penance had to be done. This was not merely a theoretical norm found in church legislation and the collections of legal material compiled by church lawyers; we know that such penances were actually imposed after the battles of Fontenoy (841) and Soissons (923). On the other hand, ecclesiastics acted as if the ability to bear arms was a condition of full membership both of the church and of civil society, at least for male members of the political elite. Those who had had penances imposed for any grave sin were expected to renounce the *cingulum militare*, the soldier's belt, for the duration of their penance (which in theory might be lifelong). Moreover, the ninth century saw the beginnings of what would later become a full-fledged clerical justification of warfare: the help of God and the saints was invoked against the pagan enemies of Christian rulers and their followers in the form of masses and benedictions. Even penitents who had renounced their soldier's belt were expected to take up arms against pagan incursions.

The paradox of praising warriors for their defence of Christianity and the church while treating them as murderers for doing so outlived the period treated in this chapter, but a more morally coherent attitude to warfare and its morality was slowly emerging in the ninth and tenth centuries. One way of achieving this was to reconceptualize society as consisting of 'those who pray, those who fight and those who work (on the land)'. This division, wherever it is found, is never a mere division; it carries with it the implication that each of the groups has its own proper and legitimate sphere of action, and that each needs the other two to be able to fulfil its function. It is first found hinted at in the works of Carolingian intellectuals of the school of Auxerre in the mid-ninth century and then articulated by King Alfred of Wessex at the end of it, to be taken up with increasing frequency by clerical thinkers in France and England from the late tenth century onwards. It is a model to think with rather than to impose thought: it could be used to legitimize royal authority as well as the practice of arms, but as a view of Christian society it clearly had implications for all warriors. The process, by which the ritual of conferring arms on young males when they reached adulthood (originally a quite secular affair) became the clericalized ritual of becoming a knight, has a chronology which is still much disputed; but it is clear that the clerical elements were already more explicit and more fully articulated by the early eleventh century than they had been in the ninth.

It is yet another paradox that this development took place during a period when warfare was directed less and less against the pagan Other beyond the frontier and more and more against members of the same universal community, that of Christianity. The period from the eighth to the tenth century in Continental Western Europe saw a slow evolution away from large-scale imperial structures sustained by the massive exercise of military power. By the year 1000 such 'states', and the kind of warfare which had gone with them, were becoming archaic, at least in what had been the Frankish empire: the dominion of English rulers over their Celtic peripheries, and indeed the more fragile and short-lived empires of Boleslas Chrobry of Poland, and of Scandinavian war-kings like Cnut and Olaf, showed that as late as the eleventh century such things were still possible on the European periphery. But the future would belong to more expensive and intensive forms of warfare, based on stone fortifications and on armies where not only the leaders but all the followers were fully armed: at least in its early stages, such warfare was less likely to result in substantial losses, and it is perhaps significant that there were few engagements in post-Frankish Europe with really heavy casualties between 950 and 1050. The old forms of warfare could still be found in wars of expansion, but where this happened (in Spain, southern Italy, the near East, and on the Celtic and Slavic peripheries) it was now territorial rather than tributary expansion. In any case, the main thrust of European warfare in the high middle ages was against neighbours and within kingdoms themselves. War was as endemic as it had ever been, but it came to be marked by increasing costs, and by a rate of return which rarely covered them: the need for those who waged it to tax ever more heavily to pay for it was visible on the horizon.

3 THE VIKINGS

H. B. CLARKE

THE Vikings are almost as elusive to us today as they were to their contemporaries. We pursue them through historical records at our peril. There is a fundamental imbalance between Scandinavian and non-Scandinavian sources—in broad terms between what was buried in the ground and what was written down. The art of warfare is usually presented and understood from the perspective of its practitioners. Viking values are represented, often enigmatically, in skaldic poetry and runic inscriptions. A limited number of defensive sites have been identified in the homelands and abroad, some with urban connotations. Most eloquently of all, Scandinavian sources speak to us voicelessly through the remains of their dead, in the shape of skeletons of humans and domestic animals, and of weapons, ships, and other equipment. But the great bulk of the written record comes from the Vikings' opponents, who were naturally hostile and hardly objective. Danes and Norwegians feature prominently in annals and chronicles composed by English, Frankish, and Irish clerics and monks; Swedes are mentioned occasionally by Arabic and Greek observers. Few of these writers are likely to have witnessed at first hand the battles and sieges that they describe, although they may have looked captured and collaborating Vikings directly in the eye. Asser, the Welsh cleric and bishop of Sherborne, claims in his biography of King Alfred to have been shown both the solitary thorn-tree round which Danes and English had clashed at Ashdown in 870 and the fort at Countisbury where a Viking force had been confronted in 878. The preponderance of non-Scandinavian written accounts has lent to Vikings a somewhat distant, other-worldly character, which at the same time is part of their enduring appeal. This other-worldly quality has been reinforced by over-reliance on much later texts, principally Scandinavian and non-Scandinavian chronicles and sagas.

The word 'Viking' (Old Norse *víkingr*) has always been problematic. In the early Viking Age it seems to have denoted an inhabitant of Víken—the coastal district round Oslofjord and Skagerrak in southern Norway. Vikings in that sense may have been trading across the North Sea well before *c.*790. But in the course of time the word came to mean 'sea pirate' and this remains its normal usage in all languages. Like most medieval warriors, Vikings were fighters by vocation rather than by profession, in that they did not constitute standing armies. Nevertheless they clearly had an *esprit de corps* of a well-developed nature, for which the best evidence emanates not from the field of battle but from the realm of religion. In the ninth century and the first half of the tenth, Western European sources depict Vikings as Gentiles, heathens, or pagans, that is as non-Christians. Scandinavian paganism of the Viking Age deserves to be taken seriously. During the Saxon wars, Germanic neighbours of the Danes had demonstrated a courageous attachment to their paganism in the face of brutal Carolingian aggression and many Scandinavians may have had a similar attitude. A polytheistic religious system offered to warriors, and to those who composed skaldic verses in their honour, a specialized, high-status god of war, Odin. Animal sacrifices to him were probably made each spring for success on military campaigns. Valhalla (*Valhǫll*) as a paradise for fallen comrades must have acted as a spur to bravery on the battlefield. The psychological comfort to be derived from this concept is impossible to gauge, but we may reasonably assume that its power was at least equal to that of Heaven or Paradise for Christians. Just as the cult of Thor, controller of elemental forces, may account in part for the almost reckless adventurousness displayed by Vikings as seafarers, so may the cult of Odin have underpinned their equally renowned reputation as doughty fighters.

The hierarchy of pagan gods was matched by that of

Odin, here represented by a bronze figurine from Linby in Skåne (once in Denmark, now in Sweden), was the Scandinavian god of war and of a select band of dead warriors who were attended by valkyries. Blind in one eye, Odin's attributes were complex and convoluted. Cunning, demonic, pitiless and violent, he brings us close to the Viking mentality.

their human adherents and inventors. At its apex, as in much of Europe at this time, were men who were called, or liked to call themselves, king (*cununc*). As in the lands of their victims, so in the homelands multiple kingship was the norm. This custom, coupled with widespread recognition of the claims of sons born outside wedlock, resulted in political instability at home and abroad. Everywhere kings were war-leaders, often young and dying young, like the five killed at *Brunanburh* (the still unidentified site in England) in 937. Some Scandinavian war- leaders were royal exiles: a clear example is Gudurm, a nephew of Horic I of Denmark, who according to the *Annals of Fulda* was driven out and lived a piratical existence. Another is his contemporary Roric, who had lived among the Saxons before gathering a force of Danes and embarking on a career of piracy. In this context we should always remember that east Frankish kings, whether Carolingian or Saxon, were neighbours of Danish kings, separated only by the 'Danish march' south of the defensive boundary known as the Danevirke (the 'Danish work' [of fortification]). Thus in 873 envoys of King Sigifrid sought peace on account of border disputes between the Danes and the Saxons, in order that merchants might trade in safety. Being on the same social level, Scandinavian kings were able to make marriage alliances with their Western counterparts: Godefrid and the Carolingian Gisela in 883 are a case in point. And, of course, Vikings forged military alliances with their Christian rivals whenever it suited both sides, as in 862 when the joint Scandinavian kings of Dublin plundered Meath in association with Aed Finnliath, king of the Northern Uí Néill.

In early medieval Scandinavia, as elsewhere in Europe, royal families arose out of a wider aristocratic milieu in which non-royal warlords were numerous. One of the first Viking commanders whose name we know, Sǫxulfr, is described in the *Annals of Ulster* as *toísech* 'chief', 'leader' at the time of his death in 837. In Old Norse he would have been a jarl, the ancestor of English 'earl'. Scandinavian kings and jarls sometimes acted in conjunction with one another; alternatively they could be rivals, as in 893 when Dublin Vikings divided their loyalty between a former king's son and a jarl. In large Viking armies there were probably several chieftains to every king: during the fighting in Wessex over the winter of 870–1, nine Danish jarls and one king died according to the *Anglo-Saxon Chronicle*. Below the level of jarl there were lesser leaders called holds (Old English *holdas*) in Anglo-Saxon sources. This military hierarchy is illustrated by the list of aristocratic casualties at the battle of Tettenhall in 910, which includes two kings, two jarls, and at least five holds. All are named by the English annalists; at this social level people tended to be acquainted with the main war-leaders. At a further stage in the Edwardian conquest of eastern England, a surviving jarl and an unstated number of holds submitted to the West Saxon king. That they 'sought to have him as their lord and protector' was a source of satisfaction; there was nothing incongruous about it. Accordingly Scandinavian armies operating abroad were normally under royal or aristocratic command and Vikings should not be thought of as an undisciplined rabble. Their leaders, on the contrary, sought fame as well as fortune and would have wished their deeds to be commemorated in skaldic verses and in runic inscriptions.

The size of Viking armies has been much debated, for we have only their opponents' word for it. Kings presumably commanded larger forces than jarls, while some of the Danish armies seeking to conquer England in the late Viking Age were of a quite different order from Norwegian raiding parties in the early Viking Age. It is usual, and wise, to adopt a cautious approach to the

Rune-stone raised *c.*1000 in memory of a Viking chieftain named Sibbe, at Karlevi on the Swedish island of Öland. Such monuments were public and were intended to be permanent memorials to a warrior's reputation. The inscription includes an authentic stanza of skaldic verse composed in a technically elaborate metre—itself a subtle form of flattery.

Gravestone from Lindisfarne, Northumbria, depicting a Viking war-band in action. The island monastery was attacked in the summer of 793, probably by raiders from western Norway. The theme of this gravestone is the Day of Judgement and the warriors wielding axes and swords symbolize divine punishment—a typical early medieval reaction to earthly trials and tribulations.

credibility of figures given in Western annals and chronicles. Irish annalists are notably restrained in their estimates of casualties on the Scandinavian side. When in 837 the men of Brega, north of Dublin, 'routed' a plundering war-band, a total of six score Vikings are reported to have been killed. In 917, this time in Munster, only about a hundred men fell between the two sides, despite the fact that the fighting lasted for several hours. The main exception to this restraint comes in 848 when, in four battles in different parts of Ireland, 240, 500, 700, and 1,200 Viking dead are claimed—successes that were duly noted in the *Annals of St-Bertin*. Contemporary Irish sources are less oppositional than their English and Frankish counterparts, perhaps because it was relatively common for Irishmen to fight side by side with Scandinavian allies. The post-Viking Age propaganda tract *Cogad Gaedel re Gallaib* (The War of the Irish with the Foreigners) is completely out of step in this regard. The probability is that most Viking armies numbered hundreds rather than thousands: a 'large force'

(Old Irish *sluagh mór*) of Vikings defeated along with their Southern Uí Néill and Leinster allies in 868 is defined realistically as '300 or more'. Much smaller armies could easily have struck terror into civilian populations and could have occasioned widespread destruction and misery. The argument that Viking armies were essentially small does not deny this fundamental reality.

In the second half of the ninth century a Danish 'great army' was at large in England and in Francia, both countries rich in potential for financial and political gain. Referred to in Old English as *micel here* and in Latin as *magnus exercitus*, this force was clearly regarded as being out of the ordinary. Led by several kings and numerous jarls it did not arrive all at once, but at intervals starting in East Anglia in 865. Successful in Northumbria and in East Anglia, though not in Wessex, the great army was reinforced in the spring of 871 and again in 878 after another defeat by the West Saxons. A year later this new great army crossed over to Francia, where its mixed fortunes are summarized in the *Anglo-Saxon Chronicle*. This was the army that conducted the sustained yet unsuccessful siege of Paris in 885–6 and which, following another defeat in 891, returned to England as 'the great Danish army, which we have spoken about before'. By no means a single cohesive force, it had broken up into two parts in England in 874 and again in 876, and in Francia in 884. Finally, at Bridgnorth on the River Severn in the summer of 896, the great army dispersed, into East Anglia, Northumbria, and the Seine region of France. There is no possibility of ascertaining the size of this army at any stage in its chequered history and the same is true of those latter-day great armies, even if they are not so called, which were brought over to England from Scandinavia by King Sven Forkbeard and others in the early eleventh century. The most spectacular great army, however, was commanded in 1066 by a mere duke—William of Normandy, descendant of the Scandinavian Rollo—and several counts, as we see them portrayed on the Bayeux Tapestry. There the fleet has all the appearance of a Viking one, to the extent of transporting horses across the English Channel as a Danish forerunner had done in 892. Instead of a kingdom in England, the objective was the kingdom of England, and of course the Anglo-Danish opposition was famously defeated.

The question of how Viking armies, great and small, were recruited and organized is fraught with difficulty, for lack of contemporary evidence. There is a danger of reading back into the Viking Age the more formalized institutional arrangements of high medieval Scandinavia. In northern Europe state formation was hesitant, held back to some degree by intense dynastic rivalry that caused parts of one country to be taken over by another. From the Viking Age itself, the best evidence for effective state formation assumes the form of five administrative sites in Danish territory: Aggersborg and Fyrkat in Jutland,

Nonnebakken on Fyn, Trelleborg on Sjælland, and another Trelleborg in Skåne. Built with military precision, though not primarily for military purposes, these centres may represent a revival of Danish political fortunes under the Jelling kings. Even so, there is no justification for the view that methods of military recruitment were more advanced in late Viking Age Scandinavia. Essentially warriors were recruited and maintained by informal, highly personalized means. They joined with, and fought for, leaders whose military prowess might guarantee material and political gain. Attacks on monasteries would yield a quick profit in terms of provisions and loot, whereas long-drawn-out campaigns motivated by political aspirations created severe logistical problems, the most immediate of which was an adequate and constant food supply. In 1006 Danish forces were provided with food 'throughout England', whilst in 1013 both Sven Forkbeard and Thorkell the Tall demanded food for the coming winter. On the field of battle, Viking loyalties were represented practically and symbolically by their leaders' standards: in 865 Count Robert of Angers slew over 500 Vikings and sent their standards and weapons to King Charles the Bald; thirteen years later the West Saxons captured Ubbe's raven banner, a symbol of the cult of the war god Odin.

Archaeologically the Viking period in Scandinavia constitutes part of the late Iron Age, which is another reason why we should not presuppose the existence of higher levels of political and social organization than are likely to have been the case. The paganism of this prehistoric culture has left us a precious resource in the shape of thousands of weapons accompanying male burials. In addition Gotlandic memorial stones provide valuable indications, despite their relative crudity as images. There can be little doubt that the supreme weapon of war was the sword. Viking swords were used as slashing instruments, like machetes, as is shown by the mutilated bones found in some graves. Their double-edged blades, usually between 70 and 80 centimetres long, were light and flexible. Swordsmanship required great agility to avoid enemy blows and to inflict injury or death. Superior weapons were pattern-welded from a bundle of thin rods of iron which, when hammered into shape and fitted with steel cutting edges, were immensely strong. Despite the prohibitions of Frankish rulers, blades were imported into Scandinavia from the Rhineland and some of these are inscribed with the name Ulfberht—presumably a highly skilled craftsmen who enjoyed a reputation akin to that of Antonio Stradivari in an entirely different context. Imported blades may have been finished off in Scandinavian workshops, as is suggested by the extensive deposits of slag over much of the site at Hedeby (German Haithabu) in southern Jutland. There is a certain irony in the Danish peace offering sent with messengers to Louis the German in 873: it was a sword with a golden hilt.

Sword hilts as classified by Jan Petersen in 1920 still constitute the basis of a complicated dating system, to which scholars have clung as tenaciously as the Dublin Norsemen held on to the sword of Carlus, a war trophy last heard of in 1029.

There were two main types of spear—a lighter one for throwing like a javelin at the start of a pitched battle, and a heavier one for thrusting at the enemy in the subsequent fighting at close quarters. Many spearheads

A selection of Viking offensive and defensive equipment from Norway, including the Gjermundbu helmet. The sword, spear, and axe were standard offensive weapons, while the metal helmet and round shield were for bodily protection. Unlike the other items displayed here, metal helmets are rare finds and may have been owned mainly by kings and chieftains.

recovered from graves and from settlement sites are plain and unadorned, but others are decorated on the socket by grooves inlaid with silver, copper, or brass, or some combination of these metals, producing a glittering effect. The heavier type was sometimes fitted with wings to prevent over-penetration in the body of the victim; it has been suggested that these, too, were Carolingian imports to judge by the phrase *vigra vestrænna* 'western war-lances' in a comparatively early poem *Haraldskvæði*. Axes were used by Vikings in fighting, though their presence in graves might simply reflect their utility as general-purpose tools in a culture that relied extensively on heavy timber. Not many axes uncovered as grave-goods are decorated, but a notable exception is the famous ceremonial weapon from Mammen in Jutland. The grave in which it was found has been dated dendrochronologically to 970–971, in the reign of Harald Bluetooth. During the eleventh century a long-handled, broad-bladed battleaxe was developed and was employed with devastating effect against Norman cavalry at Hastings by Harold Godwinesson's Anglo-Danish household troops (*huscarlas*). Evidence of bows and arrows has come from pagan graves, but again their utility in hunting might account for their presence. The lack of grave-goods from Christian opponents of Vikings makes it virtually impossible to compare the quality of Scandinavian and non-Scandinavian weaponry. At the beginning of the Viking Age the Irish had shorter swords, but once native kings reacted to greater Viking pressure after 837 they scored many victories over the foreigners, perhaps with the aid of weapons captured in earlier engagements.

Defensive equipment used by Vikings included circular shields about a metre across. Normally only the metal boss survives, but lime-wood appears to have been favoured. This might be covered with leather and fitted with a metal rim. Shields were painted in bright colours and devices on them form the subject of some of the earliest skaldic verses. They were comparatively fragile, too, and their loss in battle is symbolized in the Gokstad ship-burial in southern Norway by the provision of two shields for each crew member. From a Frankish source we have the fascinating detail that shield-sellers and other traders following in the path of the imperial army in 876 were obstructing a narrow escape route. A hoisted shield was a (deceptive) sign of surrender on the part of Danes entrapped in a stronghold six years later. Contrary to popular conception, a typical Viking helmet may have been made of leather, similar to those depicted on Gotlandic memorial stones which are conical in shape and provided with a nose-guard. Viking helmets were certainly hornless, like the best preserved Scandinavian specimen found at Gjermundbu in southern Norway. Leather may also have been the usual form of body protection, perhaps reinforced with bone plaques and worn over an inner garment.

At the battle of Stamford Bridge, east of York, in 1066 the heroic Norwegian defending the bridge single-handedly is said to have been stabbed to death under his corselet. Mail shirts seem to have been rare and the preserve of men of high status, while the bear-coats associated with frenzied and indomitable berserkers (*berserkir*) are a feature of later literary sources rather than contemporary historical ones. Protective gear, even when not made of metal, may have contributed to mass drownings of Vikings who found themselves on the losing side. This phenomenon is recorded, for example, in 891 at the River Dyle in the Low Countries and in 947 at the River Boyne in eastern Ireland.

Scandinavian warfare conducted outside the homelands must have been influenced in terms of strategy and tactics by those of their opponents. There was no uniform, Viking method of warfare. Scandinavians and their Celtic, Germanic, and Slavic antagonists were possessed of a comparable range of offensive and defensive personal equipment and normally fought land battles on foot. Western European written sources offer a few pointers in the direction of pre-battle manoeuvres and formations. The most important strategy in this context was to avoid pitched battles whenever possible. Vikings were perceived to be vulnerable in open country, as the *Anglo-Saxon Chronicle* observes, especially when their whereabouts was known, depriving them of the element of surprise. In 876 the Danish great army slipped past the West Saxons on its way from Cambridge to Wareham and subsequently 'stole away' from Wareham by night. Similarly Guthrum's part of the same army arrived at Chippenham in January 878 'by stealth'. Four years later, in another winter manoeuvre, Danish Vikings were able to follow tracks left in the snow by departing Franks. On occasion it proved necessary to disencumber themselves before undertaking military operations, as when in 893 and again in 895 the Danes placed their womenfolk (many of them probably English by birth), ships, and other property in East Anglia for safety. Horse-mounted scouts were no doubt used extensively by armies in general, including Viking ones, but they are rarely indicated in our texts. Whenever a pitched battle could not be avoided, it was essential of course to choose one's ground to advantage and to appear resolute. If we are to believe the annalists recording events in 1003, Sven Forkbeard's army was able to look that of Ealdorman Ælfric in the eye, and to cause the English war-leader to feign illness and his men to disperse.

Great set-piece battles of the Viking Age, such as *Brunanburh* (937), Clontarf (1014), and Hastings (1066), were probably preceded by quite elaborate marshalling of troops. At Ashdown the Danes formed themselves into two divisions, one led by two kings and the other by all the jarls. According to a description of the second battle of Corbridge in the *Annals of Ulster*, there were four batallions of Vikings, all under different leaders. One of these commanded by Ragnall, the king of Waterford, lay in wait out of sight and its assault on the Scottish rear won the day. The shouted negotiations that preceded the poetic account of the battle of Maldon may or may not reflect historical actuality, but at least the precise site of this heroic episode has been identified with a fair degree of certainty. An element of surprise would have been decisive on many an occasion. Guthrum's defeat at Edington in May 878 was brought about in this way. From the Danes' perspective, King Alfred's

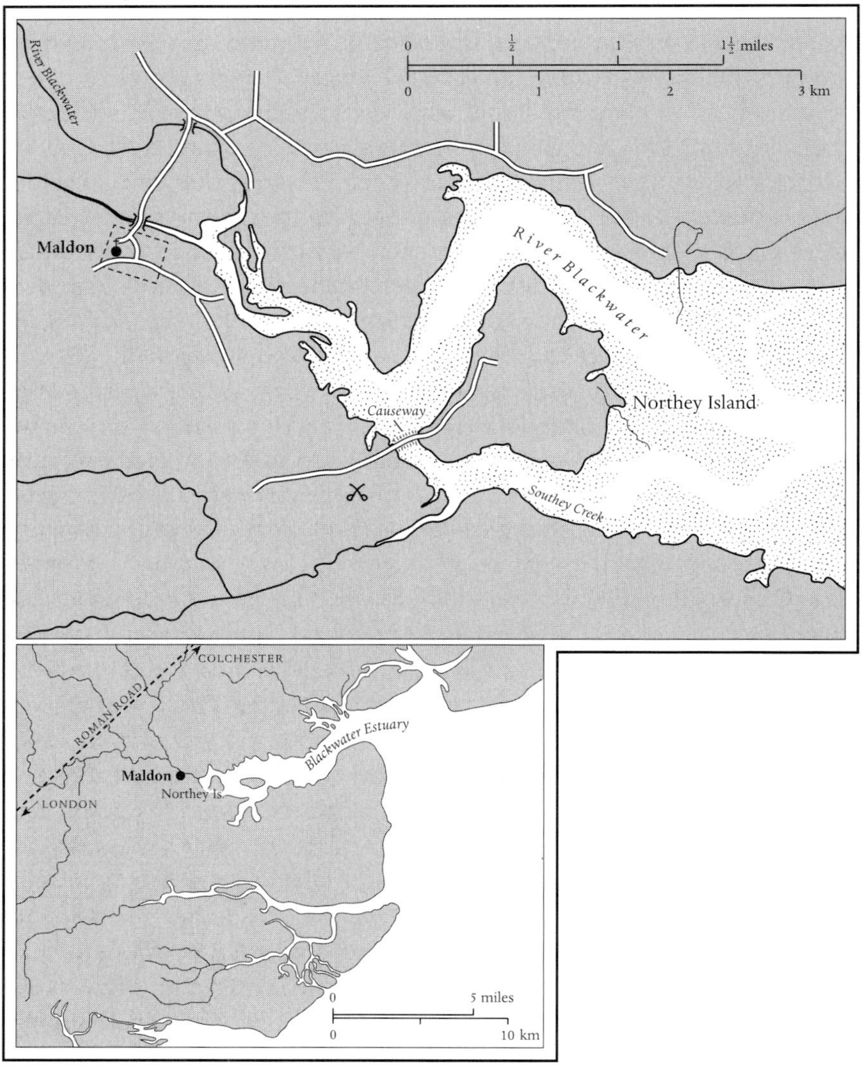

THE PRESUMED SITE OF THE BATTLE OF MALDON, ESSEX, FOUGHT IN 991.

mounted force crossing over the north-western angle of Salisbury Plain at first light would have been invisible until it came charging down the steep scarp of Edington Hill. After what may have been a relatively brief military encounter, the Danes retreated northwards to their fortified encampment at Chippenham, where they surrendered a fortnight later. Similarly Harald Haardrada's Norwegians were taken by surprise at Stamford Bridge. Contrary to their popular reputation, Viking armies were frequently beaten. An analysis of battles against the Irish in which Dublin Norsemen participated, down to and including the epic contest at Clontarf, places them on the losing side far more often than not. One obvious reason for this is that they were outnumbered and, in hand-to-hand fighting, numbers count. Irish annalists describe the losers' fate in matter-of-fact language: in 926, for example, 200 Vikings were beheaded; in 948 the survivors of another major defeat were taken prisoner and no doubt sold into slavery. Lurid Viking methods of dispatching vanquished warlords, especially blood-eagling, belong to the realm of imaginative literature.

The commonest types of warfare in which Vikings engaged assumed the low-level forms of raiding and skirmishing. Many of these casual encounters with local forces and even local populations occurred as Vikings sought food and human captives. The detailed account in the *Annals of Fulda* for 873 of a raid by an inveterate Viking called Rudolf implies that the tactic was to kill the menfolk in the Ostergau of Frisia and then to take possession of their women, children, and property. In 917 Danes based at Leicester and Northampton made a night-time raid southwards, capturing men and cattle. When monasteries were targeted by Vikings some of their victims were undoubtedly monks, but others were probably members of local defence forces. Irish monasteries were repositories not only of ecclesiastical treasures but also of the wealth of laymen, who would have tried to protect it. Christian armies were sometimes led by abbots and bishops with relatively small forces at their command. In 882 Bishop Wala of Metz made a rash attack on Danish Vikings and brought upon himself both death and posthumous censureship by Archbishop Hincmar of Reims for having taken up arms. Nonetheless in the following year Liubert, the archbishop of Mainz, also with a small force, killed a number of Vikings and recovered their plunder. In northern France in 859 we hear about a sworn association of 'common people' who fought bravely against Danish Vikings, whilst in 894 a raiding party returning from the siege of Exeter was put to flight by the townspeople of Chichester. Low-level warfare was probably the norm in the vicinity of the greater Russian rivers used as trade routes, where Swedish Vikings (Varangians) conducted regular forays in order to gather tribute in the form of furs, honey, skins, and wax, and of course slaves, for sale in southern markets.

In the vastness of Russia, ships remained the only feasible means of long-distance transportation; so essential were they that ingenious methods were devised for hauling them over watersheds and around the Dnepr rapids. But in the narrower confines and more open landscapes of Western Europe, horses were used extensively by Viking armies. The Danish great army spent the winter of 865–6 in East Anglia equipping itself with horses; after its defeat by the Franks at Saucourt-en-Vimeu in August 881 it did the same; and in 892 it crossed over the English Channel from Boulogne 'horses and all'. The section of the army that returned to England in late 884 was subsequently deprived of its Frankish horses by King Alfred's relieving force. In an earlier phase of the Alfredian wars, Guthrum's Danes had outridden the West Saxons on their journey from Wareham to Exeter. A great deal of Viking raiding conducted overland depended on horses for mobility as well as convenience. In 866 about 400 Vikings, allied with Bretons, came up the Loire with their horses and then attacked and sacked the town of Le Mans. A detail from the *Annals of Ulster* illustrates in a precise way the power of the horse: on 26 February 943 Dublin Vikings defeated and killed the energetic northern king, Muirchertach of the Leather Cloaks, whose chief church at Armagh 56 kilometres away was plundered by them on the very next day. Not surprisingly that

Memorial stone from Lärbro, on the Baltic island of Gotland, showing the prominence given to horses in the Viking homelands. Other signs of an attachment to these animals are collars, stirrups, and spurs, sometimes manufactured at least in part from precious metals, as well as skeletons of horses interred with their former owners inside chamber-graves and in or alongside ship-burials.

most exploitative of late Viking Age commanders, Sven Forkbeard, was provided with food and horses by the cowed and war-weary English in 1013. Having left ships and hostages with his son Cnut, Sven rode with the main part of his army around southern England, taking more hostages, with the result that by the time he 'turned northward to his ships . . . all the nation regarded him as full king'. Æthelred II's kingdom had been conquered on horseback over half a century before the battle of Hastings!

England was won by Danes by different military tactics from those used by Normans, their Frenchified descendants. Nevertheless the Bayeux Tapestry shows Norman cavalrymen holding spears aloft like javelins, as well as under arm in couched-lance style. Horses were often at or near the scene of military actions involving Vikings. At the siege of Buttington, situated where Offa's Dyke meets the Severn near Welshpool, the encircled Danes were forced by lack of food to eat most of their horses. After Edmund Ironside's victory at Otford in Kent in 1016, Danish warriors retreated on horseback to the island of Sheppey; their horses had presumably been stationed somewhere near the field of battle. Raiding parties would have been horse-mounted for the most part, like that conducted in Brega in the year 1000 by the Dublin Norsemen and their Leinster allies in advance of the main army of their new overlord, Brian Bórama; in the event most of them were killed by Mael Sechnaill's men. A few years earlier, in 994, Olaf Tryggvason and Sven Forkbeard had ravaged coastal districts of south-eastern England and 'finally they seized horses and rode as widely as they wished and continued to do indescribable damage'. After their defeat at Saucourt, Danish Vikings indulged in a Cromwellian touch: in the course of extensive pillaging, including the royal palace at Aachen, they stabled their horses in the king's chapel. On another occasion they turned the advantages of having a steed against its aristocratic rider: according to the *Annals of St-Vaast* and Regino of Prüm, the east Frankish margrave Henry rode headlong into a pit excavated in advance and was there killed. The same ruse finds a literary echo towards the end of *Orkneyinga Saga*, where Sven Asleifarson is entrapped in a Dublin street.

In populated areas outside the homelands Scandinavians were vulnerable, whether operating as raiders, traders, or settlers, or some combination of these activities. Just like their victims, Vikings needed protection and security. To start with, their most precious possessions were the ships by which they arrived. Naval encampments designed to protect these were such a novel and distinctive phenomenon in mid-ninth-century Ireland that a descriptive word was coined from two Latin components. A *longphort* (plural *longphuirt*) is expressive of ship defence and among the first recorded examples were those at Annagassan (Co. Louth) and Dublin. Naval bases of this kind had the immediate effect of extending the range of inland forays in 841—about 120 and 90 kilometres, respectively. Natural islands were ideal as lairs for fleets, since elaborate defences would not have been required. Some of these were relatively large and situated off the coast: good examples are Noirmoutier in western France and Sheppey and Thanet in south-eastern England. Other island bases were smaller and upriver or, in Ireland, in big lakes and inlets such as Lough Neagh and Strangford Lough. Provided they had adequate supplies, Vikings could feel tolerably safe. In 863 a party of Danes withstood a two-pronged siege for several weeks on an island in the Rhine, despite the fact that it was winter-time, before retreating. Adrevald of Fleury gives us the clearest written account of such a base, on an island in the Loire near his great monastery. Here Vikings secured their ships, erected huts to live in, and kept prisoners in chains, and from here they ventured on plundering forays aboard ship and on horseback. Major naval bases attracted the covetous eyes of other Vikings: in 851 Norwegian Dublin was ransacked and burnt by Danish Vikings; ten years later a substantial ship-borne force attacked the Danish fort on the island of Oissel in the Seine upstream from Rouen.

To identify and to investigate archaeologically relatively short-lived encampments, and thus to describe their design, has not been easy. The standard Viking practice was probably to excavate a ditch and to build a bank inside it, as at Repton; indeed the Danish fort under construction at Louvain at the time of the Frankish assault in 891 was surrounded by a ditch 'after their fashion'. According to Asser, the winter camp at Reading had gates and extensive use

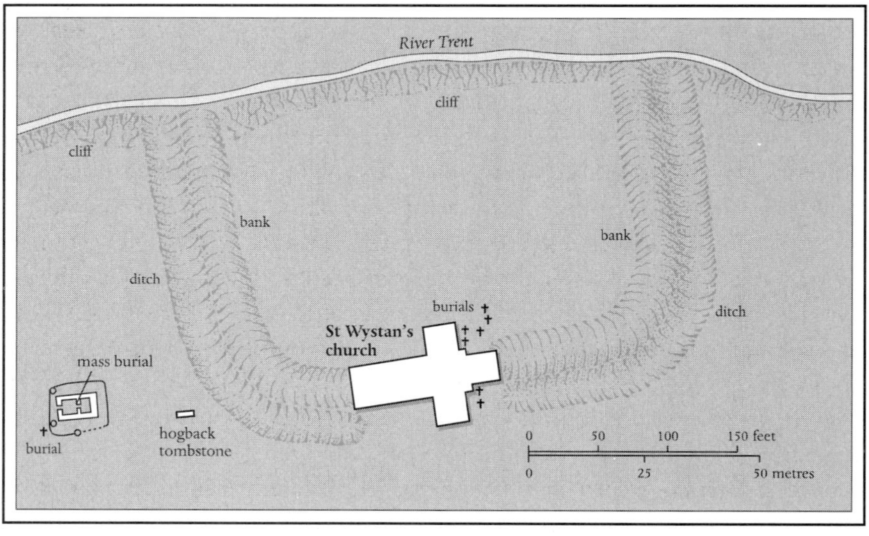

PLAN OF THE DANISH WINTER CAMP AT REPTON, DERBYSHIRE, BUILT IN 873.

was presumably made of timber for such purposes. The site at Jeufosse selected by Danes in the winter of 856–7 is praised by a Western annalist for its excellence as a base-camp. At Nijmegen in 880–1 they did even better, taking over the king's palace and building fortifications that proved to be too strong for the royal army. On the other hand, a year or so later, having barricaded themselves in a large farmstead at Avaux in the Low Countries, predatory Vikings decided to decamp by moonlight, but were subsequently defeated on their way back to their ships. Winter camps had to be stocked with provisions, a necessity that exposed the aggressors themselves to attack. The Fulda annalist tells us explicitly that the Frankish tactic at Asselt on the Meuse in 887 was to ambush unsuspecting Vikings outside their stronghold. Two years earlier a war-band took control of Hesbaye and its hinterland, gathering crops of various kinds and assembling a workforce of male and female slaves, only to find itself besieged, deprived of its supplies, and forced to make an overnight escape. Similarly an English army obliged the Danes to abandon Chester towards the end of 893 by seizing cattle and by burning corn or feeding it to their horses.

Vikings are rarely recorded besieging mere forts: at the unidentified site of *Wigingamere* in south-eastern England a large Danish army attacked 'long into the day' in the critical year of 917, but gave up when it met with stiff resistance. Quite the opposite occurred at defended towns that were full of loot, for Vikings were capable of mounting and maintaining prolonged sieges. An early example is Bordeaux, beginning in 847. In the following year the besiegers were beaten off by Charles the Bald's forces, but subsequently, possibly by means of a night attack, the Vikings broke through the defences and ravaged and burnt the town. Their persistence had been rewarded. Danes made elaborate preparations for a siege of London in 1016, digging a large ditch parallel to the southern bank of the Thames and dragging their ships upstream of the bridge. The town on the northern bank was then surrounded by another ditch, with the result that no one could get in or out. Time and again towns in Western Europe were targeted. Their usual fate was to be subjected to plundering and burning, like Bonn and Cologne in 881; occasionally they were captured and taken over for lengthy periods, as happened to York in 866 and London five years later. Viking siege techniques were probably similar to those of their contemporaries: exotic strategems, such as Harald Haardrada's supposed use of small birds fitted with burning shavings of fir tied to their backs, whereby to set fire to a Sicilian town, belong firmly to a saga writer's imagination. In due course Vikings built defences for their own urban creations, as at Birka and Hedeby in the homelands, or at Dublin in Ireland. The two Scandinavian ones were abandoned during the Viking Age itself and

The Gokstad ship viewed from the helmsman's position. With a beam of 5.3 metres this vessel is surprisingly spacious amidships. There were no fixed benches and the crewmen probably sat on their sea-chests when they took to the oars. Either singly or lashed together with ropes, ships like this would have formed fighting platforms for Vikings and their opponents.

their mid-tenth-century ramparts can be traced in their entirety. At Dublin, on the other hand, the fortifications have been only partially revealed by archaeological excavations, notably at Wood Quay. There the sequence consisted essentially of earthen banks, reinforced by timber, dated *c.*950 and *c.*1000, culminating in a stone wall of *c.*1100.

Viking attacks of all kinds were heavily dependent for their success on Scandinavian mastery of shipbuilding and navigation. Ships conveyed not only warriors and sometimes horses, but also that element of surprise which has always been decisive in military history. The bewildering mobility of Vikings that so struck contemporaries owed much to their ships. That mobility was demonstrated spectacularly in 859–60, when Danes sailed through the Straits of Gibraltar and up the Rhône as far north as Valence, before retreating to an island base and then setting off for Italy where they attacked Pisa and other towns. In 1005, as the *Anglo-Saxon Chronicle* ruefully remarks, the Danish fleet left England for home, yet 'let little time elapse before it came back'. Scandinavians in the Viking Age deployed many types of ship, as the extensive vocabulary in Old Norse implies, but the classic warship of the first half of the period is probably still best represented by the one discovered at Gokstad, in southern Norway, in 1880. With its sixteen pairs of oars it would have had a crew of about 35 men. This ship was built in the last years of the ninth century, at precisely the time when King Alfred was experimenting with 'longships' that were roughly twice as big as those of the Danes and equipped with 60 or more oars. These details from a Norwegian ship-burial and from an English text are in perfect accord. Later ships were probably bigger, like that which Earl Godwin gave to King Harthacnut in 1040 and which was manned by 80 warriors. In an incident off the north-east coast of Ireland in 986 the crewmen of three Danish ships were captured; 140 of them were executed and the rest were sold into slavery, implying a complement for each ship of at least 60 and possibly more. Ships of both types were deployed on the open sea and along the greater rivers: in 844, for example, Vikings sailed up the Garonne as far as Toulouse. In more confined spaces their crews took to the oars, as on the Lympne in Kent in 892 and on the Lea north of London two years later.

By the twelfth century there was an obligation on the inhabitants of coastal districts in the Scandinavian homelands to build and man ships for both defensive and offensive purposes. This obligation, known as leidang (*leiðangr*), is probably to be interpreted as an expression of growing royal power, along with

Memorial stone from Smiss, Gotland, showing a ship full of Viking warriors. Though crudely represented, visible features of the vessel include ornamented stem- and stern-posts, the steering oar to starboard, the mast and supporting stays, and the interwoven sail-cloth. The crewmen wear conical helmets and carry shields. The upper panel depicts two men in single combat.

other developments such as the foundation of bishoprics, the protection of townspeople, and the minting of coins. The antiquity of this system of naval military service is highly uncertain, again for lack of contemporary evidence. Warships were sophisticated in their construction and required carefully selected timber that had to be transported, materials such as rivets, ropes, and sail-cloth, and skilled craftsmen. In one English reference we have a precise indication of the average cost of building a warship—£345 5*s*. In terms of late Anglo-Saxon notional prices, this was the equivalent of over 4,000 cows. Since a typical Norwegian farmer may have had only a dozen or so, Scandinavian warlords would have disposed of considerable tributary resources in order to assemble a fleet of any size. Social mechanisms of military obligation must be presumed to have lain in the realm of customary dues, which were incurred by the war-band itself when fleets operated abroad. This we can deduce from allusions to ship repairs and even ship construction in Western European sources. In June 866, for example, a group of Vikings moved from their island base near the monastery of St-Denis and sailed down the Seine until they reached a suitable place for both purposes, as well as to take delivery of tribute from the local Frankish population. Four years earlier Weland's warriors had chosen Jumièges on the same river in order to repair their ships and to await the spring equinox, before making for the open sea.

There has been much debate among scholars about the size of Viking fleets. Contemporary written records offer two types of figure. One is small, precise, and usually associated with circumstantial details. Thus a mere six crews inflicted severe damage on the Isle of Wight in 896, while seven ravaged Southampton and killed or captured most of the inhabitants in 980. The other type of figure is much bigger and normally a round number, suggestive of an estimate. The more conservative of these figures are perfectly credible: the Norwegian fleet that menaced eastern Ireland in 837 in two equal halves clearly heralded a change of policy and the 67 shiploads of warriors who sacked Nantes six years later may have been part of it. Large fleets needed correspondingly large resources: a Danish one based on the Isle of Wight in 998 was exploiting Hampshire and Sussex for its food supply. Sea battles may be distinguished in the same way. Most were probably small-scale skirmishes of the kind that we hear about in Alfred's reign, as in 882 when the opposition consisted of four ships' crews, two of which were killed and the others captured. Land-based chroniclers have little to say about major naval battles fought among the Scandinavians themselves. In 852 a Norwegian fleet of 160 ships was attacked by Danish Vikings off the Irish coast over the space of three days and nights, whilst in 914 a 'naval battle' (*bellum navale*) was fought between the rival grandsons of former kings of Dublin. Two large-scale naval battles in Scandinavia had important political consequences for Norway: at Hafrsfjord, near Stavanger, Harald Finehair defeated a coalition of rival warlords *c.*870, and at Svold, in the Baltic Sea, Olaf Tryggvason lost his life in a contest with his Danish contemporary, Sven Forkbeard, in the year 1000.

Of greater importance than the role of the Viking ship as a mobile platform for conventional fighting was its utility as a mode of conveyance. As we are informed in 1003, 'Sven went back to the sea, where he knew his ships were'. Armies campaigning among hostile populations depended on their ships as a means of departure as much as they did for their arrival. Their opponents would naturally endeavour to deny them access: only those raiders who could swim out to their waiting ships were able to escape from English pursuers in north Devon and Somerset in 914. In 855 and again in 865 Vikings based on the Loire tried to reach Poitiers about 75 kilometres away on foot, on the first occasion unsuccessfully. The *Anglo-Saxon Chronicle* cites the distance that loot and provisions were carried back to the coast in 1006—over 50 miles—the Danes taunting the inhabitants of Winchester as they marched past their gate. On big Continental waterways the progress of a Viking fleet could serve as an advance warning to the local people, as in 853 when relics and treasures were removed to safety from Tours. Such predictions were less possible further away from the main rivers: six years later the townspeople of Noyon were subjected to a night-time attack by Vikings based on the Seine, at least 85 kilometres to the south-west, and the bishop and other noblemen were taken captive. Fleets sometimes lent support to land-based forces by co-ordinating their movements: this happened along the south coast of England late in 876 as the Danish great army proceeded overland from Wareham to Exeter, though a substantial number of these ships were lost in a storm off Swanage. But the essential role of the ship was to facilitate raiding and profit-taking. The Fulda annalist wrote sorrowfully in 854 about Vikings 'who for twenty years continuously had cruelly afflicted with fire and slaughter and pillage those places on the borders of Francia which were accessible by ship'.

That military activity shaded off imperceptibly into economic activity was characteristic of the Viking Age. The classic early nineteenth-century view of warfare enunciated by Carl von Clausewitz is that it amounts to a continuation of political intercourse with the admixture of different means; in the case of the Vikings we might see warfare as often as not as a form of economic intercourse. In the autumn of 865, for example, Vikings took over the great monastery north of Paris at St-Denis and spent about twenty days stripping it of movable wealth, carrying booty to their ships each day before returning to base-camp not far away. A similar operation by Dublin Vikings at Clonmacnoise on the Shannon in 936 required only a two-night stopover. In cases such

Mixed hoard of gold, silver, and beads from Hon in south-eastern Norway. Among the gold objects are a large trefoil-shaped mount from Francia and a finger-ring from England. Carolingian coins were fitted with attachments to make them adaptable for necklaces, suggesting that Viking Age womenfolk may have encouraged their menfolk to engage in piracy.

as these, there was no overt political agenda; the motive was easy profit and most of the loot from Britain and Ireland that has been discovered in western Norway in particular must have originated in this way, the beneficiaries including womenfolk whose grave-goods betray the piratical inclinations of their menfolk. Stolen goods could find a ready market elsewhere, as when Danish raiders in Kent in 1048 subsequently made for Flanders where they sold what they had stolen and then went back home. One plundering tactic, therefore, was simply for Viking raiders to turn up, in the words of the *Annals of St-Bertin*, 'with their usual surprise attack'. For Christian communities major church festivals were a time of danger: in 929 Kildare was raided from Dublin on St Brigid's Day, when the place would have been full of pilgrims; in 986 Iona was attacked by Danes on Christmas night, when the community was preoccupied with its devotions. Another tactic was more complex—to threaten destructive violence with a view to exacting tribute. Vikings engaged in this process in the west Frankish kingdom in 866 had come equipped not only with weapons, but also with their own balance-scales for weighing the 4,000 pounds of silver.

The profits of Viking warfare assumed several different forms. Most basic were food and drink, for such provisions enabled warriors to continue to pursue their warlike activities. In 864, for instance, Rodulf Haraldsson and his men received as tribute not only cash, but also flour, livestock, wine, and cider. In Ireland cattle on the hoof were the standard tribute among the native population and Vikings took advantage of this tradition as early as 798. Norwegians, on the other hand, were accustomed to exploiting their own seas for large creatures, which accounts for 'a great slaughter of porpoises' by them off the east coast of Ireland in 828. A second form of profit was human beings. High-status people would be ransomed whenever possible; low-status people and others for whom payment was not forthcoming would be retained or sold as slaves. A spectacular ransom was paid in 858 for Abbot Louis of St-Denis and his brother, Gauzlin: 686 pounds of gold and 3,250 pounds of silver. The upcountry bishop of Archenfield, on the Anglo-Welsh border, was delivered at a cost of £40 donated by the West Saxon king in 914. The alternative was death, as in the case of Archbishop Ælfheah of Canterbury who was brutally murdered in 1012 when payment of the Danes' demand for £3,000 was not forthcoming. A third form of profit was land on which to settle. The entry in the *Anglo-Saxon Chronicle* for 896 may imply that Vikings might purchase property, but land must often have been obtained by force of arms. Large-scale political takeovers would have facilitated the acquisition of farmland, as in Northumbria (866–7), East Anglia (869–70), and Mercia (873–4), all of which were to receive Danish settlers in due course. Even earlier, land-taking had occurred in the Scottish Isles and the kingdom of Dublin had been established *c.*853. Accordingly food and drink, bullion and cash, land and labour were among the considerable profits of Viking warfare.

In effect Vikings were competing among themselves, and with the natives of the countries in which they raided, traded, and settled, for wealth. Amid all the aristocratic and dynastic competition of the Viking Age, the greatest prize was the kingdom of England, which was won initially by the West Saxons in 910–27, by the Danes in 1013–16, and by the Normans in 1066–71. A final Danish challenge failed to materialize in 1085–6. Behind the aggression, brutality, and destructiveness, there was calculating rationality. From our own distant perspective, filtered through external sources for the most part, it has become fashionable to portray Vikings as catalysts of economic and political change. By dishoarding monastic treasuries, wealth was released for more productive purposes, even though some of it was simply rehoarded in Scandinavia. There is an element of truth in this argument, but any temptation to glamorize Vikings should be resisted. Vikings divested of bear-coats, horned helmets, a predilection for blood-eagling, and devilishly ingenious siege tactics are Vikings demythologized, yet they become all the more credible as brave and resourceful fighters. As such they were celebrated by contemporary skalds and their deeds were further elaborated to the point of fictionalization by later generations of saga writers. With that in mind, the modern Icelandic author, Halldor Laxness, published a subtly satirical novel entitled *Gerpla* in 1956; two years afterwards this appeared in English as *The Happy Warriors*. According to the book's own publicity, 'the inescapable conclusion is that the legendary heroes were not larger than life after all; they were what would nowadays be called misfits, and a nuisance to everyone'. More than that, their historical antecedents brought untold misery, injury, and death to tens of thousands of men, women, and children. But warfare was not a Viking monopoly; Vikings were a Scandinavian manifestation of a universal scourge.

4 AN AGE OF EXPANSION c.1020–1204

JOHN GILLINGHAM

The Rise of the Empire of the Franks

In the eyes of Muslims and Greeks eleventh-century Western Europeans (whom the Muslims called Franks and whom the Greeks sometimes called Franks and sometimes Celts) were loud-mouthed and crude barbarians whose only skills lay in fighting and in the manufacture of arms. During the later eleventh and twelfth centuries these barbarians enjoyed a period of unusually sustained military success and expansion. A great historian Ibn-al-Athir, looking back from his vantage point in early thirteenth-century Mosul, described it as the 'rise of the empire of the Franks'. For Ibn-al-Athir two key dates were 1085, the capture of Toledo, and 1091, the completion of the Norman conquest of Sicily. Had he been writing in Edinburgh instead of Mosul, he might have started with 1066, the year of Hastings when, in the words of the Bayeux Tapestry, 'both Franks and English fell in battle'. Underlying the rise of the empire of the 'Franks' were demographic growth and economic expansion—developments which put more resources and money into the hands of the ruling elites of Western Europe. Since they were warrior elites, they chose to spend more on war: on arms, armour, horses, ships, and fortifications. The scale of military operations increased. Even more than before, Western aristocratic society became an aggressive society where knights and their followers, archers and crossbowmen, pushed back the frontiers of their dominions, east against the Slavs and towards Jerusalem, south into Greek and Muslim South Italy and Spain, north and west into England, Wales, and Ireland, building castles wherever they went. By the mid-twelfth century an author such as the German Helmold of Bosau could

This English manuscript illustrates the quantity of iron—for tools as well as for weapons and armour—consumed by the arms industry. As shown here, from the twelfth century onwards rich societies manufactured coats of mail even for warhorses.

envisage expansion as being planned on a Europe-wide scale. According to him, those organizing the great crusade of 1147 decided that one army should go to the Orient, a second to Spain, and a third against the pagan Slavs.

The Lure of Gold

In some cases—for example the twelfth-century campaigns against Celts and Slavs—this expansion was underpinned by an industrial and technological advantage possessed by the English and German aggressors, their capacity to produce arms and armour superior both in quantity and quality to those available to the people who were trying, in vain, to hold on to the lands of their fathers. But neither of the dramatic eleventh-century events highlighted by Ibn-al-Athir can be explained in terms of an imbalance of military technology. Indeed Spain and South Italy were highly developed, urbanized, and very wealthy societies—in all of 'Western' Europe (geographically speaking) they were the only two regions where gold coin continued to be used. This, of course, was why mercenaries and adventurers, men such as Roger de Tosny and Harald Sigurdson, made for these theatres of war. In the 1020s Roger de Tosny fought for Barcelona against its Muslim neighbours; then went back to Normandy—where he was known as 'Roger the Spaniard'—and used his wealth to found the abbey of Conches *c.*1035. Harald Sigurdson went to Constantinople, saw service with the Greeks in Sicily and then returned home to Norway with such 'an immense hoard of money and gold and treasure' that he was able to become king in 1047. As Harald Haardrada, 'the thunderbolt of the North' he invaded England in 1066. All he won was the proverbial six foot of English soil, but the other invader, Duke William of Normandy, conquered a land that his chaplain called 'a treasure-house of Araby', so abundant was it in gold and precious metals. But if it is easy to explain why those who 'sought wealth by soldiering' in the eleventh century were attracted to South Italy, Spain, and England, it is not so easy to explain why the invaders, fighting against defenders with resources at least as great, should have won the upper hand.

Eleventh-Century Spain

Eleventh-century al-Andalus remained a wealthy, urbanized, and culturally sophisticated society, extending over the greater part—and the more fertile part—of the landmass of modern Spain, but after the death of Abd al-Malik in 1008 the Ummayad Caliphate of Córdoba fell apart into 30 or so warring city-states, the 'party' or *taifa* states. For its manpower the Cordoban war-machine had come to rely heavily on 'imports': Slavs and Berbers. The former were boys captured in war in North East Europe, castrated and then transported to Cordoba where they were trained as slave-soldiers, the Mamluks of al-Andalus. When developments along the Slav–German frontier led to the drying up of this source of slaves, the *taifa* kings were unable to find an alternative supply and as rulers of small states they were conscious of the risks of relying on large numbers of Berber tribesmen from nearby North Africa. Their consequential lack of fighting men meant that they became increasingly vulnerable to military pressure from the Christian north. Where once the Muslims had regularly raided the Christians, the boot was now well and truly on the other foot.

Christian rulers exploited their military dominance to consolidate their power and enhance their status. The counts of Barcelona began to mint their own gold coin; Castile became a kingdom in 1035; the lords of Aragon became kings in 1076; Portugal became a kingdom after 1140. Their strategy was to use military pressure, raiding, ravaging, and looting, to extract tribute (*parias*). According to the memoirs which Abd Allah, emir of Granada, wrote in the 1090s, Alfonso VI of Leon-Castile (1065–1109) 'spoke to me softly saying "I will not subject you to anything more than the payment of tribute"—which he fixed at 10,000 mitqals a year—"but if you do not pay up in good time you will receive a visit from my ambassador and you will find his stay rather expensive." I accepted his terms for I knew that paying 10,000 a year for protection was better than the devastation of the land.' Alfonso VI's father, Fernando I (1035–65), had been the first great exponent of this protection racket, at one time collecting the rich *parias* of Zaragoza, Toledo, Badajoz, and Seville. They had made him rich enough to endow Cluny in 1055 with an annual gift of 1,000 pieces of gold—more than this great abbey's entire income from land; in 1077 Alfonso VI was to double his father's gift.

Inevitably there was rivalry between the Christian states for control of these rich pickings. In these circumstances Muslims might sometimes fight for Christians and vice versa, as when the Cid took service with the emir of Zaragoza. Nonetheless the existence of the religious frontier between Christian and Muslim meant that war between them was thought of as normal, indeed admirable. But for decades, despite having the upper hand, and with rare exceptions such as the capture of Coimbra in 1064, the Christians deliberately refrained from territorial expansion. According to Abd Allah, they knew that they lacked the human resources which would have enabled them to retain, colonize, and profit from any territory they conquered. Their intention, he believed, was 'to set the Muslim princes against each other and continually take money from them'. It would have been foolish to kill the goose that laid the golden egg.

But the Toledan goose became so weakened that in the 1080s, almost inexorably, Alfonso VI was drawn into taking it over. Excited by the capture of this great city, the old capital of Visigothic Spain and a strategic centre from which roads radiated out in all directions, Alfonso and his allies pressed forward. In 1094 a second major Muslim centre fell when the Cid captured Valencia. But the tide of war had already turned. Shattered by the fall of Toledo, the *taifa* rulers had been reluctantly driven to turn for help to a powerful fellow Muslim, even though they regarded him as much a crude barbarian as the Christians. This was Yusuf ibn Tashufin, Almoravid emir of a wide North African empire. The strongly religious outlook of the Almoravids, their disapproval of what they regarded as the decadent softness of *taifa* society, their abolition of non-Koranic taxes, and their promise to put an end to the threat of Christian raids—a promise backed up by the dispatch of African military resources (including camels)—all combined to make them irresistible in post-1085 al-

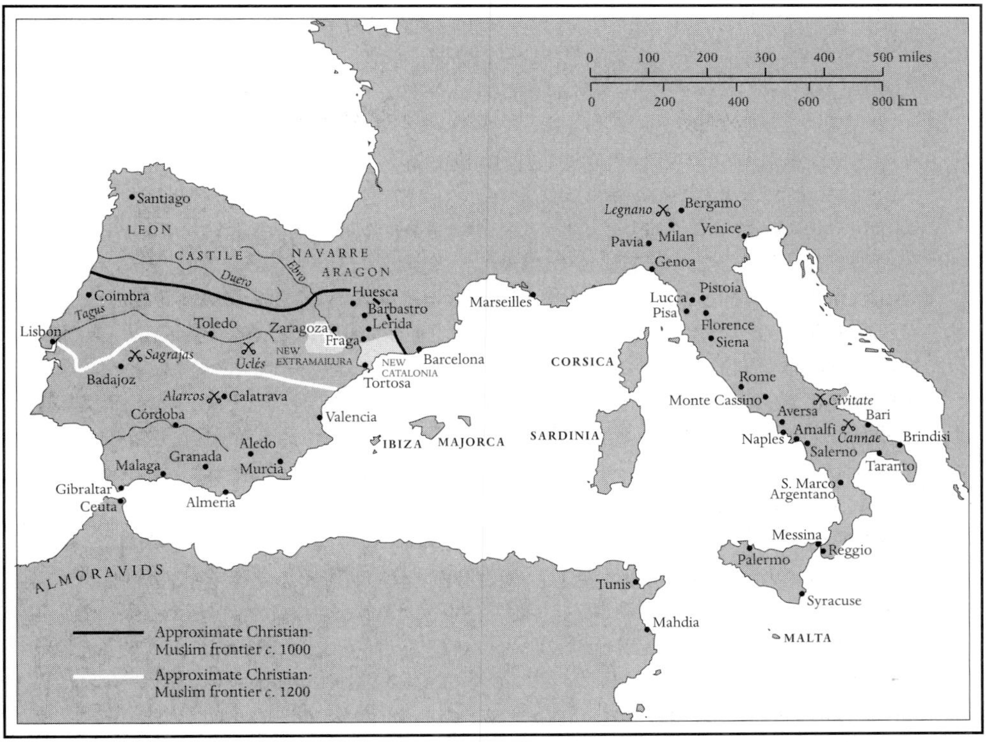

THE WESTERN MEDITERRANEAN, FROM SPAIN TO ITALY, *c*.1000–*c*.1200

Andalus. From the moment of their arrival in Spain they were to enjoy over thirty years of virtually unbroken success. Yusuf defeated Alfonso VI in battle at Sagrajas in 1086; Alfonso's only son met his death in battle at their hands at Uclés in 1108. Angered by the failure of the *taifa* kings to help him when he besieged Toledo itself in 1090, Yusuf turned against them. Their Christian protectors failed to protect and one by one they were added to the Almoravid empire. Even in the north-east where the kings of Aragon with French help had some success in pushing down the Ebro, taking Huesca in 1096 and Barbastro in 1100, Almoravid expansion continued apace. They recaptured Valencia in 1102, took over Zaragoza (1106) and recaptured Majorca and Ibiza. By 1117 all the former *taifa* states had been eliminated; the political map of Spain completely redrawn. Roughly speaking Christians held the upper hand until 1085; then Muslims until *c*.1118. The way the tide of war turned, first *c*.1010 then after 1085, suggests that it was political rather than military factors which were decisive. As in the history of the crusades, the key variable was the degree of fragmentation in the Muslim world.

The Normans in the South

From *c.*1000 a motley crew of mercenaries from France and northern Italy as well as from Normandy drifted into South Italy where they took service with either the Byzantine government or any one of a number of rival Lombard rulers. Late eleventh-century authors, who knew the end of the story and were usually writing for Norman patrons, give the impression that such was Norman bravery, cunning, and ruthlessness, and by so much did they outclass their enemies in the arts of war, that once they had found their way there they were bound to end up as masters of Greek South Italy and Muslim Sicily. According to William of Apulia, 'the people of Gaul are more powerful than any other people in force of arms'. Twentieth-century authors sometimes agree, suggesting that in the charge of their mounted knights the Normans possessed a military arm that swept all before it. It is not a view which stands up to analysis.

Their normal technique was to seize a castle and use it as a base from which to terrorize the surrounding district into submission, as Robert of Hauteville, known as Guiscard, 'the Weasel', did from San Marco Argentano in Calabria. According to Amatus of Montecassino, another Norman, Richard of Aversa, 'carried off everything he could and gave it away, keeping little . . . in this way the land about was plundered and the number of his knights multiplied'. Decades of this kind of brigandage made the Normans thoroughly unpopular and Pope Leo IX organized a coalition of Byzantines and Lombards against them. This forced the various Norman bands to unite their forces and they managed to bring the pope's army, which included a contingent of Swabian troops, to battle at Civitate on 17 June 1053, before it was joined by the Greeks. At Civitate, it has been said, 'the old world of Germanic infantry tactics went down before the new chivalry of heavy cavalry.' But according to William of Apulia's *Deeds of Robert Guiscard*, once the pope's Lombards had ridden away in flight, the 700 Swabian foot soldiers who remained put up a prolonged and stout resistance against several thousand Normans. If anything Civitate demonstrates the strength in battle of infantry even when hugely outnumbered. Leo IX was taken prisoner and forced to recognize the Norman acquisitions. But the few lordships they had obtained by this date were hardly impressive. As yet, apart perhaps from Humphrey of Hauteville's Melfi, they controlled none of the major centres.

Only after 1059 did the Normans make spectacular gains, and for this there were two principal reasons. The first was the growing pressure of the Seljuk Turks on Anatolia. As late as 1038 Constantinople had shown real interest in the West, sending an expedition under its foremost general, George Maniaces, to recover Sicily. He captured Messina and Syracuse, but was recalled in disgrace in 1040—the fate of many 'too successful' Byzantine generals from Belisarius onwards. What mattered was that 1038–40 was the last time that Constantinople felt able to give so high a priority to its most western provinces, indeed it was increasingly reluctant to provide the governors of Apulia and Calabria with resources adequate to maintain the regional status quo. In 1058–9 there occurred the first serious breaches in Byzantine defences in Anatolia, and soon afterwards the Normans made their first major inroads. In 1060 Guiscard, recently given the title 'duke of Apulia and Calabria, future duke of Sicily' by Pope Nicholas II, occupied Reggio, Brindisi, and Taranto. Next year Robert's younger brother Roger crossed the Straits and seized Messina—the first step into the politically disunited society of Muslim Sicily. On the whole the two brothers cooperated well, and from 1060 until their deaths, Robert's in 1085 and Roger's in 1101, they dominated the region. This was the second principal reason for Norman success after 1059: the continuity of leadership provided by two extraordinarily able—and long-lived—conquistadores. The Cid's exploits as a warlord made him a Spanish hero; Guiscard was to achieve international fame as, in the words of his epitaph, 'the terror of the world'. Something of the impression he made can be gleaned from the character sketch composed by the Greek princess, Anna Comnena: 'that Norman braggart Robert, notorious for his power-lust, of obscure origin, overbearing, thoroughly villainous, a brave fighter and very cunning, wonderfully built, and utterly determined.'

In 1068 the braggart began a siege and naval blockade of Bari, the main stronghold of imperial Byzantine power in South Italy, at a time when the soldier-emperor Romanos Diogenes was increasingly preoccupied with the eastern campaign that was to end with his defeat and capture at Mantzikert. After a three-year blockade, Bari surrendered in 1071. Immediately Robert and Roger turned their attention to Palermo, the metropolis of Muslim Sicily. It surrendered in January 1072. Only after the fall of these two great cities was there an air of inevitability about the Norman conquest of the south. Amalfi was taken in 1073, Salerno in 1077, Syracuse in 1085, the last fortresses in Sicily and Malta in 1091. The critical battles which sealed the fates of both Bari and Palermo were not won by the much vaunted Norman cavalry, they were not even land battles, but naval battles, fought when fleets tried, in vain, to break the blockades. Given the length of the coastlines of South Italy and Sicily in relation to landmass, it is not surprising that sea power should have been critical.

In the Mediterranean

The Muslim loss of Sicily and Malta completed the ruin of their once impressive chain of possessions along the trunk routes of the Mediterranean. In this the Pisans and the Genoese had played a major role, even occasionally acting in concert (see Chapter 11, pp. 249). In a series of raids, beginning in 1015, they wrested control of Corsica and Sardinia from the Muslims. They launched raids on North African ports such as Mahdia (1087). In the Mediterranean the principal warship was the oared galley, single-masted and lateen-rigged. Given their limited water-storage capacity, galleys had a restricted range and they tended to hug land, since lack of freeboard meant they were easily swamped. But they were capable of high speed over short distances, and more manoeuvrable than sailing ships in estuaries and coastal waters. Hence they were ideally suited to coastal raids and attacks on ports. Although Muslim ships were of the same types as Christian, geography favoured the latter. They had the advantage of prevailing weather and current patterns, more suitable harbours on the northern shores, and of the fact that the major Mediterranean islands were nearer the northern shore (see Chapter 11, p. 231). After 1091 the Muslims retained only the Balearics and the ports of western Andalusia.

On the Northern Frontiers

The more powerful northern rulers, such as the kings of Germany and England, liked to think of their poorer neighbours as tributary peoples. They were encouraged in this belief by the way exiles turned to them for help. In Britain, for example, the sons of Duncan of Scotland appealed for help against Macbeth in 1054, and Edgar the Scot turned to William Rufus against Donald Ban in 1097. The numerous succession disputes within the Hungarian, Bohemian, Polish, Abodrite, and Danish ruling dynasties presented German kings with many opportunities for military intervention—and they sometimes took them. But conquest was ruled out by the logistical problems involved in maintaining armies for long periods in relatively thinly populated countries. (One index of eleventh-century England's prosperity is the fact that it was conquered twice.) Elsewhere only a loose overlordship was feasible, and dependent rulers tended to become independent—and stop paying tribute—as soon as they sat reasonably securely on their thrones. The kings of Germany (throughout this period) and the kings of England (especially after 1066) had many other more pressing concerns and tended to leave the business of enforcement of their superiority to marcher lords—in Germany, to the Saxon and Bavarian aristocracy. So these frontiers long remained war-zones between fairly evenly-matched powers. Beyond these frontiers successful warrior-kings often pursued overlordships of their own, such as that obtained by Gruffudd ap Llywelyn of Gwynedd over the other Welsh kings from 1055 to 1063, or in Ireland the 'high-kingships' won by Diarmait mac Maíl na mBó of Leinster (1042–72) or Muirchertach O'Brien of Munster (1086–1114). The vast expanses of Eastern Europe enabled Polish kings such as Boleslav II and Boleslav III to strike out from their centres at Gniezno, Poznan, and Cracow, in the direction of Pomerania and the Baltic fishing grounds, or even as far east as Kiev, in the construction of overlordships which were on a much grander scale, but just as ephemeral.

Wars in the North

Overlordship meant tribute and tribute meant raiding. Everywhere from *taifa* Spain to the far North where the Norse raided Laps to enforce a tribute of reindeer, the basic form of war was the raid, the *chevauchée* (see also Chapter 5, p. 98). In urbanized societies such as Spain and Italy the raid was not enough; ultimately wars were decided by sieges and blockades. By contrast in societies

A passage from a twelfth-century epic, the *Chanson des Lorrains*, provides an apt commentary on this scene from the Maciejowski Bible: 'a surge of fear sweeps over the countryside. Everywhere you can see helmets glinting in the sun, pennons waving in the breeze, the plain covered with horsemen. Money, cattle, mules and sheep are all seized.' Here the mail armour of the prisoners shows they can afford ransoms.

such as those in the Celtic, Scandinavian, and Slav worlds, where towns and markets were few and where wealth was dispersed widely through the countryside, the raid was virtually the only form of war. Here, in pillage economies, plunder and tribute were central to the circulation of wealth. Kings and other war-leaders mounted raids on their neighbours either to seize slaves and livestock or by burning and destroying to enforce the payment of tribute, probably itself paid in livestock. (Obviously the sea-kings who used oared warships built in the northern tradition (see Chapter 11, p. 234), clinker-built and square-rigged, for their raids did not go in for cattle-rustling, but concentrated on slaves and precious metals.) On land the job of most of those who rode with a raiding party was to round up the prey; there was no need for them to be heavily armed. When the going got tough they scattered and left the fighting to the well-armed few, the nobles. Farmers, their families, and their livestock were escorted to a place of refuge as soon as an alarm was given, but often the slow-moving convoy would be caught and a running fight would develop between the fightingmen. Even if raiders achieved initial surprise, they would not want to kill their prey by over-driving, so in this case too

Trim Castle. Although its curtain walls were added in the thirteenth century, dendro-chronological dating shows that the keep was built for Hugh de Lacy (d.1186), lord of Meath and Henry II's governor of Ireland. At a time when no Irish king was building in stone on anything like this scale, it symbolized the power and ambition of an English aristocrat suspected of wanting to be king of Ireland.

a running fight between their well-armed rear-guard and the defenders determined to recover their own was almost inevitable. In some of these battles casualties among the nobles could be very high.

Castles and Wars in the West

From the time of the early eleventh-century building boom observed by Ralph Glaber, by far the most important aspect of the increased investment in war in Western Europe was the money spent on fortification (see further, Chapter 8, pp. 170–3). In the military architecture of the time, though with more evident purpose, there was that same striving after height visible in contemporary church architecture. It was characterized by towers which 'soared to the sky', tower-houses in towns and towers perched on artificial mounds (mottes) in the countryside. Compared with other forms of fortification the castle was tall and small. Too small to admit more than a small proportion of the local population, it protected them only indirectly, depending on the capacity of the garrison to harass invading forces and inhibit ravaging. But castles were instruments of power and independent-minded lords found them highly desirable. Raymond III of Rouergue built a castle on the rock at Conques to impose the yoke of his lordship, as he himself (according to *The Miracles of St Foy*, *c*.1020) put it, on those who did not want to accept it. Rights to tax, justice, and all profits of local lordship readily fell into the hands of castellans. The problem for princes was to retain the loyalty of castellans. In about 1030 the Poitevin lord Hugh of Lusignan composed an account of his disputes with Duke William of Aquitaine. This narrative, the *Conventum*, suggests that in Western Europe small-scale wars were a normal continuation of local politics by other means. Castles were both the main bones of contention between them, and the focal points around which the campaigns revolved. Even in principalities such as Flanders and Normandy where the rulers on the whole contained the castellans, this was far from being a stable situation. According to William of Jumièges, when the boy William became duke of Normandy in 1035, the province was reduced to chaos as 'many Normans hatched plots and rebellions once they felt secure behind newly built earthworks and fortifications'. A century later Suger's *Life* of Louis VI suggests that even the king of France was troubled by lords who defied him from behind their castle walls.

There were many other causes of wars. Virtually everywhere from Scotland to Spain and from Brittany to Bohemia succession to royal or ducal office was only decided after a power-struggle, often a war, between brothers or cousins. Intermarriage between the ruling dynasties meant that wars of succession quite often reached the level of wars between states (indeed this remained the case well beyond the middle ages). Occasionally such dynastic wars resulted in conquests as dramatic as the Norman Conquest of England or the Hohenstaufen (German) conquest of Sicily. In urbanized Italy cities fought to control food supply and trade routes. War was the common experience not just of the peoples who lived on the frontiers of Europe, but in almost every part of Europe—though England was often an exception.

Conquest and Control of Territory: England

Where the control of territory was disputed, pitched battles could be decisive, especially in those regions where castle building had not yet proliferated. The stories of the Norman Conquest of England and of the Saxon war in Germany offer illuminating illustrations. They point up two crucial issues in medieval warfare: the relative importance of cavalry and infantry, and the impact of new techniques of fortification.

Between Cnut's conquest in 1015–16 and the overwhelming events of 1066 England's unusually centralized government kept the peace to the economic benefit of its people. Towns were managed by royal officers, and there were very few castles. The kings kept a permanent fleet of hired Danish ships and men at London until 1051; from Edward the Confessor's reign Kentish ports provided naval patrols in the Narrow Seas. Great magnates such as Earl Godwin and his sons used fleets, not castles, to pursue their political ends—as when they reasserted their dominance over Edward in 1052. In 1063 Harold burned Gruffudd ap Llywelyn's ships as they lay at Rhuddlan, and then took his own fleet from Bristol round Wales to put an abrupt end to Llywelyn's power. But in these years, except on the Scottish and Welsh borders, the English had very little direct experience of war.

In 1066 Harold stationed his fleet at the Isle of Wight with every reasonable expectation of being able to deal with William's expeditionary force, but the Norman duke delayed sailing until the English fleet returned to London for re-provisioning. However William's fleet was blown off course and ended up at St-Valéry-sur-Somme. When he eventually sailed from there, Harold was in Yorkshire meeting Haardrada at the Battle of Stamford Bridge and so William was able to establish a beachhead virtually unimpeded. On 14 October 1066 William outmanouevred Harold, though whether this was enough to win the battle of Hastings can never be determined with any certainty; Harold was still able to draw up his troops in a strong defensive position. It is possible that William's army, recruited from all over northern France, possessed a decisive advantage in its missile-delivery systems—either a technological edge in the shape of the crossbow, seemingly a weapon unknown to the English, or perhaps simply an advantage in the number of archers present. The contemporary French author of *The Song of Hastings* wrote of 'the French, versed in strategems, skilled in warfare' and of the English as 'a people ignorant of war'. This too may have been significant in deciding the outcome—since the success of the French cavalry's feigned flight suggests practice on one side and inexperience on the other.

In the critical weeks after Hastings such was the disarray within the English leadership that none of the fortified towns which might have resisted William—Dover, Canterbury, Wallingford, and above all Winchester and London—did so. Not until early 1068 did an English city, Exeter, show what English fortifications might have achieved. Although Exeter surrendered after an eighteen-day siege, it did so only after inflicting heavy losses on William's army and inducing him to offer favourable terms. William, of course, was keenly aware of the strategic problem posed by the towns. Hence his systematic policy of building castles in the major towns. He was equally aware of the strategic problem of the north—hence the 'Harrying of the North', probably the most systematic burning and destroying in medieval history. But one type

Widely regarded as a diabolical weapon, the crossbow carved on this late eleventh-century capital from the cathedral of St Sernin, Toulouse, is shown being spanned. Spanning, even by a demon, took time. The crossbow's rate of fire was much slower than that of the 'ordinary' bow, but not even the well-armoured knight was safe from its penetrative power. Both bow and crossbow were banned by the Lateran Council of 1139; the ban had no effect.

of problem at least William had not had to face, he was not confronted by a landscape of castles as he would have been in France, as indeed he had been when conquering Maine in the early 1060s. In William's camp there were men who believed that, no matter how brave its soldiers, a land without castles was virtually indefensible. William set about remedying the situation from the moment he disembarked late in September 1066 and constructed the castles of Pevensey and Hastings. His men followed suit. As many as 500 castles may have been built by the end of his reign (1087).

Conquest and Control of Territory: The Battles for Saxony

The battles for England in 1066 have been endlessly fought over by historians. Less well-known are the battles between the Saxons and the Salian (i.e. Frankish) Kings of Germany, Henry IV and Henry V—even though they were the action highlights of the most important war in Germany before the Thirty Years War. The war was fought in three phases, 1073–80, 1085–9, and 1112–15. Each phase was precipitated by the king moving into Saxony in order to exert, as he saw it, traditional royal authority there. Each phase ended with the king driven out by the Saxons who saw him as a tyrant trying to overturn their cherished liberties—in part by building too many castles such as the Harzburg, near the great Salian palace of Goslar, in a previously fairly castle-free zone. In all three phases battles mattered. In the second phase Henry IV was defeated at Pleichfeld in August 1086 by dismounted enemies who fought on foot around their standard. The third phase was settled when Henry V was defeated by Lothar of Supplingenburg, duke of the Saxons, at the battle of Welfesholz in February 1115. But it is the first phase which is best known, thanks in large part to *The Book of the Saxon War*, a vivid narrative written by Bruno of Merseburg, a clerk who was himself deeply involved in the events he describes. Few descriptions of eleventh-century warfare are as penetrating as Bruno's. Although the revolt began with the Saxon siege of Harzburg in 1073–4, Bruno's war does not revolve around sieges but around what he calls the first, second, third, and fourth battles.

The first battle occurred on the Unstrut on 9 June 1075. According to Bruno, Henry IV attacked the Saxons while they were still expecting negotiation, and despite the desperate confusion, exacerbated by dust, in which contingents on both sides took to flight, the advantage he stole then was sufficient to win the day. He followed this up by ravaging Saxony more ruthlessly than any heathen, until in July logistical difficulties forced him to withdraw. When he mustered a second army of invasion in October, after the harvest, the Saxons surrendered. It was in the aftermath of this triumph that Henry took the fateful step of pronouncing the deposition of Pope Gregory VII, an overconfident move that led to the great quarrel between 'Empire and Papacy' and to the election of the Swabian duke Rudolf of Rheinfelden as a rival king in March 1077.

Bruno's second battle took place at Mellrichstadt on 7 August 1078 when Henry successfully forestalled a conjuction between the Saxon and Swabian forces. No sooner had battle been joined than many Saxons fled. The runaways were set upon and robbed by the people of the district. Among those to suffer this humiliation was the bishop of Merseburg who gave Bruno an account of his misfortunes (and that more than once, Bruno remarks). However in another part of the field, Otto of Nordheim's Saxons drove Henry's troops far in the direction of Würzburg. As Otto's men returned, exhausted, they could see another force in occupation of the field of battle, and when their scouts failed to report back, they concluded it was the enemy—though it was in fact another Saxon contingent. They returned home victorious, believing they had lost. Henry quickly exploited the confusion about the outcome

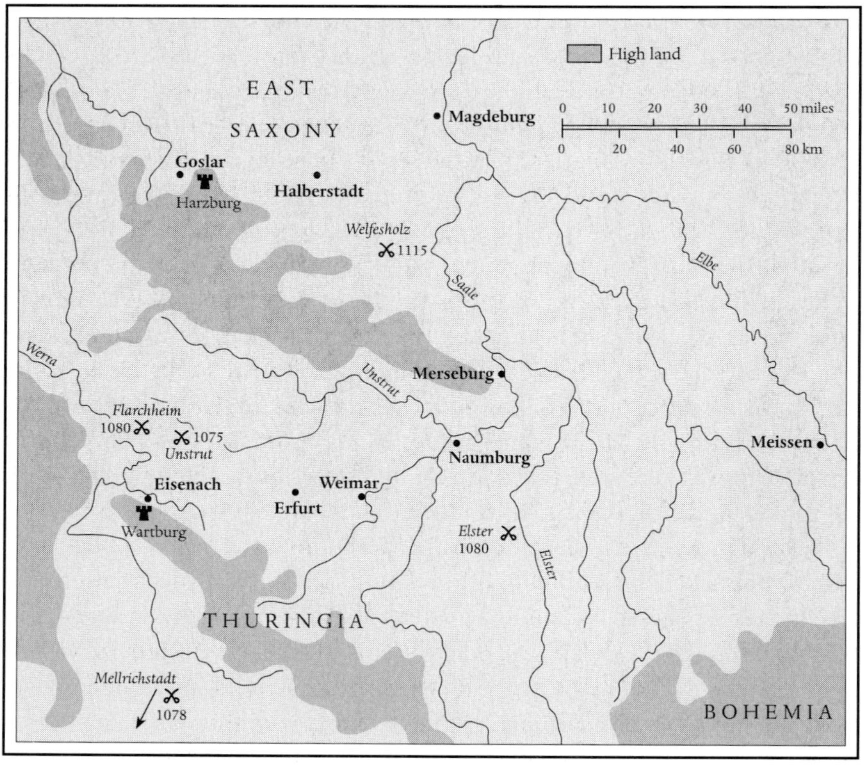

THE SAXON WARS OF HENRY IV AND V, 1073–1115

of Mellrichstadt, attracting men to his banner by announcing that Saxon losses had been so heavy that their land now lay defenceless. When his assembled troops learned the truth, he led them on a ravaging expedition against Rudolf's Swabian lands instead.

Bruno's third battle was fought at Flarchheim on 27 January 1080. Again Henry invaded Saxony and again he surprised his enemies, outmanoeuvring them and taking them in the rear. However Otto and Rudolf managed to regroup and fought back so fiercely that Henry himself fled. When he halted to rest his weary troops near the Wartburg, the castle garrison made a sudden sally and successfully plundered the immense treasures of the royal camp.

The fourth battle took place on 15 October 1080 when Henry, to avenge this humiliation, launched his second invasion of the year—he was, wrote Bruno, 'tireless in war'. Bruno's account of a campaign that came uncomfortably close to Merseburg is particularly detailed. When Henry's scouts reported that Rudolf and Otto had mustered a large army against him near Eisenach, he ordered the bulk of his troops to march in the direction of Erfurt, while his swiftest cavalry made for the Goslar district where they were to burn settlements and then rejoin the main army as fast as possible. The strategem worked. The Saxons reacted to the news from Goslar by rushing there, and then, when they realized they had been deceived, by rushing back in an attempt to defend Erfurt. Even though in their haste they left many troops, both horse and foot, behind at Goslar, they were too late. Henry sacked Erfurt and moved on to ravage the countryside around Naumburg. However the Saxons were moving much faster, even through hilly country, than Henry's ravaging and plundering army, and they were able to get back in time to defend Naumburg itself. On 14 October Henry camped on the banks of the Elster. Why did he halt there? Bruno confessed he was at a loss to know whether the Salian king was following a battle-seeking strategy—despite having lost his last two battles—or whether he was now waiting for reinforcements from Meissen and Bohemia before marching in overwhelming force via Merseburg and Magdeburg to ravage the whole of Saxony. Whatever his intentions, next morning Henry offered battle. Although the Saxons were tired by their pursuit, they decided to attack. Since most of their foot soldiers had been left behind, the infantry needed strengthening and many of the cavalry were ordered to dismount. As they advanced their clerics chanted the 82nd Psalm. Henry himself fled as soon as hand-to-hand fighting began, but his men did not; they drove some of the Saxons into flight. Rudolf of Rheinfelden was seriously—and, it transpired, fatally—wounded. In the Salian camp, men were already beginning to celebrate victory when to their astonishment they saw the Saxon foot led by Otto of Nordheim advancing against them. The camp fell before their determined assault. Then—and for Bruno this was the critical moment—Otto prevented his men from succumbing to the temptation of looting the king's treasures; he made them turn instead to challenge the large detachment of Henry's army which was still in possession of the field of battle and thought it had won. Once again Otto led the foot in a victorious attack—allegedly against superior numbers. Only then were the Saxons allowed to enjoy the rich spoils of Henry's camp. Bruno ended his narrative with the proud report that when Henry tried to organize another campaign, his men told him they would rather go round the whole world than ever again try to invade Saxony.

Bruno's war was decided not by capturing strongpoints but by winning battles. None of his four battles was a clash between besieging and relieving armies—the characteristic scenario for battle in a well-fortified zone. His war was fought in East Saxony and Thuringia, a region which, though disturbed by the throes of encastellation, was still much less urbanized and encastellated, i.e. much less 'modern', than, say, the Rhineland. Like England in 1015–16 and 1066, this was a theatre of war in which contestants were more willing to risk battle than they would be in a densely fortified country. Bruno represented Henry IV's supporters, many of whom came from the prosperous Rhineland, as men who looked down on the Saxons, seeing them as backwoodsmen, 'rustics without military expertise, short on both horses and knightly skills'. Few authors have bettered his descriptions of the terror and sheer confusion of battle, but he was also clear that with intelligent leadership—he described Otto of Nordheim as 'prudent in war'—disciplined infantry could beat well-equipped cavalry.

Cavalry and Archery in Battle

As the battles for Saxony as well as the battles at Civitate and Hastings demonstrate, eleventh-century knights were far from being the masters of the battlefield. It is, however, sometimes suggested that by the twelfth century they had discovered how to use a couched lance, and that this new technique then enabled them to drive all before them. True, the couched lance, having behind it the weight and power of the moving horse and rider, could penetrate a hauberk and was an ideal weapon in the joust, the head-on confrontation of knight against knight which marked the beginning of many a clash between bodies of cavalry both in tournament and real battle. But there is no evidence that the couched lance was new and the technique was in any case useless against infantry (for a slightly different view, see Chapter 9, p. 188). The likelihood is that couching the lance was one of a number of options which had

A scene from a Life of St Edmund *c.*1135. The battle is already over and knights, couching their lances, pursue a demoralized enemy. The couched lance was for use against cavalry; other methods worked better against infantry, whether they stood and fought or whether, as here, they were being finished off.

long been available to horsemen. The Normans in the Bayeux Tapestry are shown throwing or jabbing down with their lances not because they had not yet learned the 'new' technique, but because they were attacking infantry in close formation. Cavalry operating alone had no chance against well-disciplined infantry. Horses are too sensible to impale themselves on a hedge of spears. Only when the formation had been disrupted was it possible to drive home a charge. The risky tactic of feigned flight might occasionally work, but missile weapons offered by far the most effective way of disrupting infantry, particularly if, drawn up in defensive formation, they presented an immobile target.

When Anna Comnena wrote that 'a mounted Celt is irresistible', she drew attention not to a particular technique of lance management, but to the fact that the knight's shield and armour made him virtually invulnerable to arrows. This is why one of the standard Latin words for a knight was *loricatus*—the man wearing a metal hauberk. When Anna elaborated the circumstances in which the knight was irresistible and moved from the poetic 'he would bore his way through the walls of Babylon' to the realistic, she wrote, 'inspired by passion they are irresistible, their leaders as well as their rank and file charging into the midst of the enemy line with abandon—so long as the opposition everywhere gives ground'. Historians have too often missed that last crucial proviso. Cavalry were devastatingly effective when it came to finishing off and pursuing troops who were already beaten; of least use when the outcome of a battle still hung in the balance.

Castle Warfare

As castles proliferated, so the nature of warfare changed. Twelfth-century battles remained frightening and risky, for even though fewer commanders were killed in them than in the eleventh, the political consequences of being taken prisoner (as Robert Curthose was at Tinchebrai in 1106 and Stephen was at Lincoln in 1141) were catastrophic. On the other hand, battles from which the losing commander escaped still left the victor with the problem of capturing strongholds, and the more densely fortified the region, the greater the problem. Wars could be won without battles. Roger II of Sicily avoided battle but defeated the military alliance ranged against him and took over the mainland territories after the death of Guiscard's grandson, Duke William of Apulia, in 1127. Geoffrey of Anjou conquered Normandy (1136–44) and Henry VI conquered Sicily (1195), both without battle. Apart from a river-battle for Château-Gaillard, there were no battles when Philip Augustus drove King John out of Anjou, Normandy, and much of Poitou in 1203–4. Not surprisingly commanders became increasingly reluctant to risk battle. Only when very confident would they offer it, and in those circumstances their opponent was almost certain to avoid it—as Philip Augustus fled from Richard I at Fréteval (1194) and Gisors (1198), preferring to suffer the humiliation and losses incurred in flight rather than risk potential disaster. Thus battles became rarer, and when they did occur, it was generally in the context of a siege, as at Lincoln in 1141 or at Carcano in 1160.

Even more than before wars revolved around the winning or losing of strongholds. But they, of course, were hard to take, and became even more so as increasingly they were built or rebuilt in stone. Stone walls could sometimes be undermined or breached. With the development of siege towers and better artillery the technology available to the besieger (if he could afford it) continued to improve (see further, Chapter 8, pp. 171–4). But even if the walls had been breached casualties in a direct assault were so high that it was very rare that troops would risk it—despite the incentive of the right to unrestricted plunder which they would then be allowed by the custom of war. The best chance was surprise, as when King David of Scotland attacked Wark in 1138, at dawn on a mid-winter morning. An alternative was intimidation. For example in 1113 Henry V threatened to hang his prisoner, Mouzon's lord, if Mouzon were not handed over. In 1146 Roger of Berkeley was 'hanged' three times outside the walls of his own castle, before being returned half-dead to prison. On neither occasion did the threat work. In the new climate of chivalry (see p. 83) it was unlikely that such threats would be carried out—and defenders guessed as much.

Since direct attacks were so problematic, the usual tactic was a more indirect one, an attack on

The counterweight trebuchet—the most advanced piece of siege artillery in the world of *c*.1200. The sling in which the projectiles were placed added to the velocity with which they were flung into the air in a high arc.

the castle's economic base. In the late twelfth-century metrical *Chronicle* composed by Jordan Fantosme, the author put some advice on how to make war into the mouth of Count Philip of Flanders, one of the most respected commanders of the time. Speaking to King Louis VII, he envisages William king of Scots invading England as Louis's ally:

> Let him aid you in war, swiftly and without delay
> Destroy your foes and lay waste their country,
> By fire and burning let all be set alight
> That nothing be left for them, either in wood or meadow
> Of which in the morning they could have a meal;
> Then with his united force let him besiege their castles,
> Thus should war be begun: such is my advice.
> First lay waste the land.

Precisely because castles were so hard to take, even campaigns targeted against them began with ravaging, and many campaigns did not get beyond these destructive—and profitable—preliminaries.

If a siege was eventually laid, then some of the besieging forces would garrison counter-castles or entrench themselves in siege-works, but others would remain highly mobile. In a closely pressed siege, the attackers would want a rapid response force ready to take swift advantage of any opening created by a sortie by the defenders. When William of Normandy blockaded Domfront, he 'went out riding by day and night, or lay hidden under cover to see whether attacks could be launched against those who were trying to bring in supplies and messages, or who were trying to ambush his foragers'. Lightly armed foragers and ravagers needed to be escorted by heavily armed patrols. The Abodrite prince Niklot was killed in 1160, ambushed by Saxon knights as he attacked their foragers. When the Cid laid siege to Valencia in July 1093, one of his tactics was to launch hit and run raids on its suburbs, fields, and gardens. Warfare, in other words, remained a war of movement both in the preliminaries to siege and during siege. In this kind of warfare, rather than in battle, cavalry was in its element.

After a tough winter, food shortages brought Valencia's defenders to agree terms of surrender in June 1094. This was how William took Domfront. It was the usual pattern. The offer of generous terms might persuade defenders to surrender earlier rather than later. David of Scotland eventually won Wark in 1138 by agreeing not only to let the garrison go free but also to provide them with horses to replace the ones which hunger had forced them to eat. Other besiegers in other circumstances took a tougher line. Conrad III intended to imprison the defenders of Weinsberg (to which he laid siege in 1141) and would only agree to let their women go with whatever they could carry. They carried out their men.

Once taken, a strongpoint could then become a base from which further destructive raids could be launched. William of Poitiers' summary of how William the Bastard conquered Maine illustrates the combination of ravaging, taking strongholds, and further ravaging. 'He sowed terror in the land by his frequent and lengthy invasions; he devastated vineyards, fields and estates; he seized neighbouring strongpoints and where advisable put garrisons in them; in short he incessantly inflicted innumerable calamities upon the land.' According to Otto of Freising, Frederick of Staufen, the duke of Swabia, advanced 'down the Rhine building first one castle in a suitable site and subjecting all the surrounding country to his power, and then moving on and building another, in this way gradually subjecting to his will the entire country from Basle to Mainz, the richest part of the realm. It was said of him that he always hauled a castle with him at the tail of his horse.' Richard I's base for the recovery of the Norman Vexin from Philip Augustus was the new castle, Château-Gaillard, which in 1196–7 he built at Andeli only five miles from the French king's fortress at Gaillon. Aggressive commanders sometimes seized castles situated deep in enemy territory and used them as bases from which to disrupt agriculture and trade. For example, after conquering Toledo in 1085, Alfonso VI placed a garrison in Aledo—far to the south of his effective rule—and managed to keep it there, a thorn in Muslim flesh, until 1092.

Italy

No society was more encastellated than Italy, the richest part of Europe. Phenomenal economic growth went hand in hand with acute political fragmentation. By 1200 there were as many as two hundred independent city-states, the communes. In this fiercely competitive society the threat of armed violence was never far away. Rich families built castles in the countryside and tower-houses in town. Benjamin of Tudela said of Genoa, which he visited in the 1160s, that 'each householder has a tower in his house and at times of strife they fight each other from the tops of the towers'. At Pisa, he alleged, there were 10,000 such houses. City governments tried to set legal limits to the height of towers. Aggrieved neighbours took more direct action, bringing up their own siege artillery.

As the urban population grew so walls had to be extended time and again, sometimes enclosing an area three or four times greater than the Roman walls had done. In the early twelfth-century *Liber Pergaminus*—the earliest surviving literary work in praise of a commune—among Bergamo's other excellent

A German illustration of a siege in Italy showing men of high rank (note the shields with heraldic designs) in the thick of the fighting. In England in 1144 Geoffrey de Mandeville was fatally wounded at the siege of Burwell by an arrow in the face, but the great helms shown here—fashionable from the late twelfth century onwards—gave better protection against missiles than had earlier forms of helmet.

qualities were its formidable walls and its military strength. As each city tried to extend the area from which it could require deliveries of grain and on which it could levy taxes and military service, so it came into conflict with its neighbours. By the mid-eleventh century Pavia and Milan were at each other's throats—a rivalry which was to last for centuries. Florence was generally at odds with Lucca, Pistoia, and Siena. Gradually both smaller towns and rural aristocrats succumbed to the power and lure of the greater towns. By the mid-twelfth century a German historian, Otto bishop of Freising, noted with astonishment that 'practically the whole land is divided between the cities'.

In the eleventh and twelfth centuries the German kings found it hard to exercise the authority in Italy which their Ottonian predecessors had enjoyed. The famous *carroccio* of Milan is first mentioned in 1039 in the context of a campaign against the 'imperialists'. Frederick Barbarossa made a huge effort to revive imperial power in Italy. Barbarossa himself, in a letter written in 1157, described his first campaign in 1155. 'Because this land had become arrogant and rebellious, we entered Lombardy in force and destroyed almost all its strongholds [*castella*]'. In the next few sentences Frederick used the verb 'destroy' five more times. He exaggerated his success, but he had clearly found a lot to destroy. So it was in all his Italian campaigns. Being defeated in battle at Legnano at the hands of Milanese forces in 1176 was simply the final straw. What had worn him down was the fact that in a protracted war, and despite his shrewd exploitation of inter-city rivalries, he found the wealth, fortifications, and military resources of a coalition of cities led by Milan too much for him. What he destroyed they rebuilt. In the end (1177) he had to give up. In this period few dynastic rulers could match the military achievements of the 'businessmen' of Milan, Genoa, Pisa, and Venice.

Chivalry and Tournaments

Where local wars were endemic and the dominance of the castle led to protracted campaigns with sieges usually ending in negotiated surrender, it made sense for a convention to develop whereby the wealthy (i.e. those with negotiable assets) would be taken prisoner rather than—as so often before—be killed or mutilated. For the elite such a convention offered both financial gain (ransom) and an insurance policy against the day when they were on the losing side. The new knightly code of values—chivalry—did not benefit 'ordinary' soldiers. For example when Henry II captured Stephen's castle of Crowmarsh in 1153 he spared the knights but executed 60 archers—another indication of their effectiveness. At the same time knights found a new arena where they could both hone their military skills and meet socially to share ideas and values. From the 1120s onwards effective body armour was sufficiently widely available to permit the development of a realistic game of group combat—the tournament.

Colonial Wars

Demographic and economic developments had a dramatic effect on the equilibrium of raid and reprisal which in the eleventh century had so often characterized war on the northern frontiers. In the twelfth century the quest to maintain overlordship was replaced in many regions by a policy of conquest accompanied by settlement and economic development. An early sign came in 1092 when William Rufus took Carlisle from the Scots, built a castle and then, in the words of the *Anglo-Saxon Chronicle*, 'sent many farmers there with wives and livestock to live there and cultivate the land'. In Henry I's reign many colonists moved from England into South Wales, founding the earliest towns in Wales. The king even planted a colony of Flemings in Dyfed where 'they occupied the whole cantref called Rhos and drove away all the [native] inhabitants'. The anonymous author of the *Gesta Stephani* wrote that by 1135 the intruders had 'added Wales to their dominion and fortified it with numberless castles, imposed law and order on the people and made the land so productive . . . that it might easily have been thought a second England'. From 1169 onwards English soldiers and settlers moved into Ireland, building castles, towns, villages, mills, and bridges, pushing the native Irish back into the least fertile parts, bogs and uplands. Both Welsh and Irish lost territory partly because they were politically disunited—the invasion of Ireland began, for example, when the exiled King Diarmait of Leinster begged for help against Ruaidri Ua Conchobair of Connacht—but partly also because the English iron industry hugely outproduced them in terms of armour and fire-power (arrow heads and crossbow bolts).

Irishmen, wrote Gerald of Wales in 1188, always carry an axe and are all too ready to use it. This thirteenth-century English representation of a barefoot Irish axeman reflects the view, widely held from the twelfth century onwards, that the Irish, like the Scots and Welsh, went 'naked' into battle. Their lack of armour left them so vulnerable to archery that they rarely got close enough to use the dreaded axe.

A similar process underpinned by the same economic and technological superiority occurred to the north-east of Germany, in Brandenburg and along the Baltic coast towards Mecklenburg. In the 1140s Count Adolf of Holstein drove many Slavs out of Wagria and sent messengers as far afield as Flanders, Holland, Frisia, and Westphalia to recruit new settlers. In Helmold of Bosau's words 'an innumerable multitude of different peoples came at his call, and bringing their families and possessions arrived in the land which he had promised them.' Towns such as Lübeck were developed and by 1172 it seemed to Helmold that 'all the country of the Slavs between the Elbe and the Baltic reaching from the River Eider as far east as Schwerin, once a dangerous wasteland, was now made into one great colony of Saxons, in which cities, villages and churches multiplied'. In the 1170s and 1180s the initiative lay with Danish fleets rather than with German knights. They destroyed Wendish sea-power, and by the 1190s were raiding the Estonian and Livonian coasts. In 1200 Riga was established as a trading centre and a base for further expansion. In the winning of the Baltic, Danes and Germans exploited the technological superiority given them by the cog, the new ship of the northern waters. In battle against traditional longships, the cog's high freeboard gave it the advantage, maximized when the stability of its deep, heavy hull was used to build fighting castles fore and aft, and even a topcastle at the masthead—the quest for height in marine architecture (see Chapter 11, p. 236).

In the West population growth meant the end of labour-shortage and the end of slavery. In consequence from the twelfth century onwards when English and German armies invaded Celtic and Slav lands they no longer went hunting for human cattle. Celts and Slavs, however, living in more thinly populated regions still used slave labour and consequently, when they raided, they continued to target not just property but also the 'civilian population', especially women. This practice Westerners now condemned as barbarous. English and German awareness of the material and technological edge which they enjoyed over the Celts and Slavs whose lands they were occupying took on a moral dimension; this created an attitude of cultural superiority which was to have long-lasting consequences.

Twelfth-Century Spain

Colonization and settlement played an increasingly important role in another theatre of war: Spain. Despite all their successes between 1086 and 1117, the Almoravids failed to recapture Toledo. Although it became an increasingly exposed frontier bastion, it held out. In part this may have been because the kings of Castile held the inner lines of communication, but it was also because

Castles at sea, fore and aft, and at the masthead, are shown in this picture of fighting at sea from a French version of Vegetius' military handbook. Crossbows too are prominently displayed. When Anna Comnena commented on what she called these 'diabolical machines' of the Franks, noting their great range and penetrative power, it was in the context of a naval engagement.

with some success they pursued a policy of offering legal and tax privileges to settlers brave enough to settle in the hitherto underpopulated sheep- and cattle-raising country which was Toledo's hinterland.

At the same time more strenuous efforts were made to get help from across the Pyrenees—often from knights already familiar with the pilgrim road to Santiago, the *camino francés* (French road). According to al-Maqqari, in 1117 Alfonso I 'the Battler' of Aragon 'sent messengers to the lands of France summoning all the Christian nations there to help him. Rallying to his call, they came to his standards like swarms of locusts or ants.' Next year he captured Zaragoza—the first serious setback to be suffered by the Almoravids. In 1125 'the Battler' led a great raid as far as Malaga and returned with, allegedly, no less than 10,000 Andalusian Christian families whom he settled in the Ebro

Valley. His death in 1134 might have been the signal for a Muslim revival, but in its African bases the Almoravid regime found itself increasingly hamstrung by the opposition of a new and more fundamentalist sect, the Almohads. Under this pressure the Almoravid empire began to break up. In effect a second wave of *taifa* kingdoms swept across Spain—no less than 14 emerging between 1144 and 1146. With the return of Muslim political fragmentation, Christian rulers surged forward on all fronts. In 1147 Alfonso VII of Castile organized the grand coalition (contingents from Navarre, Aragon, and the Midi, fleets from Barcelona, Genoa, and Pisa) which captured Almeria, the main Muslim port for trade with Africa and the Eastern Mediterranean. In the same year Alfonso I of Portugal took Lisbon with help from English and Flemish crusaders. Ramon-Berenguer IV, count-king of Barcelona and Aragon, won Tortosa after long siege in 1148, then Lerida and Fraga in 1149. By 1151 Alfonso VII and Ramon-Berenguer had the confidence to plan a partition of all Spain between them.

But exactly as in the exuberant years after the capture of Toledo this confidence was misplaced—and for the same reason. Christian success precipitated decisive military intervention from North Africa. The Almohads arrived in 1148, swiftly winning control of Muslim city-states (only the kingdom of Murcia and Valencia ruled by an adventurer known to Christians as King Lobo, retaining its independence for long). The Almohads recovered Almeria in 1157 and three years later founded Gibraltar to give them a secure bridgehead in Spain. The Christians remained on the defensive, again relying on their capacity to attract settlers to hold on to newly-won lands such as the New Extremadura and New Catalonia. Just as in the crusader states the Military Orders (see further, Chapter 5, p. 95) were called upon to retain control of exposed regions, so a similar need here led to the foundation of the Orders of Calatrava (1164) and Santiago (1170). But the Almohads clearly held the upper hand whenever their caliph himself was free to campaign in Spain, as in 1171–6 and 1195–7. In the early 1170s King Lobo was overthrown. In 1195 Caliph Ya'qub won a great victory over Alfonso VIII of Castile at the battle of Alarcos. With Christian Spain in disarray as old rivalries led the kings of Leon and Navarre to ally with the Almohads, rumours spread through Europe that 600,000 Africans were about to march across the Pyrenees. In fact the threat which Almoravid fleets operating from Majorca posed to the African coast and Almoravid success in fomenting revolt in Tunisia led Ya'qub to grant Castile a truce in 1197. For the moment the mainland Christian states were saved. But with the conquest of Majorca in 1203 the Almohad advance resumed. Although the Christians now held roughly twice as much territory in Spain as in 1000 and crucially had held on to some of their greatest gains—notably

Toledo, Zaragoza, and Lisbon—in 1200 it was by no means certain that they would not go the way of Valencia and Almeria. Where 'the empire of the Franks' confronted the Muslim world, in Spain as in the crusader states, the century ended with signs that it might be tottering (but see Chapter 6, pp. 117–18).

The Lure of Land and Loot

Everywhere else, however, the frontiers continued to be pushed back. In Ireland the English crossed the Shannon and began to take over the kingdom of Connacht. A new military order founded *c.*1202 at Riga by a German bishop, the Brothers of the Knighthood of Christ in Livonia, brought an intensely religious drive to the penetration of the Baltic lands. More than earlier German soldiers and settlers had done, the Sword-brothers—as they were commonly known—insisted that pagans, especially Livs and Prussians, must be converted to Christianity. But most dramatic of all was expansion at the expense of fellow Christians. The Fourth Crusade's capture of Constantinople (1204) by an army originally intended for Egypt, amounted, at least according to Geoffrey de Villehardouin, one of the crusade's leaders, to 'the conquest of the greatest, most powerful and most strongly fortified city in the world'. In what he called 'the grandest enterprise ever' a decisive role was played by the Venetians, first in financing the crusade and building a fleet, and then in using it to strike at the very heart of a rich and ancient empire in crisis. 'Geoffrey de Villehardouin here declares that, to his knowledge, so much loot has never been gained in any city since the creation of the world.'

5 WARFARE IN THE LATIN EAST

PETER EDBURY

WHEN in 1095 Pope Urban II preached the First Crusade, he initiated a tradition of Christian holy war which was to last well beyond the medieval centuries and which came to embrace wars fought in a wide variety of different theatres and in vastly contrasting contexts. In the course of time, crusades were directed against pagans in Lithuania, Muslims in Spain, heretics in southern France and Bohemia, and against Greeks, Turks, Mongols, and Russians to name just some, and inevitably the military techniques, the types of warriors employed, and the organization of warfare differed greatly. But for many people in the middle ages the first goal of the crusades—Jerusalem and the Holy Land—continued to hold pride of place, and it is with the warfare waged in the Near East with the aim of winning or defending the places made sacred by Christ's presence on earth that this chapter is concerned.

The First Crusade attained its primary objective in 1099 with the capture of Jerusalem, and in its wake Western European warriors, clergy, and settlers were able to seize lands and establish themselves in Syria and the Holy Land. The crusaders founded a series of principalities in the East—the kingdom of Jerusalem, the counties of Tripoli and Edessa, the principality of Antioch—and the last of their strongholds were only retaken by the Muslims in 1291. At their fullest extent the lands conquered by the crusades comprised the entire Levantine coast and many inland areas including the whole of the present-day states of Israel and Lebanon. Most of these conquests were at the expense of Muslims, although the crusaders also found themselves on occasion in conflict with the Byzantine Greeks in northern Syria or with the Armenians of eastern Anatolia and Cilicia; and in 1204 the Fourth Crusade, recruited to fight the infidel, ended by sacking Christian Constantinople. The crusaders did not

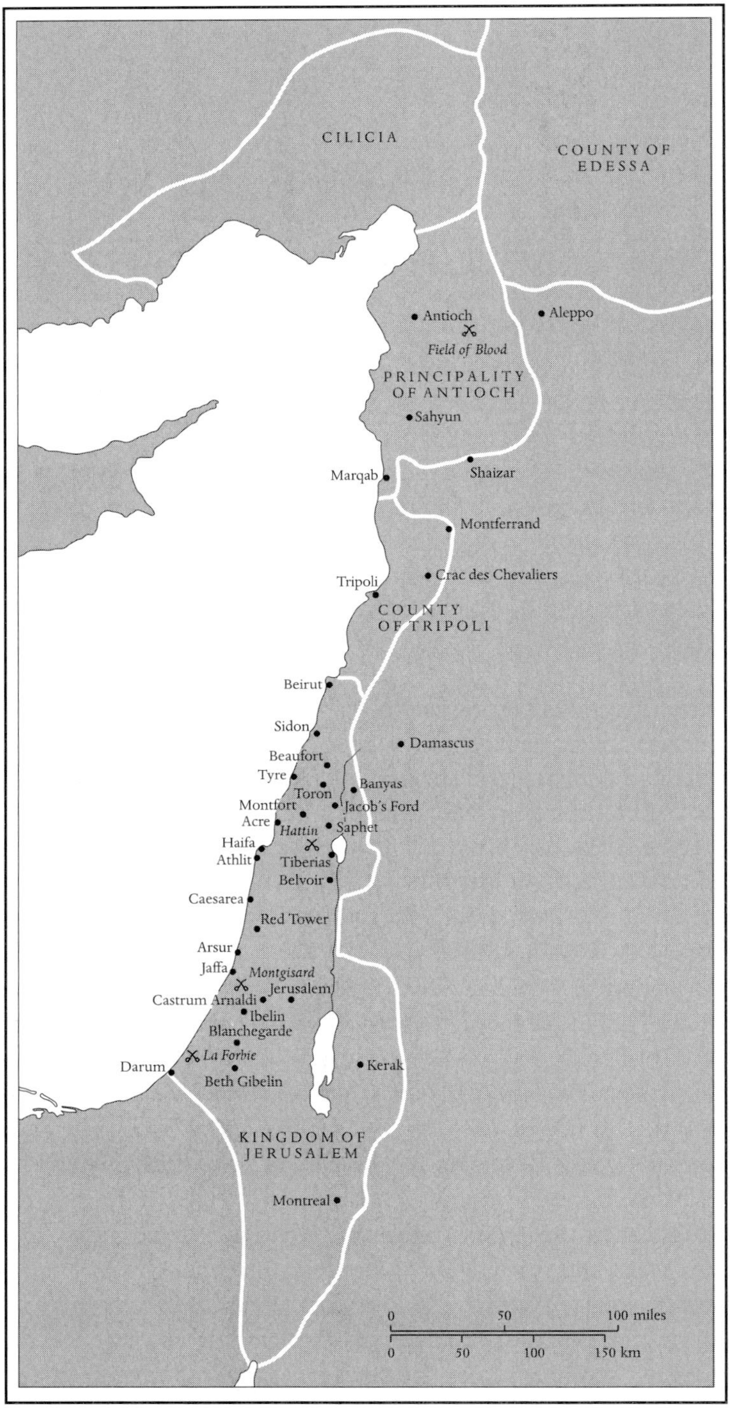

THE LATIN EAST IN THE AGE OF THE CRUSADES

see their gains in the Levant simply in terms of territorial aggrandisement. Rather, they were inspired by the belief that the shrines and the other places associated with the life of Christ and the Christians who served them should be freed from the yoke of unbelievers and delivered into the safe-keeping of the faithful.

Not surprisingly the Muslims were keen to expel these Westerners whom they regarded as intruders into the *Dar al-Islam*. There were, it is true, periods of truce, but there could be no permanent peace between Christian and Muslim, and, although a measure of accommodation could be achieved and instances of Christians forming alliances with Muslims against other Christians or Muslims did occur, in the twelfth century at least warfare persisted as a constant fact of life. To the Muslims, as to the Christians, Jerusalem was, and is, a holy city, and within a generation of the arrival of the crusaders—men fired with the idea of waging war on Christ's behalf—the Muslims were preaching the jihad (Islamic holy war) to repel them. Ultimately the Muslims were successful, but the fact that the crusader principalities lasted for almost 200 years is in itself testimony to the martial prowess and persistence of the West.

In the early twelfth century the crusaders were able to take advantage of disunity and political fragmentation in the Muslim world to expand and consolidate their gains, but by the late 1160s the balance of power was beginning to tilt decidedly in favour of the Muslims as successive rulers were able to unite more and more of the Islamic lands in the Near East under their sway. The Muslims had to hand greater resources of wealth and manpower than the Christians, and, once a ruler emerged who could provide adroit political leadership and military direction, it was perhaps inevitable that the Europeans would be forced on to the defensive. Such a ruler was Saladin, who from 1174 was ruling in both Damascus and Egypt and so for the first time since the arrival of the crusaders in the late 1090s had control over all the Muslim lands bordering the kingdom of Jerusalem. In 1187 Saladin defeated the Christians in battle at Hattin (in Galilee) and went on to capture Jerusalem itself and almost all the other crusader territories. Until 1187 the Christians had been able to mount a vigorous defence of their possessions. Now it required a new crusade, the Third (1188–92), to give their presence in the East a new lease of life. But despite some successes, the Christians never regained their former territorial power. Except for a brief period between 1229 and 1244 they were denied possession of Jerusalem, and the area under their control was largely restricted to the coastal regions. Even so, they were able to retain this attenuated position for another century. After the Third Crusade the character of warfare in the Latin East changed. It was now rare for the Christians to be able to go on to the offensive unless they were joined by a crusading expedition from the West. Instead we find much longer periods of truce and much greater emphasis on the defensive use of fortifications.

It will be immediately clear from this brief sketch that warfare and needs of defence loom large in any account of the Christians in the Levant during the twelfth and thirteenth centuries. The Westerners brought with them to the East ideas of how to wage war and how to build and utilize fortifications, and during the two centuries under consideration their practices continued to be affected by contemporary changes in the West. But they also learnt from their experiences of warfare with their Muslim and Byzantine neighbours, and in the process they were able to work out for themselves their own solutions to problems of recruitment, strategy, and castle design.

Throughout the history of the Latin East, pride of place was assigned to the heavily armed mounted warrior, the knight. Knightly arms and equipment would seem to have kept pace with developments in the West, and, as in the West, during the course of the twelfth and thirteenth centuries the knight's social standing steadily rose. But the number of knights that could be retained permanently as fief-holders was limited. A list drawn up in the mid-1180s suggests that the king of Jerusalem could call on the services of no more than about 675 feudatories, which in the context of the need to defend fortresses and conduct campaigns virtually every year suggests that there was a severe shortage. How many other knights—mercenaries or volunteers—the kings could recruit is not known. Towards the end of the twelfth century the sources begin to refer to mounted sergeants, presumably men whose arms and equipment were similar to the knights' but who lacked their status in society. Here too the emergence of this class paralleled developments in the West.

In Syria the crusaders' chief enemies were the Turkish rulers of Damascus, Aleppo, and the other Muslim cities of the hinterland, and such potentates employed Turkish horsemen whose equipment and techniques differed markedly from the Westerners' (see further, Chapter 9, p. 190). These warriors were lightly armed mounted archers whose speed and ability to manoeuvre in formation while firing a rapid barrage of arrows from the saddle had from the time of the First Crusade posed major problems for the heavier Western knights whose standard technique was the massed charge with the couched lance. The effectiveness of the Turkish mounted archers is beyond doubt, although it seems that their arrows had limited capacity for penetrating armour. Before long the Christians were employing troops armed and equipped in the Turkish manner and known in the sources as 'turcopoles'. Some may have been recruited from among the indigenous Christian communities in the Levant, while others would have been of Western extraction, perhaps the sons of mixed marriages between crusaders and local women.

For cavalry forces to be effective they needed infantry. Whether as archers, crossbowmen, spearmen, or sappers, their role, and also their training and efficiency, would have varied considerably. When confronted by the Turkish mounted archers, their job was to keep them at bay long enough for their horses to tire and so allow the Christian knights to pick the optimum moment for their charge. To be able to stand firm under fire from volleys of Turkish arrows required courage and discipline, but it was often essential for Christian success. If the cavalry charge, when it came, proved ineffective, it would be difficult for the knights to regroup and repeat the operation, and so patience was needed in choosing the best possible opportunity. Turkish mounted archers could be particularly dangerous when deployed against a Christian army on the march. Troops strung out in a long line with their baggage train were especially vulnerable to the Turks' ability to approach, discharge their arrows, and then make a rapid retreat, and the only way to counter this harassment was by organizing the column in close formation and maintaining strict discipline. The most famous instance of this technique occurred in 1191 at Arsur when on the Third Crusade King Richard the Lionheart was marching south towards Jaffa. The infantry shielded the flank and the knights of the military orders the rear. In the event the Christian cavalry charge seems to have been launched before the king gave the order, but, although the Christians had much the better of the encounter, the main Muslim army was able to regroup and resume harassing Richard's forces almost immediately.

In siege warfare, the foot soldiers, and especially those skilled in operating siege machinery or in techniques of mining, were of the utmost importance. Evidence for how the infantry was recruited is sparse, but it would appear that the towns and the greater churches had responsibilities. Recent research has suggested that there may have been far more Western settlers in the Holy Land than used to be thought, with ecclesiastical and presumably also secular landlords promoting Frankish settlement in the countryside, and it looks as if it was from these settlers as well as from the burgesses in the towns that the infantry was drawn.

It is evident that the crusaders lacked sufficient resources of manpower or money to garrison their defences adequately and at the same time also take the offensive against the Muslims. This shortage of manpower may explain the generous terms under which fiefs were held. In contrast to the situation in England, kings and lords were anxious that the feudatories should serve in person when summoned but were not much concerned with profiting from entry fines, control of wardships, or those other fiscal aspects of fief-holding familiar from England and elsewhere in the West and known collectively as feudal incidents. It is doubtless significant in this respect that in the Latin East there was no systematized institution of scutage (payment in lieu of service): if a vassal wished to avoid service he had to surrender his fief for a year and a day. Manpower shortages meant that rulers were cautious about committing their armies to pitched battle, and in the thirteenth century they came to rely increasingly on fortifications and a largely passive defence strategy. In 1187 it would seem that King Guy had to strip many of the fortifications of their garrisons in order to raise a field army large enough to challenge Saladin's invasion, and, with this army destroyed at Hattin, the Muslims encountered few cities or castles with enough armed men to put up any meaningful resistance.

The simple fact was that throughout their existence the Latin states in the East needed financial and human resources from Western Europe to sustain their position. Right from the start it would seem that warriors were coming to the East as pilgrims and remaining there for one or more campaigning season, thus providing a useful adjunct to the military strength furnished by the more permanent settlers. In some cases young men who had yet to enter their inheritances would occupy themselves in this manner. But sometimes major aristocrats from the West—for example Count Fulk V of Anjou or the successive counts of Flanders, Thierry of Alsace and his son Philip—would spend time in the East, sharing in the military action. It is also clear that almost until the loss of the last strongholds in 1291, well-born immigrants from the West could still gain entry into the aristocracy of Latin Syria, and there was ample scope for Westerners of more lowly origin to find military employment.

The biggest contingents of armed men to come to the aid of the Latin East were of course those recruited for specific crusades. There were many more crusading expeditions to the East than the handful of numbered campaigns familiar from the standard modern accounts, but it has to be said that apart from the First Crusade and, to a lesser extent, the Third, and despite the high hopes that the crusaders themselves often entertained, these expeditions had only limited or temporary success. Increasingly people were becoming aware that Western crusaders might succeed only in destroying the existing *modus vivendi* with the Muslims and that, once they had returned home, they would leave the Christian defenders of Latin Syria dangerously exposed to retaliation. It was with this thought in mind that King Louis IX, who was in the East between 1248 and 1254, established a standing garrison at Acre, the capital of the kingdom now that Jerusalem was lost, at French royal expense. This French force remained in being until 1291.

Not only did the Latin East look to the West for manpower, it also relied heavily on Europe for money to pay for its military expenditure. Crusading was expensive, and the costs were borne by the crusaders themselves, their families, their lords and, increasingly from the end of the twelfth century, by taxes levied on the Church in the West. In addition, the capacity of the Christians in the Levant to sustain their military resources benefited from a transference of wealth from Europe—directly in the form of donations or legacies, and less directly thanks to Western endowments for churches in the East and to the large numbers of European pilgrims to the Holy Land who by their very presence there would have bolstered the local economy. Monetary historians are in no doubt that large quantities of Western silver flowed into the crusader states and had a considerable impact on the economy of the region, and, though a good deal of that bullion would have arrived as a consequence of the thriving long-distance trade with the Levant which developed during the course of the twelfth century, much would have resulted from the piety of Christians in Europe.

But for the historian, the most striking and at the same time the most direct way in which the West channelled wealth and manpower into the defence of the Latin East was through the institutions known as the military orders. The Hospital of Saint John began as a religious corporation attending to the needs of pilgrims, and throughout its history it has continued to provide accommodation and medical care. From the early twelfth century the Hospital in Jerusalem was arranging armed escorts for pilgrims taking the route from Jaffa to Jerusalem and then on to the Jordan and the other pilgrimage sites—evidently a very necessary precaution—and it was a small step from supplying armed guards to garrisoning fortresses along the way or making troops available when the king was on campaign. The process whereby the members of the Order themselves came to serve in a military capacity is controversial, but what is clear is that their services were much appreciated and led directly to their acquiring substantial landed endowments in Western Europe which were to provide them with the wherewithal to diversify and extend their activities. The beginnings of the other leading Order, the Templars, differed in that the earliest members seem to have been drawn from an association of warriors whose original vocation had from the outset been the protection of pilgrims to Jerusalem. In about 1120 King Baldwin II gave them the al-Aqsa mosque in Jerusalem, which popular tradition identified with Solomon's Temple, to be their headquarters, and it was from this building that they took their name. Like the Hospitallers, their military function expanded, and they too received lavish endowments in Western Europe. By the middle decades of the twelfth century both the Templars and the Hospitallers were powerful ecclesiastical corporations whose military might had reached significant propor-

tions. In the East they came to acquire lands and castles, including many in northern Syria, well away from the principal pilgrimage shrines, but most of their endowments were in the West, and it was from the West that they drew most of their recruits. Their wealth and military role meant that they also acquired considerable political influence. As warriors, the brothers of both Orders were respected and feared by the Muslims. Their reputation for military discipline when on campaign was recognized as early as the 1140s when King Louis VII of France had the Templars organize his own forces while moving through hostile territory in Asia Minor during the Second Crusade, and such was their prowess and devotion to the Christian cause that Saladin had all the Templar and Hospitaller prisoners taken at Hattin executed. In the thirteenth century their wealth and resources probably equalled those of the secular lords in the East.

Both institutions employed mercenaries and allowed volunteers to fight under their banner for limited periods, but they were led by brother-knights who, as professed members of a religious order sworn to obedience, poverty, and chastity, counted as members of the regular clergy. The concept of men

For many people, the Hospitaller castle of Crac des Chevaliers epitomizes crusader military architecture. The existing structure dates mainly from the first half of the thirteenth century. It formed the centre of a Hospitaller lordship straddling the main route between the Christian Tripoli on the Mediterranean coast and Muslim Hamah.

subject to monastic discipline who could at the same time bear arms and shed blood was a radical departure from the commonly held view that clergy should eschew violence. But the idea of the 'armed monk' proved popular. It was soon to be copied in Spain and elsewhere. Perhaps the most famous of these later foundations was the Teutonic Order. This originated at the close of the twelfth century in the Holy Land, where it continued to play an active military role until 1291, but it is chiefly remembered for its activities in the Baltic region, fighting the pagans of Lithuania.

Warfare in the East shared many characteristics with contemporary warfare elsewhere. Major pitched battles were few, and when they did occur it was frequently in the context of attempts to raise sieges. Thus the Christian disaster at Hattin in 1187 came about when what may well have been the largest army ever mustered by the Franks in the East—the best estimates suggest 18,000 men of whom 1,200 were heavily armoured knights, 4,000 light cavalry, and the rest foot—allowed itself to be outmanoeuvred and stranded in a waterless area when attempting to advance against an even larger Muslim force besieging Tiberias. When Christian and Muslim armies did meet in open combat as at the Field of Blood in 1119 or at La Forbie in 1244, the Christians could suffer serious losses, although, as in these two instances, the Muslims were not always able to capitalize on their success. Generally the Christians adopted the more prudent tactics of not exposing their field armies to the risk of full-scale conflict, not least because they could not afford the loss of too many men.

But although prudence and the occasional spectacular defeat may have characterized much of the military action of the Franks settled in the East, the continued survival of Christian rule testifies to their strengths and effectiveness. As in all frontier societies, the essential elements were the raid (or *chevauchée*, see Chapter 4, pp. 67–9) and the use of fortifications and sieges. Raiding was perhaps the commonest form of military activity for both Christians and Muslims. Its objectives varied. At one level, campaigns designed to devastate the countryside would impoverish the enemy and destroy morale, thus making siege operations and permanent annexation at a later date more likely to succeed. Mounted warriors could move fairly freely, and, provided they took sensible precautions such as attending to reconnaissance and avoiding passing too close to the enemy's castles, they could normally use their mobility to avoid encountering serious opposition. Occasionally exploits of this type did come to grief, as for example in 1177 when Saladin led a large *chevauchée* into southern Palestine only to be badly mauled by a hastily assembled and much smaller Christian army at Montgisard. The Christians became adept at handling Muslim raiding parties. Perhaps the classic example was Saladin's raid of 1183. Then the regent of the kingdom and his men were able to garrison their strong points, occupy the main sources of water in the areas in which the Muslims were operating and shadow their forces. There was no attempt to challenge them in open conflict, although presumably there would have been skirmishes with small bands of foragers. The strategy was one of damage-limitation, and the Muslims duly withdrew without having achieved any major success.

Other raids might be little more than rustling exploits, perhaps directed against the nomadic Bedouin pastoralists. William of Tyre recorded a particularly spectacular example led by King Baldwin III of Jerusalem in person in 1157, but it is clear that smaller scale exploits of this type were common. Frequently these were simply instances of stealing livestock, but rulers also sought to coerce the tribesmen into paying tribute, and the occasional show of strength or a punitive attack would have been needed to enforce earlier agreements. Rather similar were the attacks on merchant caravans. In the 1180s the Christian lord of the Transjordan region, Reynald of Châtillon, staged at least two major raids on Muslim convoys moving between Damascus and Mecca. Supposedly it was these actions that precipitated Saladin's invasion of 1187 and the battle of Hattin, but how far Reynald was simply being opportunistic and how far he was using force to assert his claims to make the Muslims pay tolls when passing within range of his fortresses is not clear.

Raiding and tribute-taking were inextricably linked. In the early decades of the twelfth century the princes of Antioch were able to place the Muslim rulers of nearby Aleppo and Shaizar under tribute. If the payments were to continue there would have to be continuous military pressure, and it has recently been suggested that the situation closely paralleled the subjection that the kings of the Spanish kingdoms were able to exert at this period over the neighbouring Muslim *taifa* kingdoms (see Chapter 4, pp. 61–3). In his writings Usamah ibn Munqidh, a member of the family that ruled in Shaizar in the first half of the twelfth century, has left an impression of the low-level military activity on the border that characterized relations between Christians and Muslims. It was a question of petty raiding and skirmishing in an attempt to probe the weaknesses of the opposition and assert localized dominance. At a rather later date the Templars and Hospitallers from their strongholds in northern Syria were able to exact tribute from the Isma'ili sect of the Assassins who from the 1130s had established themselves in the mountains between the county of Tripoli and the principality of Antioch—a fact that belies their fearsome reputation which gave their name to the English language. Far more ambitious were the attempts of the kings of Jerusalem in the 1160s to place Egypt under tribute. The regime there was unstable, but successive campaigns designed to assert Frankish dominance alarmed Nur al-Din, the Muslim ruler of Damascus (1154–74), who sent his own troops to intervene. The war in Egypt became a race between Christian Jerusalem and Muslim Syria to see which could seize power first and so pre-empt the other's ambitions. It was a race the Muslims won, and their triumph led directly to the rise of Saladin.

Sometimes the Christians and Muslims would agree to put an end to border warfare and seek ways of sharing the frontier zone by tallaging the rural population in a condominium. It is difficult to assess how successful such compromise arrangements were, but in the second half of the thirteenth century, when the Muslims were extending their control at Christian expense, agreements between the two sides carefully defined which rural settlements each were to possess and which, if any, were to be shared.

The most tangible reminders of warfare in the Latin East are of course the castles which to this day dot the landscape. Some, such as Crac des Chevaliers, Sahyun, Marqab, Belvoir, or Kerak, provide spectacular testimony to the achievements of the military architects and masons who built them (see further, Chapter 8, p. 176). Situated on hills and ridges, often in an inhospitable terrain, it is easy to see why in the past they have fired the imagination of people such as T. E. Lawrence, who was originally drawn to the Near East in order to study them. Of all the crusader castles, the most famous has to be the Hospitaller fortress known Crac des Chevaliers situated in the hills to the north-east of Tripoli. Most of the structure, which exhibits considerable sophistication in its design, dates from the thirteenth century, and in its heyday the castle could have held a garrison of 2,000 men. The problem with these castles is that they are so impressive that it is all too easy to forget the less spectacular fortifications in the countryside or the urban fortifications, and attach more significance to these famous places than perhaps they deserve.

When the crusaders arrived in the East they came to a land with comparatively few fortresses. In Palestine there were walled towns along the coast, and Jerusalem itself was well defended, but there were not many castles. Further north, where for a century or more the Byzantines had confronted their Muslim neighbours, they were more numerous, and pose the question of how far the designs of the crusaders' own castles were influenced by Byzantine or Arab prototypes. The crusaders occupied existing strongholds—the castles at Sahyun and Crac des Chevaliers had originally been built by the Byzantines and Arabs, respectively—but the consensus among modern scholars is that they adapted little of what they found when they came to build their own structures. Instead it would seem that they relied far more on the traditions of castle building with which they were familiar in the West. For example, characteristic of much of France, notably Anjou and Poitou, was the donjon, the square tower, often with interior stone vaulting which contributed to the structural solidity, and the crusaders were to build many such towers in the East, often with a cistern at the base. Elsewhere in the West where the terrain lent itself to this type of construction, the Europeans were siting castles on hills or ridges, making the most of the natural escarpments which frequently meant that only on one side, where the ridge abutted the massif, did they need to build elaborate defences. This sort of fortification was not of course unique to Western Europeans, but in the East, where the crusaders built a number of strongholds of this type, they employed their own characteristic designs for the towers, crenellations, and the internal arrangements. The castles of the Latin East necessarily varied greatly in scale, but, insofar as it is possible to pinpoint specific influences on their design, the models seem to have been Western rather than Eastern. In particular they avoided fortified enclosures consisting of a curtain wall with semi-circular flanking towers, preferring instead the square donjon or a fortified complex with one or more donjon-like towers flanked by curtain walls with smaller square projecting towers. Unlike the Byzantines and the Muslims, it was very rare, at least in the twelfth century, for the crusaders to build circular or semi-circular towers. At Sahyun, a ridge castle where the Byzantines had excavated a deep ditch to separate the fortress from the adjacent hill, the crusaders took full advantage of the ditch but found the Byzantine structures inadequate. They redesigned and rebuilt the castle, employing noticeably better quality masonry. The end-result was altogether more formidable.

In the early years of the Latin states in the East, the new rulers concentrated their efforts on capturing and holding existing fortified sites. The kings of Jerusalem were particularly keen to bring the cities of the coast under their rule, and in almost every instance they needed naval support in order to do so. Occupation of the coast and its urban fortifications had major strategic implications. Christian control precluded the use of these places by Muslim warships, with the result that the Egyptian navy, the only significant Muslim sea-borne force in Eastern Mediterranean waters, had nowhere to take on fresh water and supplies and so found that its operational range was severely curtailed. That in turn meant that the seas around the coasts of Syria and Palestine were correspondingly safer for Christian shipping. This security was very necessary, for although the armies of the First Crusade had travelled overland across the Balkans and Asia Minor to reach Jerusalem, it was immediately clear to the crusaders that in the future merchants, pilgrims, and settlers would find it far easier to travel by sea. The Christian capture of Tyre in 1124, following a major victory by a Venetian fleet over the Egyptians off the coast of Palestine the previous year, was crucial in this respect as it meant that the Muslims now had no naval facilities north of Ascalon.

Above: the crusaders besiege Tyre (1124). (From a French manuscript of the third quarter of the thirteenth century.) Tyre and the other Muslim-held cities on the coast needed to be invaded by both land and sea. Note the defenders dropping rocks from a great height into the boat attempting to approach the walls.

Originally built by King Baldwin I of Jerusalem in 1115, Montreal, to the south east of the Dead Sea, helped establish Frankish control over the roads from Damascus and both Egypt and Mecca. It fell to Saladin in 1189 after a long siege.

The Christians seem not to have engaged in much castle-building during the first two decades of the twelfth century. One early—and ambitious—example of a new fortification was Montreal (al-Shaubak) beyond the Dead Sea near the ancient city of Petra. Montreal dates from 1115 and was designed to assert control over the caravan routes between Damascus and Mecca. Another new castle was at Toron, built, so we are told, as a refuge for troops from Tiberias campaigning against Tyre. Toron is an appreciable distance from Tyre, but building castles as part of a long-term offensive strategy for investing major centres was a tactic employed elsewhere. During the First Crusade small forts were constructed outside Antioch during the siege of 1097–8. Later, during the siege of Tripoli (1103–9), Raymond of St Gilles erected a fortress known as *Mons Peregrinus* overlooking the town. With the Christian capture of Tyre, the one remaining Muslim stronghold on the Palestinian coast was Ascalon, and during the 1130s and early 1140s the Franks built a series of castles—*Castrum Arnaldi*, Bethgibelin, Ibelin, Blanchegarde—to serve as bases for attacks on Ascalon and its environs. Ascalon duly fell to the Christians in 1153.

After the capture of Tyre in 1124, the kingdom of Jerusalem was much less exposed to Muslim attack, and this state of affairs was to last until about 1170. But it was precisely during these middle decades of the twelfth century that large numbers of for the most part quite small fortifications were put up. It would be natural to associate the construction of castles with external danger, but for this period at least no such correlation is possible. The castles just mentioned that faced Ascalon were all built after the Muslim garrisons there had stopped posing a major threat to the security of the Christian-controlled areas of southern Palestine, and it is for that reason that historians have concluded that their primary purpose was offensive, not defensive, and can point to the fact that they also provided the nuclei for rural settlement, feasible now that the military danger had receded. But there were many more castles dating from these middle years of the twelfth century, mostly in the lordships of Arsur and Caesarea or in the royal domain around Jerusalem and Acre—areas that remained virtually free from external attack during these decades. A recent count has suggested that the fortifications of this date in these areas may have amounted to more than half the total of 162 fortified sites identified within the area occupied by the kingdom of Jerusalem. They were clearly not being built as defences against Muslim attack, and so we need to consider what alternative purposes they would have had. There is no doubt that they functioned as centres for rural administration, and it may well be that they should be seen as evidence for more intensive exploitation of the countryside. In many cases the structures, perhaps consisting simply of a donjon and associated outbuildings, sometimes with an outer perimeter wall, should be seen as fortified manor houses. Maybe there were still sufficient brigands in the countryside to make this type of defence necessary. Maybe there was a need to overawe the local peasantry. In some instances they were clearly intended to provide a focal point for rural settlement for Frankish settlers from the West, and it could well be that, as in the West, the local landholder regarded the possession of fortifications as a symbol and assertion of his own status in society. The conclusion to which such considerations point is that at least in the middle decades of the twelfth century these fortifications denote confidence and an expanding economy rather than fear of invasion or a preoccupation with the neighbouring Muslims. It should be called to mind that in many parts of Europe at the same period this same phenomenon, which historians have dubbed *incastellamento*, was in full swing for much the same reasons (see Chapter 8, pp. 164–5), and it has been suggested that in the mid-twelfth century

The Red Tower (Burj al-Ahmar). Situated south east of Caesarea, the remains of this two-storey vaulted *donjon* provide a good example of the small fortress or fortified manor-house that would have functioned as a local centre for rural administration. Many such fortresses were erected in the course of the twelfth century.

The Red Tower (Burj al-Ahmar): plan from excavations carried out by the British School of Archaeology in Jerusalem in 1983.

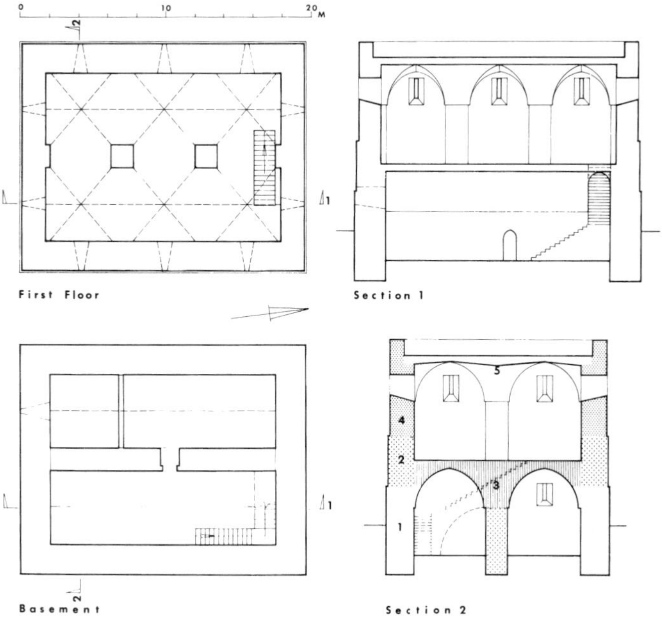

the countryside in the heartlands of the kingdom of Jerusalem was no less secure and enjoyed just as much local prosperity as many regions of the West.

After the late 1160s the situation changed. The comparative security gave way to a series of damaging Muslim raids as Nur al-Din and then Saladin were able to take the offensive. During the 1170s and 1180s these attacks became more frequent and succeeded in penetrating more deeply into Christian-held territory, culminating in the Hattin campaign of 1187. The Christians in the kingdom of Jerusalem responded with a marked increase of castle building in the key frontier areas, and it would seem that this was first time in the kingdom's history that a defensive building strategy had been adopted. There is some evidence to suggest that the two great castles of the Transjordan region, Montreal and Kerak, were enlarged and strengthened at this time. In the late 1160s a fortress was built at Darum on the direct coast approach to Ascalon from Egypt. In the north of the kingdom, in the area closest to the Muslim centre of power at Damascus, the castles at Belvoir and Saphet, acquired by the Hospitallers and Templars respectively, were extensively rebuilt. At Saphet the construction is not clear—there was further rebuilding in the mid-thirteenth century and considerable earthquake damage subsequently—but at Belvoir excavation has revealed a precocious example of a concentric design. Evidently it was much admired: in the 1190s the new Frankish rulers of Cyprus had a castle built at Paphos with a ground plan which though smaller was otherwise virtually identical. The Franks also set to work to build a castle at Jacob's Ford to the north of the Lake of Tiberias athwart one of the most obvious routes into Christian territory from the direction of Damascus, but Saladin reacted swiftly and in 1179 the still-incomplete fortress was captured and destroyed. All these fortresses were constructed on a massive

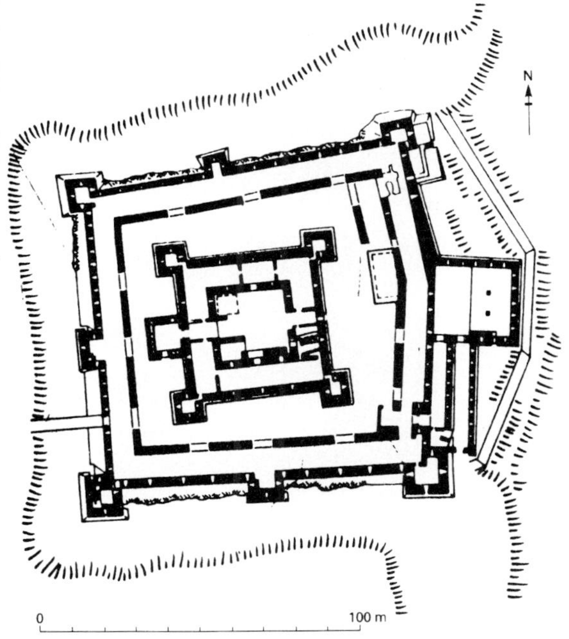

Belvoir Castle. The Hospitallers built this castle in southern Galilee during the years leading up to the Hattin (1187) and the collapse of the kingdom of Jerusalem. It consists of an almost square inner court with towers at each corner surrounded by an outer court. Note the elaborately fortified entrance to the right of the plan.

King Louis IX rebuilt the fortifications at Caesarea in 1251. The walls originally stood to a greater height above the existing talus, but when the city was taken by the Muslims in 1265 the higher sections were toppled into the moat. The moat itself was designed to be flooded by the sea, thus rendering mining operations impossible.

scale. After the battle of Hattin, Saphet, Belvoir, Kerak, and Montreal together with Beaufort in the lordship of Sidon were the fortresses which almost alone resisted Saladin's victorious progress. Darum was the one fortified site in southern Palestine apart from Jerusalem itself which Saladin decided not to slight when confronted with Richard the Lionheart's advance into that region in 1191.

Despite the partial recovery effected by the Third Crusade after the collapse of the kingdom of Jerusalem in 1187, the Christian-held territory at the close of the twelfth century must have been largely in ruins. Only Tyre had successfully resisted Saladin's assaults, and, what with a two-year siege of Acre and a systematic scorched earth policy adopted by the Muslims in southern Palestine, both the defences and the economy would need extensive restoration. King Richard's works at Ascalon and Darum were destroyed under the terms of the 1192 truce which signalled the end of the crusade, and his rebuilding at Jaffa was nullified by the Muslim capture of the town in 1197. New defences elsewhere took time. The castle of Beirut was restored during the first decade of the new century. At Caesarea work was put in hand in 1217, but interrupted by a Muslim assault two years later. At Sidon and Jaffa we have to wait until the late 1220s before the crusaders could restore the fortifications. Major new castles were build at Athlit on the coast south of Haifa (for the Templars) beginning in the winter of 1217–18, and at Montfort in the hills north-east of Acre (for the Teutonic Knights) beginning in about 1227. In 1240–1 Richard of Cornwall built a fortress at Ascalon, and at precisely the same time work was started on restoring the Templar castle at Saphet in Galilee. It was also during the first half of the thirteenth century that the Hospitallers remodelled their two major strongholds in the north, Marqab and Crac des Chevaliers. Between 1250 and 1254 King Louis IX of France strengthened the fortifications of Acre, Caesarea, Jaffa, and Sidon, but in 1260, when Palestine was threatened for the first time with Mongol invasion, the master of the Templars voiced the opinion that in the kingdom of Jerusalem only Tyre and Acre and two Templar fortresses—presumably Saphet and Athlit—and one fortress belonging to the Teutonic Knights—Montfort—were in a state to offer serious resistance. He also mentioned three Templar castles in the principality of Antioch and two Templar and two Hospitaller fortresses in the county of Tripoli.

The Templar master may have been exaggerating the plight of the Christians in the Holy Land—there is no mention of Beirut where the castle had held out for several months when besieged by the Emperor Frederick II's forces during the civil war in the early 1230s, nor of Jaffa where considerable resources had been expended on the defences in the 1250s. But his remarks do highlight the reliance by the Christians in the thirteenth century on a handful of strongly fortified sites and the fact that the castles in the countryside were mostly in the hands of the military orders. However, walled towns and their citadels were of the utmost significance, and the fact that nothing or almost nothing remains of the defences at towns such as Jaffa, Tiberias, or Beirut tends to distort the picture and allow undue attention to be given to the fortresses in the rural areas where, with fewer people bent on robbing the stonework to build their own dwellings, they survive in a better state of repair.

The whole point of building castles or placing walls around towns was to enable them to withstand sieges. Military architects were well aware of the weapons and techniques available to the enemy and tried to devise ways of countering them. The great castles had ample storerooms and frequently a good water supply. In fact there is no known instance of castle surrendering through lack of water, although in 1137 Montferrand surrendered when the food gave out, as did Kerak and Montreal in 1188 and 1189, respectively. Armies could normally only remain in the field for the duration of the campaigning season, and so the chances of a castle putting up a successful resistance was strong. At the time of the First Crusade, the Westerners had only fairly simple siege techniques. They would have been used to the need to fend off relief columns and engage the besieged garrison in exchanges of archery or in hand-

The crusaders massacre the citizens of Antioch in 1097. The massacre of civilians was commonplace when a city was taken by assault and helps explain why commanders would surrender when successful resistance seemed out of the question, even though their supplies and manpower were not yet exhausted. (From a manuscript copied in Acre in the 1280s.)

to-hand fighting should they attempt a sally. But their ideas about how to assault the walls were fairly primitive. At the capture of Jerusalem in 1099 they had scaling ladders and a movable siege tower. Scaling ladders were little use against an adequately defended circuit of walls, and towers were vulnerable to incendiary devices and were clumsy to operate. Ditches and other obstructions had to be overcome, and the tower had to be hauled into place against the wall. Only then could hand-to-hand fighting commence. There was no opportunity for surprise and plenty of chances for the defenders to meet the challenge. The remarkable thing is that at Jerusalem the use of a siege tower in the principal assault worked. At the siege of Acre during the Third Crusade the Christians used protected battering rams called 'sows' or 'cats'—a device apparently not used by the Muslims; but these too were vulnerable to Greek fire—an incendiary mixture of naptha and petroleum—which the Muslims defenders were able to put to good effect.

Where the crusaders trailed behind the Muslims was in the construction of stone-throwing machinery and in mining techniques, neither of which were in regular use in the West until the beginning of the thirteenth century. It could well be that during the twelfth and thirteenth centuries the Muslims themselves made significant advances in these areas. According to Usamah ibn Munqidh, in 1115 they used sappers from Khurasan in north-eastern Persia when attacking a Frankish-held town, and this suggests that the experts in this field were to be found much further to the east. When the 1191 Richard the Lionheart attacked Darum he is said to have employed Muslim sappers from Aleppo. Muslim expertise in mining proved crucial in inducing the surrender of the castles at Saphet (1266), Crac de Chevaliers (1271), and Marqab (1285).

The Muslims also made extensive use of machines designed to hurl stones against or over the walls of fortifications. Variously known by Western writers as 'trebuchets' (see further, Chapter 8, pp. 174–5), 'mangonels', or 'petraries', they seem to have depended on a counterweight (or human effort) to pull down the shorter arm of the beam and so release the projectile. (The use of torsion instead of a counterweight may also have been used: unfortunately the narratives rarely provide sufficient information about the technology involved for there to be any certainty.) It has been estimated that the counterweight trebuchets had a range of up to 200 metres which meant that they could be sited beyond the reach of archers whose arrows would not have been effective at more than about 140 metres. Their capabilities are not in doubt, and they could be aimed with pinpoint accuracy. Saladin employed trebuchets during his victorious campaigns of 1187 and 1188, but it was the Mamluk sultan Baybars (1260–77) who gained the maximum advantage from them. He had them constructed in prefabricated sections so that they could be erected

The crusaders besiege Nicaea. Note the Christian use of the crossbow while the Muslim archer in the tower has a simple bow. (From a manuscript copied in Acre shortly before its fall in 1291.)

speedily at the site of operations. At Beaufort in 1268 he had no less than twenty-six in operation at the end of the siege. Bombardment could knock holes in the walls and in particular destroy crenellation or the wooden hoardings which were frequently employed to give the defenders cover. Stones lobbed into the fortification would cause casualties and an extended assault would doubtless damage morale. Trebuchets would also help provide cover for miners to operate, and what is significant about many of the successful sieges of the second half of the thirteenth century is that both tactics were used in tandem. The Muslims had developed their siege techniques to such a degree that in the second half of the thirteenth century they never needed more than six weeks to reduce any of the great Frankish fortresses to submission.

The defenders might hope to put trebuchets out of action by making their destruction the object of a sally or by setting them on fire. It is also clear that they modified the design of their fortifications to take their effectiveness into account. In the thirteenth century both Christians and Muslims built fortifications with thicker walls and massive towers in an attempt to withstand bombardment, and, as at Jaffa in the 1260s, they could mount their own trebuchets on the towers. The development of concentric castles would have meant that the main stronghold was further from where the machines could be sited. It may be that the use of round or semicircular towers in the

Demoralizing the besieged. Gaining psychological advantage over the opposition has always been an essential element in warfare. Here the crusaders hurl decapitated heads into Nicaea during the seige of 1097. (From a French manuscript of the third quarter of the thirteenth century.)

thirteenth-century defences at Crac des Chevaliers, Marqab, and a few other places were also conceived as a riposte to improved artillery and were less susceptible to mining.

In 1291 the last major conflict in the history of the Latin states in the Levant was played out at Acre. The Mamluk sultan brought up a huge army. The Muslim trebuchets kept up a constant bombardment, and their archers gave solid support. All the while sappers undermined the towers at the most vulnerable corner of the defences. The defenders' sallies came to naught, and, though they fought valiantly when the Muslims began to force their way into the city through the breaches in the walls that their mines had opened, they were overwhelmed by force of numbers. Such was the impact of the defeat that the Franks surrendered Tyre and their other remaining strongholds without further resistance.

6 EUROPEAN WARFARE c.1200–1320

NORMAN HOUSLEY

Two battles fought near the start and end of this period provide us with convenient vantage points from which to begin an assessment of its characteristics. At Bouvines, between Lille and Tournai, on 27 July 1214, a French army commanded by King Philip II Augustus engaged a German-Flemish army led by the Emperor Otto IV and the count of Flanders. After a hard struggle involving a great deal of hand-to-hand fighting, Philip was victorious. The Emperor escaped, but the count of Flanders was captured and taken in triumph to be imprisoned in the Louvre. At Courtrai, south of Ghent, on 11 July 1302, an army mainly composed of the Flemish communal militias inflicted a crushing defeat on Robert of Artois's French army, killing its commander and all the other leaders of the royal host. The French appear to have lost between a third and a half of their knights, and the gilded spurs of 500 of their dead were hung up as trophies in the church of St Mary in Courtrai.

Bouvines and Courtrai present us with both similarities and differences. The two battlefields lie no more than forty miles apart, their proximity serving as a reminder of the strategic importance for France of the Flemish plain and the provinces lying immediately to its south. On both occasions political circumstances overruled the well-known and justifiable reluctance of medieval commanders to risk engaging in battle. In 1214 Philip II confronted an extremely dangerous coalition: King John of England, Otto IV, and Ferrand of Portugal, the count of Flanders. In 1302 French control over Flanders, established just two years previously, was imperilled by insurrection, the 'Matins of Bruges' of 18 May. Bouvines proved to be a decisive riposte to the challenge which Philip faced. The king saw off the German threat, confirmed his con-

It was well-armed and disciplined foot-soldiers like these who in 1302 defeated Philip the Fair's horsemen at the battle of Courtrai. This famous triumph of infantry over cavalry was an affront to the age's sense of social order as well as a massive blow to a monarchy which stood at the height of its prestige and influence.

quest of Normandy from England, and constructed a firm French hegemony over Flanders. Philip also garnered great personal renown from winning the first pitched battle which a French king had dared fight for a century; it should be added that the encounter almost cost him his life. On the other hand, the defeat at Courtrai proved to be much less important in its long-term consequences. King Philip the Fair reacted with energy to the humiliation and personally gained a victory over the Flemings at Mons-en-Pévèle two years later.

Both at Bouvines and at Courtrai the French relied primarily, though not exclusively, on their heavy cavalry. This proved disastrous in the latter engagement, but only because Robert of Artois refused to allow his skilled crossbowmen to inflict enough casualties on the massed Flemish pikemen before launching his series of charges. Courtrai was a triumph over stupidity as much as a revelation of what infantry could achieve. Both battles reveal the essentially eclectic mixture of battle tactics which characterized thirteenth-century warfare, before the devastating impact of the English longbow on Continental war-making (see Chapter 7, p. 142; Chapter 9, pp. 203–5). Nor were there major changes in the way the French royal host was recruited for the two encounters, although the shock of Courtrai did induce Philip the Fair to attempt a revival of universal military service (the *arrière-ban*) as a means of mobilizing men and money more rapidly and effectively. In terms of tactics and organization, the historian searches in vain for a 'military revolution' in this period. Instead we detect developments more fragmented and subtle: the wearing of more plate mail in response to the spreading use of crossbows, the more sophisticated deployment of infantry, more formidable stone fortifica-

tions and hence more ingenious siege techniques, especially the widespread employment of the trebuchet from about 1200 onwards (see Chapter 5, p. 109; Chapter 8, p. 174). Above all, behind these changes we see the pervasive impact on warfare of government, as the latter became more centralized, ambitious, and demanding. European war-making in the thirteenth century was arguably more conditioned than ever before by the wide variation in the capabilities of the individuals and states which were resorting to the use of force.

Before addressing these issues, some assessment must be made of the wars which were fought. Following Bouvines there was a period of some eighty years of peace between England and France. Peaceful relations were not unbroken, but the absence of a major conflict between Western Europe's two most powerful kingdoms was remarkable and the consequences for French society were profound. The problem of the *routiers*, freelance mercenaries (see Chapter 10, p. 213) who harassed religious houses and civilian communities, was dealt with, largely because so many died at Bouvines and during the Albigensian Crusade. Warfare ceased to be part of the normal pattern of French life. In addition, slowly but surely it was removed from the private domain and became a prerogative of public authority. By *c.*1284 even Philippe de Beaumanoir, a noted champion of the nobility's privileges, was ready to accept limitations on their right to go to war if it infringed royal justice. Indeed, Philippe Contamine, France's leading historian of warfare in the middle ages, has recently written of 'the great peace of the thirteenth century'. For the French nobility, war became associated above all with two forms of activity and associated loyalties which exerted a powerful appeal on the aristocratic mind: crusading and service to the Capetian dynasty.

The continuing appeal of the crusade was apparent in the Fourth and Fifth Crusades (1202–4, 1217–19), for which recruitment in France was heavy. But more important for our purposes was the Albigensian Crusade of 1209–29. This series of expeditions against the cathar heretics and their noble protectors took the form, for the most part, of gruelling sieges conducted amongst the valleys and hills of Languedoc by armies of knights and sergeants from northern France. The crusaders found their opponents well-entrenched in fortresses, and in sieges like those of Minerve and Termes in 1210, the new type of trebuchet, which derived its power from a counterweight, proved invaluable. But trebuchets were temperamental and required skilful handling by engineers who all too often fell ill, were killed, or deserted because they were unpaid. Local nobles, moreover, were infuriatingly nonchalant about breaking the terms of surrender agreements once their fortresses had been captured. Simon of Montfort, the leader of the Catholic forces, was forced to rely on the services of crusaders whose votive obligation committed them to just forty days of fighting. He therefore faced almost insurmountable problems in holding on to what he gained in the course of each summer's hard campaigning. In the winter of 1209–10, for example, it was claimed that more than forty strongholds slipped out of Simon's hands. Crusader frustration and cathar intransigence led to a brutality which was rare by the standards of thirteenth-century warfare. Massacres and burnings became commonplace; after the fall of Bram in 1210 Simon had the entire garrison blinded with the exception of one man who was placed in charge of his mutilated comrades. Nonetheless, it was only in 1226, when Louis VIII led a royal expedition to the south, that substantial progress was made.

The one important battle of the Albigensian Crusade was fought at Muret on 12 September 1213 between Simon of Montfort and the combined

This anonymous *crucesignatus* represents the monastic ideal of a crusading knight: reverential and committed to Christ's cause, but possessing the arms, equipment, and support to defeat His enemies. In reality, however, any *crucesignatus* who sported so many crosses would have been regarded by his comrades as both incongruous and vain.

forces of the house of Toulouse and the crown of Aragon. Simon secured victory at Muret in a thoroughly orthodox fashion by launching a shock cavalry charge at the disorderly Catalan lines. His success was scarcely less important for Philip Augustus than the king's own a year later at Bouvines, for it put paid to an Aragonese attempt to establish a protectorate over Languedoc. Bouvines consolidated this gain by taking England too out of the political equation, clearing the way for the extension of royal authority in the south between 1226 and 1249. Such leaps forward in Capetian power and prestige, and the administrative innovations which accompanied them, enabled Louis IX to plan his crusade to the East, in 1244–8, with a rigour and attention to detail which was unprecedented in French military history. The recruiting of troops, the raising of cash, and the provision of shipping and supplies, all showed what the Capetian monarchy was now capable of achieving, and may well have been repeated for the king's second crusade in 1267–70. But these were extraordinary efforts, and set standards which Louis's descendants were unable to match.

St Louis's two crusades met with failure, as did the next major exertion of royal strength, Philip III's invasion of Aragon in 1285. Philip's army could not take the great stronghold of Gerona and he was cut off from his supplies when most of his fleet was sunk. In military terms, none of the Capetians from Louis IX onwards enjoyed overwhelming success, but it would be a mistake to allow our knowledge of the disasters to come to shape our views of this period. For example, the French more than held their own in fighting against the English in Gascony in 1296–7. They were led on these campaigns by the same commander who was to lose at Courtrai, and who won against the Flemings at Furnes in 1297. Philip VI's reign, which was to see so much disaster, began with a brilliant victory, again over the Flemings, at Cassel in 1328. In addition, while St Louis's crusades were not crowned with military glory, the kudos derived from them gave the French monarchy incalculable benefits in terms of its image within the European community, its relations (especially financial) with the French church and the papacy, and its projection of policy to its own subjects. In the thirteenth century, the age of crusading par excellence, military balance sheets have to take such factors heavily into account.

Crusading, which offered its participants a potent blend of combat and penitence, was integral to the experience of warfare for many thousands of European soldiers in the thirteenth century. Apart from the campaigns in the East and within the heartlands of Christendom, there was much crusading in Iberia and the Baltic region. In these two areas the crusaders achieved military successes as striking as any which had occurred in the Latin East. At the battle of Las Navas de Tolosa, on 16 July 1212, Alfonso VIII of Castile inflicted a crushing defeat on the Almohads, the rulers of Muslim al-Andalus. The encounter was the most important Christian victory of the entire Reconquista, leading to a series of Castilian and Aragonese conquests, notably the Balearic islands (1229–35), Córdoba (1236), Valencia (1238), and Seville (1248). Also by 1248, the Portuguese had reached the Algarve coastline in the south. It took decades for these huge territorial gains to be effectively assimilated and colonized. Granted that the Almohads were already disunited at the time of Las Navas, this battle joined Muret and Bouvines as an encounter which had massive consequences. Indeed, it would be hard to find another example in European history of three battles, fought in consecutive years in different theatres of operation, which were so decisive in their impact.

The conquests made at much the same time in Livonia and Prussia were almost as impressive as those in Iberia. Catholic Livonia was created between 1198 and 1263, initially by bands of German crusaders, then by the military order of the Sword-brothers, and finally by the Teutonic Knights. More important for the latter was their work further south, in Prussia. The Knights were invited into northern Poland by Conrad of Masovia to counter destructive raids on his lands by the pagan Prussians. From their initial base in Kulmerland, the Knights drew on their own personnel, and the services of visiting German crusaders, to advance northwards along the Vistula basin. Stone castles were built to consolidate conquests, major examples being Balga (1239), Königsberg (1254), and Ragnit (1275). The subjugation of the natives in the name of Christ proved difficult: there were great revolts against the Order's rule in 1240 and 1260. Nonetheless, by 1320 the Knights were no longer challenged in Prussia, where they had created, and successfully colonized, the most closely governed 'order-state' of the middle ages. They needed this stable base, as well as the continuing support of the German and indeed the European nobility, for they now faced an even greater challenge in the shape of their great war against pagan Lithuania.

Mailed cavalry, stone towers manned by Knight-brethren, giant catapults and trebuchets, crossbows, and cogs added up to an overwhelming superiority in military techniques for the Germans in their war against the indigenous tribes along the Baltic. Perhaps not until the Spaniards encountered the Aztecs was such a dramatic disparity of technology to recur in a major conflict. However, it is notable how rapidly the Prussians learnt how to use at least some of their opponents' weapons. And any idea that this local imbalance represented a general ascendancy of Catholic Europe over its neighbours is readily shattered when one considers the hammer blows dealt by the Mongol Tatars during their military encounters with the central European powers. In April 1241, within the space of a few days, the Tatars crushed the Poles and Teutonic

'To be soaked in one's own sweat and blood, that I call the true bath of honour' (Henry of Laon). Fortunes as well as reputations were won and lost in the hack and thrust of close combat like this, for knights who were captured had to pay large sums for their release. It is not hard to imagine the noise, confusion, fear, and exhaustion which accompanied protracted hand-to-hand encounters.

Knights in one battle (Liegnitz) and the Hungarians in another (Mohi) (see further, Chapter 9, pp. 196–7). In both cases it was the discipline and fury of the Tatars which overwhelmed their Christian opponents. Sheer good fortune, in the form of a Tatar withdrawal shortly afterwards, saved the European powers from the threat of conquest, and from the difficult task of adapting their traditional tactics to deal with Tatar fighting techniques.

Is there, then, any underlying unity to the dramatic successes achieved in this period in Spain and the Baltic region? It cannot plausibly be argued that they were simply the military expression of population pressure. Settling what they conquered was no easy task for either the Iberian monarchies or the Teutonic Order; and in the case of a third zone of Catholic conquest, the Byzantine lands following the Fourth Crusade, it proved impossible to promote adequate settlement. The active presence in all these areas of crusading ideology and institutions naturally represents a common feature of some importance. In particular, the contribution made by the brethren of the military orders should not be underestimated. While the Knight-brothers of the Iberian orders did not play the central role enjoyed by the Sword-brothers and Teutonic Knights, they did garrison a large number of fortresses. Salvatierra castle, held by Calatrava, was a thorn in the flesh for the Almohads for some years in the early thirteenth century, and its fall in 1211 precipitated the Las Navas campaign. Without the assistance of the orders the southwards sweep of the Iberian monarchies could not have proceeded so fast. However, even in the Baltic region 'the crusading presence' does not by itself account for Catholic success. At the end of the day, it was largely coincidence that local factors, of a widely differing nature, worked to the advantage of the crusaders at both extremities of Europe.

It remains to consider warfare in the British Isles and Italy. England in the thirteenth century experienced two periods of intense military activity, the first in the Barons' Wars of the 1260s and the second during the Welsh and Scottish Wars of Edward I. Civil wars tend to be characterized by pitched battles as both sides seek a speedy resolution of the quarrel, and the Barons' War produced two major engagements at Lewes (1264) and Evesham (1265). By contrast, it is hard not to see the most important feature of Edward I's conquest of Wales in 1277–83, and certainly its most fascinating legacy, as the carefully planned network of castles which the king had constructed there (see also Chapter 8, pp. 176–9). The most important were at Rhuddlan, Flint, Conway, Harlech, Beaumaris, and Caernarvon. Michael Prestwich has recently judged them to be 'the most magnificent series of fortifications to be built in all of medieval Europe', while at the same time questioning the wisdom of Edward's strategic approach in terms of the resources required to maintain them later.

Together with Louis IX's two crusades, Edward I's Scottish wars form the most instructive of all the thirteenth-century conflicts which have to date profited from the close attention of research historians. This was principally because, like Louis's overseas ventures, they so clearly reveal the royal government tackling fundamental issues of military organization in a thorough way. The strategy adopted by Edward is less impressive, consisting as it did of sending northwards large armies with the goal of bringing the Scots to battle. This worked at Falkirk in 1298, but on other occasions it failed, either because the Scots avoided battle or because, as at Stirling Bridge in 1297 and Bannockburn in 1314, they won through innovative ways of deploying their foot soldiers. It was not until after 1320, first at Boroughbridge (1322) and more importantly at Halidon Hill (1333), that the English began implementing their own tactical changes, which were shortly to pay such huge dividends in France.

Italy witnessed probably the most constant and widespread warfare of any

European country in the thirteenth century, one result being that it attracted bands of mercenaries from virtually everywhere else. The endemic nature of the conflicts there was rooted in two sets of circumstances. First, the self-governing communes of the north and centre were engaged in cut-throat competition for land and markets. Secondly, both the popes and the kings of Sicily, until 1266 the Staufen and thereafter the Angevins, were in a position, either ex officio or for dynastic reasons, to mobilize and bring in military power on a large scale from outside the peninsula. These two dynamics interacted because the complex range of communal enmities and alliances wove intricate patterns of patronage and allegiance with the papal, imperial, and royal authorities. The resulting warfare defies ready analysis, except for the relatively clear divide between the royal south and the communal centre and north. In the kingdom of Sicily, where political authority had long been remarkably centralized, battles could be decisive. Charles of Anjou, the younger brother of Louis IX who was summoned into Italy by the pope to oust the Staufen, effectively won the *Regno* through his clear-cut victories at Benevento (1266) and Tagliacozzo (1268). On the other hand, in Tuscany and

The single combat depicted here between a French knight and Manfred of Staufen is a stylized representation of the rivalry between the Angevins and their German opponents. In 1283 complicated arrangements were made for a real-life duel between Charles I of Anjou and King Peter of Aragon, who was Manfred's son-in-law. But the encounter never took place.

Lombardy the extreme political fragmentation meant that even such a resounding victory as Frederick II's defeat of the Milanese at Cortenuova (1237) ultimately settled nothing.

Because the centre and north was a land of fortified towns and cities, sieges were commonplace. They were, however, notoriously difficult to carry through, and even a town which had been captured might be lost again shortly afterwards through bribery, treachery, or insurrection. The situation was in fact similar to what the Albigensian crusaders encountered in Languedoc. Capturing even such a relatively small town as Faenza took Frederick II six months in 1240–1; and the emperor's siege of Parma in 1248 ended in failure despite his construction of a siege camp, which he foolishly called 'Victory', on such a scale that it was all but a town itself. The virtual impossibility of inflicting a decisive defeat on one's enemy meant that warfare in Italy in this period attained a frequency which resembles that of the eleventh rather than the thirteenth century. This was viable within a society which depended to such a large degree on commerce, ease of communications, and inter-city cooperation only because of a complex system of restraints. These kept hostilities to a mutually agreed level and helped to exercise a brake on the most brutal behaviour during the conduct of military operations. At times the restraints broke down or were mutually discarded, as during the last ten years or so of Frederick II's war with the communes. The horrors of this period were graphically depicted by such chroniclers as Salimbene. But for the most part thirteenth-century Italy enables us to view the 'law of arms' (the customary conventions governing relations between hostile parties) functioning with a clarity lacking in less well-ordered and legally refined environments.

Even this short *tour d'horizon* of war-making in the thirteenth century will make it apparent that there were numerous reasons for the age's belligerence. The pursuit of dynastic rights, the conquest of enemy territory, civil war, and the winning of personal glory or honour, co-existed without apparent tension with more altruistic motives such as the defence of the realm or *patria*, the reconquest of patrimonial lands which had been seized, and service to the Christian faith through the crusade or wars of conversion. It was of course these latter causes which were pressed on rulers by canon and civil lawyers; by 1300, such men were vociferous in their espousal of the duty of the Christian prince to wage only just wars. But many rulers neither knew of nor much cared about the ideas of lawyers and theologians, and those who were personally susceptible to such arguments found little difficulty in portraying their most cherished goals in acceptable ways. As Maurice Keen put it, 'in practice a just war and a public war meant the same thing'. Documents issued in the name of men like Frederick II and Philip the Fair showed that they appreciated the desirability of communicating their military goals in a plausible manner, for many reasons. But it would be hard to sustain the argument that they or their contemporaries had an approach towards war which was *au fond* very different from that of their predecessors in the eleventh and twelfth centuries.

Where change was occurring, albeit in piecemeal fashion, was in the recruiting, paying, and supplying of armies. Recruitment of soldiers is best handled by reference to England, France, and Italy. The English kings raised their armies through a combination of household service, feudal obligations, the imposition of a more general duty to serve, and payment. The royal household provided at least the core of an army and sometimes much more than that. In 1314–15 Edward II had thirty-two bannerets and eighty-nine knights in his household, although these figures contracted sharply immediately afterwards. As for feudal obligations, in the early thirteenth century the English magnates won a major success by getting their quotas (*servitium debitum*) drastically reduced. From John's reign onwards the issuing of a feudal summons was rarely enough in itself to secure an army. It was either replaced or supplemented by distraint of knighthood (as for Edward I's first Welsh campaign of 1277), wages, and, from at least 1270 onwards, contractual service. A multiplicity of military, financial, and political factors shaped the approach which was followed on each occasion that the crown needed to raise an army. In 1282, for example, the earls wanted to serve in Wales without pay, because by responding to a feudal summons they would increase their chances of receiving any lands which the king conquered. More puzzlingly, no feudal summons was issued in the case of the Falkirk campaign of 1298 yet the majority of the cavalry were not paid either. The motive for service appears to have been general fealty to Edward I.

The situation in France was not dissimilar. Philippe Contamine has written of the royal host that fought at Bouvines that it was 'hardly an army at all, rather an episodic gathering together of small, autonomous units, a reflection of the feudal structure, easily brought together, easily dismissed at the end of the campaign, which came when requested to flesh out the modest group of household knights'. Feudal services continued to be used throughout the century, although the last occasion when the resources of the entire kingdom were called on was in 1272. Towns were usually expected to provide contingents of infantry. It is possible to reconstruct the quotas in the case of the Bouvines campaign, ranging from 1,000 due from Arras to fifty from Crandelain. Many religious houses also had military obligations to the crown: Saint-Germain-des-Près, for example, was supposed to send 150 sergeants whenever the king led his host to war.

Well before the last feudal summons of 1272, the Capetians had begun to

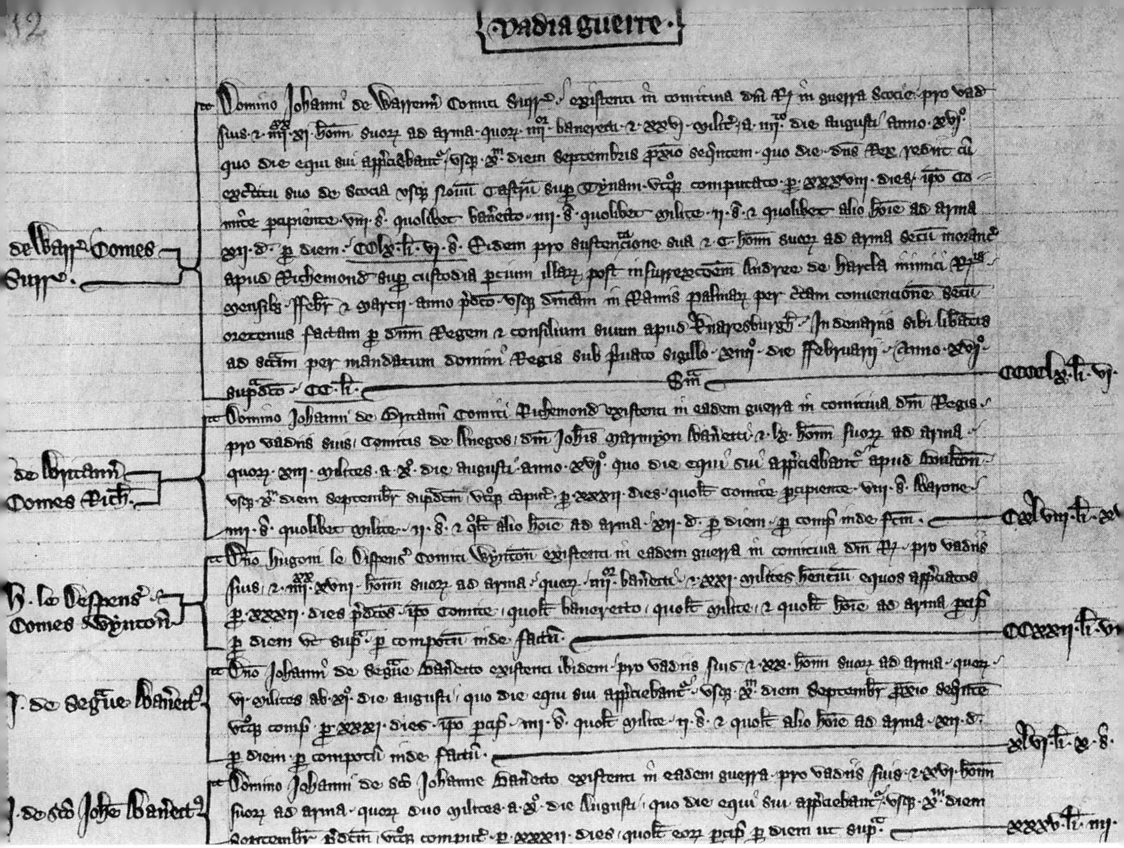

The famous dictum *pecunia nervus belli est* (money is the sinews of war) certainly applied to European warfare in the 13th century. These accounts of wages paid for cavalry service in Scotland in 1322 were compiled by clerks working for the English royal wardrobe, but their counterparts existed in all the western European states. War needed bureaucrats as well as cash.

make extensive use of wages (*vadia*), notably for St Louis's crusades and for the Aragonese crusade of 1285; all three were interesting cases because a large proportion of the combatants had a votive obligation to serve. Salaried service was particularly prominent in the large number of castle garrisons which had to be paid to man France's more troubled frontiers. Some of these were substantial; for example, in 1299 there were 32 sergeants stationed at Sainte-Livrade, 256 at Moissac, and 50 at Villefranche. When money was paid for service on campaign, on the other hand, the amounts were modest, and the concept of salary is sometimes less appropriate than that of an indemnity to cover expenses and compensate for inconvenience. By 1300 written contracts to serve were also making their appearance, at first in the feudal disguise of fief-rents (i.e. a 'fief' granted in the form not of an estate but of payment in return for the promise of service). None of these mechanisms were exclusive. As in England, we can assume that the procedure adopted was what best suited both soldiers and paymaster after a period of haggling. In 1249, for example, Alphonse of Poitiers engaged the services of Hugues le Brun, count of Angoulême, together with eleven knights, for his crusade. Hugues received wages, an annual hereditary fief-rent of 600 *livres* Poitevin, and a four-year loan of 4,000 *livres* of Tours.

In both England and France the movement towards paid service was blurred by the fact that it co-existed for many decades not just with older forms of obligation but also with a strong sense of personal allegiance to the anointed monarch who, on major campaigns, himself led his soldiers into action. The vast majority of these men were after all subjects of the king. In the Italian communes the historical continuity was much less imposing and the element of personal loyalty lacking. Many foreign soldiers were attracted by the wealth and incessant belligerence of the peninsula's governments; in turn their business-like attitude towards the engagement of their skills and expertise accentuated the appearance that Italy was in the vanguard of a movement towards a more commercial way of organizing war. To a large extent this was true also of the Angevin kings of Naples. Their commitments regularly exceeded the military service they could prise out of the feudal baronage and they hired many French and Provençal knights, sergeants, and crossbowmen. Some of these were subjects of the Angevins, but many were mercenaries pure and simple.

The result has been well analysed, in the case of Florence, by Daniel Waley. The obligation of Florentine citizens to serve in person was taken very seriously throughout our period. However, the service of the citizens was supplemented by the hiring of mercenaries, troops whose service was solely linked to the payment of wages. From about 1270 onwards their role both on campaign and in garrison duty became more significant. Waley has vigorously rebutted the idea that this reflected the demilitarization of Florentine society: 'There is no evidence that the Florence of 1300 was a city of soft, decadent businessmen who preferred to pay others to fight on their behalf.' Rather, it was due to the spread of plate mail and the increasingly heavy chargers which it necessitated, the lengthening of Florence's military agenda, and the growing pool of mercenaries who were available for hire. The contract (*condotta*; see also Chapter 10, p. 217) was therefore by 1320 a common and sophisticated feature of military life in the peninsula. By this point most cities were appointing officials with the task of negotiating the contracts. The *condotta* had already proceeded far beyond the obvious stipulations relating to salary and length of service, to include provisions about the armour to be worn, compensation for horses lost (*mendum*), disposal of booty and prisoners, and jurisdiction in the case of lawbreaking. Moreover, many contracts were by this time agreed between communes and entrepreneurs, Italians or otherwise, who had assembled into a *masnada* or *conestabularia* the troops on whose behalf they negotiated terms.

Underpinning all these changes was of course the development across the Continent of a money economy, together with the ability of governments to milk this economy in order to increase their revenues and expand their credit, and so pay for their warfare. War finance is too large and complex a topic to be dealt with here, but one point at least must be made: that in Western Europe at least, population growth, allied to burgeoning governmental receipts and an undiminished bellicosity on the part of rulers, led to considerably larger armies taking the field. Professor Contamine has estimated a threefold or fourfold increase in the military strength available to the French crown between Bouvines and Courtrai. Based on the king's expenditure, it has been reckoned that Louis IX led as many as 15,000 or even 25,000 combatants on his first crusade: extraordinary figures when it is borne in mind that these men, accompanying non-combatants, and perhaps 8,000 horses, all required shipping. Like Philip the Fair, Edward I could field an army of up to 30,000 men, a figure far beyond what King John could have hoped to achieve. Professor Prestwich has written that the Falkirk campaign of 1297 was fought by 'probably the largest single army that had been raised up to that time by an English government'. By contrast, William Marshal may well have won his victory at Lincoln in 1217 with fewer than 800 men.

These bigger armies were also more sophisticated in their make-up than their predecessors had been. In the English army the heavy cavalry were divided into three categories: bannerets, knights, and a third group made up of sergeants, squires, and valets. Amongst the French, a greater emphasis on knighthood created two groups: the dubbed, ranging from dukes to bachelor-knights, and the rest, generally termed sergeants at the start of the century and squires by its close. These categories of 'men-at-arms' hinged not solely on social status but also on the amount of mail worn and the number of chargers owned. In addition, there were mounted archers and crossbowmen, and in England the lightly armed horsemen called hobelars (see Chapter 9, p. 195). Infantry featured in some capacity in nearly all campaigns and included such specialized troops as archers, spearmen, crossbowmen, and shieldbearers (*pavesari*), who protected the crossbowmen while they reloaded.

Many units in thirteenth-century armies were remarkably well organized. As in so many spheres of medieval life, lordship was the most important cohesive force. In English and French armies it was exercised through the retinues of the kings and magnates. In 1297 the earl of Norfolk served Edward I with a retinue of five bannerets, nine knights, and seventeen men-at-arms. A few years later, during the Courtrai campaign, the lord of Varannes served Philip

IV with a force of five knights, twenty squires, a chaplain, two clerks, six chamberlains, sixty-one servants, and a washerwoman. They had at their disposal eighty-four horses. In other cases knights formed agreements, based on mutual support, known as brotherhood in arms. Infantry were commonly grouped along regional lines, each group of fighters possessing its civilian servants, chaplains, and similar auxiliaries. The militias provided by towns, particularly those of Italy, Flanders, and the frontier regions of Castile, were characterized by a high degree of organization. The men used the same equipment and armour and trained together; indeed, in many instances they worked and worshipped together. Uniforms were common by 1300: the men from Tournai wore red tunics with a silver castle on the chest and back.

Organizational neatness reached its apogee in the citizen militias of the Italian communes, in which each of the town's quarters would field a separate force fully kitted out with its requirements. Thanks to the 'Book of Montaperti' compiled by officials of the Florentine commune we possess a mass of

Their crosses show that at least some of these Catalan foot-soldiers were crusaders, probably participants in Jaume I's campaigns against the Moors of Valencia and Majorca. Their prowess and ferocity became legendary, and enabled Jaume and his successors to establish the crown of Aragon as one of the most dynamic powers in the Mediterranean region.

Together with arms, equipment, and money, armies needed food. Their requirements were met in part by direct provisioning, but more frequently by encouraging the efforts of merchants and entrepreneurs to buy up and transport supplies for the fighting men and their animals.

detail about the army which fought (and lost) the eponymous battle in 1260. Here in microcosm is the commune at war. Each *sesto* (sixth) provided both cavalry and infantry, the cavalry contingents being the responsibility of the aristocratic clans (*consorterie*). Contingents were led by standard-bearers accompanied by commissioners and councillors. The entire army was commanded by the *podestà*, the commune's chief executive official, but what really unified his composite army was the *carroccio*, the curious battle wagon drawn by oxen and carrying a miscellaneous collection of the commune's relics and blessed banners. At Montaperti the Florentine *carroccio* had a guard of fifty knights. The loss of the town *carroccio* to the enemy was considered a dire humiliation. Following the battle of Cortenuova in 1237 Frederick II had the captured Milanese *carroccio* dragged by an elephant through the streets of Milan's leading rival, Cremona. Its banners were lowered in shame and the captured *podestà* was shackled to it.

It was surely inevitable that this general movement towards larger numbers of combatants, and better ordered forces, should have its counterpart in the field of supply, in particular that of food for men and animals. Across Europe, strenuous efforts were made by governments to ensure that armies and garrisons would be adequately supplied as well as equipped. The figures available in documentary sources are on a scale simply not approached in earlier periods, so there is a danger of exaggerating the novelty of what was achieved. Nonetheless, it would be foolish not to accept the extent of the effort involved. This was the more striking insofar as it emanated from officials who were already overstretched: few new administrative organs were created. So effective was the redirection of Sicilian grain towards the supply needs of Louis IX's crusading army in Tunisia in the summer of 1270 that there were shortages not just in the north Italian cities but at Syracuse itself. In England, by the end of Edward I's wars, the compulsory purchase of foodstuffs for military purposes, known first as prise and later as purveyance, had become one of the crown's most unpopular prerogatives. In France, at the same time, a stream of safe conducts and toll exemptions were issued by the king for merchants who were busy supplying the royal host. However it was undertaken, provisioning was acknowledged to be crucially important. When it broke down prices went through the roof, morale collapsed, and relations with the local civilians, which were fraught at the best of times, were brutalized.

Shortage of weapons could be as serious as shortage of food, and by 1300 the more advanced European states were also getting used to making purchases of arms and armour in readiness for their conflicts. The records of the English, French, and Neapolitan monarchies are full of references to the buying in and auditing of such stores. In 1295, for example, the French government bought 2,000 crossbows, 1,000 padded doublets, 3,000 bascinets, and 3,000 gorgets, at Toulouse, for the war in Gascony. Trebuchet ammunition was kept in bulk and above all crossbow bolts and arrows were stored. In the Italian communes the usual practice was that hired mercenaries would provide their own armour, but the city would furnish ammunition for crossbows. The counterpart to these preparations was the ban customarily placed on the export of war materials, horses, armour, and even iron, at times of war.

Crusading to the East posed uniquely vexing problems relating to supply, and the efforts which St Louis made to ensure the adequate provisioning of his troops are well known. One of Joinville's most charming anecdotes is of the hills of wheat and barley which Louis's officials accumulated in Cyprus in anticipation of the needs of the royal army when it wintered on the island. The corn on the top sprouted in the rain and had to be removed to get at the fresh corn lying underneath. St Louis's first crusade also provides the most famous thirteenth-century example of civilian building works undertaken in association with a military venture. This was the king's construction of Aigues-Mortes in Provence, in order that his army could embark at a port located within the lands of the French crown. For Louis, as later for Philip VI, this consideration evidently outweighed such disadvantages as the ineluctable

This aerial view of the port at Aigues-Mortes communicates well the astonishing ambition of Louis IX's military planning. The energy and resources which on this occasion were harnessed for the needs of the king's planned crusade to the East would later be directed towards objectives nearer at home and yielding more obvious benefits to the French crown.

tendency of the harbour to silt up and the lack of fresh water in the vicinity. Aigues-Mortes was a response to what one historian of Louis's reign has termed 'the challenge of the crusade'. It is increasingly clear that the main impact which crusading in the East exerted on European warfare lay in the field of novel administrative demands, rather than the application in the West of specifically military lessons which had been learned in Egypt, Palestine, and Syria. There were very few of the latter, and they do not include Edward I's Welsh castles, which historians used to think were modelled on castles which Edward had observed in the Holy Land during his stay there in 1271–2.

So far in this chapter we have concentrated on the broad sweep of campaigns and the mobilization and organization of the armies which fought them; let us finally consider the fighting man of the period. Did the growing professionalism of war, and the increasingly dirigiste role of governments, affect his attitude to what he was doing? Was he different in kind from his predecessors? It is notoriously difficult to answer such questions with confidence, but they must at least be addressed. For simple reasons of evidence we can only consider the attitude of the mounted warrior, the knight, or at best the sergeant, regrettable though it is to neglect the views of those who fought on foot.

Military service, as we have seen, was provided out of obligation, voluntarily, or for pay. So much attention has been paid in recent years to the way in which these intertwined that the old view of the thirteenth century as a period of transition, from feudal, or civic, obligation towards paid service, no longer seems wholly satisfactory. Payments were already being made in 1200 while obligations still played a large part in 1320: indeed, Philip IV tried to put the clock back by reviving the old *arrière-ban*, much to the annoyance of Pierre Dubois. Dubois interpreted this as the king abjectly surrendering to the nobility's reluctance to perform their vassalic duty, but it could equally well have been an attempt to revive a sense of general obligation for France's defence, whether expressed through service or payment.

Perhaps of greater importance than what Philip was trying to do was the political and administrative effort involved in this and in similar moves in other countries. Governmental control over the waging of war became tighter in the thirteenth century than it had been in the twelfth or was to be (at least in some areas) in the fourteenth. We have seen that the freelance mercenaries known as *routiers*, who had acquired a terrible reputation for brutality in the later twelfth century, ceased to be a problem early in the thirteenth century. Their successors, the free companies, had yet to emerge. The exception, the Catalan Grand Company, was certainly extraordinary and pointed the way to the future (See further Chapter 10, p. 217). But its success was largely due to its theatre of operations, first in the Byzantine Empire and then in Frankish Greece. Since the Fourth Crusade the endemic conflict in this area had attracted a lot of Western mercenaries: as early as 1210 the Latin emperor of Constantinople, Henry, was criticized by Pope Innocent III for aggravating his shortage of fighting men by not offering the going rate for such soldiers, who were more attracted by the wages offered by Henry's Greek enemies. Elsewhere the thirteenth-century warrior was generally anchored to the service of an established authority to which the lawyers ascribed the *ius ad bellum* (right to wage war): either a secular power or, when he fought as a crusader or as a professed member of a military order, the church. Those who took the cross but accepted financial subventions while doing so, such as many who fought with St Louis in the East, were often in the service of both. The obligations of fighting men were increasingly spelled out in the form of contracts and religious vows, while the nature and limits of their service were defined juridically through the work of canon and civil lawyers.

It is safe to say that warriors had never before been subject to such controls or received such quantities of prescriptive advice; but whether this radically altered the way the fighting man saw himself and his work is another matter. A consensus about what constituted chivalric behaviour had already emerged by 1200, and may be clearly seen in the Life of William Marshal, which was written in the late 1220s. Its author focused on a characteristic blend of military excellence, faithful service to a succession of English kings, good lord-

Roland, shown here in a thirteenth-century manuscript being dubbed by his lord Charlemagne, remained an extremely attractive figure for fighting men. His combination of vassalic loyalty, military prowess, and religious devotion made him an enduring chivalric exemplar.

ship, and religious piety. William spent over two years in the Holy Land and entered the order of the Knights Templar on his deathbed in 1219. During the following decades those knights who attracted similar admiration from their contemporaries tended to have a career as crusaders, as well as being loyal vassals and active in military affairs generally. Geoffrey of Sergines, who commanded the French 'regiment' left behind at Acre by St Louis when he returned to France in 1254, was acclaimed as a hero by the poet Rutebeuf, and such men as Erard of Valéry, Otto de Grandson, and Giles of Argentine fitted much the same mould.

It is tempting to see a gulf in attitudes between such warriors and some of those who took contractual service with the Italian communes, and whose relations with their employers turned sour. One such was the Catalan marshal Diego de Rat, who was an important element in Florence's military establishment from 1305 to 1313, commanding some 200–300 cavalry and 300–500 infantry. Rat became a familiar enough figure in Florence to feature in the *Decameron*, and in 1308 the city praised him for his service. But by 1312 ill-feeling had developed between the republic and its employee over his substantial arrears of salary, and in the spring of 1313, when Florence faced a grave threat of attack from Henry VII, Rat was refusing to obey orders. Like the activities of the Catalans in Greece, this was an ominous sign of things to come, and indeed it was just nine years later, in the winter of 1322–3, that the republic first had to take military action against a large force of mercenaries who detached themselves completely from the service of the political authorities and lived by ravaging the countryside.

Appearances can however be deceptive. William Marshal's career contained its fair share of political wheeler-dealing. His efficiency as a warrior hinged on his willingness to destroy and steal the property of non-combatants, and his renowned expertise on what has been termed 'the tournament circuit' was milked for all it was worth in cash terms. William was fortunate in that circumstances enabled him to rise to prosperity while adhering sufficiently to the chivalric ideals of his day to excite the admiration of his contemporaries. In other words, it seems likely that success in thirteenth-century chivalry remained the rather volatile combination of ideals, skills, and sharp practice that it had always been. A degree of brutality in the treatment of civilians was accepted as a natural concomitant of war. Destructive raiding was a key feature of strategy, and booty an essential component of the range of rewards available to fighting men. In these circumstances it is hardly surprising that *ius in bello*, as opposed to *ius ad bellum*, received scant attention from the theorists. The attention it did receive tended to be exculpatory, as when the decretalist Raymond of Pennaforte judged that a man who set fire to another's property 'at the command of one who has the power to declare war' was innocent of arson. The behaviour of those fighters whose economic needs or sense of adventure took them far from their native lands, and exposed them to the raw winds of the market place and the temptation to switch allegiances, was probably not so different from that of their contemporaries whose military careers unfolded in more familiar settings and more 'respectable' contexts.

This is not to imply that all wars were identical in the perception of the warrior elite. A keener interest in the juridical nature of the conflict being waged led at least some warriors in the thirteenth century to make distinctions between the opponents whom they faced. Michael Prestwich has outlined a difference between the way the English fought in Wales and Scotland, on the one hand, and France, on the other. The Welsh and Scots were regarded as rebels against the crown and prisoners were executed in barbaric ways. Paradoxically, the insistence of the Scots that they were fighting a just (i.e. 'public') war compelled them to adhere to chivalric conventions in their treatment of English prisoners. In much the same way, normal chivalric *mores* were set aside during crusades, although there were substantial differences in practice between behaviour in Iberia, the Baltic, and the East. Warfare against Islamic rulers was often characterized by a courtly behaviour, conditioned by economic as well as cultural factors, which was absent from the vicious fighting in Prussia and Livonia. There can be little doubt that one reason for the horrors perpetrated during the Albigensian Crusade was the view held by some of the crusaders that the cathar heretics and their employees, the hated *routiers*, were 'beyond the pale' and that they were waging what would later be termed a *guerre mortelle*, although the normal chivalric law of arms can be seen intermittently in operation.

If the world-view and behaviour of fighting men remain at times difficult to interpret, the overall characteristics of European warfare in the thirteenth century are clear enough: an ambitious attempt by the public authorities to establish a monopoly on military activity; strenuous efforts by those authorities to mobilize the resources of their subjects more fully and effectively for war; and a growing tendency to view the practice of war through juridical spectacles. To a whiggish frame of mind these trends appear to be progressive. It is not so long since a historian of Philip the Fair's reign could describe the substitution of taxes for personal service as 'a major step towards civilization'. This is misguided. Arguably the bigger armies mobilized, albeit less frequently, around 1300, were more destructive than their predecessors. The *chevauchée* was not total war but it was far from being surgical in its impact on civilian life. The unrelenting bellicosity of Europe's rulers exerted massive fiscal demands on their subjects; the 'military state' and the 'fiscal state' were twins. Warfare became more expensive, and more of a drain on the economy. Lawyers placed few constraints on how war was waged, focusing instead on slavishly justifying the demands which their princes made. What had been achieved was 'bigger and better' wars. Moreover, there was a danger of their becoming all-consuming should the state falter in its control of the armies which it was creating. The actors were in place and the stage set for the ferocious conflicts of the late middle ages.

7 THE AGE OF THE HUNDRED YEARS WAR

CLIFFORD J. ROGERS

IN THE year 1300, the royal clerk Pierre Dubois composed an insightful work of military theory, the *Doctrine of Successful Expeditions and Shortened Wars*, for his monarch, King Philip the Fair. The central theme of the essay was that a new approach to military strategy had to be developed, because the two most common methods of using armed force against rebels or other enemies, battle and siege, had ceased to be effective. Siege warfare did not get the job done, because the castles and fortified cities which dominated the landscape of medieval Europe were too strong to be taken by assault; they could be captured by a regular siege, but this was excessively costly in time and money. 'A castle can hardly be taken within a year,' explained Dubois, 'and even if it does fall, it means more expenses for the king's purse and for his subjects than the conquest is worth.' The problem with battle, on the other hand, was that the royal army of France had become so overwhelmingly powerful that no one would dare stand up to it in open combat. An enemy faced by the advance of the Capetian host would simply retreat into his fortresses, and rely on their strength to make up for his relative lack of men-at-arms; then the king would be back to the problems of siege warfare. Dubois's resolution of this dilemma was an intelligent one, which would find much application in the practice of fourteenth-century warfare: if enemy armies hid behind stone walls, and fortresses were too strong to capture efficiently, then the solution was to direct one's efforts against softer targets, namely the villages of the countryside and the crops in the fields. By invading just before the harvest, the French could destroy the grain, vines, fruit trees, and other elements of the agricultural economy of their enemies, who would thereby be brought promptly to heel.

Dubois thus set out the basic strategic problems which the strong superiority of the defensive in thirteenth- and fourteenth-century siege warfare posed for offensive strategy, and also highlighted the most effective method by which an army superior in the field could employ its strength against an enemy anxious to avoid the test of open battle. He was, however, dramatically wrong about one thing: as all of France was soon to learn, the royal host was not so invincible as he thought. This lesson was delivered by teachers most unexpected—the weavers, shopkeepers, and artisans of Flanders.

By the beginning of the period covered in this chapter, the ferocious Flemish mercenaries who plagued England in the twelfth century had long since faded from the scene. The infantry troops of fourteenth-century Bruges, Ghent, and Ypres were quite different from their predecessors. Organized largely along guild lines into regular, uniformed militias, they were surprisingly well equipped, typically protected by mail haubergeons, steel helmets, gauntlets, shields, and often even coats of plates, and armed with bows, crossbows, pikes, or *goedendags*. These unique weapons (the name means 'hello' or 'good day') consisted of a thick, heavy wooden staff four to five feet in length, tipped with a lethal steel spike. Many of the militiamen thus armed had seen repeated service during the last decade of the previous century, thanks to the frequent conflicts between Flanders, Hainault, and Holland, and deserve to be considered veterans.

Their experiences in those campaigns, however, did not include anything like what they had to face on the hot summer afternoon of 11 July 1302. In that year the cities of Flanders, with the exception of Ghent, were in rebellion against the King of France, who had therefore dispatched an army of 2,500 men-at-arms and 8,000 infantry to break their siege of Courtrai castle, rescue the beleaguered French garrison, and suppress the revolt. King Philip probably did not anticipate that this task would involve a battle, for the Capetian army was incomparably superior to the Flemings in men-at-arms, and heavy cavalry was the acknowledged arbiter of battlefield victory or defeat. Yet, when the French troopers approached the encircled town, their enemies did not flee before them or retire behind protective fortifications. Instead, they withdrew to a carefully selected position on marshy ground outside the city, a spot where streams and ditches posed an obstacle to any attacker and protected their flanks, then drew up in battle formations with the River Lys at their backs and stood ready to greet their adversaries.

The communal infantry were ordered in four divisions, with three in line and a fourth in reserve positioned to block a sally by the besieged garrison. The soldiers were packed into a dense array, about eight deep, grouped by region

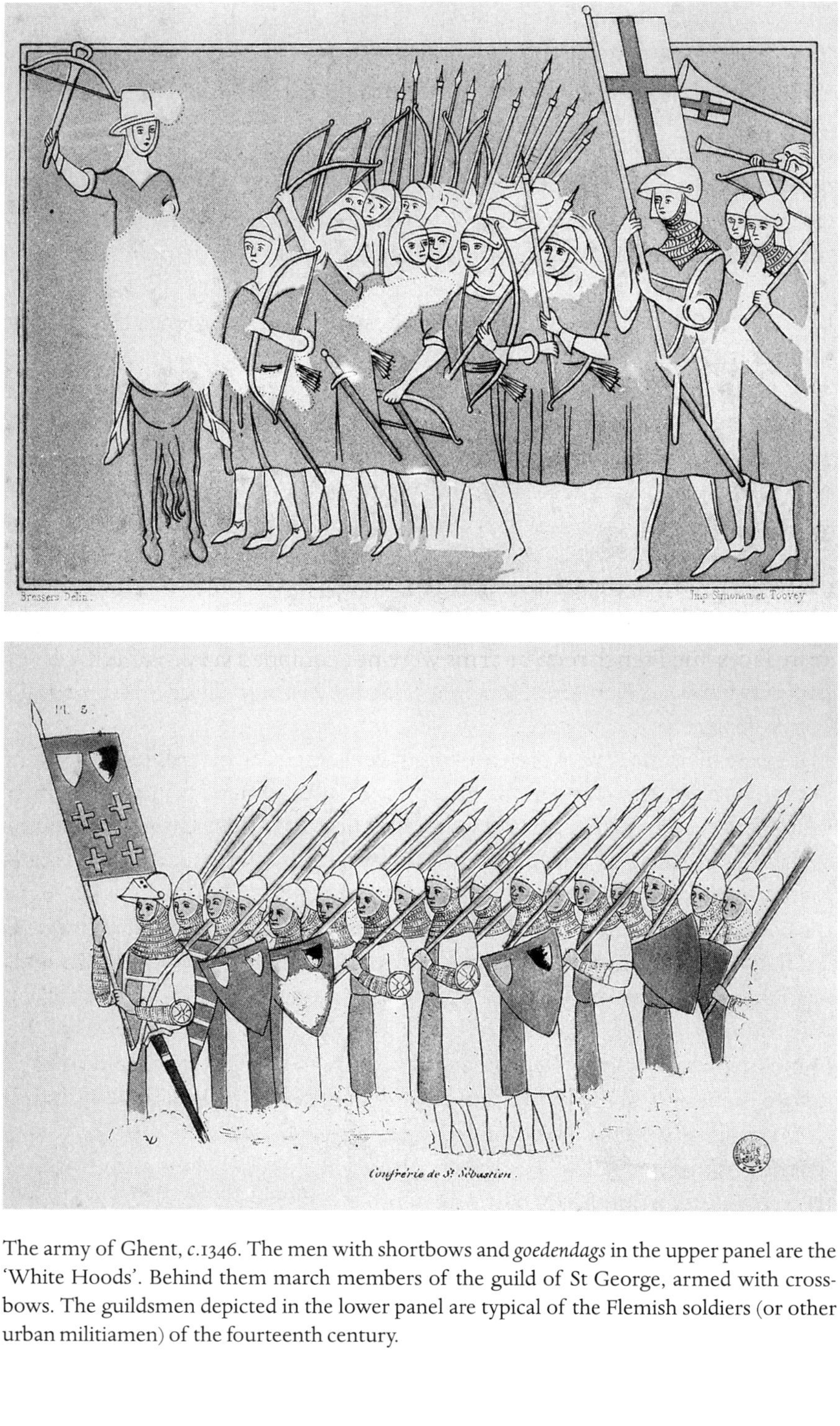

The army of Ghent, *c.*1346. The men with shortbows and *goedendags* in the upper panel are the 'White Hoods'. Behind them march members of the guild of St George, armed with crossbows. The guildsmen depicted in the lower panel are typical of the Flemish soldiers (or other urban militiamen) of the fourteenth century.

and craft so that each man knew his comrades well, a factor understood to enhance morale and cohesion. Their *goedendags*, supplemented by longer pikes in the foremost row, made a bristling hedge of wood and steel in front of them. Broad rectangular banners marked the positions of the various guilds—here a hammer, there a mason's trowel, over there a ship. Farther forward towards the French, archers and crossbowmen were dispersed.

The resolute appearance of the militiamen was enough to give pause to some of their enemies. In a council of war, one French leader suggested breaking up the Flemish formation with crossbow fire; another advised simply letting the townsmen stay where they were until they were exhausted by standing, fully armed, in the hot sun. The majority, however, saw the situation as an unexpected opportunity to gain a decisive victory of just the sort of which Dubois had lamented the rarity. They insisted on a quick attack, lest the Flemings change their minds. So, early in the afternoon, the crossbowmen of the Capetian host advanced to engage their opposite numbers with long-range missile fire. They had largely succeeded in driving the Flemish skirmishers back behind the shelter of the heavy infantry when Robert of Artois, the French commander, ordered his cavalry forward.

Aside from their lances and swords and the great helms which covered their entire faces, the French men-at-arms were not equipped very differently from the men who awaited them on foot. There were, however, two critically important distinctions between the forces about to come to blows. First, the men-at-arms, whether knights or esquires, were nobles, members of the second order, the *bellatores*, whose primary *raison d'être* (according to medieval political theory) was making war. Second, they were mounted on large, powerful warhorses, protected by 'trappers' of thick-quilted cloth, or even by mail, and painstakingly trained to charge straight forward even into a seemingly solid line of men or other horses. The stallions, like the proud men atop them, had come to assume that infantry would not stand against them, that the wall of flesh and bone which stood facing them would dissolve before they smashed into it. Then, once they had broken into the enemy formation, the men-at-arms would be riding high above a milling mass of panicky shopkeepers and artisans, who would benefit from their numbers no more than a dozen sheep beset by four wolves.

The same images would doubtless have run through the minds of many of the militiamen. Yet these were not raw levies with no experience of war, and they knew that, with a river at their backs, they could not save themselves by flight. They had nothing to gain by breaking their formation, and everything to lose, for everyone knew that an unwavering array was the key to victory. So they stood steady in their tightly formed ranks: they stood and watched the

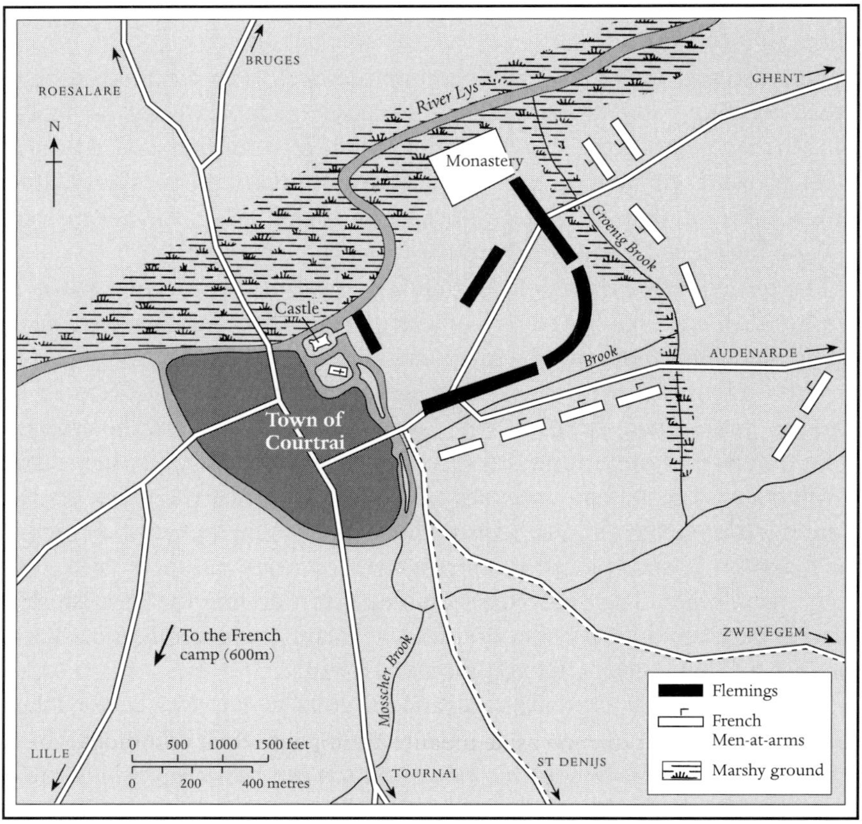

PLAN OF BATTLE OF COURTRAI, 1302

chivalry of the most powerful nation in Europe form into line, banners and pennons unfurled, trumpets blaring, steel flashing. It is difficult to imagine the sound of 2,500 heavy horses trotting forward all at once, but surely the thunder of their hooves, blended into a cacophonous din with the war-cries of the riders—*Montjoye! St Denis!*—must have struck the motionless infantrymen with an almost physical impact.

Some of the knights and esquires may also have had to struggle with fear as they rode forward, locked into their places in the French line, like the men-at-arms described in the fourteenth-century *The Vows of the Heron:*

> When we are in taverns, drinking strong wines, at our sides the ladies we desire, looking on, with their smooth throats . . . their grey eyes shining back with smiling beauty, Nature calls on us to have desiring hearts, to struggle, awaiting [their] thanks at the end. Then we could conquer . . . Oliver and Roland. But when we are in the field, on our galloping chargers, our shields 'round our necks and lances lowered . . . and our enemies are approaching us, then we would rather be deep in some cavern.

More, however, probably experienced emotions more like those described by Jean de Bueil in the fifteenth century:

> It is a joyous thing, war . . . You love your comrade so much in war . . . A great sweet feeling of loyalty and of pity fills your heart on seeing your friend so valiantly exposing his body . . . And then you are prepared to go and live or die with him, and for love not to abandon him. And out of that, there arises such a delectation, that he who has not experienced it is not fit to say what delight is. Do you think that a man who does that fears death? Not at all, for he feels so strengthened, so elated, that he does not know where he is. Truly he is afraid of nothing.

Caught up both emotionally and physically in the onrush of their line, the French cavalrymen jumped the brooks in front of them at speed, then roared forward. Some stumbled and went down, for the ground was very muddy and criss-crossed with irrigation ditches and trench-traps dug by the Flemings. The horsemen drew nearer and nearer to a collision, accelerating to a gallop from about fifty yards out. When they saw that the line of infantry did not break, did not waver, some of the men-at-arms must have lost their nerve at the last minute, and tried to turn aside before impaling themselves and their horses. Formed as they were into a tight line, however, this would only have produced chaos, for turning aside meant running into their comrades next to them, and perhaps being struck by the second line coming up behind them. Others, confident to the last or simply beyond caring, pressed on until their mounts hit the pikes which the militiamen held with their butts firmly grounded in the earth. Some of the Flemings went down, pierced by a knight's lance or trampled under a destrier's metal-shod hooves, but with eight-deep files the fallen could rapidly be replaced and the line restored. The French charge collapsed into a jumbled mass of screaming horses, cursing men, spraying blood, and splintered wood.

After a period of confused mêlée, the militiamen went over to the attack. They outnumbered the cavalrymen several times over, and still had their formation intact; the men-at-arms, on the other hand, were demoralized and had lost their cohesion and momentum. The Frenchmen were driven back, despite a counterattack by their reserve which almost succeeded in turning the tide of the battle. When the retreating horsemen backed up against banks of the brooks which they had crossed with some difficulty in their advance, their situation became desperate. Those who survived soon fled, followed by the panicked footmen of the Capetian host, who had no stomach to face the men who had just defeated their masters. The Flemings pursued on foot as best they could, striking down whatever fugitives they laid their hands on.

Over a thousand noble men-at-arms perished in this battle, 'the glory of

France made into dung and worms', a proportion which would have been considered terribly high even in the American Civil War or the Great War, and which was absolutely stunning in an era more accustomed to the low casualties of battles like Brémule or Lincoln. As Norman Housely observed in the preceding chapter, this sanguinary battle provides a convenient marking point for the end of the style of warfare that reached its peak in the thirteenth century. The first clang of the death-knoll of heavy cavalry as the dominant force on the battlefields of Western Europe had sounded.

It took some time, however, for the new military era to eclipse the old one entirely. The victory of the Flemings at Courtrai owed much to favourable terrain and the overconfidence of their opponents, and over the following years the French, proceeding more cautiously, did much better, temporarily suppressing the rebellion of Flanders after their victory at Cassel in 1328. And yet all of Europe had taken note of the townsmen's victory. The *Scalacronica* specifically notes that the Scots at Bannockburn, where their pikemen crushed the chivalry of England in 1314, were imitating the tactics of Courtrai, and the same appears to be true for the infantry of the Catalan Company which won the battle of the Kephissos against the 'Frankish' Duke of Athens in 1311. Perhaps the Swiss halberdiers who ambushed and destroyed an Austrian army of men-at-arms in the Alpine pass of Morgarten in 1315 were also inspired by the Flemings. In any case, a sort of chain reaction had begun. By 1339, the Swiss at Laupen employed formations and tactics similar to those of the militiamen of Courtrai to win an important victory over a superior enemy. The English, having learned their lesson at Bannockburn, chose 'contrary to the customs of their forefathers' to fight on foot at Dupplin Muir (1332) and Halidon Hill (1333), where they wiped out two successive Scottish armies. Wings of archers armed with powerful yew longbows with draw weights of a hundred pounds and up were angled forward from central bodies of tightly massed dismounted men-at-arms; when the Scots attacked they were shot down by the thousands and cast into complete disorder by the archers, leaving the survivors with no hope of breaking through the serried ranks of the English men-at-arms (see further, Chapter 9, pp. 203–5). The French, in their turn, after being severely defeated by the English at Crécy (1346), chose to fight mainly on foot at Poitiers (1356) and thereafter. The Black Prince brought the new tactics into Iberia, where they gave him and Pedro the Cruel victory at Nájera (1367); similar methods ensured a second Castillian defeat at the hands of the Portuguese at Aljubarrota (1385). From then until the end of the middle ages, the thunderous charge of heavy cavalry was a rare sight on medieval battlefields, and was successful even more rarely.

Looking at this detail from a fifteenth-century depiction of the battle of Poitiers, it is easy to see one reason why English armies of the fourteenth century were able to rack up a truly remarkable string of battlefield victories, triumphing over much larger enemies at Dupplin Muir, Halidon Hill, Crécy, Poitiers, Nájera, and elsewhere. A good archer could easily fire five arrows in the time it took a mounted man-at-arms to charge home from out of bow range, and those arrows could wound and madden a horse even at extreme range. At close range, a clothyard shaft could strike down a warhorse or penetrate armour to kill its rider.

This 'Infantry Revolution' of the fourteenth century involved far more than just the matter of whether men chose to fight on horseback or on foot: it also led to changes in cultural attitudes towards war, chivalry, social class, and political participation, and alterations in the composition and recruitment of armies. The key fact was that pikemen and archers were usually drawn from the common populace, rather than the aristocracy. Although some of the 'infantry' troops of the late middle ages, including the renowned English mounted archers, were provided with horses, they did not ride into battle. Thus, they needed only cheap hackneys to provide them with strategic mobility, rather than trained warhorses which typically cost from five to twenty times as much, or even far more: one destrier purchased by Edward III in 1337 cost the fabulous sum of £168, the equivalent of over eighty years' income for a prosperous peasant family. The infantrymen also typically made do with much simpler and less expensive armour (in comparison with the ever-more-elaborate plate armour of the men-at-arms), and expected far less luxury while on campaign. Furthermore, infantry armed with pole-arms (halberds, bills, pikes, etc.) did not need to invest anywhere near the 'human capital' required to train a knight or esquire to fight effectively on horseback. All this was reflected in the lower wages they received: in England a mounted archer earned only half as much as a man-at-arms, while a Welsh spearman could be hired for just a sixth of an esquire's pay. So long as money was available for wages at these levels, moreover, a power fighting a popular war could find an almost limitless supply of soldiers, since infantrymen were drawn from the mass of the population rather than the elite 2–4 per cent at the top of the social pyramid who provided the bulk of the heavy cavalry. France was so populous and so wealthy that her monarchs could continue to field armies composed mainly of men-at-arms (who after 1346 typically fought on foot, mounting only for pursuits and occasional skirmishes) despite their cost, and the same was at least partially true for the Italian states, who used their commercial wealth to hire cavalry-heavy mercenary companies (*condottieri*), but—as at Courtrai—the lower cost, easy availability, and great effectiveness of common infantry now made it possible for smaller powers to stand up to their more powerful neighbours, a fact contributing significantly to the frequent particularistic rebellions of the period, which led to greater independence for the Scots, the Portuguese, the Flemings, the Frisians (whose infantry defeated the men-at-arms of the count of Hainault at Staveren in 1345), and the Swiss, among others.

One side effect of the rising importance of common infantry was that the European battlefield became a much more sanguinary place than it had been. Noble combatants of the high middle ages expected to be taken for ransom rather than killed if defeated in combat, and battles of the twelfth and thirteenth centuries often involved no more than a few dozen deaths. Common troops, however, could not afford to pay ransoms large enough to be worth the bother, even if their inferior armour allowed them to survive long enough to surrender. In addition, the weapons and the close-order tactical systems of the new style of combat made it relatively difficult to take captives. Finally, class antipathy between noble and commoner often led to remarkably bloodthirsty behaviour by both sides. The Swiss, for example, were famous for never giving quarter: such was their ferocity that it was considered necessary, in a regulation of 1444, to forbid them from tearing out the hearts of their dead enemies. The French men-at-arms who (fighting on foot) defeated the Flemings at Westrozebeke, on the other hand, 'had no mercy on them, no more than if they had been dogs'. In contrast to the five knights who perished during the year-long Flanders war of 1127 (only one of whom was actually killed by the hand of an enemy), the death-toll at Agincourt on St Crispin's day of 1415 may have approached 10,000 men. (See the illustration from the Holkham Bible in Chapter 9, below p. 204, for an image of battlefield mortality.)

These casualties tended to be suffered almost entirely by the defeated army, especially after its formation had been broken. For infantry fighting hand-to-hand, the key to keeping losses to a minimum, and also the key to gaining the victory, was to maintain a good, solid, tight formation, 'in such close order that one could hardly throw an apple among them, without its falling on a

By the late fourteenth century, when this illumination was painted, men-at-arms normally fought on foot, rather than on horseback. Contemporary artists, however, continued to depict battle scenes as dramatic clashes of mounted knights. Because the combat shown here took place on a bridge, the artist gave us a rare glimpse of how fourteenth-century men-at-arms actually deployed and handled their weapons when fighting as heavy infantry. As usual in medieval infantry battles, the defenders (left), able to maintain better order, ultimately won the fight (near Ivry, July 1358).

bascinet or a lance'. In the words of the fourteenth-century chronicler Lopez de Ayala, good order was 'the most important thing in the world for gaining an advantage over one's enemy'; on the other hand, wrote another contemporary, 'those who are not in ordered formation are easy to defeat.' 'Two great evils', explained Christine de Pisan around 1409, '. . . can follow from a disordered formation: one is that the enemies can more easily break into it; the other is that the formations may be so compressed that they cannot fight. Thus it is necessary to keep a formation in ranks, and tight and joined together like a wall.' Of course, it was much easier for soldiers to keep such an array if they were standing still than if they were tramping over difficult ground, jumping irrigation ditches or hedges, all the while holding their heads down to keep arrows away from their ill-protected faces. Thus, there was a great advantage to be gained by holding to the tactical defensive. As Jean de Bueil wrote in the late fifteenth century, 'a formation on foot should never march forward, but should always hold steady and await its enemies . . . A force which marches before another force is defeated, unless God grants it grace.'

The defensive is inherently the stronger form of warfare, and this was especially true in the late middle ages, when this tactical superiority of the defence was combined with the equally great advantage enjoyed by the defensive in siege warfare (at least until the 1420s, when gunpowder artillery began to reverse the balance). For a belligerent with defensive aims, this made a Fabian strategy of the sort recommended by the late Roman author Vegetius (whose work was the most popular military handbook of the middle ages, frequently translated into the vernacular and borrowed heavily from by 'popularizers' like Alfonso the Wise of Castille and Christine de Pisan) potentially very effective. Philip VI of France, for example, took this approach when his kingdom was invaded by an Anglo-Imperial army under Edward III in 1339. The campaign, the first major one of the Hundred Years War, opened with a siege of Cambrai, but this was abandoned after just nineteen days, as the invaders had not made adequate logistical provisions and were running out of supplies, and the city was too strong to be taken by assault. Edward then rode through the Cambrésis, Vermandois, and Thiérache burning and plundering the countryside in an effort to provoke King Philip into giving battle, but despite the destruction of nearly two hundred villages and a few larger towns, the French resisted the temptation to attack his army. Instead, Philip's troops blocked any supply columns from reaching the Anglo-German army and implemented a virtual scorched-earth policy to hinder the invaders further. After a stand-off in which each side occupied a strong position in the unfulfilled hope that the other would accept the disadvantages inherent in taking the tactical offensive (a quite common occurrence during this period) the campaign simply fizzled out. Philip had suffered a severe blow to his kingly reputation, but Edward had expended a huge fortune and a full campaigning season without making any concrete gains. As Philip's counsellors dryly remarked, 'if the King of England wanted to conquer the realm of France, he would need to make a large number of such *chevauchées.*'

This campaign provides a concrete illustration of the problem sketched out in general terms by Dubois a generation earlier, but with a significant twist: in this case it was the weaker power which was strategically on the offensive, and so eager for battle, while the stronger army, Philip's, was unwilling to make an attack even though its enemies did not retreat behind stone fortifications. In a development not foreseen by Dubois, the walls formed by steady infantry formations had come to be almost as invulnerable as permanent fortresses. The 1339 campaign also illustrates, however, that relying on the tactical defensive in pursuit of aggressive war aims was likely to lead nowhere unless it was combined with a strategy that somehow persuaded the enemy to cooperate by taking the tactical offensive. Medieval commanders in this situation relied mainly on two techniques to pressure their adversaries into doing just that, both of which were attempted, unsuccessfully, by Edward III in the campaign discussed above. One was to besiege an important city or castle until it was about to fall, so that its owner had to make a move in order to rescue it; the other, as suggested in the *Doctrine of Successful Expeditions and Shortened Wars*, was to devastate the lands unprotected by city walls, so that the defenders would have to attack to stop the destruction.

Edward III preferred the former of these two approaches. He used it successfully in 1333 (drawing the Scots to attack his position at Halidon Hill by

Above: the devastation of the countryside was a normal part of medieval warfare, and fire was the soldiers' main tool in the work of havoc. A woman might have her house burned as retribution for failure to pay 'patis' [protection money] to enemy garrisons, or for failure to pay taxes or levies to support 'friendly' garrisons, or by an invading army bent on provoking the defending army into giving battle, or by a defending army trying to create a wasteland in which the invaders could not operate.

besieging the city of Berwick), and tried it again in 1339, 1340, and 1346–7, with the sieges of Cambrai, Tournai, and Calais, respectively. The biggest problem with this strategy however, was its cost. As noted above, a well-defended and well-fortified city could hold out against a siege for many months, and during that time the besieger had constantly to maintain an army large enough to withstand a relief army's attack. In some ways the rise of the infantry helped reduce this problem, for foot soldiers were far cheaper than men-at-arms, but this advantage was largely counteracted by the need to have them in large numbers: as Commynes said of archers (though it would be equally applicable to pikemen) 'in battles they are the most important thing in the world, but only if they are strong and in large numbers, because a few of them are useless.' The rising importance of the foot troops, thus, brought not only the opportunity but also the need to expand armies substantially. Thus, as early as the late thirteenth century, we can observe Edward I campaigning at the head of armies incorporating tens of thousands of paid archers and spearmen; by the time of his grandson, the English government's capacity to manage military endeavours had increased to the point where forces of that size could occasionally be maintained for several months, even across the Channel. This represented a major change in approaches to recruitment, organization, and above all pay.

The cost of supporting an army which averaged somewhere around 23,000 men for the two-month siege of Tournai in 1340, for example, mounted to roughly £60,000 in soldiers' wages alone; the total expenditure was several times that large. The annual peacetime revenues of the English crown at the start of Edward III's reign, by contrast, were in the area of £30,000–40,000. It is easy to see why this style of warfare strained the resources of any medieval state, even the best organized (like England) or the richest (like France) to the very breaking point, and sometimes beyond. Over the course of the last century of the medieval period, army size did fall off from the peaks achieved just before the Black Death, partly because of the rise of mounted infantry troops (who were more expensive than regular infantry, though still paid only half as much as heavy cavalrymen) and partly because of the general decline in population. The levels of military expenditure, however, remained very high.

In fact, the rapid increase in the scale and costs of making war which characterized the end of the thirteenth and start of the fourteenth centuries was, in terms of its impact on society at large, perhaps the most important aspect of the period's military developments. It was only with the greatest possible effort that the monarchs of the time were able to bear the financial burdens of war, but war gave them the greatest possible incentive to make those efforts.

The following passage from a contemporary chronicle vividly illustrates the financial difficulties of the French monarchy at the start of the Hundred Years War. The chronicler also, unwittingly, indicates the equal fiscal problems of the English king, for in fact the reason for the inactivity of Edward's allies was his failure to pay them the subsidies he had promised:

And because the King of England received no help from his German allies—even though he had paid all too dearly for it—he could do nothing, and did not try to accomplish anything further. And the King of France, leaving some men-at-arms on the frontiers, returned to Paris and gave leave for his army to depart. And because of the assembly of that army, he taxed his people very severely, for he made them pay double the subsidy which they had to pay the year before. And the tax collectors said that this was for the *arrière-ban* [the call-up of the militia] which had been proclaimed at the beginning, but in truth it could not be said to have been a real *arrière-ban*, because the army never actually went forth. And besides this common tax, everyone was required to take part in musters of arms. Then it was put to the rich men that they were not sufficiently equipped, and that they would therefore have to pay certain fines. In this year [1338], Pope Benedict granted the tithes for two years from the churches to the King of France, on condition that he not demand any other subsidy from the clergy; but the condition was not met, for there were few clerics of whatever estate or condition who didn't have to make some other aid to the King. He even asked of his own clerks of Parlement, of the chamber of inquests, and of the chamber of accounts, and even of the knights of his household, that they lend him their silver vessels in order to make coins. This they did and so he struck a great deal of money, and then before the year was over he returned to them the silver, according to the measurements which had been taken. And he continually lessened the silver content of his coinage, and so made florins out of pennies.

As expedients and emergency measures became regularized, and as taxpayers grew accustomed to year after year of heavy impositions, the agonizing stretches of the early years of the Hundred Years War became routine. By the end of the fourteenth century, taking taxation into account, the average annual revenues of the crowns of France and England had grown very substantially—a fact all the more remarkable when one considers what it meant in terms of per capita taxation over a period when the population fell by nearly half due mainly to the repeated visitations of the Black Death from 1348 on.

In England, the monarchy's greatly improved ability to squeeze money out of the community of the realm without engendering radical opposition from the taxpayer was largely the result of King Edward's superb skill in building a political consensus in favour of his policies, exercised in the rising institution of Parliament, which owed its increasing importance in this period directly to the government's need for vast sums of money in order to fight the war with

France. At various times Edward had tried a number of expedients aimed at extracting money or military service against popular opposition, and had been forcefully reminded of the limited coercive powers provided by a fourteenth-century state apparatus, even one as relatively well developed as England's. Thus, in general he was careful to secure the co-operation of the Commons in his efforts to raise the huge amounts of cash required by his initial strategy for fighting the Hundred Years War, which involved paying massive subsidies to the Continental allies who provided the great majority of his soldiers in 1339–40.

The story of the three Parliaments called between October 1339 and May 1340 provides the best illustration of the interrelationships between war finances and the rising importance of the Commons. At the first of the three sessions, the royal government requested a large subsidy in order to pay some of the debts arising from the just-finished Cambrésis campaign, and to make possible a renewed effort in the spring. The Commons complained of the heavy taxes they had already paid, and took the highly unusual step of refusing to grant an aid until they had returned to their communities to get popular approval for a new subsidy. When Parliament met again in January of 1340, the Commons agreed to a large subsidy of 30,000 sacks of wool, but only if the King would grant a list of petitions, the most significant of which were an audit of the accounts of all the royal ministers and tax-collectors, and the creation of a committee of Peers, answerable only to Parliament, to oversee future military expenditures. Since Edward was still on the Continent, his representatives could only agree to forward the Commons' offer to him, and dismiss the Parliament until May. Then the assembly was told of the massive debts the prosecution of the war had created, and

> how our lord the King needed to be assisted with a great aid, or he would be dishonoured forever, and his lands on both sides of the sea in great peril; for he would lose his allies, and he would have to return personally to Brussels, and remain imprisoned there until the sums for which he was obligated had been fully paid. But if he were granted an aid, all these difficulties would cease, and the enterprise which he had undertaken would be brought, with the help of God, to a good conclusion, and peace and calm restored for all.

There was some compromising on both sides, and after the King accepted a somewhat reduced list of petitions (which did however include the audit of his officials' accounts by a parliamentary committee) the community of the realm granted him a tithe of the wheat, wool, and lambs produced in the counties, and a ninth of the goods of the burgesses. This process, notes G. L. Harriss, marked 'the first emergence of the Commons as an independent political force'. By 1369, thanks to the continuing demands of war finance and recruitment, the MPs elected by the free landholders of the shires had secured all the powers they were to hold for the next two hundred years.

However willing and effective Parliament might be as a tool for raising revenues, however, it simply could not sustain costs like the ones stemming from the Low Countries campaigns of 1339 and 1340. As Dubois had predicted, a siege-based strategy had proved both ineffective and ruinously expensive. Thus, when the war reopened in 1346, the English turned to a new strategic approach. In 1346, 1349, 1355, 1356, and 1359 Plantagenet troops launched major *chevauchées* into almost every corner of France, laying waste broad bands of territory (typically some fifteen miles wide) along the lines of their passage. Once the armies reached areas away from the heavily defended frontier areas, they were able to destroy sizeable towns and even cities as well as the smaller settlements of the countryside: on the Crécy *chevauchée*, for example, the towns of Caen, Cherbourg, St-Lô, Lisieux, Barfleur, Carentan, Valonges, Gisors, Vernon, Poissy, St-Germain-en-Laye, St Cloud, Pontoise, Poix, Longueville, Neufchâtel, Le Crotoy, and Étaples, and the suburbs of Beauvais, Montreuil-sur-Mer, and Boulogne, were all more-or-less destroyed, along with nearly a dozen others. In one of the two major *chevauchées* of 1355, the Black Prince rode from Bordeaux to the Mediterranean and back, destroying some 500 castles, towns, villages, and hamlets, along with Limoux and the suburbs of Toulouse, Carcassonne, and Narbonne, some of the largest cities of France. By 1359–60, when a large English army rode from Calais to Reims to Burgundy to Paris, France was left 'overwhelmed, and trampled under foot', 'on the verge of destruction', and 'tormented and war-ravaged' from one end to the other.

Devastation, as noted above, was an important method of provoking an enemy into giving battle. It was only the need to try to stop the destruction of their realm that led the French to fight (and suffer defeat) at Crécy in 1346 and Poitiers a decade later. Devastation served more purposes than that, however. It also enriched the raiders, demoralized and impoverished their enemies, and gave the people of the raided country (from bottom to top of the social hierarchy) an immediate and direct reason to desire peace, gained by accepting the invaders' demands if it could not be achieved by defeating them in battle. In explaining why he had accepted the humiliating 1360 Treaty of Brétigny, which called for the surrender of a full third of France to English sovereignty, King Jean II made this clear:

> because of the said wars many mortal battles have been fought, people slaughtered, churches pillaged, bodies destroyed and souls lost, maids and virgins deflowered,

The Norman city of Caen was one of the many sacked and burned during Edward III's Crécy *chevauchée* of 1346. 'The tourn & the subbarbus vnto the bare wallys of al thing that myghte be bore & caryed out, was robbid and despoyled', observes the *Brut* chronicle. The destruction of the city served both to enrich the English soldiers and to encourage other towns to negotiate surrenders instead of fighting until they were captured by assault, as Caen was.

respectable wives and widows dishonored, towns, manors and buildings burnt, and robberies, oppressions, and ambushes on the roads and highways committed. Justice has failed because of them, the Christian faith has chilled and commerce has perished, and so many other evils and horrible deeds have followed from these wars that they cannot be said, numbered or written . . .

Considering all this, 'and that it seemed in truth that even greater evils could have followed in time to come' if the war continued, he had been compelled to accept the English demands. The devastation of the North of England in the 1320s, similarly, led directly to the 'Cowardice Peace' of 1328, by which the young Edward III surrendered his claim to suzerainty over Scotland.

Thus, the direct inflicting of misery and harm on the enemy population was one of the three main tools in the hands of the medieval commander, along with battle and siege. This may seem surprising given the widespread modern idea of the late middle ages as a time of high chivalry, but the contradiction is a false one, for nothing in the late medieval conception of chivalry forbade direct attacks on the 'civilian' population, just as nothing prevented the bombing of Dresden or Nagasaki in the twentieth century: the population at large was seen as the mast of the enemy's ship of state, and so a legitimate target of attack, for it was only by the support of the commons that a king could wage war. 'If sometimes the innocent must suffer along with the guilty' in such attacks, wrote Honoré Bouvet, 'it cannot be otherwise' (see further, Chapter 12, pp. 261–3).

One of the reasons, then, that a battlefield victory could yield decisive results was that it enabled the winning side to proceed with what H. J. Hewitt aptly called the 'work of havoc', with all its political implications, largely free from interference. Of course, that was no new revelation: the high stakes wagered in a general engagement were the reason for the popularity of Vegetian strategy for armies on the strategic defensive, as already noted. In the mid- to late-fourteenth century, the Scots and the French in particular refined this old strategic approach in order to trump the English *chevauchée* strategy which had proven so effective in the period up to 1360. This required two basic changes. First, the strategic defenders had to strengthen their resolve to avoid battle so that they could resist the pull of honour and the push of shame which impelled them towards fighting an invader. The many victories of defensively arrayed infantry armies from 1302 onwards made this increasingly practicable. Second, they had to reduce their physical vulnerability to devastation, lest they find themselves escaping the frying-pan of battlefield defeat only to burn up in the fire of economic and social collapse (like France in 1358–60). The French achieved this by making immense expenditures on two waves of refortification inspired by the events of 1346 and 1355–6, which secured the urban centres of the realm, and by improving their ability to 'shadow' an invading army, forcing it to keep concentrated and ready for battle (and thus preventing it from spreading out to inflict widespread destruction), which minimized the damage to the countryside. In the 1380s they persuaded King John of Castile to employ similar methods against the Duke of Lancaster's expeditionary force:

> We will make war wisely, by garrisons, for two or three months, or for a whole season, if need be, and allow the English and Portuguese to *chevauchée* through Galicia and

elsewhere, if they can. If they conquer some towns, what of it? We will recapture the towns immediately, once they have left the area. They will only have borrowed them. . . . So the best way to decimate and defeat them is to decline to fight them, and let them *chevauchée* wherever they may.

The resolute pursuit of such a strategy by the defender, though it might be painful, left the attacking side little choice but to attempt a gradual conquest based on a series of sieges. If the fortifications dominating a given area could be captured and garrisoned, then control of that area would be effectively secured, and the burden of the initiative would be shifted to the other side to try to get it back. Such a 'gradualist' strategy was used for example by Henry V in his conquest of Normandy from 1417.

As Dubois had observed, however, capturing a strong castle or town by force was a 'lengthy, dangerous, and arduous' process, and expensive as well. A besieging army might harass the garrison by arcing trebuchet-stones over the walls, could try to overtop the walls with mobile siege towers or to slowly dig a mine under them, but none of these techniques was likely to make a rapid assault possible. Thus, by far the best way to capture such strongholds was simply to persuade the men guarding them to hand them over. This was most often accomplished through bribery, threats, or some combination of the two. It was common for a besieging army to engage in bombardment and assaults simultaneously with negotiations. Usually the attackers would threaten dire consequences if they succeeded in taking the place by storm, while promising favourable treatment for the garrison and inhabitants in case of an agreement to surrender. The longer the resistance, the less favourable the terms would generally become, and the greater would be the chance that the place would be captured by assault, in which case the defenders were usually slaughtered without mercy. If a garrison surrendered reasonably promptly, on the other hand, the soldiers could expect to be allowed to keep their accumulated plunder and take it with them under a safe-conduct escort to the nearest friendly fortification (see further, Chapter 8, pp. 182–3).

These pressures were set in balance with the defenders' desire to hold out on their lord's behalf as long as possible; over time the scales tipped more and more in favour of surrender, which was the ultimate outcome far more often than assault. Of course, this calculus was greatly influenced by each side's assessment of the probability of a relief army coming to break the siege, of the strength of the fortifications, of the relative logistic problems facing the adversaries, etc. If an invading army was sufficiently strong, hope of relief sufficiently remote, and the enthusiasm of the defenders sufficiently low, whole regions could change hands through a series of negotiated surrenders in a single campaigning season. This style of warfare enabled the French, in the early 1370s, to reconquer most of the lands they had lost to the Plantagenets in 1360, and brought Normandy and Maine under English control in the years after Agincourt. When Henry V wanted to capture the castle of the town of Caen, where the garrison was holed up, for example,

> he sent worde to the lorde Montayny beyng capitain, that if he would yelde the castle by a daie, he should depart without dammage. And yf he would be foolishe and obstinate, all clemencye and favor should be from hym sequestred. When the capitain and his compaignions had well digested his message, beyng in dispaire of comfort, upon the condicions offred, [they] rendred the Castle and yelded themselves.

The fall of a particularly strong fortress, if the prospect of a relief army remained remote, could trigger a wave of other surrenders. 'When the renderynge of Roan [Rouen] was blowen throughe Normandy' in 1419, for example, 'it is in maner incredible to heare how manye tounes yelded not once desired [to surrender], & how many fortresses gave up wythout contradiccion.'

The two factors which played the greatest role in determining the success of military operations of this sort were probably reputation and the ability to raise or to fight off relief forces. The latter was important because the prospect of assistance was critical in inspiring defenders to hold out: if help was not on the way, or would clearly not be able to overcome the besiegers, then what were they holding out for? If it was inevitable that they would have to surrender, they might as well do it promptly and get generous terms, without enduring the discomforts of the siege or the risk of a catastrophic assault. Thus, in this situation, battlefield victories were neither necessary nor sufficient for conquest, but they were still highly advantageous. Henry V's victory at Agincourt paved the way for his occupation of Normandy, though the battlefield victory had to be followed up with a determined and

Just nineteen years old when she led a small army to break the siege of Orléans in 1429, Joan of Arc gave the Dauphin and his troops the confidence they needed to stand up to their English adversaries. Charles VII's coronation at Reims, which she engineered, gave the Valois party a critical advantage over the young Henry VI, and marked a true turning point in the war. This drawing was made in 1429, but the artist was inaccurate in depicting Joan in women's clothes and with long hair.

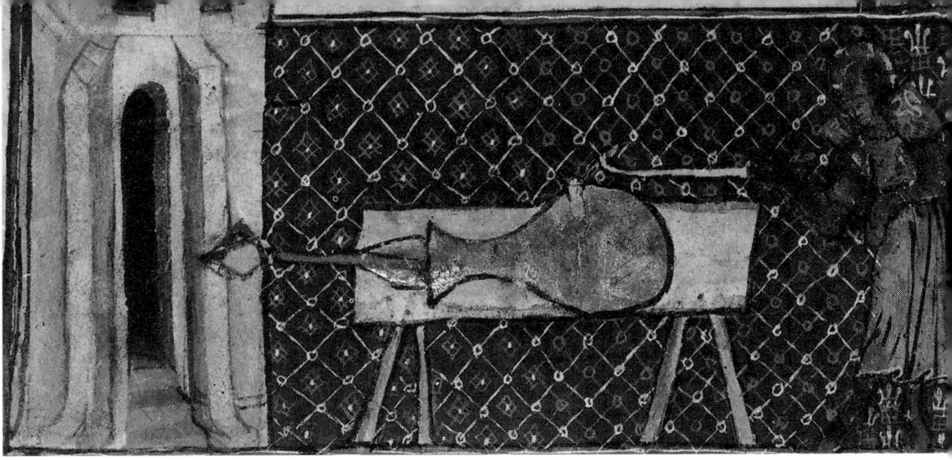

i

ii

iii

These three plates illustrate a century's development in gunpowder artillery. The illumination (i) is one of the two earliest depictions of European cannon, dating from 1327. Vase-shaped guns firing bronze bolts quickly gave way to more tubular designs, like the one shown (iii) being loaded in this page from a German Master-Gunner's Book of 1411. This type of bombard had a long, thin powder chamber behind a short barrel, typically skilfully executed campaign of conquest lasting several years; after the English defeat at Formigny in 1450, on the other hand, it took only four months to eliminate the last vestige of Lancastrian control of the duchy. The second factor, reputation, was so important because, as already noted, most sieges ended with a negotiated surrender rather than with toppled walls and a bloody assault; thus, the struggle was as much a psychological as a physical one. The more the defenders saw their eventual surrender as inevitable, the more certain they were that they would be punished severely if they held out too long, and the more confident they were of receiving good terms if they gave up quickly, the shorter the siege would be.

In Henry V's conquest of Normandy, the English developed a reputation for invincibility in battle and unwavering resolution in the prosecution of sieges that served them in very good stead for many years thereafter. The French were in a difficult situation: particularly after their defeats at Cravant in 1423 and Verneuil in 1424, they lacked the confidence to challenge English armies, and therefore left themselves no opportunity to win a victory which could restore to them the aggressiveness and *élan* without which they could not hope to reverse the tide of the war—even though English over-confidence gave them various opportunities for military success. That is why the appearance of Joan of Arc was so important. The Valois cycle of defeat and dismay had to be broken from outside, and the soldiers' belief in divine intervention did the trick. Inspired by her to defeat the English siege army at Orléans in 1428, they shook off their sense of inferiority and resumed the war in a new military environment which now, as it happened, favoured them more than ever before.

The art of war had already begun to experience something of a sea-change in the years between Agincourt and the arrival of the Maid; this was largely due to the development of gunpowder artillery capable of knocking down strong castle walls (see further, Chapter 8, pp. 180–2). By this time, cannon had

(as here) with only slightly more length than diameter. Because of the short barrel, the gun 'spat' out the stone ball it fired, rather than accelerating it more smoothly; to make this practical, the opening of the powder chamber had to be plugged with a soft wooden cylinder (in the left hand of the figure on the left), and then the ball had to be wedged in place with three triangular wedges and covered with wet loam. The firing process was so slow, and the resulting trajectories so inaccurate, that one gunner who managed to hit three different targets in the same day was required to make a pilgrimage because it was thought he had to be in league with the devil. By the 1430s, large guns with much longer barrels were being built up out of wrought-iron hoops and staves. Guns like *Dulle Griet* (ii), firing stone balls weighing hundreds of pounds at higher velocities (thanks in part to the introduction of superior 'corned' gunpowder) had the power and accuracy to bring down castle walls.

been in use in Europe for just over a century, but the early guns were far too small and weak to demolish fortifications. Instead they were used mainly as harassment weapons, lobbing large stones onto the roofs of houses within a besieged town and so increasing the misery of the defenders and encouraging them to surrender sooner rather than later. Over the years the guns grew slowly but steadily larger, until by around 1420 the largest of them fired stone balls weighing as much as 750 kg. Around the same time, a series of technological innovations (especially the development of more powerful 'corned' gunpowder) and design improvements greatly increased the efficiency of the guns. The most important of these was the simple step of lengthening the cannons' barrels so that the ball was pushed by the force of the explosion for a longer period of time, increasing its muzzle velocity and so its accuracy and hitting power. This also meant that the wet loam seal formerly used to plug the ball in the barrel could be dispensed with, so the guns fired much faster. The net result was a radical increase in the practical usefulness of the heavy artillery. It had taken Henry V seven months to capture Cherbourg and six more to gain Rouen in 1418–19, despite his use of a siege train powerful for its time. In 1450, by contrast, only sixteen days were required to leave almost the entire wall of Bayeux 'pierced and brought down', while at Blaye a year later it took only five days until 'the town walls were completely thrown down in many places'. As Pierre Dubois had observed a hundred and fifty years earlier, the superiority of the strategic defensive had in his day given the weak leverage to resist the strong, and reduced the value of the King of France's battlefield might. This 'Artillery Revolution' of the fifteenth century tended to reverse that situation. Triumph in battle (as Guicciardini remarked when the siege trains developed in the crucible of the Hundred Years War took Italy by storm in 1494) came to be the virtual equivalent of victory in war, for now the value of the Vegetian approach to strategy was severely undermined, and defence had to be defence in the field.

At the same time when cannon were dramatically tipping the strategic balance in favour of the strong over the weak, and in favour of the strategic offensive over the defensive, they also began to alter the determinants of battlefield success. Defensive tactics remained dominant, and indeed the growing prevalence and effectiveness of gunpowder weapons tended to reinforce the advantages of the defence, by allowing nations not blessed with a recruitment pool of strong yeoman archers nonetheless to enjoy some of the tactical advantages which the longbowmen provided to English armies. The Bohemian Hussites in the 1420s and 1430s, for example, used cannon and primitive 'hand culverins' (ancestors of the arquebus) to help defend the mobile fortresses which they constructed on the battlefield by chaining together lines of war-

This contemporary drawing shows the essential features of the Hussite *Wagenburg*. Troops armed with crossbows, primitive handguns, maces and flails shelter behind their war-wagons, which protect them much as the wall of the city would. The barrel of another artillery piece can be seen guarding the opening at the front of the first (bottom left) wagon. Hussite victories made such war-wagons common in eastern and central Europe of the fifteenth century.

wagons. One key difference, however, was introduced by the new weapons: now the side best provided with artillery could often compel its enemy to make an attack (or suffer interminable bombardment), and so secure for itself the advantages of the tactical defensive. By the end of the Hundred Years War, this finally provided the French with an effective counter to the English tactics which had led to Valois defeats from Crécy to Verneuil. The last two battles of the war, Formigny and Castillon, were almost the first full-scale, head-on fights to be won by the French, and in both their artillery played an important part.

Since victory or defeat on the battlefield now had such great consequences (sieges having declined into relative unimportance), Western European rulers placed ever-greater emphasis on fielding larger and more professional armies. This trend is particularly noticeable at the end of our period, with the *compagnies d'ordonnance* of France and Burgundy, which will be discussed in the concluding chapter of this book. These standing forces were very expensive, as was a good artillery train, and in general only the richest rulers of Christendom could afford them. All of this favoured the central governments of large states who benefited from a 'coercion-extraction cycle' whereby a state's military might enabled it to conquer new lands or impose new taxes on reluctant subjects, thus increasing revenues and funding a new increment of military might, and so on. Philippe de Commynes, the late-fifteenth-century soldier, politician, and historian, illustrated this circular process when he spoke of 'a prince who is powerful and has a large standing army, by the help of which he can raise money to pay his troops'. This was a new military world, one dominated by what William H. McNeill dubbed the 'Gunpowder Empires': states whose powerful armies in combination with wall-toppling cannon enabled them to consolidate their power over particularist provinces and to gobble up their smaller neighbours. Two of the first states to set out on this path were France and the Ottoman Empire. In their respective campaigns of 1453 they employed armies spearheaded by permanent, professional troops and backed by skilled artillerists and large siege trains to effect conquests which were literally epoch-making. The earl of Shrewsbury's army was wiped out by French gunners at Castillon, leading to the collapse of the pro-English rising in Gascony and (in retrospect) the end of the Hundred Years War. Meanwhile Mehmed the Conqueror, assisted by mammoth bombards among the largest ever manufactured, succeeded in the task which had frustrated his forebears for many years: the capture of Constantinople, the strongest-walled city in Europe. Thus did the 'middle ages' draw to their close, with thick clouds of black-powder smoke as their final curtain.

PART II

THE ARTS OF WARFARE

8 FORTIFICATIONS AND SIEGES IN WESTERN EUROPE *c*.800–1450

R. L. C. JONES

FROM the earliest times, the construction of physical defences produced a new form of warfare, the siege. Evidence from Crickley Hill, Gloucestershire, suggests that its ramparts, *c*.2800 BC, were assaulted and burnt down using fire arrows. Prehistoric defences were designed to protect large areas within which communities lived. But at their heart was the desire of an elite to defend its own interests, generally power and wealth. These early fortifications were based on a simple line, or lines, of defence, exploiting height and depth through a series of banks and ditches. These became more complex over time, incorporating the developed defensive ideas seen at the western entrance of Maiden Castle, Dorset, where those attacking were channelled along well-protected 'corridors' between the built-up defences. Echoes of these prehistoric measures—the simple circuit of defences surrounding large communities—can be found in the urban enceintes of the Roman Empire. In the political vacuum created by the retreat of Roman power, archaeological evidence also shows that such hillforts were reoccupied in the early medieval period. Clearly there was a continuity of defensive practice linking the prehistoric hillfort with medieval town walls.

But the middle ages also saw a break from this tradition with the emergence of the private defence or 'castle'. The pretence of defence for all was lost: castles were the unambiguous statements of powerful figures that they were prepared to invest heavily in fortifications to defend their own interests. The proliferation of these smaller defences, seldom covering more than a few acres, complicated the way war was waged. With more fortifications in the landscape, the siege began to predominate as the most effective style of warfare. Few campaigns were waged during the period 800–1450 without siege being laid to at least one, and sometimes several, key strongholds. Only where societies relied less on castles, for example in twelfth-century Ireland or thirteenth-century Wales, did siege warfare remain of secondary importance. Sieges far outnumber pitched battles, naval skirmishes, mounted raids, and all other forms of warfare during the period. Geoffrey V of Anjou conquered Normandy without a battle between 1135 and 1145 and the great warrior King Richard I, although constantly engaged in siege warfare during his ten-year reign, fought no more than two or three battles. Crusades were won and lost through the combination of major siege operations and pitched battle. In thirteenth-century Germany, the wars of succession after the death of Emperor Henry VI, the final struggle with the papacy, and the conflicts caused by the demise of the Hohenstaufen dynasty were all conducted primarily through siege action. Equally, the Christian reconquest of Moorish Spain culminated at large urban centres like Cordoba and Seville. Yet despite the relative frequency of siege action, and the scale of such operations, it was rare for the conclusion of an individual siege, either successful capture or defence, to dictate the outcome of a wider conflict. Striking exceptions can be found such as King Stephen's success at Faringdon in 1145 which marked the end of civil war with Mathilda, and the English success at the siege of Calais in 1347 which decided much more than the preceding battle at Crécy. Battle in open country remained the stage on which dynastic power could and did change hands. More often than not, however, the preliminaries to battle can be found in a single siege or in a series of military blockades, for example the battle of Lincoln during the reign of Stephen where the king himself was captured. It is clear that the stakes were higher in battle. Sieges could be actively sought, while battle was to be avoided until absolutely necessary. Nevertheless, siege brought the warring parties together and was often used, both wittingly and unwittingly, as the catalyst for decisive military action, the set-piece battle.

A castle or town under siege played a defensive role, but castles also fulfilled important offensive roles too. As operational bases for mobile forces, strongholds acted as supply bases and safe-havens for troops not actively engaged in the field. Broad areas were dominated from these places. The chronicler Suger reported that when the castle of Le Puiset—captured by King Louis VI in 1111—was under enemy control, no one dared approach within eight or ten miles of the place for fear of attack from the garrison. Capture of such threatening redoubts often meant mobilizing large field armies. Conversely, retaining control of these places became the paramount concern of those on the defensive. Aside from their military role, these fortifications also represented political power. They were administrative centres for public authorities, as well as for private lordship, where fealty was rendered and services performed. Castles became the symbols of the wealth, status, and power of those who built them. While maintaining a military function, castles were adapted over time to provide comfortable, even luxurious, accommodation for their lords; at Orford, Suffolk, for example, the twelfth-century keep was split into small rooms, and a gravity-powered water system provided a constant running supply. Dover had similar 'modern' amenities. These non-military provisions have led some scholars recently to reassess and reduce the military role of the castle (see also Chapter 5, p. 103). While certainly in part residential, their capacity to withstand siege warns against interpretations which totally ignore their military design. The functions of fortified towns were equally complex, constructed not only to defend the local population, but also to represent the town's political maturity, and most importantly to protect its economic interests. All three elements can be seen in the construction of walls around the Italian city-states. With such potentially rich pickings in towns and cities, it is easy to see why the siege was attractive to any aggressor.

In military terms at least, the design of defensive structures in Western Europe responded to the menace posed by aggressive forces, both real and perceived, whether it be the small Viking raids or large royal armies, classical siege engines or gunpowder weaponry. Siegecraft was developed to overcome defensive obstacles, from the simplest earth and timber castle to complex multi-layered stone defences. Because of their relative scale, it was easier, quicker, and less costly to adapt weaponry and siege engines than static defences. Fortifications were to play a continuous game of catch-up throughout the period, teetering on the brink of obsolescence, as military architects sought to counter the ever-changing arsenal of the aggressor. The fine balance between defensive structures and offensive weaponry characterizes the period. In actual fact few fortifications fell as a result of direct bombardment or assault. Far more surrendered due to human frailty as supplies ran low, or because relieving forces failed to come to a garrison's aid. As Robert Blondel commented in fifteenth-century Normandy, 'It is not by walls that a country is defended, but by the courage of its soldiers.' Still more strongholds, anticipating siege action, capitulated before siege was laid. The capture of Alençon in 1417 precipitated the surrender of six lesser towns and castles within a fortnight. In the same fashion, the vast majority of English-held castles in Normandy between 1449 and 1450 capitulated without resistance when faced with the overwhelming firepower of the French artillery train. In the main, however, defences appear to have kept pace with changes in weaponry. William of Holland, for example, undertook thirteen sieges between 1249 and 1251, of which only three were successfully concluded. Even a reluctance to change and adopt radically new defensive measures, notably after the introduction of the cannon, failed to prove terminal for traditional defences. Henry V's conquest of Normandy between 1417–19 was conducted through a series of sieges yet the defences of Caen, Falaise, Cherbourg, and Rouen, all built without consideration for cannon, were able to offer stiff resistance, the last for more than six months. Despite their knowledge of the potency of such weaponry, neither Henry V nor Henry VI redesigned any fortifications after the conquest of Normandy, suggesting that they considered these fortifications capable of withstanding the new firepower. The early incorporation of cannon into the defences of Western Europe, it can be argued, actually made these defences stronger than before. Embrasures for cannon were added to existing defences, for example along the south coast of England, where castles such as Carisbrooke, on the Isle of Wight, and towns such as Southampton incorporated gun loops into their design from the 1360s. By the 1390s most English fortifications were designed to take cannon, as Cooling and Bodiam castles, and the town defences of Canterbury and Winchester show. It is dangerous to assume, however, that all advantage lay with those who defended fortified places. Throughout the period if the besieger could bring to bear the whole suite of aggressive tactics—bombardment, assault, mining, and blockade—few castles or town defences were able to withstand the onslaught for long. Even the best designed castles, those described by contemporaries as 'impregnable', for example Château-Gaillard, or Crac des Chevaliers, or Cherbourg rarely lived up to their reputation. Duke William of Normandy was said never to have failed to take a castle.

It is widely accepted that the proliferation of castle building and other defensive works from around AD 1000 had its roots in fundamental social change. This was brought about, in part at least, by the external military threat of Viking, Magyar, and Saracen raids. The marauders posed serious problems, since they were able to move swiftly, either on horseback or by following rivers, to penetrate deep into the heart of Europe. Raiders moved with impunity across the countryside. The only means of slowing their progress was to build defences. Across Europe the threat was the same, but the defensive solutions adopted differed greatly. Viking raids into Francia encouraged the construction of private defences, for example, in the Charente region, and of public works: Charles the Bald at the assembly of Pitres in 864 ordered fortifications to be raised along the major rivers. Refurbished town defences as at Le Mans and Tours on the Loire, as well as fortified bridges on the Elbe and Seine resulted from this initiative and over the next twenty years much work was carried out. It proved crucial for the successful defence of Paris in 885–6. In Ireland individual communities erected tall round towers both as refuges

Defence of the Burh. The depiction of masonry defences suggests that the illuminator was influenced by classic images of siege. Some Roman defences were re-used for example at Chichester and Winchester. To guarantee the security of these locations, rural estates were required to provide both men and money, based on the number of land units as laid down in the text known as Burghal Hideage.

and lookout points against the Viking incursions. In England Alfred began to fortify the major population centres, creating an integrated system of defences or *burhs*, offering protection for the surrounding countryside. Generally a single earthen rampart was thrown up, capped with a wooden palisade, often on a naturally defensible position such as a promontory or within the bend of a river. Access points were protected by gatehouses. Elements of several of these earthwork defences can still be seen, for example at Wareham, Wallingford, and Burpham. To counter the Magyar threat, in Germany, Henry the Fowler (919–36) constructed fortress towns such as Werla, Brandenburg, and Magdeburg. Each fortress comprised a series of fortified enceintes leading to a citadel.

Knowledge of how siege was conducted in antiquity was applied, with slight modification, to early medieval siegecraft. Accounts of early sieges demonstrate that, in attack and defence, little had changed. At the siege of Barcelona in 800–1, the Moors burnt the surrounding countryside to deny their Frankish besiegers supplies and took Christian hostages. The walls were weakened by mining and bombardment from stone-throwing siege engines such as petraries and mangonels which used torsion to provide the power to launch their projectiles. It also appears that the gates were attacked with battering rams. The final assault was led by men approaching the walls under cover, the *testudo* (or 'tortoise,' an armoured roof on rollers), and the walls were scaled by means of siege towers and ladders. It is clear from this account that diverse measures had been taken in advance of the siege. Such preparation was clearly ordered in Charlemagne's *Capitulare Aquisgaranense* of 813 which provided for the organization of trains for siegeworks and the supply of the besieging army. The *Capitulare* also decreed that men should be equipped with pickaxes, hatchets, and iron-tipped stakes to make siege works. The attack on Paris during the winter of 885–6 illustrates well the state of ninth-century siegecraft. Faced with formidable defences, the Vikings were cognizant of all the methods to overcome them. According to the monk Abbo, they used bores to remove stones from the walls, mined the towers, brought up rams to batter the walls but were unable to bring their siege towers close to the walls, and used fireships to overcome the fortifications on the river. These attacks were repulsed by the defenders of the city with boiling liquids, anti-personnel darts and bolts from *ballistae*, and forked beams to shackle the rams. Rapid repairs were made at night. The variety of siege methods employed, and the defensive tactics used to counter them, are evidence that siegecraft was not in its infancy. The Carolingian success in defending Paris was a rare achievement. Faced by large area fortifications, manned by few trained soldiers, besiegers could generally expect to succeed. The sheer scale of early defences contributed to their weakness. The defensive solution was to reduce the length of the exposed front; this reduction reached its apogee with the castle.

The design of castle defences sought to counter the threat posed by any aggressive force. As siegecraft evolved so too did castle designs. In most cases, therefore, it is possible to link the great changes in military architecture seen between 800 and 1450, albeit with certain time lapses, to the mastery of available siege techniques, to the introduction of new weaponry, or to the exposure to different defensive ideas, many of which came from the East. Of these, perhaps, the last led to the most radical changes, while the first and second encouraged piecemeal, but nevertheless fundamental, improvements. These factors, individually or in combination, lie behind the five main stages of medieval castle design: the replacement of earth-and-timber castles by those constructed in stone; fortifications based around the keep or donjon; the move from square keeps and mural towers to round ones; the adoption of concentric and symmetrical plans; and early attempts to build fortifications both capable of countering and of using gunpowder weaponry.

Two forms of early fortification were commonly adopted: the ringwork

Several castles are shown on the Bayeux Tapestry. It appears that some effort has been made to reproduce a faithful rendering of each castle. Here, the embroiderers have shown the timber tower, the bridge, the gatehouse, and the ditch and counterscarp around the motte in detail. The cavalry charge, however, is probably the result of artistic licence.

and the motte-and-bailey. In origin each was designed to withstand the methods of warfare of the time, possibly inspired to some degree by the fortified winter encampments of the Vikings. At Ghent and Antwerp, for example, later defences were adapted from those first constructed by the Vikings. By retreating behind physical barriers, defenders effectively neutralized the most powerful element in any army—its cavalry. It was impossible for mounted men to breach both walls and ditches. Even when mounted assault was launched, as at Lincoln in 1217, this was probably led more by a misguided sense of honour rather than by any preconceived military advantage this might bring. The ringwork, a simple fortified enclosure of earth and timber, usually surrounding one or two major buildings, offered few other advantages to its defenders. The addition of an elevated motte, utilizing a natural or artificial mound (as much as 20 m high and up to 30 m in diameter at its top), greatly enhanced defensive options. From its dominant position, the enemy could be observed, helping defenders to coordinate their limited resources on areas of the castle which were under attack. It might also provide a platform, such as that found at Abinger, Surrey, from which missiles could be rained down on any besieging force. With a bailey, or series of baileys, livestock and other provisions could be gathered in anticipation of a lengthy siege (rendered the harder if the surrounding countryside was then scorched), while defenders could retreat behind successive lines of defence as they fell, ultimately occupying the motte itself. Quick and easy to construct, this form of fortification was predominant in many parts of Western Europe during the eleventh and twelfth centuries.

As allegiances changed and the political map was in flux there was a need for constant fortification and refortification. Earth and timber defences provided the perfect defensive solution. Their appearance across Europe, from Scandinavia, through the Low Countries, to the Mediterranean proves demonstrably the effectiveness of this defensive design as a military structure. It can be seen also in the introduction of the motte-and-bailey type of fortification into Ireland and Scotland during the twelfth century when stone-built castles were becoming more common elsewhere. Even in areas where the political situation did not dictate speedy construction, it was the motte-and-bailey that was built. From the outset, however, the design of each fortification, while sharing the common features of enclosed bailey and elevated motte, varied from site to site. Hen Domen, Montgomeryshire, the best-studied site in Britain, might be considered classic; its motte surrounded by a ditch occupying one end of a bailey enclosed with its bank and ditch. But of the five castles built during the reign of William I in Sussex, each adopted a different plan: at Hastings the motte was constructed within a prehistoric enclosure, and at Pevensey the medieval fortification was built within the masonry walls of the Roman shore fort; at Lewes it appears that the castle had two mottes, at Arundel the motte was surrounded by two baileys, whilst at Bramber the motte was raised at the centre of one large oval bailey. With such variation in one short period it is impossible to identify any clear evolution of defensive design through time. Evidence also suggests that the ringwork and motte-and-bailey co-existed happily. If on some sites the motte has been shown as a later addition, the motte-and-bailey never replaced the ringwork as the ideal castle plan.

Elsewhere in Europe during the late eleventh and early twelfth centuries other political and social factors such as the emergence of a powerful hereditary aristocracy prompted an unparalleled spread of castles. In Germany unrest in Saxony encouraged Henry IV to construct royal castles but a major cause for castle building here was the anarchy which followed the outbreak of the Investiture Contest in 1075. This led to the construction of castles not only in Germany, but also in Austria, Switzerland, and Italy. These frequently differed from those in France and England. As they were built on land which was not disputed, newly conquered, or immediately under threat, military architects could select the most naturally defensible sites, hilltops and promontories such as Karlstein bei Riechenhall and Rothenburg. Due to their elevated siting, the main defensive feature of these castles was the *Bergfried* or watchtower, not the motte. Political instability stimulated castle building, as seen in Normandy in the 1050s and in England during Stephen's reign. Attempts were made to restrict the spread of castles: the Norman *Consuetudines et Justicie* of 1091 legislated for ducal control over all castle building, prohibiting the erection of fortifications over a certain size and permitting the Duke to enter or demand the render of all castles in his duchy, whether his or not, at will. In fact, the ducal monopoly over building castles harked back to royal rights enshrined in the Carolingian Edict of Pitres; similar claims to rendability were made by other strong rulers during the twelfth and subsequent centuries.

Siegecraft in the eleventh and twelfth centuries varied little from that of earlier periods. Mangonels and *ballistae* constituted the heavy artillery deployed to weaken any defences. Mining remained an effective tactic since in most cases earth-and-timber fortifications were surrounded by dry, and not water-filled, ditches, allowing miners to approach and undermine outer defences. Assaults were focused on weak points on the outer defensive line such as gates, while relatively low ramparts and timber palisades meant that escalade was a feasible option. More importantly, these fortifications were susceptible to fire. Henry I burnt down the castles of Brionne, Montfort-sur-Risle, and Pont-Audemer, while the Bayeux Tapestry shows attackers setting light to the palisade around the motte at Dinan in 1065. Moreover, unlike the sieges of large cities such as Barcelona or Paris, where the besiegers found difficulty raising the manpower for full blockade, the small size of castles made them vulnerable. An effective method of blockade was to construct counter-castles, from which a relatively small force could survey the besieged castle, preventing the free flow of traffic to and from it, while providing a base from which to launch aerial bombardments, and a place of retreat if the besieged counter-attacked. William I constructed four counter-castles to blockade Rémalard in 1079. In 1088 William II used fortified siege towers against Rochester and in 1095 constructed counter-castles at Bamburgh. Similar tactics were used by Henry I at Arundel and in 1145, during the anarchy of Stephen's reign, Philip, son of the Earl of Gloucester, advised his father to build counter-castles from which to monitor the sallies of royalists garrisoned at Oxford. Counter-castles continued to be used throughout the period; they were perfected by the mid-fourteenth century. Siege bastilles built around Gironville in 1324–5 were constructed as raised earthen platforms, 35 m square and 2 m high and surrounded by ditches 4 m deep and 12–20 m wide. The English bastilles for the siege of Orléans in 1428–8 were similarly 30 m square and able to contain 350–400 troops within their fortifications.

By the early twelfth century, siege tactics were well understood by most military commanders. As a result, sieges regularly succeeded, prompting the need to find new defensive solutions. The improvement of building techniques, used in the construction of ecclesiastical buildings, were applied for the first time to military buildings. A natural step was to replace earth-and-timber defences with masonry. In terms of defensive options, early stone castles differed little from their wooden predecessors. Defence was still based on the holding of the outer line of defences, now stone walls rather than timber palisades. The donjon either replaced or colonized the motte, offering active defensive options by its elevation, as well as passive resistance as a place of last refuge. The earliest now-surviving stone castles were built in France during the late tenth century. As he expanded his power, Fulk Nerra, count of Anjou (987–1040) constructed castles to protect his possessions against neighbours in Blois, Brittany, and Normandy. Amongst these, Langeais possessed a stone 'keep' by 1000, while at Doué-la-Fontaine, an earlier unfortified Carolingian palace was converted into a donjon, but generally Nerra's castles were at first of the motte-and-bailey type; even amongst the highest ranks in society, initially few could afford to build extensively in stone. Thus most of the earliest stone castles in England and France were either ducal or royal establishments. Of these Rouen, the White Tower in London, and Colchester were precocious examples. But by the 1120s Henry I was reconstructing in stone many of his timber castles in Normandy, including Argentan, Arques-la-Bataille, Caen, Domfront, Falaise, and Vire. All these were dominated by massive square or rectangular keeps; elsewhere great lords, like those of Beaugency or the earls of Oxford (at Castle Heddingham, Essex) followed suit. At Gisors Henry I constructed a shell-keep surrounding the motte; other fine examples also survive at Totnes in Devon and Tamworth, Staffordshire. In Germany, there is evidence at Staufen that a stone tower and masonry walls had been erected by 1090. Castles proliferated in Léon, Castille, and Catalonia. Here, however, Christian conquerors were more often content to add elements such as keeps to earlier Moorish fortifications. Many fortresses remained garrison centres rather than feudal caputs. Despite much castle building, the fortified towns of the peninsula also remained central to defence, with Christian powers preserving the best of Moorish military architecture like the massive town walls and gates of Valencia.

Masonry offered far greater resistance against stone-throwing siege engines inherited from the Roman world. In combination with more exten-

Falaise. The two classic donjon types, the twelfth-century square keep constructed by Henry I of England and the thirteenth-century circular donjon built by Philip Augustus of France. Not only does this juxtaposition demonstrate the progress made in military architecture, but also hints at how different castle designs could be used for political purposes.

sive and more complex outworks, the threat from mining could be minimized. Masonry castles could expect to withstand siege longer, since mining operations were more difficult. The threat from fire and physical bombardment was diminished. The heightening of walls made escalade more difficult, while improved outworks including flanking towers and gatehouses offered greater cover against attacks on the walls, and water-filled moats prevented siege towers being drawn up against them. Indeed, by the mid-twelfth century even minor castles were able to resist aggressive action for considerable periods. At this period the normal duration of a siege appears to have been between four and six weeks, although there were notable exceptions: the siege of Tonbridge was decided in just two days by William II, while the siege of Norwich in 1075 and the siege of Arundel in 1102 both lasted three months. Stone fortifications, if well-provisioned, were able to withstand siege longer.

Louis VI had to besiege Amiens for two years, while it took Geoffrey V of Anjou three years to enter Montreuil-Bellay, a siege notable for the first mention of the use of Greek fire in the West. Time was an important factor, since this greatly increased the chance of relieving forces coming to the assistance of the besieged. Nevertheless, despite all these improvements, the besiegers could proceed along the same lines as before. With force, now technically more difficult, every defensive measure could be overcome. Richard I at Chalus and Frederick Barbarossa at Milan and Tortona used reconnaissance to assess the strengths and weaknesses of the fortresses that they faced. The former made great use of speed in attack to catch strongholds unprepared for siege while the latter, a master of siege warfare, was prepared to build great siege works around large Italian cities to enforce long-term blockade. Many accounts of siege at this period record the filling of wet moats or dry ditches either with rock or rubble, for example at Montreuil-Bellay, or with faggots and timber as at Shrewsbury or Acre.

A number of works detailing different siege-engine designs were produced throughout the thirteenth century, for example Villard de Honnecourt's sketchbook and Egidio Colonna's *De Regimine Principum*. This pulley-system assault tower was designed by Guido da Vigevano at the beginning of the fourteenth century, just one of a number of his innovative military ideas.

The most important innovation around 1200 was a new form of siege engine, the trebuchet. Unlike the mangonel and *ballista*, the trebuchet used counterweights. It was more powerful than its predecessors, and more accurate, since by changing the size of the counter or altering the pivotal length, it was possible to vary its range, vital to pinpoint specific targets (see also Chapter 5, p. 109). It has been estimated that a trebuchet could propel a 33 lb casting-stone about 200 yards; it could also be used to throw other missiles, including rotting carcasses, a primitive form of biological warfare. The introduction of the trebuchet shifted the balance of siege in favour of the besieger; they were much in evidence at Toulouse in 1217–18 and the many other sieges that marked the bitterly fought Albigensian Crusade in southern France. The destructive force of any projectile thrown by the trebuchet needed to be addressed if castles were to remain effective against attack. Two counter-measures were taken: increasing the height of the walls, and reducing the number of flat surfaces prone to such bombardment. The rectangular or square donjon was replaced by the round donjon just as square flanking towers were replaced by semi-circular or convex mural towers. By increasing the number of towers, flanking fire could be ranged against anyone approaching the walls. The construction of sloping talus on the walls not only dissipated the power of incoming projectiles but also allowed objects to be dropped from the wall heads which then ricocheted unpredictably towards the attackers. Elsewhere, for example at Château-Gaillard and La Roche Guyon, donjons were constructed to offer an acute peak to the most likely direction of attack. Round towers also offered greater protection against mining. Any angle in a wall proved its weakest point, exploited for example to great effect at the siege of Rochester in 1216. Nevertheless, this siege demonstrated that square keep castles could withstand royal siege; even after the collapse of the corner, the defending garrison believed the tower still to be capable of resistance and it was only the failure of relieving forces to arrive that finally forced surrender.

Round-towered castles began to be constructed in England and France in the 1130s, for example at Houdan, where the round keep was further strengthened by four round towers which projected from its line, and Etampes, built in the 1140s, designed on a four-leafed plan. Circular donjons only became dominant, however, at the start of the thirteenth century. At the peripheries of Europe, square towers continued to be built; in Ireland, for example the great square keeps of Carrickfergus and Trim were erected between 1180 and 1220. By contrast, Philip Augustus's re-fortification of Normandy after 1204 saw many square keeps either replaced by round towers or their outer fortifications improved by the addition of semi-circular angle and mural towers as at Caen and Falaise (see p. 173, and cf Trim p. 68). This period saw the introduction of castle forms which did not rely on the strength of the donjon. The Trencavel citadel at Carcassonne and the Louvre were built on a quadrangular plan around small courtyards, defended by towers at each of their four angles, a plan which was to be readopted in fourteenth-century England at Nunney and Bodiam. Similar compact fortifications also emerged in the Low Countries from the thirteenth century. The lack of building stone meant that many were constructed in brick, but exploited the low-lying nature of the land by adding extensive water defences. Muiderslot, built by Count Floris IV provides a good example of these *Wasserburgen*, a regular castle with projecting circular angle towers and a defended gatehouse totally surrounded by wide moats. At a lower social level, this was also the period when many otherwise lightly defended manor houses acquired water-filled moats.

At the same time that military architects began to understand the defensive worth of circular structures, other defensive ideas began to spread back into Western Europe from the East as the early crusades brought Christian Europe into direct contact with new ideas. Exposure to the massive fortifications at Byzantium and Jerusalem, Nicea with its four miles of walls, 240 towers, and water-filled moat, Antioch with a two-mile enceinte with 400 towers, and Tyre with a triple circuit of walls with mural towers which were said nearly to touch, greatly impressed those that saw and attacked them. The siege of Jerusalem in 1099 demonstrated how difficult these fortifications were to take. The crusaders, after filling the ditches brought up three siege towers to overlook the walls of the city. Savage bombardment failed to breach the defences. Only by scaling the walls and opening one of the town gates was the city finally reduced. Of the castles of the Holy Land the most powerful was Crac des Chevaliers, totally remodelled by the Knights Hospitallers after they acquired it from the Count of Tripoli in 1142 (see plate, pp. 96–7). Its defences were based on a concentric plan with the inner circuit of walls close to and dominating the outer line. Access to the inner citadel was through a highly complex system of twisting corridors and ramps which were overtopped on each side by high walls. Its outer line of walls was protected by regular semi-circular angle towers and deep talus offering great protection against projectiles and mining. Its overall strength derived not only from the man-made defences but the naturally-protected spur it occupied. The influence of crusader castles on the siting and design of Château-Gaillard has been long stated and clearly its triangular *châtelet* or barbican mirrors the powerful outwork to the south of Crac. Just as German castles had exploited the mountainous terrain, so too did many of the castles of southern France such as Montségur or Puylaurens. The impact of the Crusades, however, became most visible from the 1230s. At this time the great banded walls around Angers were erected, the concentric town defences of Carcassonne were perfected, and the heavily fortified town of Aigues-Mortes was constructed by Louis IX to be the port of embarkation for his crusading exploits. In Britain, ideas on concentric fortification reached their medieval apogee in Wales during Edward I's castle-building campaigns from 1277 to 1294–5. At Harlech, on an already prominent rocky outcrop, an inner line of defences dominates an outer circuit, with a massive gatehouse facing the easiest access. At Rhuddlan, the inner circuit formed an irregular hexagon, its two shortest sides occupied by two gatehouses, whilst at each

Chateau-Gaillard adopted features probably first encountered during the Crusades. The defences were made up of a series of ditches and walls. If captured the defenders could fall behind successive lines and regroup. The fortifications culminated in an unique wall built of small arcs, more resistant to projectiles, and the donjon, exhibiting enormous machicolations to improve its offensive capabilities.

angle there was a large circular tower. But Edward's most remarkable, though unfinished achievement in symmetry was Beaumaris, with two enormously powerful gatehouses protecting an inner bailey with angle towers and further mural towers placed halfway along the curtain. This inner line dominated the outer defences, akin to the defences of Crac. Surrounding marshland and the sea provided natural protection. Against these royal enterprises can be set the de Clare castle of Caerphilly begun in 1268. The inner bailey displays the same attempts at symmetry although more poorly executed. The great strength of Caerphilly, however, derived from a series of complex and unrivalled waterworks which allowed two great lakes to be flooded in times of trouble leaving the castle isolated on a small well-defended island. Where topography

dictated the plan, Edward was prepared to build more traditional fortifications such as Conway and Caernarvon, although the octagonal flanking towers of the latter mirrors Byzantium's urban defences and other features, like the decorations of the walls with banded stonework and the symbolism of the Eagle tower, have been linked with Edward's 'imperialist' ambitions. In Scotland too, some efforts were made to incorporate symmetrical, if not concentric ideas, into new defences, like the triangular plan of the castle of Caerlaverock with its gatehouse protected by twin towers at one apex, famously besieged by Edward I in 1300. Water-filled moats kept the royal siege towers at bay, but battering at the gate, an attempt to mine, and aerial bombardment finally brought the garrison to terms. In the same way, the long sieges of Château-Gaillard in 1203–4 and Crac in 1271 demonstrate the problems these fortifications posed for besiegers, capable of penetrating the outer lines of defences, generally with great loss to personnel and equipment, who were then faced with the challenge of more substantial defences.

The fourteenth century saw few innovations in England and France. Traditional and transitional castles were still constructed; for example, in the Cotentin the polygonal keep at Bricquebec or the reconstructed square keep at St-Sauveur-le-Vicomte, while in England castles became more compact, sometimes known as 'courtyard' castles, incorporating water defences in their design. In Spain unrest allowed the nobility to construct further castles, often like Fuensaldana or Penefiel or Medina del Campo based on the square donjon. In Poland and along the Baltic coast, important low-lying brick fortifications were built by the Teutonic Knights between 1291 and 1410, their plan influenced by their monastic concerns, as seen at the most impressive site of Malbork. Here the central cloister was surrounded by a machicolated gallery. Indeed the introduction of machicolations from *c.*1300, allowing defence from the wall head, marks an important stage in castle design and was widely adopted across Europe. Later, from the last quarter of the fourteenth century other architectural changes stimulated by gunpowder and combustible artillery weapons began to appear. The height of circuit walls was reduced to

Facing, above: Beaumaris, the perfection of concentric castle design. Its architect Master James of St George fully exploited the firing lines from inner and outer wards to maximize defensive potential. Its strength lay in the powerful gatehouses and complex seaward access. Welsh Edwardian castles form a discrete group, yet each final design was unique, overcoming the problems of local topography and function.

Facing, below: the fortifications at Constantinople were some of the most powerful in Europe. Seen by crusaders they were to exert influence throughout the west. At their height in 1453, there were four miles of landbound walls, nine miles of seaward walls, a vast ditch, and a hundred towers.

The beginning of the end. By the late fourteenth century castles such as Bodiam were designed for comfort and effect rather than for purely defensive reasons. Nevertheless an early attempt was made to incorporate firearms into its defences, and the internal arrangement of rooms suggests a realization that the threat from within was as important as that from without.

offer a smaller target to cannon, while the walls themselves were thickened as can be seen in the massive fortifications of southern France, for example Villeneuve-lès-Avignon and Tarascon, and reached their apotheosis in the 13 m thick walls constructed by Louis de Luxembourg, constable of France, at his castle of Ham in the 1470s. In places the whole of the ground-floor was filled with earth to resist the impact of large calibre projectiles. Mural towers were also lowered to the height of the enceinte, and strengthened to act as platforms for defensive artillery pieces. Arrowloops were widened to take the new firearms, characteristically assuming a 'key-hole' shape. Further outworks, bulwarks, and bretesches, were perfected, using low banks of earth and timber to protect against artillery, while extra-mural barbicans improved the defensive capabilities of the gatehouse. The impact of these changes and the speed of their adoption, however, should not be exaggerated. They were introduced piecemeal and slowly, to such an extent that no true artillery fortification can be said to have been constructed before 1450.

It appears that cannon were regularly used in sieges from the 1370s. There are some notably precocious examples, such as those used at Berwick in 1333, at Calais in 1347, and at Romorantin in 1356, but these remain exceptional. By 1375, however, the French were able to train 36–40 specially built artillery pieces at the castle of St-Sauveur-le Vicomte. While the potential benefits of bringing firearms to a siege could be enormous, their transport overland and siting caused logistic problems which greatly slowed any advancing force. It was reported in 1431 that 24 horses were required to pull one cannon and a further 30 carts needed to carry the accessories. In 1474, the Sire of Neufchâtel used 51 carts, 267 horses, and 151 men to transport only 12 artillery pieces. Some idea of the speed with which these pieces travelled can be gauged from other contemporary accounts. On average during the fifteenth century large artillery pieces could be moved 12 kilometres per day. In 1433, it took 13 days to take a large cannon from Dijon to Avallon, a distance of 150 kilometres. Others fared worse: in 1409 the large cannon of Auxonne, weighing some 7,700 lb was unable to be moved more than a league per day and in 1449 it took six days to move a cannon from Rennes to Fougères (47 kilometres), a daily rate of 8 kilometres. Yet these statistics compare not so unfavourably with the movement of the traditional siege engines. It took 10 days to take siege engines from London to the siege of Bytham in 1221, an average of 16 kilometres per day. It is unsurprising to find that wherever possible alternative routes were taken for both siege engines and cannon alike; the most efficient means was by river or sea, as during the preparations for the siege of Berwick in 1304.

It is uncertain how effective the early cannon were. At Dortmund in 1388, 27 cm calibre stones were ineffective against its walls, and in 1409 at the castle of Vellexon, the firing of 1,200 projectiles ranging between 700–850 lb also failed to bring down the defences.

The German *Feuerwerkbuch* in its several versions was widely read throughout Europe during the fifteenth and sixteenth centuries. Derivative of, but distinct from, Konrad Kyeser's *Bellifortis* (1405), this page from a *Feuerwerkbuch* manuscript (1420s) depicts a number of weapons: cannon, handguns, and crossbows firing incendiary bolts. Note the countermeasures being taken by the defenders to remove these devices from the roofs.

Moreover, large cannon could not compete with the traditional engines in terms of speed of fire. Five shots per day were released from a single cannon at the siege of Ypres in 1383 and sixteen years later at Tannenburg some large cannon only fired once a day. These rates, however, generally improved over time; moreover, medium calibre weapons could be loaded and fired more quickly. At Tannenburg 6 per day from smaller guns was recorded and at Dortmund 14 per day. By the mid-fifteenth century great advances had been made. In 1428 the English guns at Orléans could release 124 shots over twenty-four hours, and at the siege of Rheinfelden in 1445, these weapons fired at a rate of 74 per day. Standardization, modest calibre, and their greater speed of fire meant that by the fifteenth century these weapons were now far more efficient than traditional siege engines. Christine de Pisan had already estimated that 262,000 projectiles from traditional engines would be required to overcome the defences of a well-fortified town, but that only 52,170 would be required if firearms were used, a reduction of over 5:1.

Siege was a slow business. It was inevitable that conventions of siege would be established at every stage. These were affected by the rules of the just war and the code of chivalry in just the same way as battle. It was therefore vital to establish when a siege began and when it was concluded. The firing of a shot from a siege engine, later from a cannon, or the throwing of a javelin or spear or pebble, often symbolized the commencement. White flags, the handing over of keys (as at Dinan on the Bayeux Tapestry) and other acts demonstrated that surrender had been offered. By treating with the enemy, a defending captain could reduce the destruction to his town or castle and its population on its surrender. But conditions for surrender too were carefully codified. At Berwick in 1352, Richard Tempest was required to endure three months of siege before negotiations could begin. Often, however, hostilities were suspended, offering the chance of relief from external forces for the besieged. In such instances the rules were strict: for the besiegers, no further siege engines or men could be brought up into position, while the besieged were forbidden to make repairs. The giving of hostages sought to strengthen any such truce. On occasion, the terms were broken and hostages put to death. Even if a relieving army arrived, it was required to come prepared for battle, often at a time and place appointed by the besieger. At Grancey in 1434 it is reported that the armies were to meet 'above Guiot Rigoigne's house on the right hand side towards Sentenorges, where there are two trees'. Advantage was with the besiegers with their foreknowledge of the field and the ability to occupy the best position. If no relief came within the time set, then the besieged garrison was obliged to surrender. If unconditional, much was made of this. Those leaving were sometimes forced to come out barefoot, as at Stirling in 1304, or at Calais where in 1347 the six most prominent citizens had to wear halters around their necks when they brought out the keys of the town to Edward III. Negotiation played a large part in the siege. The safety of negotiators, often clerics, was recognized by both sides. If, however, the stronghold was taken by storm, the successful had almost complete control over the defeated, inflicting rape, enslavement, murder, and the seizure of property; terrible massacres followed many successful sieges during the Albigensian Crusade and the Black Prince notoriously sacked Limoges after its recapture in 1370, though the number of civilian victims remains uncertain.

In this chapter the focus has been on the attack and defence of castles, the evolution of their design, and the changing weaponry ranged against them. The emergence of the private defence separates the middle ages from other periods in which the emphasis was placed on public, communal defence, though most major towns and many smaller ones spent heavily on their defences in this period, and successful sieges of towns, especially during the Hundred Years War, constituted some of the most notable military achievements of the age. In the main the evolution of medieval town defences mirrored the advances made in castle design, though borrowings were not all in one direction: masons were sent to view the town gate at Rennes when the castle of Blain was remodelled in the 1430s. Despite improved weaponry, the major tactics of siege—assault, bombardment, mining, and blockade—changed little. Similarities in the siege tactics used against Constantinople by the Russian Prince Oleg in 907 and later, successfully, by the Turks in 1453 bear this out, while the capability of castles such as Château-Gaillard, built in an earlier era, to withstand artillery siege at the end of the middle ages also demonstrates the longevity of castle designs against ever-changing firepower. The period is notable for its underlying continuity of practice in attack and defence. One of the many reasons for this remained a continuous adherence to the advice offered to besiegers and the besieged in Vegetius' *De Re Militari*, first copied by the Carolingians. Six chapters of this text are devoted to fortification including where to site a stronghold, how the walls, ditches, and gatehouses should be built, and how to counter fire and eliminate injury to personnel. Four chapters deal with preparations for siege such as building defensive siege engines and provisioning, and a further 18 chapters are concerned with siege strategies for both attack and defence. Vegetius remained the textbook for all military commanders and was studied down to the end of the middle ages.

It is perhaps not surprising, given the predominance of siege during the medieval period, and the scale of the operations which affected all strata of society, that numerous accounts of sieges have come down to us through chronicle and other literary sources. Few other events can have had such a

profound effect on national and local psyche and morale; this is perhaps why the siege became the literary metaphor or allegory for the struggle between good and evil in didactic texts, or those reflecting the lovers' tribulations. It is important, however, not to overestimate the importance of actual sieges. Of the thousands of fortifications constructed across Europe at this period only a minority were besieged. Many survived several hundred years, frequently refurbished and adapted to new circumstances, without their efficacy ever being tested in earnest. For most of the time, castles and town defences were not directly threatened by assault or blockade; though it cannot be tackled here the story of fortifications in peacetime is an equally fascinating history.

Siege of Rhodes, 1480. The vast numbers of men and weapons deployed in late medieval sieges is perfectly demonstrated in this scene. The improvements to town defences can be seen by the double circuit of masonry walls, the regular flanking towers, and the cannon embrasures placed in the advanced line of walls.

9 ARMS, ARMOUR, AND HORSES

ANDREW AYTON

If medieval warfare is to be represented by a single image, encapsulating both its distinctiveness and the predominant role played by the military elite, that image must surely be the mounted, armoured warrior. For while the armies of the Roman Empire and early modern Europe were dominated by foot soldiers, the corresponding role in those of the middle ages was played by men on horseback. The armoured knight, mounted on a colourfully caparisoned warhorse, is an indelible symbol of medieval Western Europe: he graces the folios of countless illuminated manuscripts and springs to life in the word pictures of the chroniclers of chivalry. Admittedly, artistic and literary works should be interpreted with caution. Primarily produced for, and often by, men of gentle blood, such sources offer an idealized image of warfare which concentrates on the role of the aristocratic warrior almost to the exclusion of other, often more numerous participants. The reality of war could be very different. Disciplined and resolute infantry proved, on many occasions, to be more than a match for heavy cavalry on the battlefield. Foot soldiers assumed a particularly important role in siege warfare. Yet, to recognize the aristocratic bias of some of our sources and to give due acknowledgement to the role of infantry is not to deny that, in essence, the middle ages was an equestrian age of war. Reconstruction of the reality of medieval warfare reveals a complex and varied picture, but one in which the mounted warrior is an ubiquitous, irrepressible figure.

There were, of course, many kinds of mounted warrior. Any survey of war from the eighth century to the sixteenth should not neglect the impact on Christendom of the ferocious 'horse peoples' of the steppe. The Magyars in the late ninth and tenth centuries and the Mongols in the thirteenth campaigned with breathtaking discipline and brutality. Their consummate horsemanship may be compared with that of the Seljuk Turks, whom the Byzantines, themselves heavily dependent on cavalry, encountered in Asia Minor and whom Western European crusaders fought in Outremer. Equestrian warriors of equal distinction were the Ottoman Turks, who began their advance into the Balkans in the mid-fourteenth century. The medieval West was no less militarily dependent on the horse. The *chevauchée*, or fast-moving raid by a mounted force, was a commonplace feature of medieval warfare. Armies might be mounted for the march, thereby achieving mobility and strategic flexibility, even if, like the Anglo-Saxons and Vikings, and the English during the Hundred Years War, the intention was to dismount to fight. On the battlefield, heavily armoured horsemen could play a decisive role, particularly if charges (and, perhaps, feigned retreats) were well-timed, delivered in disciplined, close-order fashion, and backed up by infantry or combined with archery. This remained as much the case in the fifteenth century as it had been in the eleventh.

Above and beyond strategy and tactics, it was the close association of the military aristocracy of Christendom with the warhorse that ensured that the agenda in medieval warfare would be set by the armoured man on horseback. At once an expensive symbol of wealth and status and, as St Anselm put it, the 'faithful companion' of the chivalric warrior, the warhorse raised the military elite above the rest of society. Acquiring suitable warhorses and the arms and armour required for mounted combat involved a substantial capital outlay. In the eleventh century the most expensive items of equipment, because their manufacture involved skilled, time-consuming work with materials which were in short supply, were the hauberk or

Nowhere is the association of noble equine and knightly warrior more powerfully illustrated than in the equestrian monuments of Italy, the grandest series of which commemorate the Scaligeri lords of Verona. Here, the effigy of Cangrande I della Scala (d.1329), life-size with grinning face and drawn sword, astride a caparisoned warhorse, makes an arresting statement of aristocratic authority.

mailshirt, composed of perhaps 25,000 rings, and costing, as James Campbell has observed, 'something like the annual income from quite a big village'; and the sword, which would take even longer to make (a modern estimate is 200 hours). A good warhorse would have cost at least as much as a hauberk. Examination of mid-fourteenth-century horse valuation inventories suggests that an English knight at that time would think nothing of spending £25 on a high-quality warhorse. Purchase of arms and armour befitting his status, plus additional horses and equipment, could easily bring the overall cost of preparing for war to £40 or £50. To put such sums in perspective, £40 per annum in landed income was regarded by the crown as sufficient to support knighthood. It was also roughly the amount that a knight would receive in wages for a year's service in the king's army. Comparable data suggest that an aspiring man-at-arms in mid- to late fifteenth-century France faced a similar financial outlay.

The provenance of the heavily armoured, aristocratic equestrian warrior has excited much debate. It has been argued, most notably by Lynn White, that it was the arrival of the stirrup in eighth-century Western Europe that prompted the emergence of cavalry capable of 'mounted shock combat', with lance held tightly 'couched' under the right arm; and that, moreover, since warhorses, armour, weapons, and military training required landed endowment for their maintenance, it was in effect the stirrup which was responsible for the establishment of a feudal aristocracy of equestrian warriors. More recent research, by Bernard Bachrach among others, has suggested that the solid fighting platform necessary for a rider to engage in mounted shock combat depended upon a combination of stirrup, wrap-around saddle with rigid cantle (back plate), and double girthing or breast-collars. With the rider thus 'locked onto the horse's back in a sort of cock-pit', it was possible, experimentally from the later eleventh century, and with greater regularity in the twelfth, to level a couched lance with the assurance of the combined weight of horse and rider behind it. Furthermore, historians no longer accept that the medieval aristocratic elite was actually brought into being by advances in horse-related technology. Rather, an existing military aristocracy—great lords and the household knights whom they armed and horsed—adopted new equipment when it became available, and pursued the tactical possibilities which that equipment offered. Those possibilities could not ensure battlefield supremacy for the knightly warrior. Nor was he the only important component in field armies. But the elite distinction of mounted shock combat, associated as it was with the emergence of chivalry as an aristocratic code of martial conventions and behaviour, gave rise to an image of the nobleman as equestrian warrior which, while being firmly grounded in reality, proved irresistible to manuscript illuminators and authors of romance literature. Although presenting an idealized world, such artistic works reflected the martial *mentalité* of the nobleman while contributing to its further elaboration and dissemination; and they leave us in no doubt that the warhorse was at the heart of the medieval aristocrat's lifestyle and mental world.

The role of the caparisoned warhorse as conveyor of aristocratic heraldic identity in battle and tournament is vividly illustrated in this depiction of Ulrich von Lichtenstein, the Styrian knight who achieved chivalric fame through his great jousting tours of 1227 and 1240.

This was perhaps most clearly displayed on the tournament field. It is surely significant that tournaments begin to appear in the sources in the early twelfth century. Apparently connected with the emergence of the new cavalry tactics, the tourney provided a training ground for individual skills with lance and sword, and team manoeuvres by *conrois* of knights. They also offered opportunities for reputations in arms to be made or enhanced, although that depended upon the identification of individuals amidst the dust and confusion of a mêlée. It was probably this need for recognition on the tournament field, as well as the similar demands of the battlefield, which brought about the development of heraldry in the early twelfth century. Along with lance pennons, surcoats, and smooth shields, the caparisoned warhorse was emblazoned with heraldic devices, thereby becoming a perfect vehicle for the expression of individual identity and family honour within the military elite. A similar message was conveyed by the martial equestrian figures which, until the fourteenth century, were so commonly to be found on aristocratic seals, and by the ceremonial involvement of warhorses, decked out in heraldic caparisons, in the funerals of later medieval noblemen.

Yet the warhorse was, if anything, more closely identified with the warrior elites of the oriental nomadic peoples who came into contact with Christendom during the middle ages. Theirs, however, was a very different kind of mounted warrior. A natural horseman, resourceful and self-sufficient, his equipment was lighter than that of his Western counterpart and his equestrian skills more refined, attuned to exploiting the potential of his nimble, hardy mount and necessary for wielding the composite bow—a powerful shortbow 'fitted together with glue', as Fulcher of Chartres described it—from the saddle. That could be a devastating weapon: the Magyars 'killed few with their swords but thousands with their arrows', noted Abbot Regino of Prüm. The Turks were also adept as lancers. Nomadic societies were, of course, wholly dependent on the horse. The lightning raids launched by their warrior elites in search of booty, slaves, and tribute were essential to the economic and social life of these peoples; in particular, they reinforced the social order over which the military elite, contemptuous of those who toiled on the land, presided. Among pagan nomads, the central role of the horse in a warrior's life was solemnly marked at the time of his burial. The inclusion of equine remains (skull and lower legs), along with saddle and stirrups, sabre, bow, and quiver is characteristic of Magyar warrior graves in the Carpathian basin. The Cumans continued to provide horse burials for their nobility into the fourteenth century, several generations after their settlement in the Christian kingdom of Hungary. The place of the horse in the warrior cultures of the Islamic Turks appears, to the modern observer, less archaic. Expressions of feeling for horses, of appreciation for their courage and endurance, by men of letters who were also warriors, such as Usāmah ibn Munqidh (1095–1188), were the products of a more refined—and settled—civilization. That some of the 'horse peoples' were able to adapt to a sedentary life, to establish permanent armies supported by state revenues, and to combine their martial energies with the inspirational force of a war-making religion, were developments of great military significance, as was shown only too clearly in the defeat of the Mongols by Baybars' Mamluks at Ain Jalut in 1260, and in the Ottoman Turks' relentless campaigns of conquest in Europe and the Middle East in the fifteenth and sixteenth centuries.

The contrasting military cultures of Western Europe and of the oriental horse peoples rested upon very different kinds of warhorse, and also on different approaches to horse management. The warhorse of the medieval West has excited much debate, particularly with regard to size and conformation. In the absence of direct documentary evidence or a substantial quantity of skeletal remains, estimates of warhorse size have been based upon scrutiny of iconographical evidence—with all the interpretative difficulties which that entails—and of such artefacts as horse-shoes, bits, and horse armour, backed up by indirect documentary evidence (for example, records of the dimensions of horse-transport vessels) and practical field experimentation. Insofar as conclusions can be drawn from this evidence, it would seem that the 'typical' later medieval warhorse was of the order of 14 to 15 hands in height—not a large animal by modern standards; and that there had been some increase in average size and weight from the eleventh to the fourteenth century, in response to the demands of mounted shock combat and the burden of armour. That burden certainly grew. Equine armour is mentioned in the sources from the later twelfth century. Initially it took the form of a mail trapper. From the mid-thirteenth century, we also find horse barding made of hardened leather (*cuir-bouilli*) or plates of metal, the latter most commonly on the head (chanfron) and chest (peytral). The overall weight of protection for horse and man reached its peak in the fourteenth century, when mail and plate armour were being combined; indeed, it has been suggested that a late fourteenth-century warhorse may have been required to carry over 100 lbs more than its counterpart of the Anglo-Norman period. As a consequence, the warhorse of the later middle ages needed to be more substantial than those which are so vigorously depicted in the Bayeux Tapestry.

Royal and aristocratic records cast much light on the breeding of warhorses and the emergence of the *magnus equus* in later medieval Western Europe. Prompted (as one English royal writ put it) by the 'scarcity of great horses suitable for war', programmes of warhorse acquisition and breeding were set in motion in later thirteenth-century England and France, continuing into the era of the Hundred Years War. High-quality horseflesh was imported from Spain, Lombardy, and the Low Countries. Distribution among the military elite was facilitated by horse fairs, such as those in Champagne and at Smithfield, and by gifts and exchanges between domestic breeders. The product of this selective breeding, the late medieval 'great horse' was noted for its strength and capacity for aggression (only stallions were used as warhorses in the medieval West), its stamina and mobility, and its noble bearing. We should be cautious, however, of thinking in terms of 'armour-carrying equine juggernauts', even in the case of the destrier, the true *magnus equus*. Animals of exceptional size are mentioned in the sources, but there is simply no evidence that the typical 'great horse' of the later middle ages stood as high as 18 hands. Fifteen to 16 hands seems more likely, though whether we should be visualizing a heavily-built hunter, or perhaps a cob, remains open to discussion. What is clear is that only a small proportion of the warhorses ridden by men-at-arms were destriers. Indeed, in fourteenth-century England, the courser, whose mobility and stamina made it an ideal horse for *chevauchées*, emerged as the preferred mount of the wealthier section of the military elite, while the majority of warhorses were either rounceys (*runcini*) or described simply as 'horses' (*equi*; *chivals*). Even more revealing of the hierarchies within the military elite are the valuation data recorded in horse appraisal inventories. The *dignitas* and wealth of the great magnate were celebrated in the high quality of his destrier, just as the more meagre resources of the humble man-at-arms were reflected in the modest value of his rouncey. For example, records of horses lost at the battle of Cassel in 1328 include the dauphin de Viennois' mount, valued at 600 livres tournois, while the mean value for the dauphin's esquires was 49 l.t. That horse values on English inventories of the same period might range from £5 to £100 highlights not only the disparities of wealth within the military elite, but also that there was no such thing as a 'typical' warhorse.

It was said of the English knightly community on the eve of Bannockburn that 'they glory in their warhorses and equipment'. Robert Bruce's reputed remark would apply equally well to the military elite of much of medieval Europe. It is something of a surprise, therefore, to find a fourteenth-century Arab poet, Abou Bekr ibn Bedr, dismissing the Western warhorse as the 'softest and worst' of breeds. The Islamic conquests of Iberia and Sicily had, after all, brought superior oriental breeds and an advanced equestrian culture to the attention of the West. The Moors introduced to Spain the Barb, the Turkmene, and the Arabian, and made full use of the indigenous breeds, including the Andalusian. This rich mix of breeding stock had a profound effect on the development of the warhorse in Western Europe, beginning with the Franks in the eighth century. The high reputation of Spanish horses endured into the later medieval period: as Charles of Anjou so memorably remarked, 'all the sense of Spain is in the heads of the horses'. The Normans acquired Spanish horses, through gifts or involvement in the Reconquista, and bred from them in the favourable conditions of Normandy, with results which were celebrated with such verve in the Bayeux Tapestry. Their conquest of Sicily brought them into contact with a further source of superior Barb and Arabian equines, while at the southern end of the Italian peninsula they gained access to another excellent horse-breeding region, Apulia and Calabria. At a somewhat later date, Apulian stallions were bred with larger mares in the lusher pastures of Lombardy to produce the substantial warhorses for which that region became renowned. Late medieval readers of Geoffrey Chaucer's Squire's Tale would have readily recognized the quality of the 'horse of brass', compared as it is with 'a steede of Lumbardye' and 'a gentil Poilleys [Apulian] courser'.

The horses which had been bred in Western Europe to provide a robust platform for the shock tactics of heavily armoured knights seemed clumsy and unmanoeuvrable to the Turks. They were less intelligent, less sensitively trained, and less well suited to endurance in a hot climate than the Seljuks' light-moving Turkmene and Arab horses. The latter, it has been suggested, were of a similar height, or somewhat smaller, than Western warhorses, but they were a good deal lighter: 700 to 900 lbs, as compared with 1,200 to 1,300 lbs. The nimbleness and stamina of the Turkmene and Arab horses were essential to the mobile, skirmishing warfare at which the Turks, in common with all 'horse peoples', excelled. The crusaders' stock response, especially by men newly arrived in the Latin East, was to bring their weight to bear in a massed charge. This could be effective if well-timed, but it was also an inflexible tactic. All too often the Turkish light horsemen withdrew or dispersed before impact, only to re-engage with archery from a distance when the crusaders had come to a disordered halt, their horses blown and vulnerable. The Turks accepted close combat, with lance, sword, and mace, only when a decisive advantage had been gained.

The equestrian cultures of the military elites of both Christendom and its enemies had a profound influence on the organization of war and the conduct of campaigns during the middle ages. In Western Europe the mobilization of native military aristocracies, or the employment of mercenaries, tended to give rise to relatively small armies. These, as we find with the *familia regis* of the Anglo-Norman kings, the White Company in fourteenth-century Italy, or the brethren of the Teutonic Order in Livonia and Prussia could be highly effective, professional fighting units, capable of rapid movement and independent action. Alternatively, the military elite could provide a heavy cavalry core to a larger army, with massed infantry back-up. In the case of France, this 'core' might well be large: in September 1340, Philip VI may have had as many as 28,000 men-at-arms in various theatres of war. No other Western prince could call on such numbers. The only way for an English king to raise so large an army was to draw heavily on infantry. For the Falkirk campaign of 1298, Edward I's 3,000 heavy cavalry were accompanied by over 25,700 foot soldiers. Troops recruited, perhaps forcibly, from the common population might well be poorly equipped and lacking in either discipline or experience of war; but, equally, the presence of infantry did bring some military advantages. The usefulness of foot soldiers in siege work is self-evident. Moreover, heavy cavalry and infantry—including archers—could be combined to tactical advantage on the battlefield. Indeed, it was standard practice to do so, although such cooperation did not guarantee success. We should not forget that the French began their attack at Crécy with Genoese crossbowmen, and that the English tried, in vain, to deploy their archers at Bannockburn.

For all their potential in siege or battle, the employment of foot soldiers

Comēt le grant pouple bataillerent acōtre le iour de iugemēt par orguil e par envie e par coveitise.

Coment le cōmoune gent. checun leva acōtre autre e vou dra autre ocire p̄ le aver, pur lu
rise. E ceo est dunt nous esperoims breu q̄ le iour de dreit iugemēt for mēt aproche.

would have serious consequences for campaign mobility: the true *chevauchée* could only be conducted by horsemen. One solution to this problem was to supplement the military elite with light cavalry or mounted infantry. Perhaps the most colourful light cavalry to be deployed in Western Europe were the stradiots from Dalmatia, Albania, and Greece, who were recruited by Venice to fight the Turks and introduced to the Italian peninsula after 1479. Lightly armed, with breast-plate and shield, light lance and crossbow, and mounted on swift, hardy, little horses (which were 'all good Turkish ones', relates Philippe de Commynes), they were ferocious fighters and became notorious for their practice of headhunting for monetary reward. Apparently less barbaric was the English *hobelar*, or lightly armed lancer, who emerged during the Scottish Wars of Independence, and the mounted archer, who first appears in the records in the early 1330s. The mounted archer's hackney was relatively inexpensive, costing about £1, but it enabled the potency of the bowman's missile weapon, used alongside dismounted men-at-arms in disciplined tactical formations, to be combined with mobility away from the battlefield. Mounting a bowman for transport was not a wholly new idea; mounted crossbowmen, and occasionally mounted archers, are to be found in the armies of the Angevin kings, for example. The innovation lay in the scale with which it was done by Edward III and his successors, with a ratio of two, three, or more mounted archers for each man-at-arms commonplace during the Hundred Years War.

Indigenous horse archers in the oriental mould were absent from Western Europe. The isolated images of individual horse archers in Western sources—such as the last scene in the Bayeux Tapestry, depicting the pursuit, and Matthew Paris's illustration of the battle of Bouvines (1214)—are little more than enigmatic curiosities, while those in the mid-thirteenth-century Maciejowski Bible are firmly associated with the forces of evil (who are also equipped with round shields), apparently reflecting knowledge of Islamic armies. The celebrated English archer of the Hundred Years War dismounted before drawing his bowstring. Apart from the practical difficulties of using a long-staved bow from the saddle, few English yeomen would have possessed the horse-handling skills required to shoot at the gallop. The English bowmen employed at Törcsvár in Transylvania towards the end of Louis the Great's reign would, therefore, have been mounted archers in the Western European

Heavy cavalry and infantry. The Day of Judgement in the Holkham Bible Picture Book (*c.*1325–1330) distinguishes the mounted, knightly mêlée of 'le grant pouple' from the foot combat of 'le commoune gent'. The costly horses and equipment of the military elite set them apart from lightly armed infantry; but success on the battlefield would often depend upon the tactical combination of mounted men and foot soldiers.

sense; but it was in this part of Europe that the equestrian skills required for horse archery still flourished. Admittedly, in the aftermath of the Magyars' defeat at the battle of the Lech in 955 and following German involvement in the foundation of the Christian kingdom, Western-style mailed cavalry formed the core of Hungarian armies. Yet the employment of steppe peoples—the Pechenegs, Szeklers, and Cumans—as auxiliary light cavalry gave Hungarian armies a distinctive, hybrid character and a tactical edge. The advantages of tactical combination of heavy cavalry and horse archers were displayed with decisive results at the battle of Dürnkrut (Marchfield) in 1278, when the Hungarian armoured cavalry and their Cuman auxiliaries played an important part in Emperor Rudolf I's momentous victory. This hybrid military system was further developed under Louis the Great. His Italian adventures in the 1340s and 1350s were pursued with armies composed of 'lances', each of which consisted of a heavily armoured man-at-arms and a group of lightly equipped horse archers. In the later fifteenth century, it was light cavalry (the original 'hussars') who provided the rapid reaction forces which backed-up Hungary's southern frontier fortifications and launched raids (*portyák*) into Ottoman territory. So dominant was light cavalry in King Matthias Corvinus's army that the capabilities and limitations of these troops effectively determined the way in which that army fought.

Armies wholly composed of mounted men offered strategic opportunities which were inconceivable for those reliant on infantry. The English *chevauchées* in France during the fourteenth century achieved an impact disproportionate to the size of the armies involved, while the Mongols' devastating assault on eastern Europe in 1241–2, meticulously planned and executed with remarkable coordination, is surely the ultimate medieval Blitzkrieg by horsepower.

This depiction of an incident from the legend of St Ladislas in the Illuminated Chronicle (*c.*1360) provides a glimpse of the Hungarian armies of the reign of Louis the Great (1342–1382). Western-style knightly warriors are supported by lightly equipped mounted archers, apparently of Cumanian or Iasian origin. Note the use of composite bows.

Towns, castles, and river crossings could be taken by surprise by a mounted force, just as besieged garrisons could be more rapidly relieved. Yet armies so dependent on the horse tended to be less adept at siege warfare. Indeed, *chevauchée*-style warfare encouraged fortification. The flame of Hungarian resistance to the Mongols was maintained in a handful of stone fortresses, while the energy of many an English expedition in France was sapped by the frustrations of siege warfare. The military possibilities of mobile, mounted armies were also limited to some degree by logistical constraints. Although usually small by later standards, such armies still required large numbers of horses. Apart from his primary warhorse, a knight would need a good remount, a palfrey for riding on the march, a rouncey for his servant, and one or more sumpters for his baggage. The fifteenth-century 'lance', a team of men servicing the needs of a man-at-arms, would demand even more horses. Keeping this large pool of equines well-fed and healthy would have been a major preoccupation for a medieval commander; campaigning in winter could pose particularly severe problems. A plentiful supply of water was specially important, since a horse needs at least four gallons a day. So desperately short of water were the English during a *chevauchée* in 1355 that they gave their horses wine to drink, with results which can easily be imagined.

For hardiness, no Western European warhorses could rival those of the Mongols. These stocky, gelded ponies were capable of sixty miles a day, yet unlike Western European warhorses, which required regular supplies of grain, Mongol mounts could subsist on grazing. They were even able to find grass under a layer of snow. Yet their horses were, in a sense, the Mongols' Achilles heel. Each warrior needed a string of remounts and while huge herds of horses could easily be sustained on the grasslands of the Mongolian steppe, the available pasture to the west of the Great Hungarian Plain was insufficient to maintain the nomadic war machine. The strategy of the horse peoples was, therefore, always likely to be hampered by the constraints of pasture in Europe. River passage posed less of a problem to the Mongols; they were only temporarily held up by the mighty Danube and crossed when it froze over. Nor did their expeditions depend upon solving that other major logistical problem for medieval commanders: how to transport horses by sea.

Developing solutions to that problem had long been a central feature of warfare between Mediterranean states, but the crusading era brought with it a pressing demand for horse-transports which were suitable for long-haul voyages. By the mid-twelfth century, warhorses might be shipped in round-bottomed sailing vessels or in flat-bottomed, oared *tarides*. The largest of the round ships provided ample capacity (an 800-ton ship could carry 100 horses), but were deep-water vessels, requiring wharf facilities for unloading. The carrying capacity of *tarides* was smaller (twenty to forty mounts), but offered the invaluable advantage of allowing horses to be beach-landed through the stern. Where northern waters are concerned, it is Duke William of Normandy's large-scale shipping of warhorses to England in 1066 which immediately springs to mind. According to the Bayeux Tapestry, the horses were carried in open-decked longships. On arrival, the ships were tilted over on the beach to allow the horses to step over the gunwales. However, in order to appreciate the problems involved in the regular transportation of large numbers of horses, we should turn our attention to the Hundred Years War. Since the English war effort hinged on the transportation of armies to the Continent, and their strategy of *chevauchées* depended on mounted forces, it was necessary to ship thousands of horses every time that a major expedition was launched. An Exchequer record tells us, for example, that 8,464 horses were taken to France in 1370 in Sir Robert Knolles's expeditionary force—an army which had a contractual strength of 2,000 men-at-arms and 2,000 mounted archers. Given that a typical horse-transport vessel, a cog, could carry thirty equines, the shipping of even a moderately sized army would involve a fleet of several hundred ships. The majority were requisitioned merchantmen, many of which had to be refitted to carry horses. Not surprisingly, it was often difficult to raise sufficient numbers of vessels. Indeed, it seems likely that such logistical constraints operated as a check on army size. But if we find the English acquiring horses upon arrival in France, as was often the case with expeditions to Gascony, that may have been prompted as much by anxiety over the effects of long-haul voyages as by shipping shortages. Quite apart from the losses sustained in bad weather, a combination of insufficient water, inappropriate diet, muscle wastage and mental stress would have left horses debilitated, vulnerable to disease, and generally unfit for immediate service.

If the warhorse separated the aristocratic warrior symbolically from his social inferiors, so too did his armour, whether hauberk or full harness of plate, and his weapons, particularly his lance and sword. But behind the symbolism lay a real military advantage; and with arms and armour, as in the conduct of war, it was the equestrian warrior who was at the centre of developments. Most advances in protective equipment and weaponry were either servicing his needs or intended as challenges to his tactical authority.

It was noted earlier that the mounted *miles* began to adopt the couched lance technique in the later eleventh century. At this time, as can be seen in the Bayeux Tapestry, such a warrior was equipped with a long, knee-length hauberk composed of interlinked rings, slit front and back to facilitate riding and worn over a padded undergarment. Such a mailshirt would probably have weighed about 25 lbs, which could not be regarded as excessively heavy, nor likely to restrict freedom of movement. The *miles* wore a conical helmet, with nasal, over a mail coif or hood. On his left arm he bore a large, kite-shaped shield, while in his right hand he carried the lance, about nine to ten feet in length and fashioned from ash or applewood. While many of the mounted *milites* of the Bayeux Tapestry are shown with lances, some are wielding the straight, double-edged sword, that most noble of weapons, which combined military utility with powerful symbolism. Associated with Rhineland sword makers, the crucial change in sword design had occurred in the ninth century, with the emergence of elegantly tapered blades, which shifted the centre of gravity from the point to the hilt, thereby greatly improving the handling qualities of the weapon. At Hastings, then, a high-quality knightly sword would have been light (2 to 3 lbs) and well balanced, and a formidable weapon when wielded from the elevated position of a warhorse's back. Beyond its function as a weapon, the sword was a symbol of the military elite's power and lordship, with a mystical quality which derived from the fusion of pagan and Christian ritual. That so many medieval swords have been found in rivers and lakes cannot be attributed to carelessness; rather it tells that the legend of Excalibur was based on living practices recalling the pre-Christian past which persisted long after the knight's sword had become an essential part of the religious ceremonial of chivalry.

The varied available sources, including seals, illuminated manuscripts, and sculpture, suggest that the knight's equipment changed comparatively little during the twelfth century. The most significant developments, during the second half of the century, were the appearance of mail mittens and the long surcoat (or 'coat armour') worn over the mail shirt, the widespread use of chausses (mail leggings), and experimentation with helmet design, which led in the early thirteenth century to the great helm, which was worn over the coif and padded arming cap. In its early form, the helm was usually cylindrical and flat-topped. It offered better protection, particularly against missile weapons, but restricted visibility and ventilation. Shield design was also undergoing some change. Having become triangular-shaped by the early thirteenth century, shields were gradually reduced in size as that century progressed.

The essentials of the transition from twelfth-century mail harness to the fully developed plate armour of the fifteenth century may be briskly summarized. Iron plate or hardened leather defences for the elbows, knees, and shins first appeared in the mid-thirteenth century, and during the following hundred and fifty years protection for arms and hands, legs and feet became steadily more complete. From the mid- to late thirteenth century, the torso of a well-equipped knight would be protected by a surcoat of cloth or leather lined with

Left: the great seal of Henry III (1216–1272) shows a typically equipped knight after the adoption of the great helm and surcoat, but before the advent of plate armour for the torso or limbs. The elegance and poise of the king's warhorse reflects the words of Jordanus Ruffus, a mid-thirteenth-century veterinary surgeon: 'No animal is more noble than the horse, since it is by horses that princes, magnates and knights are separated from lesser people'.

Right: the seal of Stephen the junior king of Hungary suggests that the equipment of the western European knight and his straight-legged posture on the back of a massively-built, yet elegant, warhorse had become firmly established in the kingdom of the Magyars by the 1260s. The ethos of western chivalry was less readily adopted by the Hungarian nobility, rooted as they were in the archaic traditions of their nomadic past.

metal plates—a coat of plates, which by the mid- to late fourteenth century would be supplemented, or wholly replaced, by a solid breast-plate. Underneath, a mail haubergeon continued to be worn, while it was still usual to wear coat armour on the outside, although there was much local variation in this. In England, for example, the surcoat was replaced by the short, tight-fitting jupon. Meanwhile, in the early to mid-fourteenth century, the visored bascinet with attached mail aventail to protect the neck was replacing the round-topped great helm and coif for practical campaigning purposes. Visors came in a variety of forms. The simplest, common in Germany and Italy, consisted of a nasal which when not hooked to the brow of the bascinet would hang from the aventail at the chin. Often, indeed, men fought in bascinets without any form of visor. With the development of a fully articulated harness of plate armour, the abandonment of the now largely redundant shield, and the stripping away of the fabric which hitherto had customarily covered the metal, we have reached the 'white' armour of the early to mid-fifteenth century. The emergence of plate armour also prompted a change in the knight's *arme blanche*. The sword with a flat blade, which provided an effective cutting edge against mail, was gradually replaced during the fourteenth century by one with a stiffer blade tapering to an acute, often reinforced point, designed for a thrusting action against plate armour.

Unless provided by a lord or patron, or possibly in fulfilment of a local community's military obligations, the equipment of an aspiring man-at-arms would be his own responsibility. Although the mass-produced plate armour of the later middle ages may have been relatively less expensive than the mail hauberks of earlier centuries, equipping for war from scratch remained a costly business. Consequently, the quality of a man's arms and armour would have offered as clear an indication of his place in the social hierarchy of the military elite as the value of his warhorse. Much of the surviving evidence depicts the up-to-date harness of well-heeled noblemen; but, in reality, warfare in fourteenth-century Europe involved a heterogenous multitude of noble *juvenes* without prospects and sub-genteel free lances, many of whom would have fought in armour of uneven quality. Some, indeed, would have had second-hand, or even hired, harness, acquired from such international arms merchants as Francesco di Marco Datini. Fortunately, unlike warhorses, which were all too prone to disease or

The memorial brass of Sir Hugh Hastings (d.1347) in Elsing church, Norfolk. With flanking figures representing some of Hastings' companions in arms, this is an intriguingly varied ensemble of body armour from the mid-fourteenth century. Note the visored bascinets, the skirted jupons, a curiously shaped kettle hat (bottom right), a pole-axe (bottom left) and the mounted figure of St George above Hastings' head.

injury, armour would need to be purchased only occasionally; and to judge from will bequests and inventories, even gentry families were often in possession of substantial armories. Of all knightly equipment, a sword might have the most varied 'life story', passing through many hands, by purchase, bequest, gift, or seizure, its blade honed and re-hilted according to necessity and taste, perhaps coming to rest finally in a church, a grave, or a river.

While it may be tempting to attribute the emergence of iron plate armour to advances in technology, this would be unconvincing, since the skills required to produce such armour had existed in Western Europe since the eleventh and twelfth centuries. Rather, the transformation of the man-at-arms' body armour during the later middle ages should be viewed as a response to the challenges of the battlefield. The defeat of heavy cavalry by armies fighting on foot was one of the most striking features of warfare during the early to mid-fourteenth century; indeed, some historians have identified an 'infantry revolution' in these events. This is not to deny that infantry had long shown its mettle against cavalry—as when the hedge of pikes of the Lombard communal militia successfully resisted the assault of the imperial heavy cavalry at Legnano (1176) and Cortenuova (1237). Effective military operations in the Latin East, as for example the celebrated march from Acre to Jaffa in August–September 1191, depended upon close cooperation between heavy cavalry and foot soldiers, the latter screening the knights and their vulnerable warhorses, with crossbowmen keeping Turkish horse archers at a distance. Yet what we see at the turn of the fourteenth century is something rather different: armies built around foot soldiers, with little or no involvement for aristocratic warriors, and bound together by a solidarity founded upon common purpose and high morale. Armies of this kind triumphed repeatedly over the flower of European chivalry, with the trend being set at Courtrai (1302), Bannockburn (1314), and Mortgarten (1315). The vividly carved scenes on the Courtrai chest show the Flemish communal armies as well-equipped foot soldiers, uniformed, and fighting beneath guild banners. A wealth of pictorial evidence suggests that the urban militias of Italy were equipped to a similar standard. With the Scots and Swiss, however, we find smaller armies drawn in the main from the men of the countryside, peasant infantry fighting in the cause of independence. A front-line Scottish pikeman might have been equipped in mail haubergeon or quilted aketon, with an iron cap or kettle hat, and gauntlets, but most of those behind him in the schiltrom would have lacked body armour.

How was it that such armies were able to inflict bloody and humiliating defeats on the knightly elite? On occasion the explanation is to be found in a well-timed ambush. The rout of Charles I's Hungarian army by the Wallachians in the defile at Posada in November 1330 is reminiscent of the battle of Mortgarten, in which the Swiss ambushed a column of Austrian heavy cavalry-men in a mountain pass, butchering them 'like sheep in the shambles'. Even in set-piece battles, choice of ground and effective exploitation of it were usually important. That long-established ruse, the digging of ditches or pits to impede the deployment of cavalry, proved effective at Courtrai, Bannockburn, and elsewhere, while at Kephissos in 1311, the Catalan Company took up position behind a marsh. But also essential were well-ordered tactical formations, disciplined, resolute demeanour, and the use of effective weaponry. The arms which brought success were essentially a response to the heavy cavalry of the military elite. The Scots' schiltroms were hedgehog-like formations, impenetrable thickets of pikes, and capable of offensive movement against armoured cavalry. In addition to pikes, the Flemings had the *goedendag*, the Swiss, the halberd: both were long-handled weapons designed for striking men-at-arms in the saddle and pulling them to the ground.

The battle of Posada, 1330. Lured into a defile in the southern Carpathians, Charles I's Hungarian army, depicted here as consisting of mounted knights, are ambushed and heavily defeated by Wallachians wielding no more than rocks and composite bows.

Much has been written about the impact of English archery in the fourteenth century, and for some historians this forms a central feature of the 'infantry revolution'. It is not that archery was a new feature of warfare. Nor, indeed, does the evidence suggest that Edwardian bows had staves significantly longer than those used in the past (the point being that the longer the bow, the greater its potential power). What made English archery so devastating in the fourteenth century was the sheer numbers of bowmen employed, the English crown having successfully exploited the native pool of countrymen skilled with the bow. Massed archery by men able to unleash perhaps a

The battle of Shrewsbury, 1403: one of the lively, well-observed scenes from the 'pictorial life' of Richard Beauchamp, earl of Warwick (d.1439). English archers, who had proved so effective in the French wars, are here deployed by both sides, whilst the knights and esquires of Henry IV's army, having remounted for the pursuit, employ couched lances.

dozen shafts per minute would produce an arrow storm, which at ranges of up to 200 yards left men clad in mail and early plate armour, and particularly horses, vulnerable to injury, while causing confusion and loss of order in attacking formations. As plate armour became more complete, a bodkin-headed arrow was developed to pierce it. Far from being left behind by advances in armour technology, the English archer, particularly if mounted, had become a versatile fighting man who could make a living out of soldiering. His bow was inexpensive; although the best were made from imported Spanish or Italian yew, they could be bought for a shilling. The archer's body armour was usually quite light—a brigandine or padded jerkin, with an open-fronted bascinet or kettle hat—but he was capable of participating effectively in mêlées if necessary.

For all the potency of the English longbow from the mid-fourteenth century, the crossbow had a longer-term influence on medieval warfare and may well have been the principal stimulus behind the emergence of the great helm and the development of plate armour in the thirteenth century. It had been known and widely used from the mid-eleventh century. During the thirteenth century the improved, composite crossbow spread throughout Europe; thereafter it was the most important missile weapon in many parts of Christendom. Although not a fast-shooting weapon, and perhaps more suited to siege warfare than the battlefield, it was powerful and versatile, and was also less dependent than the longbow on physical strength and lengthy training. Mail offered little protection against crossbow bolts (quarrels) and given that the steel crossbows of the fifteenth century could have a draw weight of 1,000 lbs (the string being pulled by means of a windlass), it is likely that the crossbow maintained its position as a penetrative weapon against plate armour rather more successfully than the longbow.

Despite the efforts of pikeman and archer, the emergence of potent, infantry-based armies in various parts of Europe in the fourteenth and fifteenth centuries did not dislodge the aristocratic warrior from the battlefield. In part, this was due to flexibility of tactical response. One solution was to abandon warhorses and fight on foot, thereby reducing vulnerability to missile weapons, while stiffening fighting resolve. This is what the Milanese did with success at Arbedo in 1422 when faced by a phalanx of Swiss pikemen. There had been a long tradition of such methods in England, from the shield-wall at Hastings to the battles of the Standard in 1138 and Lincoln in 1141; and after a long intermission, the tactical combination of dismounted men-at-arms and archers was revived during the reign of Edward III. Such tactics were well suited to the war in France where numerical inferiority usually necessitated a defensive posture. In the face of Flemish and English tactics, the French knightly elite responded by fighting on foot, but lacking effective supporting bowmen or pikemen, and often obliged to attack on unfavourable ground, these experiments almost invariably led to defeat, on occasion with disastrous results, as at Poitiers (1356), Nicopolis (1396), and Agincourt (1415).

For some historians, the survival of the heavily armoured, equestrian warrior in later medieval Europe can be explained by reference to the supposed social prejudice and military inflexibility of the aristocracy; but a more convincing explanation would focus on improvements in armour and equipment. The production of iron and steel plate armour with improved tensile strength and tested for resistance to crossbow bolts at close range, and with skilfully designed glancing surfaces, to resist pike, arrow and lance, enhanced the man-at-arms' security. Although uncomfortable in hot weather, the full plate armour of the fifteenth century did not significantly affect mobility, since the weight of such armour—a complete harness might weigh 50 to 60 lbs—was more evenly distributed than a coat of mail, and would probably be less than the combination of mail and plate commonly worn in the fourteenth century. By 1450 plate defences for a man-at-arms' horse had extended beyond the head and chest to provide as complete a protective cover as was practicable, although, given that this might weigh 60 to 70 lbs, such harness called for strong horses and a ready supply of remounts. By the mid-fifteenth century there were clear stylistic contrasts between northern Italian 'classical' and southern German 'gothic' armours, no doubt reflecting their different cultural roots, but also the different military contexts. The mounted combat of Italian *condottieri* was best served by smooth, rounded plates, designed to deflect sword and lance, while the greater threat of longbow and crossbow north of the Alps prompted armour with grooved, rippled surfaces. Similarly, choice from the various new forms of helmet which replaced the visored bascinet in the fifteenth century appears to have depended on expected battlefield conditions. The sallet, particularly the long-tailed, 'sou'-wester' form, was preferred by the English, French, and Burgundians, while the barbuta (having a T-shaped face opening) and armet (a visored helmet) were favoured in Italy.

The development of full plate armour for both man and horse, combined with the use of the *arrêt de cuirasse*—a bracket on the breast-plate to support a heavier lance,

South German armour, *c.*1475–1485. Protected by such plate armour, the man-at-arms and his warhorse were less vulnerable to pike thrusts and projectile weapons. But his elite military function depended on the support of his *lance*, which in 1470s Burgundy consisted of a page, an armed servant, and three archers, all mounted, together with a crossbowman, a hand-gunner, and a pike-man.

ensured that the heavy cavalryman in the fifteenth century remained a formidable warrior when intelligently employed. Most obviously this might involve using cavalry in concert with archers and pikemen; at the very least, the mobility of horsemen at the end of a battle could convert a marginal advantage into a decisive victory. Another possibility was the piecemeal commitment of squadrons in rotation, to maintain battlefield control and a steady supply of fresh troops, a tactic made famous by the *condottiere*, Braccio, as at San Egidio in 1416. It was this continuing tactical potency, combined with the strategic possibilities offered by horsemen, which explains why most major Continental armies of this period, including the newly established permanent armies of France, Burgundy, Milan, and Venice, were built around heavily armoured mounted warriors. More than half of the French army which began the Italian war in 1494 consisted of heavy cavalry. Even the Hungarian army of Matthias Corvinus, dominated as it was by light cavalry, had a substantial core of heavily armoured cavalrymen, who formed about 10 per cent of the 28,000 men at the Wiener Neustadt review of 1486.

It was only during the sixteenth century that the balance of advantage on the battlefield swung decisively against heavy cavalry. Among the forces for change were more effective hand-held firearms and field artillery. Early cannon had occasionally been used on fourteenth-century battlefields, as in Sir John Hawkwood's ambush of the Veronese at Castagnaro in 1387; but slow rate of fire, modest range, and immobility severely limited the effectiveness of such weapons, which seemed more suited to field fortifications than *chevauchées*. Greater mobility, at least for the march, was achieved by the Hussites, who mounted their cannon on carts. For battle, however, these guns were dug-in, being incorporated into the Hussites' distinctive wagon-forts (*Wagenburgs*), which were mobile field fortifications formed out of wagons and manned by handgunners, crossbowmen, and men wielding chain flails (see also Chapter 7, p. 158). The Hussites were admittedly something of a military anomaly, but by the mid-fifteenth century cannon and handguns were beginning to make their mark on battlefields across Europe. At Caravaggio in 1448, the smoke from Francesco Sforza's Milanese handgunners was said to have obscured the battlefield. (In Italy at least, it seems that low cost and ease of use lay behind the replacement of the crossbow by the handgun.) In the same year, gunpowder weapons played a prominent part in the battle of Kosovo Polje. János Hunyadi's Hungarian army, well equipped with firearms, inflicted heavy casualties on Murad II's Ottoman host before, at last, being overwhelmed by weight of numbers.

It is perhaps appropriate to end this chapter with the titanic confrontation between two peoples who had originated as horse-borne nomads of the steppe and who, in their different ways, had sought to adapt to the changing technology of war. It was the Ottomans who were to be the more successful in realizing the tactical potential of hand-held guns and field artillery, for their decisive triumphs over the Egyptian Mamlukes at Marj Dabiq (1515) and Raydaniya (1516), and the Hungarians at Mohács (1526) rested on the effective deployment of firepower, as part of a truly formidable military machine. At Mohács, the Hungarian heavy cavalry was halted by the professional corps of handgun-wielding foot soldiers, the janissaries, backed-up by field artillery: a defeat, taking little more than two hours, which was in effect the destruction of a medieval army by an early modern one. The mounted warrior of the middle ages had finally been brought down by the forces of the future.

10 MERCENARIES

MICHAEL MALLETT

THE oft-quoted remark of Richard Fitz Neal in his preface to the *Dialogus de Scaccario* about the supreme importance of money in war has been shown by J. O. Prestwich to have been as much a commonplace in 1179 when he wrote it as it seems today. 'Money appears necessary not only in time of war but also in peace' Richard wrote, adding that 'in war it is poured out in fortifying castles, in soldiers' wages, and in numerous other ways, depending on the nature of the persons paid, for the preservation of the kingdom.' This was his way of explaining the central position of the Exchequer in the wars of Henry II. It introduces us to a concept of paid military service which was already clearly established in his day alongside more traditional concepts of military obligation. However, this chapter is not just about paid military service; the introduction of pay in various guises may have aroused the envy and suspicions of the feudal class, and the wrath of the Church, but it was not generally a matter of either surprise or despite by the eleventh century. Early examples of pay took many forms: money fiefs, supplements to obligatory service, subsistence allowances, rewards, and indeed pay to attract service, pay to create profit. It is the concept of fighting for profit, together with the gradual emergence of a concept of 'foreignness', which distinguish the true mercenary, the subject of this chapter, from the ordinary paid soldier.

Hence the problem is not just one of assessing the growth of the money economy, the accumulation of treasure, the raising of war taxes, the development of scutage (a payment in lieu of personal service), and other forms of commutation. Indeed as paid military service became a standard feature of European warfare by the end of the thirteenth century, these factors have to be taken for granted and form part of a quite different study. It is the motivation of mercenaries, soldiers who fought for profit and not in the cause of their native land or lord, and the circumstances and nature of their employment that we have to try to identify.

Here it is not profitable to spend too much time on the vexed question of the perception of who was a 'foreigner'. The emergence of independent and increasingly centrally administered states where distinctions between local, 'national', 'own' troops, and 'foreign' troops became gradually apparent has also to be accepted without too much attempt at further definition. War itself was a primary factor in creating the distinctions and encouraging the patriotism and xenophobia which led to a certain suspicion of 'foreign' troops. Even so, the distinction between foreign and native forces is not always sharp: the occasional repressive actions of centralizing governments were sometimes best supported and carried out by 'foreign' troops when their loyalty was deemed more to be relied on than that of subjects.

Both supply of money and the changing needs of government are demand factors; what we need to examine more carefully at the start of a study of medieval mercenaries are rather supply factors. What did mercenaries have to offer? The answer in this period was not just general military expertise and experience, but increasingly specialist skills, particularly of infantry. It was the growing sophistication of warfare which created the mercenary, together with a series of local environmental factors which made certain specific areas good recruiting grounds for soldiers. Underemployment, whether in a pastoral economy or in a rapidly expanding city, has to be a part of the equation.

But at the heart of the equation is the problem of loyalty. Mercenaries, in the middle ages as now, stand accused of fragile loyalty, loyalty dependent entirely on regular and often extravagant pay, and a concern for personal survival. But the middle ages saw a very clear distinction between the loyalty of the errant adventurer or the free company, and the loyalty of the household knight or the long-serving bodyguard. The real categorization of mercenaries is one of length of service; long service established personal bonds just as strong as those between vassal and lord; it created commitments as binding as those of emerging patriotism and nationality, once again blurring any tidy distinction between native and foreigner.

The central theme of this chapter is that, while mercenary service, in terms of service for pay, became increasingly accepted and organized from at least the middle of the eleventh century, there was a real change in the perception of the issue from the later thirteenth century. This had little to do with economic growth, much more to do with changes in the nature of society, of government, and of warfare. The thirteenth century was a period in which the universality of the Church, of crusading, of the early universities, of the widespread use of Latin, was giving way to the creation of more local identities and loyalties, to concern with frontiers and problems of long-term defence, to vernaculars and lay culture. The monopoly of military skills held in the central middle ages by select bodies of aristocratic cavalry was being challenged by the emergence of mass infantry, often with new specialist skills, and of concepts of more general military obligation. The thirteenth century is the period in which the mercenary became distinguished by his foreignness and his expertise; and it is on this period and that which followed it that I shall concentrate most attention, avoiding, however, the exaggerations of the hallowed generalization of the 'age of the mercenary'!

While it is probably true that elements of hired military service survived throughout the early middle ages, the main characteristics of the barbarian tribes which came to dominate Western Europe with the decline of the Roman Empire were the bonds of personal obligation and dependence within societies organized for war. As conditions eventually became more settled in the eleventh century, we hear increasingly of forms of selective service, of commutation of obligations, and of the maintenance of fighting men by collective contributions. This was particularly true in Anglo-Saxon England. However the Norman enterprises of the mid-eleventh century were something of a turning point. William the Conqueror, in order to assemble a force sufficient for his purposes in the invasion of England relied heavily on volunteers from Brittany, Flanders, Champagne, and even Italy, and the military strength which he maintained in being during the early years of the Conquest was also significantly dependent on paid volunteers. There was indeed eventually a settlement of William's knights on the land and the re-creation of a system of military obligation, but it was never adequate for defence of the realm from significant threat and particularly not for the defence of Normandy. The Anglo-Norman kings came to rely on a permanent military household made up partly of royal vassals in constant attendance and partly of volunteers, often landless younger sons of feudatories, who were maintained by the King and generously rewarded after any military action. Significant numbers of these household knights came from outside the bounds of the Anglo-Norman state. It was the household, the *familia regis* that provided the core and the leadership of the armies of William I and William II, the latter in particular being described as 'militum mercator et solidator' (a great buyer and purveyor of soldiers). A particular moment which is often cited by the main authorities on this particular period of military activity was the treaty of 1101 by which Count Robert of Flanders undertook to provide Henry I with

The Bayeux tapestry illustrates William the Conqueror's knights at the Battle of Hastings (1066). Many of these were mercenaries, attracted into Norman service from outside the duchy, who made up the core of William's cavalry.

1,000 Flemish knights for service in England and Normandy. These knights were to be incorporated temporarily into the royal household and maintained by Henry at his own expense; this was already an indication of the potential size of the household in arms. Count Robert was to receive a fee of £500 for providing these troops which places him in the role of a very early military contractor.

There is a good deal less evidence of such use of volunteers and paid troops by the early Capetian kings whose sphere of influence and military potential were a good deal less than those of the Normans. However in the Holy Roman Empire the same pressures to supplement the limited obligation for military service were being felt by the Emperors, particularly in campaigns in Italy. With the twelfth century came the Crusades, offering an outlet to military adventurism and at the same time prompting a greater concern amongst Western European monarchs to husband and nourish their military households. It was Henry I of England's military household which in 1124 at Bourgthéroulde defeated a Norman baronial rebellion, an event which provides us with a classic contemporary distinction, in the words of the chronicler Orderic Vitalis, between the hireling knights of the King fighting for their reputation and their wages, and the Norman nobility fighting for their honour.

At Bourgthéroulde, despite Orderic's attempt to portray the royal troops as 'peasants and common soldiers', the battle was clearly still one between mounted knights. But the hiring of infantry became an increasingly common feature of twelfth-century military practice. Louis VII, as he began to gather together the threads of central authority in France hired crossbowmen, and the civil wars of Stephen's reign in England were filled with the activities of both cavalry and infantry mercenaries.

By the mid-twelfth century the sustained use of royal household troops, particularly in the exercise of government central power in both France and the Anglo-Norman empire, the proliferation of castles and of siege warfare, and the growth of urban populations, all pointed towards a growing role for infantry in the warfare of the day. It was the use of infantry that could expand the size of armies beyond the narrow limits of the feudal class; it was infantry that could storm cities and bring sieges to an abrupt end. It was also small companies of infantry that provided the long-serving paid garrisons of castles. A clear role for the mercenary was beginning to define itself.

It is not clear whether the companies of infantry mercenaries which became a feature of the warfare of the second half of the twelfth century emerged as a result of expanding population and underemployment or whether royal initiative and deliberate recruitment was the key factor. Certainly they were seen by contemporaries in two quite different ways: on the one hand, they were denounced as brigands and outlaws, roving in ill-disciplined bands to despoil the countryside and brutalize the population; on the other, they appear as effective and coherent military units, led by increasingly prestigious captains and often provided with uniform equipment and arms by royal officials. The phenomenon was clearly a mixed one, and the same company, led by a Mercadier or a Cadoc, could give useful, indeed invaluable, service if properly paid and directed, and yet become a disorderly and dangerous rabble when out of employment and beyond the reach of royal justice. The names given to these companies—Brabançons, Aragonais, Navarrais, and 'Cotteraux'—reveal their tendency to originate in the poorer rural areas and on the fringes of the Flemish cities. The last name is thought to originate either from their lowly status (cotters) or from their use of the dagger (couteau) rather than the sword. Certainly the non-feudal nature of their employment and status is clear, and the increasing use by the companies of the bow and the crossbow added to the fear and despite which they aroused.

Henry II used these troops extensively in his French lands, both to suppress baronial revolt and to ward off the growing pressures from the Capetian kings. It was quickly clear that he could not expect effective service from his English knights across the Channel, except on a voluntary basis, and so the levying of scutage became a standard feature of his financial administration and the means by which the mercenaries were paid. However Louis VII and, particularly, Philippe Augustus also quickly learnt the value of the companies, and the Emperors too began to employ Brabançons in their campaigns in Italy and eastern France. The problem was that even the Anglo-Norman state did not have the resources to maintain the companies in times of peace and truce, and so there was an endless process of short-term employment and often longer term dismissal with all the implications of this for the security of the countryside. The outcry of the Church and the ban on the employment of mercenary companies at the 3rd Lateran Council in 1179 had little practical effect as long as the service they gave was useful. But monarchs did learn that such service was most effectively directed outside their frontiers, so as to avoid both the worst impact of demobilization and the growing dislike of their subjects for such troops. Henry II is thought to have used the Continental companies only once in England on a significant scale, in 1174; John, on the other hand, aroused bitter criticism for his lack of restraint in this respect.

The role of townsmen as infantry in this period was particularly apparent in Italy but initially in the form of urban militias rather than mercenary companies. The army of the Lombard League which defeated Barbarossa at Legnano in 1176 was in part made up of the militias of the cities of the League, moderately well-trained, undoubtably paid at least living expenses while on campaign, and on this occasion supported by cavalry. The specialist skills which converted elements of these militias into true mercenaries were however already emerging. The use of the crossbow as the main weapon for the defence of galleys led to large numbers of Genoese, Pisans, and Venetians acquiring this skill and, in the case particularly of the Genoese, selling their services abroad. Italy also provides the example of another professional mercenary group in this period, the Saracen archers of Frederick II. The colony of 35,000–40,000 Saracens settled round Lucera by the Emperor provided him and his successors with a skilled force of 5,000–6,000 archers, mostly on foot but some mounted, until 1266, when it was annihilated by the Angevin cavalry at Benevento.

The destruction of the Saracens coincided with a sharp decline in the role elsewhere of the Brabançons and other mercenary companies of the period. These relatively small infantry companies, rarely more than 1,000 in size, had proved vulnerable to concerted mass attack, and the tendency in Western Europe, by the second half of the thirteenth century, was towards the employment of larger numbers of increasingly professional cavalry and the development of general obligations for military service amongst the populations at large to provide infantry. Detailed studies of Edward I's English armies have been very influential in defining the move towards contractual employment of cavalry companies made up of enfeoffed knights banneret alongside increasing numbers of paid knights bachelor and professional men at arms. Improvements over the next century in armour and weapons, and an emphasis on collective training, ensured that the cavalry remained at the forefront of European armies. On the other hand, the tendency of the late thirteenth century was also towards the use of mass infantry. This was not necessarily at the expense of skills as was illustrated by the effectiveness of the English archers and the Swiss pikemen; but in both these cases a part of their success lay in their use in large, disciplined numbers. Soldiering was becoming a way of life for many foot soldiers as it had long been for the knights. By the fourteenth century, pay was an essential component of this life and also by that time the term 'mercenary' was being reserved for the adventurer and the companies of 'foreign' specialist troops who continued to be sought after. The Hundred Years War between the English and French monarchies was to confirm these trends.

The long series of wars which started in 1337 involved an English crown which still controlled Gascony, and (under Henry V) regained for a time Normandy, and a French crown the authority of which was only grudgingly recognized in many outlying parts of France. Gascons, as subjects of the English crown, appeared in large numbers in English armies throughout the wars, as did Bretons and Flemish who saw themselves as natural allies of England against the pretensions of the French crown. In French armies Normans, Burgundians, Poitevins, and others fought somewhat uneasily side by side, but long experience of such comradeship undoubtedly played a major part in creating a sort of national feeling. The terms 'English' and 'French' became more meaningful as the wars went on. But there was always a role for adventurers, allied auxiliaries, and true mercenaries in the armies. Blind King John of Bohemia and his knights fought at Crécy in the French army as did large companies of Genoese crossbowmen; half of John of Gaunt's captains on his expedition to France in 1373 were 'foreigners', particularly Gascons and Flemings but including three Castillians; Piedmontese knights and Scottish archers fought for Charles VII in the 1420s. However the moments at which mercenaries became particularly apparent were the moments of truce and peace when large parts of the armies were disbanded and the phenomenon of the free company re-emerged. The 1360s, following the peace of Brétigny, was such a moment; mixed companies of English, reluctant to return home, and of French temporarily deprived of royal pay, became adventurers seeking booty and employment. These were essentially footloose companies of professionals led by their natural leaders; more than a hundred such companies

At the Battle of Crecy (1346) Genoese crossbowmen confronted English longbowmen. The Genoese were placed in the vanguard of the advancing French army which put them at an immediate disadvantage. The crossbow was a much more effective weapon in static siege warfare than in the turmoil of a battle.

have been identified and they gravitated first towards Southern France where political authority was weakly established, and then on towards opportunities and possible employment in Italy and Spain. Charles V of France learnt many lessons about the dangers of sudden demobilization and the need to create greater permanence amongst his troops as he struggled to track down and destroy the companies which were ravaging his kingdom. They were lessons which were not easily absorbed and the same problem arose after the peace of Arras in 1435 when the 'Écorcheurs', mostly French by this time, became a threat and prompted Charles VII's better-known *ordonnances* for the organization of a standing army.

The arrival of the foreign companies in Italy and the development of mercenary activity in that area is a very familiar story. It is a story which goes back much further than the fourteenth century and the truces of the Hundred Years War. Early urbanization, the accumulation of wealth in the towns of north and central Italy, and the relative weakness of feudal institutions, all pointed the way towards paid military service at an early stage. As already discussed the towns provided abundant infantry manpower, and the growing rivalries amongst them led to frequent confrontations, skirmishes, and sieges.

The urban militias which conducted these campaigns were provided with subsistence, but it was not long before the escalating local warfare began to create opportunities for more permanent and lucrative employment for hired troops. Rural nobility with their followers, exiles, dispossessed and under-employed peasants, all contributed to a pool of manpower which the urban authorities could call on. The more successful a city was in expanding against and taking over its neighbours, the more it required a system of permanent defence beyond its walls with castles and professional garrisons. The gradual decline of communal republicanism and its replacement by a series of urban lordships or *Signorie* in the later thirteenth century encouraged this process as did the relative weakness by this time of the central authorities of pope and emperor.

A large number of potential employers, abundant wealth both to be earned and looted, pleasant campaigning conditions, these were the attractions of the Italian military scene which began to draw in fighters from other parts of Europe. Italy was also a forming-up point for crusading armies and an objective for Norman, Imperial, and Angevin expeditions many of which left a residue of ultramontane troops ready to exploit the opportunities available. By the end of the thirteenth century the organized mercenary company, operating either as a collective or under the command of a chosen leader, was a common feature.

One of the largest and best-known of these companies, the existence of which spanned the turn of the thirteenth and fourteenth centuries, was the Catalan Company. This formed itself during the wars in Sicily between Aragonese and Angevins, but was partly made up of Almogavars, Aragonese rural troops who had for years earned their living in the border warfare of the Reconquista. After the peace of Caltabellota in 1302 which settled the fate of Sicily, the Company, some 6,000 strong, took service with the Byzantine emperor against the advancing Turks, and in 1311, still in Byzantine service, it overthrew Walter of Brienne, the Duke of Athens, and seized his principality. From this base the Catalans were able to conduct a profitable military activity until 1388.

The story of the Catalan Company was an exceptional, and only initially an Italian, one. However, the fourteenth century did see companies of similar size appearing in the peninsular and often extending their activities over several years. While initially such enterprises often operated on a sort of collective basis, electing their leaders, and deciding on and negotiating contracts with employers through chosen representatives, it was inevitable that successful leaders should emerge to take control and give continuity. The contracts for military service were known as *condotte*, the contractors whose names began to appear on them were the *condottieri*. The service which was contracted for was initially of a very short-term nature. Italian city-states were seeking additional protection or an increment to their strike power for a summer season at the most and often just a matter of weeks. The presence of the companies beyond the moment of immediate need was certainly not encouraged but it was not simple to get them to withdraw, and the inevitable gaps between contracts and the long winter months created the conditions of uncontrolled marauding so often associated with this phase of Italian warfare.

Much of the manpower and the leadership of these companies during the first half of the fourteenth century was non-Italian. Germans were particularly prominent at this stage with the Great Company of Werner von Urslingen appearing in 1342. During the period between 1320 and 1360 over 700 German cavalry leaders have been identified as being active in Italy, and as many as 10,000 men-at-arms. Werner von Urslingen remained the most prominent figure throughout the 1340s when he organized successive companies to manipulate and terrorize the Italian cities. The only solution to this problem of very large companies of well-armed men spending much of their time devastating the countryside was for leagues of cities to pool their resources to resist them. But the political instability of the period made this a rare possibility. By 1347 Werner von Urslingen had new allies in the form of Hungarian troops coming to support the Angevin Queen of Naples, Joanna I, who had married the younger brother of King Louis of Hungary. By the late 1340s other leaders had also emerged; Conrad von Landau, a long-term associate of Werner, now came to the fore, as did the Provençal ex-hospitaller Montreal d'Albarno, known in Italy as Fra Moriale. The union of these three leaders produced the largest company yet seen in Italy which, on behalf of Joanna I, defeated the Neapolitan baronage at Meleto in 1349 and took over half a million florins' worth of booty. This was the beginning of a decade which was dominated by the Great Company of Fra Moriale and Conard von Landau. This company, over 10,000 strong, established a remarkable continuity in these years, holding cities to ransom and creating extraordinary wealth. The execution of Fra Moriale in Rome in 1354 did not disturb this continuity which went on until Conrad's death in 1363. While ultramontane troops, particularly Germans and Hungarians, but increasingly also southern French, continued to dominate in these companies up to the 1360s, it is important also to see strong Italian elements. Members of the Visconti and Ordelaffi families were prominent amongst the leaders of the companies, usually with very specific political agendas to regain control in their native cities. Undoubtedly substantial numbers of Italians fought in the great companies, and some of the smaller companies were predominantly Italian. But, of course, at this time a

Sienese, or a Pisan, or a Bolognese was as much of an enemy to a Florentine as a German was, and possibly more distrusted and feared because of long-standing local rivalries. The depredations of a German company were a temporary phenomenon which could be bought off; those of a rival city-state were aimed either at takeover or at least at economic strangulation.

After 1360 the scene changed as the free companies from the wars in France began to reach Italy. The most prominent of these was the White Company, eventually led by the English knight, John Hawkwood, but initially made up of mixed elements and leaders from the Anglo-French wars. However the White Company was always associated with the English methods of warfare, the use of archers and dismounted men-at-arms giving each other mutual support, and under Hawkwood's leadership it became a highly disciplined and effective force which Italian states became increasingly anxious to employ on a long-term basis.

The last three decades of the fourteenth century were a formative period in the history of mercenary warfare in Italy. The main Italian states were beginning to emerge from the maelstrom of political life in the communal period. As the Visconti gradually established their authority in Milan and western Lombardy, the Florentines extended the control of their city over large parts of central Tuscany. At the same time the Avignon popes were devoting huge resources to restoring order within the Papal States, and Venice was beginning to exert greater influence on the political situation in eastern Lombardy, prior to its decisive moves to establishing formal authority after 1404. The governments of these states were becoming stronger, more organized, better financed; they began to think more seriously about the permanent defence of their larger states. But, given the availability of large professional mercenary companies, of experienced leaders like Hawkwood, and a generation of Italian captains who were emerging in the 1370s, and given also the inevitable reluctance of the governments of the larger states to entrust defence to the untested loyalty of their new subjects, a military system based on extended and better managed contracts to experienced mercenaries became an obvious development. The process was a gradual one; foreign companies began to meet sterner resistance, the wars in France resumed and created counter attractions and obligations, assured pay began to look more attractive than casual booty. At the same time Italian leaders began to emerge strongly; men like Alberigo da Barbiano, Jacopo dal Verme, and Facino Cane saw the advantage of creating semi-permanent links with Giangaleazzo Visconti, just as Hawkwood began to associate himself more and more with Florence.

There was indeed a rapid decline of the foreign companies in the last decades of the fourteenth century. Alberigo da Barbiano's famous victory

The great equestrian fresco of Sir John Hawkwood painted by Paolo Uccello on the north wall of the nave in Florence cathedral *c.*1436, was a tribute to the English captain's long service as Captain General of the Florentine army in the late fourteenth century.

over the Breton companies at Marino in 1379 became a sort of symbol of the recovery of Italian military prowess and of the end of a humiliating and damaging period of dominance by foreign mercenaries. However Alberigo's Company of St George was little different in function or intention from those which preceded it or which it defeated; Italians had played a considerable part in the warfare of the previous decades, and Hawkwood remained for a further fifteen years as the most feared and respected soldier in Italy. His later years were spent largely in the service of Florence with lands, a castle, and a large salary for life provided to encourage his fidelity as captain-general. But he died in 1394 whilst preparing to return to England, leaving behind him a military scene which was in an advanced stage of transition.

The most powerful state in Italy at the turn of the century was undoubtedly the duchy of Milan where Giangaleazzo Visconti had attracted to his service a bevy of leading captains, including Jacopo dal Verme, a Veronese noble who was his captain-general for thirty years. Milanese expansionism inevitably provoked its main neighbours, Florence and Venice, into taking similar steps to protect themselves, and although the death of Giangaleazzo in 1402 led to a temporary break-up of the Milanese state, the threat of Milanese expansion had returned by the 1420s. The competition between the three states then continued until the peace of Lodi in 1454 and was the context for a stabilization of the mercenary tradition in northern and central Italy. The role of Venice in this was particularly important. Venice, long accustomed to maintaining a permanent military stance in its empire in the eastern Mediterranean with garrisons and galley squadrons, became involved in a quite dramatic way in the occupation and defence of a *terraferma* empire in the period between 1404 and 1427. The speed with which Vicenza, Verona, and Padua were absorbed, followed quickly by Friuli, and then Brescia and Bergamo, led to a perception of the problem of how to maintain effective military strength which was more coherent than that of its neighbours. A determined search for good captains, a gradual extension of the length of the

The Italian *lance* in the mid-fifteenth century consisted of three men: the man-at-arms himself, his sergeant, and his page. This illustration of a pay parade in Siena shows such a group receiving pay direct from the communal officials.

condotte to allow first for year-round service and then for service for two or three years, the allocation of permanent billets and enfeoffed lands to the captains who accepted these contracts, the erection of a system of military administration which watched over and served the companies, and the realization that regular pay was the key to faithful mercenary service, these were the mechanisms which Venice in this period succeeded in implementing rather more effectively than any of the other Italian states. They were the essential mechanisms of standing armies, applied to an Italian situation in which the majority of the troops were still mercenaries in the ordinary sense of the word. Venice's leading captains in the early years of the century all came from outside the new expanded state, and the companies which they brought with them contained few Venetian subjects in this period. The same remained true of Milan and Florence, although the Visconti were more inclined to use local nobility as lesser captains. The major captains in the first half of the fifteenth century, Jacopo dal Verme, Francesco Carmagnola, Musio and Francesco Sforza, Braccio da Montone, Niccolò Piccinino, Gattamelata, rarely served under a flag that could be described as their own. But their service was often sustained, their companies were surprisingly permanent and well organized, their moves were watched with admiration and satisfaction as much as suspicion. Only one of them, Francesco Sforza, established himself as a ruler; only one, Carmagnola, was executed for suspected infidelity.

This relative maturity of mercenary institutions was a good deal less apparent in the south of Italy where the political instability created by the Angevin–Aragonese rivalry for control of Naples, and the prolonged crisis of the Schism discouraged such developments. Many of the captains mentioned above came originally from the Papal States and had learnt their soldiering in the endemic local warfare of the area and the spasmodic papal attempts to control this. Many also saw service on one side or other of the warring factions in Naples. In these circumstances the *condottieri* behaved inevitably in a more volatile, self-interested fashion; desertions and treachery were rife, and booty continued to be more common than pay. It is interesting that despite the continuation of these unsettled conditions through the 1430s and into the 1440s, many of the leading captains had by then abandoned the uncertain prospects of the south to seek their fortunes in the more controlled and disciplined world of north and central Italy.

The establishment of Alfonso V of Aragon on the throne of Naples in 1442 and the growing recognition accorded to Eugenius IV as Pope as the influence of the Council of Basle declined led to a gradual lessening of this difference between north and south in Italy. In fact both the Papal State and the kingdom of Naples had greater possibilities of raising military manpower within their own frontiers that did the northern states. Nevertheless the tensions that existed between the two states led to kings of Naples seeking to attract *condottieri* from the Roman baronial families into their service in order to weaken the Pope and create disruption in Rome. At the same time the Popes of the second half of the century did their best to prevent the warlike signorial families of Umbria and the Romagna from taking service in the north.

The wars in Lombardy in the 1430s and 1440s were in many ways a high point of conflict in later medieval Italy. Armies of over 20,000 men on either side confronted each other in the Lombard plain; armies which had become reasonably stable in terms of their composition and organization, and in which one senior captain changing sides could significantly affect the balance of power. Francesco Sforza used his substantial company in this way as he worked towards political control in Milan in the vacuum created by the death of Filippo Maria Visconti (1447) without male heir. His cousin Michele Attendolo Sforza, on the other hand, lacking perhaps the same political ambition and military prowess, but nevertheless controlling as large a company (details of the organization of which have survived to us) timed his moves less well. During a career as a major *condottiere* spanning nearly twenty-five years, Michele (or Micheletto as he was usually known) moved at long intervals from papal service to that of Florence and back again, and eventually served Venice as captain-general for seven years in the 1440s. He came from the Romagna, as did his better known cousin, and a significant proportion of his troops were Romagnol recruited by his local agents and dispatched to wherever the company was based. That company, normally consisting of about 600 lances and 400 infantry, also contained soldiers from all over Italy and at least 20 *capisquadra* many of whom came from aristocratic families and were on their way to themselves building a career as *condottieri*. As a reward for his services to Venice, Micheletto was given the important garrison town of Castelfranco, in the Trevigiano, as a fief and base. However his career fell apart when he was dismissed and his company disbanded after he lost the battle of Caravaggio to his cousin Francesco in 1448.

After his dismissal many of Micheletto's lances were taken into the direct service of Venice as *lanze spezzate* (individual detachments, which could be combined together to form a company). In doing this Venice was following a clear trend by the middle of the fifteenth century of the better organized Italian states taking the opportunity, on the death or retirement of a *condottiere*, of retaining their troops in composite companies commanded by captains chosen by the government. To see this as a deliberate attempt to reduce the mercenary element in Italian armies is probably misleading; the prime consideration was the retention of good troops who had probably spent some time

under their former leader in the service of the particular state. It was common Venetian practice to give command of a company of *lanze spezzate* to a minor *condottiere* who already had his own company but who had given faithful and effective service.

After the succession of Francesco Sforza as the new Duke of Milan in 1450, the Milanese army began to emerge as the prototype of the later fifteenth-century Italian army in which certain mercenary institutions survived but the overall impression was one of a large standing army which could be expanded rapidly when needed. Army lists of the 1470s reveal an organization which paid about 20,000 troops in peacetime and anticipated a doubling of the number if needed in war. At the heart of the permanent force were companies of *lanze spezzate* commanded by four chosen captains who formed part of the ducal entourage, and an equivalent force known as the *famiglia ducale* which served as the Duke's bodyguard. There were then the senior *condottieri* on long-term contracts which bound them to maintain their companies at half strength in peacetime, and the main feudatories, including the sons and brothers of the Duke, who were *condottieri 'ad discretionem'* with no specific obligations or pay in peacetime but clear expectations for service in time of war. Finally over 18,000 infantry, many of whom were in permanent service as garrison troops etc. were included in the mobilization plans. The bulk of this force, therefore, was based firmly within the frontiers of the state, although some of the senior *condottieri*, such as the Marquis of Mantua, had their own independent bases where they maintained their companies. Mobilization did not mean a hurried search for new companies to hire but a more or less measured increase in the size of the existing companies, supervised by government officials.

Inevitably, after the peace of Lodi and the ending of a period of almost continuous warfare in Lombardy in which Neapolitan and papal armies had become involved by the early 1450s, the second half of the century with only spasmodic outbreaks of fighting has been seen in military terms as an anti-climax. However, more recent historical perceptions of the Italian scene in the second half of the fifteen century have emphasized the considerable political and diplomatic tensions which existed between the states, the need for a constant state of military preparedness, and the effectiveness of the armies which were brought into action on frequent occasions during the period. It has to be remembered that some of the most distinguished names in the annals of the

The Battle of San Romano (1432) was a much vaunted minor victory of the Florentines over the Sienese. Paolo Uccello painted three scenes from the battle for the Medici palace in the 1450s, and here illustrates the final phase when Michele Attendolo led his contingent of the Florentine army into an attack on the Sienese rearguard.

condottieri belong to the post-Lodi period: Bartolomeo Colleoni, Venetian captain-general for twenty years, garrisoning the western frontiers of the Venetian state from his base at Malpaga; Federigo da Montefeltro, the most famed and trusted soldier of his day, Duke of Urbino, commander of the papal army, sought after in every emergency; Roberto da Sanseverino, linked to the Sforza but a brooding spirit with a progeny of ambitious soldier sons whose restlessness added to the tensions of the period; the rising generation of leaders who were to play a prominent part in the Italian Wars after 1494, Gian Giacomo Trivulzio, Niccolò Orsini Count of Pitigliano, Francesco Gonzaga. These were all *condottieri*; they continued to receive contracts of employment from states within which they had not been born, but nevertheless it is increasingly difficult to describe their role as that of mercenaries.

If the mercenary element in Italian warfare becomes difficult to define in the later fifteenth century, there is less of a problem if one looks again outside Italy. Italian *condottieri* with their companies fought abroad, notably in the Burgundian army of Charles the Bold in the 1470s. Charles was an admirer of the skills and organization of the Italian companies and tried hard to persuade

Bartolomeo Colleoni to take service with him. English archers also found employment in Charles's army, but these foreign mercenaries made up a relatively small part of the reorganized Burgundian army of which the Duke was so proud, and which was already a mélange of different linguistic and ethnic groups from within the frontiers of the composite state of Burgundy.

Many of the handgunners and arquebusmen of the later fifteenth century came from Flemish and German cities, and spread out across Europe to appear in the armies of the Wars of the Roses and the Christian Reconquista in Spain. Balkan light cavalry gave a new dimension to European cavalry warfare, particularly the Albanian stradiots which fought for Venice and spread into other Italian armies.

However, the mercenaries par excellence of the second half of the fifteenth century were the Swiss pikemen and their later imitators, the south German *Landsknechte*. The tradition of the peasants and shepherds of the Swiss uplands fighting in large contingents with pike and halberd went back a long way, but it was in the early fourteenth century that they began to offer their services as mercenaries, initially to the towns of the plain like Zurich. Victories over Austrian heavy cavalry like that at Sempach in 1386 spread the reputation of the Swiss as brave and determined fighters who achieved high levels of physical fitness and disciplined mass manoeuvre in their training. By the early fifteenth century, requests were beginning to reach the Diet of the Swiss Confederation for the hire of large bodies of these troops. However, it was their defeat of the new and vaunted army of Charles the Bold in the successive battles of Grandson, Morat, and Nancy in 1476–7, that convinced the major European states that their armies were not complete without a large contingent of pike infantry (see further Chapter 13, p. 287). Louis XI aban-

Above: the Swiss pike infantry were the most noted mercenaries of the late fifteenth century. Their discipline and training enabled them to withstand cavalry charges, and their victories over Charles the Bold of Burgundy in the 1470s gave them a reputation which opened up possibilities of large-scale employment, particularly in French armies.

Left: the introduction on a large scale of hand-held firearms in the fifteenth century contributed greatly to the importance of infantry. The new skills were particularly to be found amongst men recruited from the Flemish and German cities. Companies of such troops, mixed with pikemen, tended to march and fight in phalanxes.

doned the experiments with the free archer militia, begun by Charles VII, and hired Swiss instead. Maximilian, King of the Romans, hired Swiss and German *Landsknechte*, groups of young men who shifted from brigandage in the south German countryside to mercenary military service at this time and imitated the method of the Swiss, for his war against France in 1486. Italian states sought to hire Swiss, or train some of their own troops in the same style as a poor substitute. For the next fifty years, one of the major debates amongst military men was on how to beat the Swiss.

By the end of the fifteenth century, two entirely contradictory ideas about the employment of mercenaries were circulating. On one side, Italian humanists deplored the use of hired soldiers to defend states which should have been developing their own military potential. They looked back to the Roman legion, citizens fighting for their country, with nostalgia and a good deal of misunderstanding. Niccolò Machiavelli, who inherited this tradition, denounced the *condottieri* as 'disunited, thirsty for power, undisciplined and disloyal; they are brave amongst their friends and cowards before their enemies; they have no fear of God, they do not keep faith with their fellow men; they avoid defeat just so long as they avoid battle; in peacetime you are despoiled by them, and in wartime by the enemy.' The exaggerations of this position are obvious; there were decisive victors and significant losses in Italian mercenary warfare; the *condottieri* of the later fifteenth century were very different from those of the fourteenth which Machiavelli appeared to be describing; his experiences were those of Florence, always the most backward of the Italian states in terms of the development of organized military institutions. Above all he was a rhetorician seeking to convince in the early sixteenth century that good infantry should be the core of every army and that, ideally, those infantry should be citizens defending hearth and home. This, of course, brings us to the other side of the contradiction; the most effective troops at this moment were the Swiss infantry; they were usually fighting as mercenaries. Machiavelli recognized and applauded their quality, but closed his eyes to their standing; Florence was not prepared to pay for Swiss, and so created the less effective solution of a rural militia. Other states and rulers, and above all the King of France, were however more than prepared to pay, and their enthusiasm to hire Swiss infantry was reflected in agreements with the authorities of the Swiss confederation for freedom to recruit them in substantial numbers.

To conclude that around 1500 the secret to success in war lay in the ability to hire expensive Swiss mercenaries would, of course, be misleading. Mercenaries, in the sense that we have defined them for the late middle ages, formed only a small part, perhaps a quarter to a third, of most European armies. An

In this early sixteenth-century drawing, attributed, probably erroneously, to Durer, pike infantry, presumably German *Landsknechte*, form up in a square to fight. By this time such infantry made up the largest element in most European armies.

increasingly professional and well-trained cavalry, maintained in royal and princely households, or in the *compagnies d'ordonnances* in France and Burgundy, and by the 1490s under similar conditions in Spain, remained the core of armies. Increasingly expensive artillery trains, which none but princes could afford to maintain, were at the same time becoming more essential to the business of warfare. Nevertheless, mercenaries who could provide specialist skills, which for a variety of reasons seemed to be only available in particular parts of Europe, were still highly prized. As long as the need for a 'national' infantry, though perceived, remained in practical terms a distant ideal they would continue to be an important factor on the military scene, and in the calculations of states seeking domination.

11 NAVAL WARFARE AFTER THE VIKING AGE *c.*1100–1500

FELIPE FERNÁNDEZ-ARMESTO

The Problem in Context

'One of the greatest victories ever in that part of the world,' in the estimation of a sixteenth-century chronicler, was won off the Malabar coast on 18 March 1506. A Portuguese squadron of nine ships, which triumphed over the fleet of the Zamorin of Calicut, allegedly 250-sail strong, helped to establish a pattern which was already becoming discernible in European encounters with distant enemies. European naval superiority enabled expeditions to operate successfully, far from home, against adversaries better endowed in every other kind of resource.

This was not only true at sea. The critical moment of the conquest of Mexico was the capture of a lake-bound city 7,350 feet above sea level, with the aid of brigantines built and launched on the shores of the lake. A little later, even more conspicuously, the conquest of Siberia—the largest and most enduring of the empires acquired by European arms in the sixteenth century—was of an enormous hinterland with little access to the sea; but it was very largely a conquest of rivers, which were the highways of communication in the region. Russian superiority in river warfare was as decisive in Siberia as was Portuguese naval supremacy in the Indian Ocean or that of the Spanish in lake-borne warfare in Mexico.

We know little of the medieval background from which these world-beating traditions of naval warfare emerged or of the maritime culture in Europe which bred them. Medieval chroniclers were almost always land-lubbers, whose descriptions of sea fights were conventional and ill informed. Artists who depicted battle scenes were rarely interested in realism. Official records give little more than clues about the structure and equipment of ships. Treatises of tactics, which are in good supply to historians of land warfare, are virtually non-existent for the seas. Marine archaeology has only recently begun to yield additional information. In recent years, moreover, naval history has been out of fashion, except as a small department of maritime history—partly as a reaction against the obsession of earlier generations, who took 'the influence of sea power on history' as an article of credal authority. The material in this chapter must therefore be more tentative than much in the rest of this book.

The Framework of Nature

During the age of sail, the outcome of fighting at sea depended on nature. Weather, currents, rocks, shoals, winds, and seasonal severities were the extra enemies with which both sides in any encounter had to contend. Europe has two sharply differentiated types of maritime environment, which bred their own technical and, to a lesser extent, strategic and tactical practices in the middle ages.

The Mediterranean, together with the Black Sea, is a tideless and, by general standards, placid body of water with broadly predictable winds and currents. Since it lies entirely within narrow latitudes, it has a fairly consistent climate, except in the northernmost bays of the Black Sea, which freeze in winter. Atlantic-side and Baltic Europe, by contrast, is lashed by a more powerful, capricious and changeable ocean which stretches over a wide climatic band. Climatic conditions had inescapable strategic implications. To some extent, these corresponded to universal rules of naval warfare under sail. In attack, the 'weather gauge' is usually decisive: in other words it is of critical advantage to make one's attack with a following wind. Havens are easiest to defend if they lie to windward. Since westerlies prevail over most of the coasts of Europe, and right across the Mediterranean, these facts give some communities a natural historic advantage. Most of the great ports of Atlantic-side Europe are on lee shores but England has a uniquely long windward coast well furnished with natural harbours; only Sweden, Scotland, and Denmark share this advantage, albeit to a lesser extent. In Mediterranean conflicts, thanks to the winds, relatively westerly powers tended to have an advantage. The racing current, moreover, which powers eastward through the Strait of Gibraltar, flows anti-clockwise along the southern shore of the sea. In consequence, in the great ideological conflict of the middle ages—between Islam, which generally occupied most of the southern and eastern shores, and Christendom in the north and west—the balance of advantage lay on the Christian side. In seaborne warfare, speed of access to critical stations is vital; the return voyage is relatively unimportant for an expedition whose aim is to seize or relieve a point on land.

The Technological Process

Naval historians like to stress the cost of naval war and the magnitude of the logistical effort it demands, but in our period it was relatively economical, compared with expenditure on knights, seige works, and fortifications. For most of the period, few fighting ships were purpose-built at public expense and the opportunities of recouping costs by seizing plunder and prizes were considerable. Only very gradually did naval expenditure overtake the costs of land warfare, as warships became more specialized and land forces less so. The full effects of this change were not felt until after our period was over. Nevertheless, the cheapness of naval warfare was a function of its scale. The occasional great campaigns, in which vast quantities of shipping were taken out of the regular economy and exposed to immolation in hazardous battles, could represent a terrible, if short-lived, strain.

Weapons apart, navigation was the most important aspect of technology for battle fleets, which often took those aboard outside familiar waters. Haven-finding was essential for keeping fleets at sea; precise navigation was essential for getting them to the right place. Most of the technical aids of the period seem hopelessly inadequate to these tasks and it is not surprising that experienced navigators, in regions they knew at first-hand, kept close to the coasts and navigated between landmarks. Advice from a treatise of about 1190 represents an early stage of the reception in Europe of the navigator's most rudimentary tool: when the moon and stars are enveloped in darkness, Guyot de Provins explained, all the sailor need do is place, inside a straw floating in a basin of water, a pin well rubbed 'with an ugly brown stone that draws iron to itself'. The compass was made serviceable in the thirteenth century by being balanced on a point, so that it could rotate freely against a fixed scale, usually divided between thirty-two compass-points. Other tools for navigators were gradually and imperfectly absorbed in the course of the middle ages, but their reception tended to be delayed and their impact diminished by the natural conservatism of a traditional craft.

Mariners' astrolabes, for instance, which enabled navigators to calculate their latitude from the height of the sun or the Pole Star above the horizon, were already available by the start of our period. Few ships, however, were carrying astrolabes even by the period's end. Tables for determining latitude according to the hours of sunlight were easier to use but demanded more

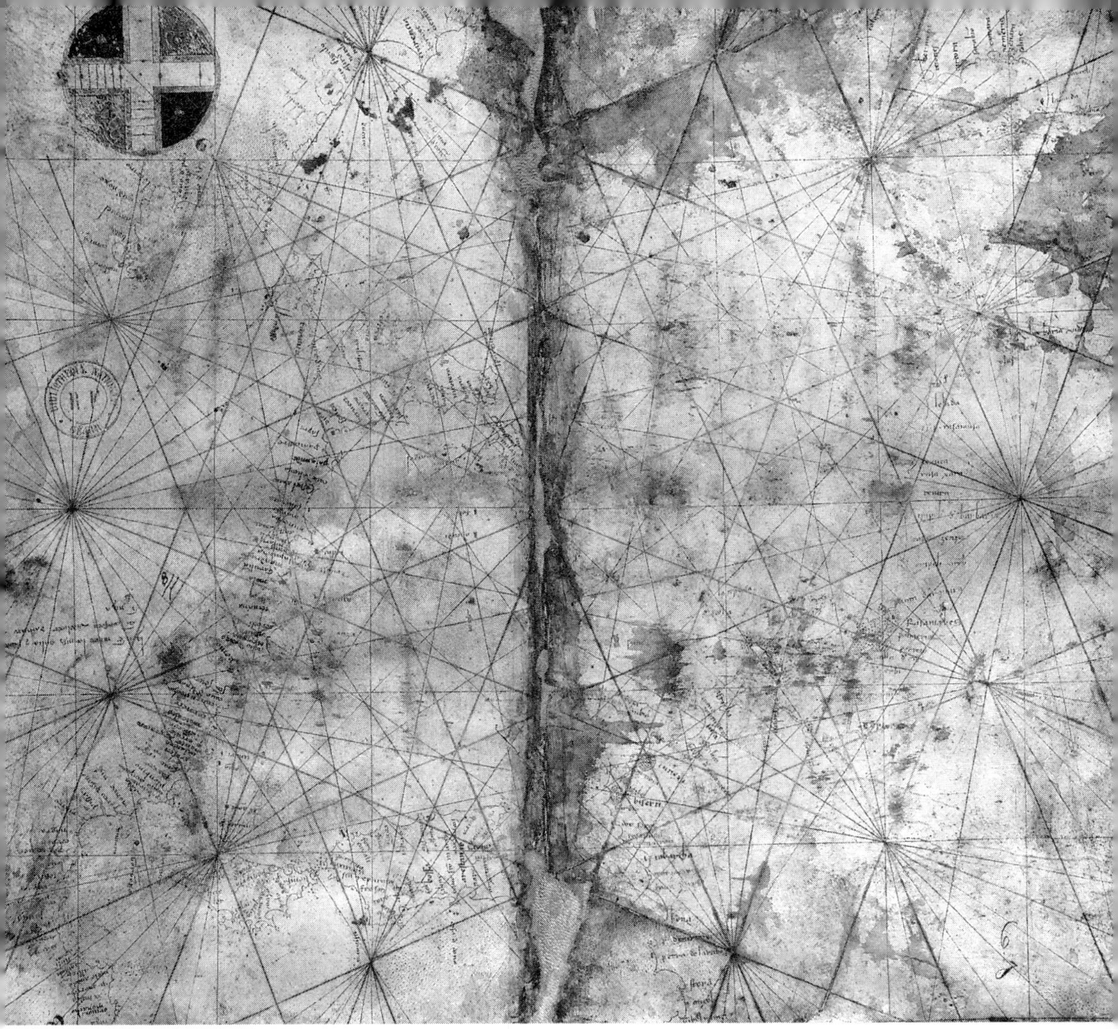

Warfare took navigators from the Atlantic and Mediterranean into each other's spheres, where they had to contend with the dangers of unknown coasts and narrows (and, in northern waters, tides). This created a demand for sailing directions, which survive in original form for the Mediterranean from the early thirteenth century. They soon began to be cast in the form of charts, criss-crossed with compass bearings, which were probably less useful for practical navigators than written directions in which detailed pilotage information could be included.

accurate timekeeping than most mariners could manage with the sole means at their disposal: sandclocks turned by ships' boys. The so-called 'sun compass'—a small gnomon for casting a shadow on a wooden board—might have been useful for determining one's latitude relative to one's starting-point; but we lack evidence that navigators carried it in our period.

In view of the dearth of useful technical aids it is hard to resist the impression that navigators relied on the sheer accumulation of practical craftsmanship and lore to guide them in unknown waters. From the thirteenth century onwards, compilers of navigational manuals distilled vicarious experience into sailing directions which could genuinely assist a navigator without much prior local knowledge. 'Portolan charts' began to present similar information in graphic form at about the same period. The earliest clear reference is to the chart which accompanied St Louis on his crusade to Tunis in 1270.

At the start of our period, there were marked technical differences between Mediterranean and Atlantic Europe in shipbuilding. In both areas, the shipwright's was a numinous craft, sanctified by the sacred images in which ships were associated in the pictorial imaginations of the time: the ark of salvation, the storm-tossed barque, and the ship of fools. Much of our knowledge of medieval shipyards comes from pictures of Noah. Underlain by this conceptual continuity were differences in technique which arose from differences in the environment. Atlantic and northern shipwrights built for heavier seas. Durability was their main criterion. They characteristically built up their hulls plank by plank, laying planks to overlap along their entire length and fitting them together with nails. The Mediterranean tradition preferred to work frame-first: planks were nailed to the frame and laid edge-to-edge. The latter method was more economical. It demanded less wood in all and far fewer nails; once the frame was built, most of the rest of the work could be entrusted to less specialized labour. In partial consequence, frame-first construction gradually spread all over Europe until by the end of our period it was the normal method everywhere. For warships, however, Atlantic-side shipyards generally remained willing to invest in the robust effect of overlapping planks, even though, from the early fifteenth century, these were invariably attached to skeleton frames.

Warships—in the sense of ships designed for battle—were relatively rare. Warfare demanded more troop transports and supply vessels than floating battle-stations and, in any case, merchant ships could be adapted for fighting whenever the need arose. In times of conflict, therefore, shipping of every kind was impressed: availability was more important than suitability. Navies were scraped together by means of ship-levying powers on maritime communities, which compounded for taxes

Until late-medieval developments in rigging improved ships' manoeuvrability under sail, oared vessels were essential for warfare in normal weather conditions. Byzantine *dromons* were rowed in battle from the lower deck, as shown in this late eleventh-century illustration, with the upper deck cleared for action, apart from the tiller at the stern.

with ships; or they were bought or hired—crews and all—on the international market.

Maritime states usually had some warships permanently at their disposal, for even in time of peace coasts had to be patrolled and customs duties enforced. Purpose-built warships also existed in private hands, commissioned by individuals with piracy in mind, and could be appropriated by the state in wartime. From 1104, the Venetian state maintained the famous arsenal—over 30 hectares of shipyards by the sixteenth century. From 1284 the rulers of the Arago-Catalan state had their own yard, specializing in war galleys, at Barcelona, where the eight parallel aisles built for Pere III in 1378 can still be seen. From 1294 to 1418 the French crown had its *Clos des Galées* in Rouen, which employed, at its height, sixty-four carpenters and twenty-three caulkers, along with oar-makers, sawyers, sail-makers, stitchers, rope-walkers, lightermen, and warehousemen. Philip the Good, Duke of Burgundy from 1419 to 1467, whose wars and crusading projects created exceptional demand for shipping, founded a shipyard of his own in Bruges, staffed by Portuguese technicians. England had no royal shipyard, but Henry V maintained purpose-built ships of his own as well as borrowing them from others: an ex-pirate vessel, the *Craccher*, was for instance loaned by John Hawley of Dartmouth. Such loans were not acts of generosity: Henry V was one of the few monarchs of the European middle ages who were serious about curtailing their own subjects' piracy.

At the start of our period, warships, whether on the Atlantic-side or Mediterranean-side of Europe, were almost invariably driven by oars.

Rigging was light by modern standards and only oars could provide the manoeuvrability demanded in battle, or keep a vessel safe in the locations, often close to the shore, where battles commonly took place.

Gradually, however, oars were replaced by sails, especially on the Atlantic seaboard. With additional masts and more sails of differing size and shapes, ships could be controlled almost as well as by oars, while frame-first construction permitted rudders to be fitted to stern-posts rising from the keel: formerly, ships were steered by tillers dangled from the starboard towards the stern. These improvements in manoeuvrability, which were introduced gradually from the twelfth century onwards, freed ships from the economic and logistic burden of vast crews of oarsmen. Oar-power dominated Baltic warfare until 1210, when the crusading order of Sword-brothers switched to sail-driven cogs, which helped them extend their control along the whole coast of Livonia. King John of England had forty-five galleys in 1204 and built twenty more between 1209 and 1212. Edward I's order for a battle fleet in 1294 was for twenty galleys of 120 oars each. A hundred years later, however, only small oared craft formed part of England's navy, in which the fighting vanguard was entirely sail-driven. French shipbuilding changed faster. The French at Sluys in 1340 had 170 sailing ships as well as the royal galleys: many of them were certainly intended for the fray.

To a lesser extent, the oar-less craft played a growing role in Mediterranean warfare, too. The Florentine chronicler, Giovanni Villani, with characteristic exaggeration, dated the start of this innovation to 1304 when pirates from Gascony invaded the Mediterranean with ships so impressive that 'henceforth Genoese, Venetians and Catalans began to use cogs. . . . This was a great change for our navy.' In the fifteenth century, the Venetian state commissioned large sailing warships specifically for operations against corsair galleys.

Once free of oar-power, ships could be built higher, with corresponding advantages in battle for hurlers of missiles and intimidators of the foe: the tactics favoured throughout the period made height a critical source of advantage. To hoist tubs full of archers to the masthead was an old Byzantine trick, which Venetian galley-masters adopted. Rickety superstructures, which came to be known as 'castles', cluttered the prows of ships; shipwrights strained to add height even at the risk of making vessels top-heavy. The clearest demonstration of the advantages of height is in the record of sailing-ships in combat with galleys: countless engagements demonstrated that it was virtually impossible for oar-driven craft to capture tall vessels, even with huge advantages in numbers—like those of the reputed 150 Turkish boats that swarmed ineffectively round four Christian sailing ships in the Bosphorus during the siege of Constantinople of 1453, or the score of Genoese craft that hopelessly

In an early thirteenth-century Sicilian manuscript, a galley cleaves a monster-haunted sea. Although no sails are up, the vessel is not about to engage, though a ram is fixed to the prow. Most of the personnel shown are professional oarsmen, of whom there were two teams, signified by the two banks of oars; on engagement, up to a third of them would double as fighting men. The presence of warriors is evident from the upraised halberds and lances. The vessel is steered by two tillers to enhance manoeuvrability.

hounded the big Venetian merchantman, the *Rocafortis*, across the Aegean in 1264.

In the Mediterranean, galleys tended to get faster. The Catalan galleys of the late thirteenth century, at the time of the conquest of Sicily, had between 100 and 150 oars; by the mid-fourteenth century, complements of between 170 and 200 oars were not unusual, while the dimensions of the vessels had not grown significantly. Light galleys pursued and pinned down the foe while more heavily armed vessels followed to decide the action. The oarsmen had to be heavily armoured, with cuirasse, collar, helmet, and shield. Despite their place in the popular imagination, 'galley slaves' or prisoners condemned to the oar were never numerous and were rarely relied on in war. Oarsmen were professionals who doubled as fighters; once battle was joined, speed could be sacrificed in favour of battle strength and up to a third of the oarsmen could become fighters.

The Tactical Pattern

Deliberately to sink an enemy ship would have appeared shockingly wasteful. The use of divers to hole enemy ships below the waterline was known and recommended by theorists but seems to have been rarely practised. For the object of battle was to capture the enemy's vessels. At Sluys, as many as 190 French ships were said to have been captured; none sank—though so many lives were lost that the chronicler Froissart reckoned the king saved 200,000 florins in wages. Vessels might, of course, be lost in battle through uncontrollable fire, or irremediably holed by excessive zeal in ramming, or scuttled after capture if unseaworthy or if the victors could not man them.

Ships fought at close quarters with short-range missiles, then grappled or rammed for boarding. The first objectives of an encounter were blinding with lime, battering with stones, and burning with 'Greek fire'—a lost recipe of medieval technology, inextinguishable in water. A digest of naval tactics from

'Greek fire' was ignited by a substance, combustible in water, of which the recipe is lost. Together with short-range missiles and blasts of blinding lime and fire-bombs, it was used prior to boarding, to distract the enemy crew and cripple rather than destroy the ship. Normally, a hand-held siphon with a bronze tube at the prow was used to project it.

ancient treatises, compiled for Philip IV of France, recommended opening the engagement by flinging pots of pitch, sulphur, resin, and oil onto the enemy's decks to assist combustion. It was a blast of lime, borne on the wind, that overpowered the crew of the ship carrying the siege train of Prince Louis of France to England in February 1217. Protection against lime and stones was supplied chiefly by stringing nets above the defenders; flame-throwers could be resisted, it was said, by felt soaked in vinegar or urine and spread across the decks. In a defensive role, or to force ships out of harbour, fire ships might be used, as they were—to great effect—by Castilian galleys at La Rochelle in June 1372, when blazing boats were towed into the midst of the English fleet.

As the ships closed, crossbowmen were the decisive arm. According to the chauvinistic Catalan chronicler of the fourteenth century, Ramon Muntaner, 'The Catalans learn about it with their mother's milk and the other people in the world do not. Therefore the Catalans are the sovereign crossbowmen of the world. . . . Like the stone thrown by a war machine, nothing fails them.' Catalan proficiency in archery was supported by special tactics. When Pere II's fleet confronted that of Charles of Anjou off Malta in September 1283, the Catalans were ordered by message 'passed from ship to ship' to withstand the enemy missiles with their shields and not to respond except with archery. The outcome, according to the chronicle tradition, was that 4,500 French were taken prisoner.

At close quarters, Philip IV's digest recommended a range of devices: ripping the enemy's sails with arrows specially fitted with long points, spraying his decks with slippery soap, cutting his ropes with scythes, ramming with a heavy beam, fortified with iron tips and swung from the height of the mainmast, and, 'if he is weaker than you, grappling.' Ramming or grappling was the prelude to an even closer-fought fight with missiles followed by boarding.

As far as is known from a few surviving inventories, the weapons carried on board ships reflected more or less this range of tactics. When inventoried in 1416, Henry V's biggest ship had seven breech-loading guns, twenty bows, over 100 spears, 60 sail-ripping darts, crane-lines for winching weaponry between fighting decks, and grapnels with chains twelve fathoms long. It must not be supposed that the inventory was complete as most equipment was surely not stowed aboard, but it is probably a representative selection. Artillery detonated by gunpowder came into use during the period, but only as a supplement to existing weaponry, within the framework of traditional tactics. Numbers of guns increased massively in the fifteenth century, though it is not clear that they grew in effectiveness or influenced tactics much. Overwhelmingly, they were short-range, small-calibre, swivel-mounted breechloaders; anti-personnel weapons, not ship-smashers.

The Conceptual Imperatives

There is something Homeric about the pattern of war these tactics represent: ships duelled with each other in single combat; their fighting crews closed in a mêlée that might be determined by individual prowess. The way wars were fought depended on how they were conceived in the adversaries' minds and, at least as much as land warfare—more, perhaps, as time went on—the naval warfare of our period was shaped by the great aristocratic ethos of the high and late middle ages: the 'cult' of chivalry, which warriors' deeds were meant to express. There is no need to dwell on the perennial objectives of war, for greed, power-lust, and various religious or moral pretexts for bloodshed are always with us. What was peculiar to the warfare of Latin Christendom was that it was animated by belief in the ennobling effect of great 'deeds' of adventure. As chivalry infused seafaring, it made naval service attractive for more than the hope of prize money. The sea became a field fit for kings.

A chivalric treatise of the mid-fifteenth century tells us that the French aristocracy eschewed the sea as an ignoble medium—but the writer was responding to a debate which had already been won by spokesmen for the sea. Almost from the emergence of the genre, the sea was

The chivalric representation of naval warfare is strong in this illumination of the Duke of Bourbon's departure on crusade to Barbary in 1390: the ships are as gaily caparisoned as any war-steed, with pennants, scutcheons, heralds' horns, and helmed knights.

seen in chivalric literature as a suitable environment for deeds of knightly endeavour. In the thirteenth century, one of the great spokesmen of the chivalric ethos in the Iberian peninsula was Jaume I, King of Aragon and Count of Barcelona. When he described his conquest of Majorca in 1229, he revealed that he saw maritime war as a means of chivalric adventure par excellence. There was 'more honour' in conquering a single kingdom 'in the midst of the sea, where God has been pleased to put it' than three on dry land.

A metaphor quickly established itself, which was to be a commonplace for the rest of the middle ages: the ship, in the words of King Alfonso X of Castile, was 'the horse of them that fight by sea'. St Louis planned to create the Order of the Ship for participants in his Tunis crusade. The Order of the Dragon, instituted by the Count of Foix in the early fifteenth century, honoured members who fought at sea with emerald insignia. By the time of Columbus, the Portuguese poet, Gil Vicente, could liken a ship at once to a warhorse and a lovely woman without incongruity, for all three were almost equipollent images in the chivalric tradition. Anyone who contemplates late medieval pictures of fighting ships, caparisoned with pennants as gaily as any warhorse, can grasp how, in the imagination of the time, the sea could be a knightly battlefield and the waves ridden like jennets.

No text better illustrates the influence of this tradition on the conduct of war than the chronicle of the deeds of Count Pero Niño, written by his standard-bearer in the second quarter of the fifteenth century. A treatise of chivalry, as well as an account of campaigns, *El victorial* celebrates a knight never vanquished in joust or war or love, whose greatest battles were fought at sea; and 'to win a battle is the greatest good and the greatest glory of life.' When the author discourses on the mutability of life, his interlocutors are Fortune and the Wind, whose 'mother' is the sea 'and therein is my chief office'. This helps to explain an important advantage of a maritime milieu for the teller of chivalric tales: it is on the sea, with its rapid cycles of storm and calm, that the wheel of fortune revolves most briskly.

At one level, sea warfare was an extension of land warfare. Set-piece battles were rare and usually occurred in the context of the activities on which naval strategy was commonly bent: the transport of armies and the blockade of ports. Inevitably, however, campaigns of this sort suggested strictly maritime strategies. It became conceivable to fight for the control or even the monopolization of sea-lanes and the extension of what might be called a territorial attitude over the sea: seizure of rights of jurisdiction over disputes arising on it and exploitation of its trade for tolls. At the level of grand strategy, some of the aims of naval warfare declared in medieval sources seem stunningly ambitious. English monarchs called themselves 'roys des mers' and aspired to the 'sovereignty of the sea'. An influential political poem of 1437, the *Libelle of Englische Polycye*, anticipated some of the language of the ages of Drake and Nelson, stressing the imperatives of maritime defence for an island-kingdom. Similar language was sometimes used in the Mediterranean, such as Muntaner's dictum, 'It is important that he who would conquer Sardinia rule the sea.'

Late medieval warfare in the Mediterranean was therefore increasingly influenced by strictly maritime considerations: instead of being used as an adjunct to land wars, mainly to transport armies and assist in seiges, ships were deployed to control commercial access to ports and sea lanes. The ideal of naval strategy was represented by the claim of the chronicler, Bernat Desclot, that in the early fourteenth century 'no fish could go swimming without the King of Aragon's leave.' In practice, no such monopoly was ever established anywhere but major powers, such as England, Venice, Genoa, the Hanseatic League, and the House of Barcelona, achieved preponderance, at various times, on particular routes and coasts. This way of conceiving grand strategy was carried by early modern invaders from Western Europe across the oceans of the world, to the consternation and, perhaps, the confusion of indigenous powers.

The Siren of Piracy

Even at its most commonplace, the grand strategy of maritime 'lordship' never displaced the small wars of mutually predatory shipping. Pirate

Seasonal constraints on shipping help to explain the long, grinding nature of Baltic wars: the progress of the northern crusades was set back, year by year, as what was won by way of sea on summer cruises was lost on land in winter to ski-soldiery and guerrilla warfare. In a wood-cut from the greatest history of the north—a labour of love by the sixteenth-century Catholic exile, Olaus Magnus—'pirate maidens' defend the Finnish harbour of Hangö.

operations could be extensive—more so than official campaigns, especially in the piracy 'black spots' found in narrows and channels, such as the Strait of Otranto, the Skaggerak, or the Straits of Dover, where for centuries the men of the Cinque Ports terrorized other people's shipping, and the Sicilian Channel, which ships are obliged to use if they want to avoid the whirlpool of the Strait of Messina 'between Scylla and Charybdis'.

At certain levels, piracy is hard to distinguish from other kinds of warfare. Savari de Mauléon fought on crusade against Albigensians and Saracens before setting up as a sea-predator: Philip Augustus offered him great lordships for his services. Eustace the Monk, a nobleman from Artois and escapee from the monastic life of St Wulmer, was invaluable in support of Prince Louis's invasion of England in 1216 while terrorizing the Channel from his base on Sark. He grew rich enough to invest his son with jewelled armour and renowned enough to be hailed by the chronicler, William the Breton, as 'a knight most accomplished by land and sea'. Guillaume Coulon, who wrecked a fleet off Lisbon in 1476 when Columbus was on board, was reviled as a murderer by his Venetian and other victims but in France was honoured as an admiral and knight of the Order of Saint-Michel. States routinely authorized acts of piracy against enemy shipping in wartime.

Strictly understood, however, piracy is only a limited form of war. It depends on the trades it feeds off and therefore seeks to interrupt or exploit them, not block them altogether. Control of trade was part of statecraft, for trade yielded tolls; but, as in other periods, opinion in the middle ages was divided on the question of whether war was a cost-effective way of garnering commerce. The association of trading ports known as the Hanse, which played a major role in the trade of the north from the late twelfth century, was capable of organizing war fleets when necessary: generally, however, its policy-makers, who were merchants themselves with vocations geared to peace, relied on economic warfare—embargoes, preferential tariffs, subsidies. Violence was a gambler's option: if it worked, it could be practised at a profit.

The Courses of War

The Atlantic Side

Our period can be said to have opened in a sea-power vacuum, vacated by vanished hegemonies—those of the Norse in the Atlantic zone and of Muslim powers and the Byzantine empire in the Mediterranean. New powers emerged only slowly. In the French case, the chronicle tradition represents what must have been a gradual process as a sudden experience, analogous to a religious conversion. On a morning in 1213, King Philip Augustus woke up with a vision of the possible conquest of England. He 'ordered the ports throughout the country to collect all their ships together, with their crews, and to build new ones in great plenty.' Formerly, French kings' rule had been almost restricted to a landlocked domain. Now—especially in the reign of Philip Augustus—France seemed to drive for the sea in every direction, and was transformed with relative suddenness into a Mediterranean and Atlantic power. Normandy was conquered by 1214, La Rochelle in 1224. The Albigensian Crusade provided a pretext and framework for the incorporation of the south, with its Mediterranean ports, into what we think of as France by 1229.

France's main maritime rival for the rest of the middle ages was already a naval power: the dominions of the English crown straddled the Irish Sea and the English Channel. A permanent navy was maintained at least from early in the reign of King John—perhaps from that of his predecessor, Richard I, who had shown some flair as a naval commander in the Mediterranean on the Third Crusade and in river-war along the Seine. After the failure of the efforts of Louis of France, doomed by the defeat of Eustace the Monk off Sandwich in 1217, no French invasion of England materialized, though a threat in 1264 flung the country into something like a panic. Sea-power was used only for transporting English expeditions across the Channel or for exchanges of raids and acts of piracy, until 1337, when Edward III's claim to the throne of France raised the stakes and made control of the Channel vital for both crowns in what promised to be a prolonged war on French soil.

At first it seemed unlikely that the issue at sea could be decisively resolved. French naval forces appeared strong enough, in numerical terms, to impede English cross-channel communications; indeed, the French struck the first blow of the war in the spring of 1338, when some of their ships raided Portsmouth and the Isle of Wight. Although Edward was able to land an army in Flanders shortly afterwards, it would evidently be hard for him to keep it supplied or reinforced without substantial help from Continental allies. Re-crossing the Channel in June 1340, after a brief return to England, he encountered a French fleet of daunting proportions at anchor off Sluys. According to one account, the outcome of the battle of Sluys was the result of the refusal of the French to escape when the tide and wind were against them. 'Honi soit qui s'en ira d'içi,' replied the treasurer of the fleet when discretion was proposed by one of the Genoese technicians advising him. The English adopted the usual tactics of inferior forces: using the weather gauge to stand off from the enemy within bowshot-range until his forces were depleted by slaughter. Like so many famous English victories on land in the Hundred Years War, Sluys was a triumph of long-range archery. The English gained command of the Channel—the freedom to transport armies unopposed. Edward III's new

The Battle of Sluys in 1340 is depicted by the illuminator as an engagement hand-to-hand, in the chivalric tradition, with the broad-beamed fighting hulks in the role of chargers. In reality, it was like so many English land victories of the Hundred Years' War—a triumph of long-range archery.

coinage showed him enthroned on board ship. The victories of Crécy and Poitiers were, in a strict sense, part of the consequences. The English advantage was confirmed in 1347, when the capture of Calais gave English shipping a privileged position in the narrowest part of the Channel—an advantage maintained until the 1550s.

The most promising French response was the intrusion of Castilian ships into the Channel from 1350: they were expert in the guerrilla warfare of the sea, but their attempts to wrest control of the straits were never fully successful. Thanks to the permanent advantage which possession of the English shore conferred by virtue of wind and weather in the Channel and the North Sea, the French never succeeded in reversing English naval dominance for long. The most they could achieve were successful raids, effected by their own ships or those of their Castilian allies, at, for example, Winchelsea (1360), Portsmouth (1369), Gravesend (1380), and a string of ports from Rye to Portsmouth (1377). By taking a wide berth out into the North Sea, the French could send fleets to Scotland in support of Scots military actions, but the prevailing winds made direct attacks on the east coast of England highly unlikely to succeed. If any doubt lingered over the balance of advantage in the northern seas, it was dispelled by events of 1416, when the English were able to relieve the blockade of Harfleur and ensure control of access to the Seine by defeating a Genoese galley fleet. The French shipyard at Rouen was dismantled. England's military power waned in the fifteenth century and her vulnerability to invasion was demonstrated by the landing of the future Henry VII in 1485; but her naval supremacy in home waters would not again be challenged by a foreign state until the cruise of the Spanish Armada in 1588.

The Mediterranean

The trajectory of naval warfare in the Mediterranean had some similarities with that in the north: a power vacuum at the start of our period, in which new contenders arose and disputed mastery of the sea. By *c.*1100 the naval war against Islam had already been won by Christians. Westerners were masters of Corsica, Sardinia, Sicily, southern Italy, and the coasts of Palestine and Syria. The difficulty of dominating the Mediterranean from its eastern end had also affected Byzantine sea power. Byzantium was already in the process of being reduced to minor importance as a naval power by comparison with some rivals further west.

The Egyptian Fatimid fleet, which had once been a formidable force is almost unmentioned in the records after the first decade of the 1100s: it continued to exist, and could put up to seventy galleys at sea in the mid-twelfth century, but it became confined to a largely defensive role. By 1110, the crusaders held almost all the Levantine ports; thereafter, the operation of Egyptian galleys against Christian shipping was practically limited to home coasts: they had virtually no friendly ports to the north in which to water. Turkish naval power, which would be invincible by the end of our period, had hardly been foreshadowed. In the 1090s Syrian collaborators provided free-lance Seljuk war-chiefs with ships that briefly seized Lesbos and Chios and even threatened Constantinople; but the crusades forced the Seljuks back; the coasts were not recovered for Islam for another hundred years or so. The crusader states depended on long and apparently vulnerable communications by sea along lanes that led back to the central and western Mediterranean. Yet they were hardly jeopardized by seaborne counter-attack. Saladin created a navy of sixty galleys almost from nothing in the 1170s, but he used it

Guarded by Amazons, Ramon de Cardona's tomb in Bellpuig commemorates one of the most successful exponents of amphibian warfare in the early sixteenth century and illustrates the use of galleys as troop transports. The shallow-draughted vessels are close inshore and the task force is landed in boats. Cardona's use of seaborne expeditions contributed decisively to Spanish campaigns of conquest in Italy. On his tomb, however, an episode from a North African campaign against Muslim enemies is suitably depicted, while the Muslims' captives cower in a corner of the composition.

conservatively and with patchy success until it was captured almost in its entirety by the fleet of the Third Crusade at Acre in 1191.

The Christian reconquest of the Mediterranean had been effected, in part, by collaboration among Christian powers. Venetian, Pisan, Genoese, and Byzantine ships acted together to establish and supply the crusader states of the Levant in their early years. Successful allies, however, usually fall out. Relative security from credal enemies left the victors free to fight among themselves. The twelfth century was an era of open competition in the Mediterranean for the control of trade, by means which included violence, between powers in uneasy equipoise. In the twelfth century, Sicily was perhaps the strongest of them. It maintained the only permanent navy west of the twenty-second meridian, but the extinction of its Norman dynasty in 1194 marked the end of its potential for maritime empire. Pisa was a major naval power of the twelfth and thirteenth centuries: its war against Amalfi in 1135–7 effectively dashed all prospect of that port emerging as an imperial metropolis; and the contribution of its ships, with those of Genoa, was decisive in the destruction of the Norman Kingdom of Sicily; but Pisa made a poor choice of allies in thirteenth-century wars and, after a series of setbacks which left it isolated, at the battle of Meloria in 1284 it suffered a blow at Genoese hands from which its navy never recovered. So many prisoners were taken that 'to see Pisans', it was said, 'you must go to Genoa.'

Three rivals stood the course of these wars: the Genoese and Venetian republics and the House of Barcelona. At different times and in overlapping areas of the Mediterranean, all three established seaborne 'empires'—zones of preponderance or control over favoured routes and coasts. The possibilities were demonstrated in 1204, when Constantinople fell to a mixed host of Westerners and Venice carved a maritime empire out of the spoils. The Republic became mistress of 'one quarter and one half of a quarter' of Byzantine territory. At first, Genoa responded with energetic corsair warfare, which had effectively failed when the peace settlement of 1218 nominally restored to Genoese merchants the right to live and trade in Constantinople. In practice, however, they remained victims of the Venetian hegemony until 1261, when Byzantine irredentists recaptured Constantinople and the uneasy parity of the Genoese and Venetian traders was restored.

Genoa acquired an empire of its own—albeit one much less tightly centralized than that of Venice: it comprised, at first, an autonomous merchant-quarter in Constantinople and scattered settlements along the northern shore of the Black Sea, ruled by a representative of the Genoese government. By Byzantine grants of 1267 and 1304, the alum-producing island of Chios became the fief of a Genoese family. Around the middle of the fourteenth century its status was transformed by the intrusion of direct rule from Genoa. The Aegean was effectively divided between Genoese and Venetian spheres. Venice dominated the route to Constantinople via the Dalmatian coast and the Ionian islands, whereas Genoa controlled an alternative route by way of Chios and the eastern shore.

Eastern Mediterranean rivalry between Genoa and Venice was paralleled in some ways in the western rivalry between Genoa and the dominions of the House of Barcelona. Catalans were relative latecomers to the arena. They enjoyed privileged natural access to the entire strategic springboard of the western Mediterranean—the island bases, the Maghribi ports; but while the islands were in the unfriendly hands of Muslim emirs, they were trapped by the anti-clockwise flow of the coastal currents. But by 1229 the power of the count-kings of Barcelona and Aragon and the wealth of their merchant-subjects had developed to the point where they could raise enough ships and a large enough host to attempt conquest. By representing the venture as a holy war, Jaume I was able to induce the landlubber aristocracy of Aragon to take part in the campaign. Once Majorca was in his hands, Ibiza and Formentera fell with relative ease. The island-empire was extended in the 1280s and 1290s, when Minorca and Sicily were conquered. In the 1320s an aggressive imperial policy reduced parts of Sardinia to precarious obedience.

Meanwhile, vassals of members of the House of Barcelona made conquests even further east, in Jarbah, Qarqanah, and parts of mainland Greece. The impression of a growing maritime empire, reaching out towards the east—perhaps to the Holy Land, perhaps to the spice trade, perhaps both—was re-inforced by the propaganda of count-kings who represented themselves as crusaders. The easterly vassal-states were, however, only nominally Catalan in character and, for most of the time, tenuously linked by juridical ties with the other dominions of the House of Barcelona. Catalan naval operations in the eastern Mediterranean were made in alliance with Venice or Genoa and were generally determined by western Mediterranean strategic considerations. If the island-conquests of the House of Barcelona stretched eastward, towards the lands of saints and spices, they also strewed the way south, towards the Maghrib, the land of gold. They were strategic points d'appui of economic warfare across the African trade routes of other trading states. From 1271 onwards, at intervals over a period of about a century, the naval strength of the count-kings was used in part to exact a series of favourable commercial treaties governing access to the major ports from Ceuta to Tunis.

Of the well integrated Catalan world, the easternmost part, from the 1280s, was Sicily. For the count-king Pere II its conquest was a chivalresque adventure in dynastic self-aggrandisement; for his merchant-subjects, it was the key to a well-stocked granary, a way-station to the eastern Mediterranean and, above all, a screen for the lucrative Barbary trade, which terminated in Maghribi ports. Normally ruled by a cadet-line of the House of Barcelona, the island was vaunted as 'the head and protectress of all the Catalans', a vital part of the outworks of Catalonia's medieval trade. Had Sardinia become fully part of the Catalan system the western Mediterranean would have been a 'Catalan lake'. But indigenous resistance, prolonged for over a century, forced repeated concessions to Genoa and Pisa. The Catalans paid heavily for what was, in effect, a political and commercial condominium. By a cheaper policy—without acquiring sovereign conquests further afield than Corsica—Genoa ended with a greater share of western Mediterranean trade than her Catalan rivals.

Thus, between them, Venice, Genoa, and a Spanish state established a sort of armed equilibrium—a surface tension which covered the Mediterranean. It was broken at the end of our period by the irruption of a new maritime power. The Turkish vocation for the sea did not spring suddenly and fully armed into existence. From the early fourteenth century, pirate-nests on the Levantine shores of the Mediterranean were run by Turkish chieftains, some of whom allegedly had fleets of hundreds of vessels at their command. The greater the extent of coastline conquered by their land forces, as Ottoman imperialism stole west, the greater the opportunities for Turkish-operated corsairs to stay at sea, with access to watering-stations and supplies from on shore. Throughout the fourteenth century, however, these were unambitious enterprises, limited to small ships and hit-and-run tactics.

From the 1390s, the Ottoman sultan Bayezid I began to build up a permanent fleet of his own, but without embracing a radically different strategy from the independent operators who preceded him. Set-piece battles usually occurred in spite of Turkish intentions and resulted in Turkish defeats. As late as 1466, a Venetian merchant in Constantinople claimed that for a successful engagement Turkish ships needed to outnumber Venetians by four or five to one. By that date, however, Ottoman investment in naval strength was probably higher than that of any Christian state. The far-seeing sultans, Mehmed I and Bayezid II, realized that the momentum of their conquests by land had to be supported—if it were to continue—by power at sea. After the long generations of experiment without success in set-piece battles, Bayezid's navy humiliated that of Venice in the war of 1499–1503. Never, since Romans reluctantly took to the sea against Carthage, had a naval vocation been so successfully embraced by so unlikely a power. The balance of naval strength between Christendom and Islam, as it had lasted for four hundred years, was reversed, at least in the eastern Mediterranean, and a new era can properly be said to have begun.

Retrospect and Prospect

In the long run, sea power in the European middle ages was more influenced by the outcome of conflicts on land than the other way round. Coastal strongholds could be established by naval forces but control of hostile hinterlands could not be permanently sustained by the same means. The Third Crusade recaptured the Levantine coast but could not re-take Jerusalem or restore the crusader states. Venetian sea-power delivered Constantinople into Latin hands in 1204; but the Latin Empire lasted only until 1261 and Byzantium's permanent losses were all in or beyond the Aegean. St Louis captured Damietta by sea in 1249 but had to relinquish it after a defeat on land the following year.

To some extent, the fate of the English 'empire' in France illustrates the same principles: only its maritime fringe was held for long; and the Channel Islands were never lost to French sovereignty; but the ultimate fate of the rest was determined by campaigns on land, where the English were at a long-term disadvantage.

Thus the great events of European history—the making and unmaking of states, the expansion and limitation of Christendom—happened, to some extent, in spite of the sea. For world history, however, Europe's medieval naval apprenticeship had grave implications. When European warfare was exported into the world arena of the early modern period, and met aggressive and dynamic imperial states in other parts of the world, it was carried by ships onto the home grounds of distant enemies and could deploy the resources of a long, rich, and varied maritime experience. In competition for world resources, European maritime powers had the advantage of an unbeatably long reach.

12 WAR AND THE NON-COMBATANT IN THE MIDDLE AGES

CHRISTOPHER ALLMAND

IN A sense the problem facing the non-combatant in time of war may be said to be one of relationships. In the second century AD, the poet Juvenal introduced into literature the theme of the relationship between the soldier and those (the *togati*) whom, in modern parlance, we call non-combatants. From the last of his *Satires* we learn that it was a very one-sided affair, the odds being heavily stacked in favour of the soldier, the unfair advantage of whose calling was held up to critical scrutiny. The reluctance of the non-combatant to use force against a soldier, or to complain of ill-treatment suffered at his hands, as well as the great advantages enjoyed by the soldier when cases came before the courts, were all emphasized. Juvenal was claiming that a soldier's power made any challenge to what he might do most unlikely. He was also making it clear that legal practices (such as placing cases involving soldiers at the head of the queue, whereas others normally waited a long time for justice) emphasized the difference between soldier and non-combatant in Roman society.

The well-defined position of the Roman soldier made it relatively easy to see who, in that age, was what we would call a civilian. The use of the word in English is modern (the *OED* citing the first known use of the term 'civilian' in this sense as dating from 1766) while in French the word 'civil', used as a noun, dates from the early nineteenth century. Did the middle ages have any comparable idea of who the non-combatant was? Did he have any sort of status, moral or legal? Although there was no word to describe his position within the law, it is clear from early on that the person who, because of age, gender, or occupation, did not normally bear arms belonged to that category of persons who might be regarded as non-combatant. Furthermore, it is clear that at certain times in the middle ages the position of such persons caused great concern.

From the very early middle ages the non-combatant (the *inermis*, or unarmed person), one of the majority of any population who did not bear arms in time of conflict, was already deeply involved in violence. He and his property, movable and immovable, were targets of attack by both Christians and non-Christians alike. In the century or so which followed the death of Charlemagne and the breakdown of the Carolingian order, unruly knights—among others—used their military power to disturb and destroy the livelihoods of persons who lived off the land. On the many frontiers of the Christian world, populations might experience attack from those whose style of making war was the raid aimed at the seizure of booty and plunder, both human and material, or at the harrying of the countryside and the destruction of the sources of production, sometimes prior to permanent settlement. The Magyar invasions and early Viking attacks, as well as the advances made by the Moors into the Iberian peninsula in the ninth century, all brought fear and terror to those caught up in them. The displacement of populations, the loss of material goods, captivity for those taken away for what might be lifelong slavery, were the fate of many in different parts of Europe at this period.

Border and frontier societies were particularly vulnerable, the raid being the characteristic form of war waged by and on those who lived on them. Dangerous as were attacks from outside, tenth-century Frankish society was even more anxious about the self-inflicted wounds, mainly in the form of attacks by lay magnates and the gangs whom they protected, upon the lands of the Church, and the effects which such lawless activity was having upon contemporary society in general. A dialogue, *De statu sanctae ecclesiae*, written about 920, demanded that spiritual penalties be imposed against those who attacked sacrilegiously the sources of the Church's wealth. What would develop into the 'Peace of God' (*Pax Dei*) movement would prove to be broader in scope. In 857 Charles the Bald had already taken steps to protect not only church lands and the clergy, but nuns, widows, orphans, and the poor (*pauperes*) from acts of violence. A century or more later, in a world in which public authority was in steep decline, and crop failure and floods were seen as marks of divine disapproval, the Church would assume responsibility for trying to restore peace to society. The feud which led to local conflict, a characteristic of these societies, had to be brought to an end. It could only be achieved by arousing public opinion and getting things done.

In this respect a meeting between the bishop of Le Puy and his people, held in 975, had more than symbolic importance. On this occasion the bishop sought the peoples' advice on what to do; and he won the important support of his noble kinsmen in his attempt to impose an oath upon men that they would respect the property of the Church and of the *pauperes*. In 989 a local ecclesiastical council meeting at Charroux, near Poitiers, ordered strong penalties against those who had attacked churches or unarmed clerks, or who robbed peasants and *pauperes* of their animals. Over the next half a century or so a series of local councils in Francia issued similar decrees against those violating the peace of people who could not adequately protect themselves.

None can doubt the importance of the 'Peace of God' movement as evidence of a growing consciousness that certain categories of persons should be placed beyond the the realm of violence (whether that violence resulted from internal disorder or from external attack). Yet, powerful as excommunication or interdict might be, neither resolved the problem of seemingly endemic disorder. Further steps were called for. Having banned acts of violence against certain groups (the clergy, pilgrims, merchants, and the ubiquitous *pauperes*), the Church went further. At Toulouges, in 1027, a new approach was announced. The product of a widely perceived need to restore order to society, the 'Truce of God', or *Treuga Dei* as it was called, was an attempt to restrict the lawful exercise of arms to certain days of the week and to certain times of the year. Fighting on Sundays (the Lord's day) would be prohibited; so would it be on Thursdays (when the Lord had instituted the Eucharist), on Fridays (when He had died), and on Saturdays (when He had lain in the tomb). Legitimate fighting was thus limited to the three days Monday, Tuesday, and Wednesday. Furthermore, it would be banned during the weeks of Advent and Lent, and on a number of major feasts. With such restrictions increasingly in place, it is hardly surprising that an ecclesiastical council held at Narbonne in 1054 should have decreed the next (logical) step, that no Christian should kill another, 'for whoever kills a Christian undoubtedly sheds the blood of Christ'. Using its own law which, by the eleventh century, was receiving increasingly wide recognition, the Church had taken the matter of establishing peace in society as far as it could.

Encouraged and aided by the Church, it now became the turn of secular authority to set its seal upon the peace movement. In a real sense, the Crusade was an attempt to release the restless energies of the nobility, and to harness them against the enemies of Christ rather than against fellow Christians. Equally significant was the way the secular power (in Normandy, for instance) acted first with the bishops, and then more and more on its own, to impose the order associated with the duke's peace. Elsewhere, too, in Sicily and southern Italy, in Catalonia and in France, it was the secular authority which, increasingly, gave its protection to the Church, its personnel, and the non-military lay classes, or, as in Germany, which encouraged the development of *Landfrieden*,

or peace regulations for a region, to further the spread of peace movements at a local level.

The twin and complementary movements of the 'Peace' and 'Truce' of God had produced ideas and principles concerning the establishment and safeguarding of social peace which would be incorporated into the *acta* of provincial ecclesiastical councils and then into the universal canon law of the Church. These texts demonstrate that, in the late tenth century, the Church of the former Carolingian world had become acutely aware of the need to grant special protection to the security of ecclesiastics, their lands and their tenants, often among the most economically productive, whose lives and welfare were threatened by unruly plunderers, mainly laity, from within society itself. The movement was influenced both by a desire to preserve social peace and the recognition of the need to maintain levels of food production at a time of not infrequent famines and plagues. In the way that it sought to protect merchants, too, the 'Peace' reflected the perceived economic and social needs of the day.

It is useful to see how far the twelfth century judged signs of change of attitude towards the noncombatant. The evidence of Orderic Vitalis, monk of Evreux, in Normandy, a well-informed commentator on the developments of the world about him, is that of a man who lived in an area where the principles of the 'Peace' and 'Truce' of God had been formally accepted by both Church and the secular authority. From him we learn that, locally, the principles of the 'Peace of God', expressed in the decisions of the council of Rouen in 1096, were not being put fully into effect. Equally significant was the way in which he recounted incidents which enabled him to express moral judgements in favour of the poor and the weak. Robert of Rhuddlan, he recalled, had harrassed the Welsh for many years; 'some he slaughtered on the spot like cattle, others he kept for years in fetters, or forced into a harsh or unlawful slavery'. 'It is not right that Christians should so oppress their brothers who have been reborn in the faith of Christ by holy baptism.' Another story, concerning the vision of the priest, Walchelin, confirms that people generally feared soldiers (because of their propensity to vio-

Although the women in the centre of this woodcut are not under direct attack, they represent those whose lives were gravely disturbed by war. The contrast between their vulnerability and the strength and violence of soldiers pursuing a defeated enemy underlines the growing awareness of the dangers to which both non-participating civilians and their property were subject in wartime.

lence) rather than seeing them as their protectors, and Orderic depicted them carrying much plunder. The day of the lawless brigand who could act without impediment, whose activities were dreaded by 'unarmed and well-disposed and simple people', was to be condemned. On the other hand, he was full of praise for Richard II of Laigle who had shown mercy to a number of peasants whom he found huddled around a wooden cross, but whom he spared although 'he might have extorted a great price if he had been so irreverent as to capture them'.

The measures taken to protect the non-combatant in the eleventh and twelfth centuries had had some effect and had evidently won some support. The thirteenth century was to bring yet further developments. With the age of nation-states about to dawn, the defence of rights or territories would now form the bases of many wars, while armies, making use of new arms and techniques, would seek more systematically to further their rulers' aims and ambitions. With an increase in inter-state war, many more would be seeking any protection which might be accorded them. The search for how best to protect the non-combatant, far from over, for these reasons took on a new dimension and a new intensity.

That search would involve the philosopher, the theologian, and the lawyer. Long ago, in the early fifth century, St Augustine, though he stressed that ultimate peace was the only proper objective of war, had held that in a war deemed to be 'just' all might be legitimately killed. The fact that all might not be equally involved (and therefore culpable) in war was an irrelevance, and the distinction between the soldier (who fought) and the non-combatant (who did not) had not been seen as significant. By 1140, however, Gratian, when compiling his *Decretum* or compendium of the Church's law, would follow the canon law which had evolved during the age of the 'Peace of God' by exempting clerics, monks, pilgrims, women, and the unarmed *pauperes* from the violence of conflict; which brought him perceptibly closer to some kind of non-combatant immunity. Yet a century or so later, while one Dominican friar, Vincent of Beauvais, thought that those who refused counsel or aid to their rulers in time of war should be exempt from its consequences, another, the great Thomas Aquinas, never set out a clear doctrine of immunity for non-combatants.

If there was progress, it came not through clearer definitions of combatant or non-combatant, but through the new 'just war' theory developed in the thirteenth century, by Aquinas in particular. The problem was essentially how best to create conditions for orderly war. These conditions could be of two kinds. The first centred on the answer to be given to the question when and in what circumstances was it legitimate to wage war? Lawyers and philosophers insisted that, in order to be seen to be just, war would have to be officially declared, something which could be done only by a properly constituted secular authority. The formal and public declaration of a state of hostilities was seen as significant. It sought to outlaw private war by making it illegal, and therefore 'unjust'. It also made it easier to insist that spoil should be taken only as an act of war ('*in actu belli*'), thus helping to control indiscriminate attacks upon the private property of the non-combatant.

More significant was the consequential problem which Aquinas faced, namely how was a just war to be fought, and what constraints should be imposed upon those who took part in it? It was clearly accepted that, however justifiable a war might be, unreasonable violence discredited not only a particular enterprise but the entire 'just war' theory as well. The means used, therefore, must reflect the participants' proper intention when going to war, war which Augustine much earlier had stressed must be fought only as a means to peace.

This would pose the problem of proportionality, best expressed in the question 'Is a sledge hammer really needed to crack a nut?' It is clear that, by the mid-thirteenth century, the problem of how to deal with war's excesses (which could be of many kinds) was being answered at least implicitly in the teachings of Aquinas. Proportionality implied the use of only as much force as was needed to achieve a particular end. It also implied, albeit tentatively, that those not equipped to fight or those who offered no resistance should not be treated in the same way as an armed soldier might be. This implied a recognition of certain categories of persons who, whether because of their nature or their evident inability to offer resistance, should have at least a minimum of respect shown to them. Such ideas were to be incorporated into Aquinas's thinking on proportionality; in time of conflict, all who did not actively oppose force with force enjoyed certain rights, in particular the right to life and, although this is less clear, the right to the preservation of property and means of livelihood. Society was now beginning to admit that those who took no active part in war, and did not resist the soldier with force, had a right, in natural law, to protection and to life.

It was what would later be known as the Hundred Years War which was to witness important developments in the story being traced here. This conflict had certain particular characteristics having a bearing on our subject. The scale of the war, measured in terms of both space and time, was to prove greater than anything known to earlier European history. It also involved whole societies in ways no previous war had done. This was the 'great war' of the middle ages, one whose effects upon society were to be considerable and, at times, terrible, too.

Why was this so? Its battles, although well known by name, were by no means the war's most significant moments. For long periods military events could be best described in terms of raids which were far more characteristic of the war than formal battles ever were. Battles involved soldiers fighting soldiers. Raids (or *chevauchées* as they were termed) were an entirely different matter, often being carried out by men who, not always assured of pay, often served on the understanding that responsibility for seeking the means of survival in enemy country lay with them. On the Anglo-Scottish border, for instance, it was not the Scottish custom to pay soldiers, who were expected to reap their rewards through their own enterprise and initiative. The activities of the reivers in that area are well known. Since they were particularly adept at setting fire to property, the advice given to Englishmen, when raids were threatened, was to remove the thatches of their houses in order to secure the main part of the building which, built chiefly of stone, could not be set on fire so quickly. The reivers also indulged in pillage, in cattle rustling, and in taking human prisoners. The survival to this day in the Anglo-Scottish Borders of fortified towers or 'bastles' is evidence of the dangers facing the civilian population in such regions which were, at the best of times, far from peaceful. Such military activity was common to many frontier societies in Europe and elsewhere. The tactics used in the north were frequently practised by the English in France, while at times the French and their allies, notably the Castilians who provided the ships, landed on the southern coastline of England, terrifying the inhabitants of the maritime shires. This was a war of intimidation in which armed soldiers, who might number a few hundred or a few thousand men, swept across an area of countryside, often content to bypass well-defended places which offered resistance, more anxious to keep on the move (in order to avoid confrontation with an enemy army), destroying farms, barns and their contents, mills, and fish ponds, ransoming whole communities, and picking up booty to be placed in wagons specially brought for the purpose.

Why were things done in this way, and with what objectives? The tactic was scarcely a new one. It was, as it had always been, a form of psychological war intended to create maximum fear and insecurity among populations. When church bells rang in the mountainous country of central southern France, their message was not always that of summoning the faithful to prayer: they could just as well be calling them to seek the inadequate protection provided by their villages or churches, many of which had crenelated towers built on to them in the course of the fourteenth century. Shepherds and their flocks on mountain pastures (the direct descendants of those referred to in the decree of the council of Narbonne promulgated in 1054) were an easy target for groups of marauding soldiers who either killed or led away the sheep. In agricultural regions harvests, including vineyards, were regularly destroyed by soldiers who brought to nought efforts to produce food and provide a living for farmers and their families, not to mention the local communities which depended on them. Such acts of seemingly wanton destruction and the lack of confidence in the future which they all too readily induced led to entirely predictable results. Many recent studies have shown how large estates in normally rich agricultural areas contracted in time of war, the uncertainty regarding the future deterring work on outlying land which, before long, became unproductive wasteland. The tares or *zizania* of Matthew's gospel, a favourite image of contemporary preachers who warned against dangerous doctrinal tendencies, were also a reality of the agricultural scene. These quickly took hold of uncultivated land which required much patient clearing before it could once again become productive.

Was all this merely wanton destruction for destruction's sake? It must be recognized that the good of the non-combatant and his property in wartime was increasingly linked to his developing participatory role in war, to the strategies adopted by the leaders of states at war and, to a certain extent, to the effects of new weaponry now becoming available. It is clear, for instance, that the role of the non-combatant in war could not always be totally distinguished from that of the soldier. The payment of small subsidies towards the costs of war, sometimes in place of personal service, was already common in some parts of Europe by the eleventh century. Over time, the contribution of the non-combatant population was to grow, particularly from the thirteenth century onwards. Certain taxes were imposed with the specific intention of securing the defence of the whole community. In most regions the clergy were expected to contribute; and they gave their blessing to war by urging their congregations to pray for victory, and by organizing public processions to seek divine approval in war. All such activities were manifestations of different sections of communities contributing to war in different ways. Likewise, the approval of taxation in assemblies, local and national, was increasingly regarded as an entire community giving agreement, through its representatives, to the levying of financial support in time of war.

In brief, then, as wars were gradually transformed into conflicts between whole and increasingly self-conscious communities, so it became increasingly difficult to argue that even the seemingly innocent activity of the farmer who tilled the land to grow cereal products, or bred cattle or sheep, should be immune from war. Some of his produce could be used to feed armies (and their horses); other parts of the same produce (skins or wool) was a possible source of taxation (hence of public wealth) out of which armies could be paid. Even goose feathers had a military use! Our knowledge, in recent years greatly enhanced by research, of how wars were organized and paid for, demonstrates that war was becoming more and more a societal enterprise, and that even the majority who did not fight in person played an increasingly important role in providing armies with their needs. Where did the non-combatant's role end and that of the soldier begin? The line of demarcation was not at all clear.

It might then be argued—as it was—that while the person of the non-combatant should be respected unless he offered armed resistance, his property (the basis of a community's wealth which would be used to

The greater realism of late medieval art encouraged depictions of scenes such as the looting of this fine dwelling. All forms of property, treasure, wine, vessels, and plate were at the mercy of greedy and loutish soldiers, intent upon the theft of what they could take away and the destruction of what they could not.

advantage in time of war) constituted a legitimate target. In certain societies (as seen above) sources of wealth and livelihood (cattle, for instance) were traditional targets of the armed raid. By the fourteenth century, the English were launching *chevauchées* across the sea into France, raids sometimes involving armies of over 10,000 men, which had the aim of laying waste the enemy's land, destroying his means of production, securing booty for the raiders and undermining the authority of the French king who would then be seen as too weak to fulfil his royal function of providing protection for his people. The construction of walls around many French towns during the second and third quarters of the fourteenth century was a recognition that French society was actively engaged in providing refuges for those living on the *plat pays*, or surrounding countryside, when hostile forces were in the area. The term 'refugee' was to enter the language rather later, but the concept was a much older one.

If military and political aims developed, as they did at least partly in response to developments in weaponry (such as the greater effectiveness of the cannon), the non-combatant might suffer even more. In the fifteenth century, English kings abandoned the raid in favour of a policy of direct conquest.

No conquest could be effected unless all fortified towns and castles were brought under the control of the invader. Ironically, the defences built in the fourteenth century to protect communities against raids now had the opposite effect of attracting armies equipped with cannon ready to besiege and take them. Thanks to developments in technology, a siege undertaken with determination was now, more than ever, likely to be brought to a successful conclusion. Such sieges, however, could witness terrible, indiscriminate, and prolonged suffering on the part of the non-combatant population. The siege of Rouen, pressed by Henry V between July 1418 and January 1419, was the siege of a well-fortified city to which thousands, fleeing before the English army, had come in search of refuge. The accounts of it describe the sufferings of those inside the walls: the old and infirm expelled into the city's ditches in mid-winter to preserve the dwindling stocks of food for the garrison and the younger non-combatants; the effects of starvation upon men, women, and, in particular, the very young. The writing is often emotional and sympathetic (even when it is written by an English soldier) to the plight of the innocent.

It is clear that the civilian was no longer the accidental victim of war but was now becoming one of the chief targets of those who were waging a 'just' war with royal or princely authority. The reasons are not difficult to understand. That the non-combatant was an easy target is obvious enough. The evidence of inquisitions or pleadings made before the courts regarding the often deliberately caused destruction of war is reflected vividly in the chronicle evidence. Yet the vulnerability of the non-combatant was not the only reason why soldiers sought him out. It should be recalled that it was from the general population that the enemy's fighting power of the future would be drawn. Likewise, it was from the economic activity of the non-combatant population, whether that of the manufacturer of goods in a town, that of the farmer who tilled the land or of the fisherman who trawled the sea, that taxes for war, in this age an increasingly important consideration, would be raised. If the non-combatant's means of production or livelihood were diminished or destroyed, then his crucial financial contribution to the escalating costs of war would suffer the same fate. Such evidence serves as a reminder that it was the non-combatant who, in more than one sense, paid for the war. Indeed, he often paid twice. Destroy the basis of individual wealth, destroy the basis of taxation. Destroy taxation, destroy the ability of an entire society to secure its own defence. Men were not ignorant of the adverse effects of the destruction of a country's economic base upon its ability and willingness to resist an enemy. In such circumstances, might it not be thought that war waged against the non-combatant was both a legitimate and an effective means of securing victory?

In 1435, at a crucial moment of the Hundred Years War with the conflict turning in favour of the French, a leading English captain, Sir John Fastolf, presented his king with a memorandum suggesting how best to exploit this trend. Sieges, he argued, were a waste of time, men, and money; rather would it be better to teach the enemy a sharp lesson and show him who still had the power and will to be master. In pursuit of this aim, Fastolf advocated the despatch of two small forces, with the intention of 'brennyng and distruynge alle the lande as thei pas, bothe hous, corne, veignes, and alle treis that beren fruyte for mannys sustenaunce, and alle bestaile that may not be dryven, to be distroiede.' Harsh as this might seem, Fastolf was explicitly advocating a form of war aimed at the destruction of the enemy's natural resources, although there is no mention of creating human victims in a direct way. Indeed, aware that such a proposal might shock some on his own side, he emphasized that 'this cruelle werre [was] withoute any noote of tirannye' since his king, 'as a goode Cristen prince', had offered 'that alle menne of Holy Chirch, and also the comyns and labourers of the reaume of Fraunce, duelling or being oute of forteresse shuld duelle in seuerte pesible', and that the war should be conducted only 'betwixt men of werre and men of werre'. The French, Fastolf claimed in his attempt to wrong-foot the enemy, had refused such an offer, 'and be concluded to make theire werre cruelle and sharpe, without sparing of any parsone'.

Fastolf was writing for a royal council on which his fellow soldiers had influence. How might such action be regarded by contemporaries who did not share this background? We should remember that this was an age which accepted, with fatalism, the reality of divine intervention in human affairs. God decided how things should happen. The best which men could do was to pray that He would avert disaster and calamities by His divine power: '*a fame, morte et peste, libera nos, Domine*' ('From hunger, death and the plague, Lord, deliver us') was the popular litany of the time. The influence of man's sinfulness and its effects were deeply ingrained upon the contemporary mind. It is of little surprise, therefore, that war and its evil results were often regarded as a divine visitation which God permitted to happen to a people who had sinned. It was not uncommon for the enemy to be regarded as the human instrument of God's will, the flail of God ('*flagellum Dei*) punishing His people as a parent punishes a child who has done wrong. Could man, indeed should man resist the will of God? Was it not better to accept disaster in a spirit of penitence as a person accepts punishment, and then to be in a position to begin afresh, having paid the price of weakness and sin?

Not all, however, saw it that way. Many regarded an attack upon a noncombatant as a sign of weak government. Such a challenge demanded a response. Yet, what form should it take? To the question why not reform society in order to avert God's anger, it could be replied that Christ himself had said that it was better to wait for the tares to grow than to try to pull them up while they were small, for fear of uprooting the good plants with the bad. Many, therefore, should resign themselves to suffer. It was the justification for such inaction which led men to ask, with increasing frequency and bitterness, how long such a state of affairs could be allowed to continue. Taking into consideration the physical and moral sufferings increasingly experienced by society in time of war, it is hardly surprising that there should develop sympathy for those who were helpless before the power and aggressiveness of the soldier, anger that such things should be allowed to happen. And, all the while, there grew increasingly vocal demands that something be done to bring about a remedy.

What we are witnessing here is a change in the perception of the civilian's position in wartime, and, above all, what should be done to assist him in his dilemma. The principle of proportionality, so often breached, was now beginning to find increasingly widespread support. More implicit than ever in the many forms of description of what were known as 'excesses' (*exces*), such as petitions to the king describing acts carried out by soldiers against defenceless civilians for which some redress was sought, was the recognition that the victims had a right to expect something better, namely protection from such acts. The sentiment of late fourteenth-century texts, increasingly condemnatory of unjustified violence, was that of righteous indignation, protest, and criticism levelled against both those guilty of such acts and against the failure of the system (the king and the law in particular) which allowed them to happen. The chroniclers are an excellent source of such opinion, commenting openly upon the undisciplined behaviour of the soldier, all too often guilty of taking the law into his own hand, more concerned with filling his own pocket than with serving the king and society, as the developing view of the soldier's role in that society held he should. Writing in the 1360s, the Carmelite friar, Jean de Venette, had harsh words for the unruly soldiery and much sympathy for those who suffered the physical hardships of war which the French crown was too weak to prevent. In the next century, we have the evidence of the anonymous Parisian who chronicled events in France's war-torn capital, seeing developments through the eye of the non-combatant who was powerless to help bring about the end of the many conflicts from which the country had long suffered. The result was that

the men who used to have the land tilled, each dwelling in his own place with his wife and his household in peace and safety, merchants and merchant-women, clergy, monks, nuns, people of all walks of life, have been turned out of their homes, thrust forth as if they were animals, so that now these must beg who used to give, others

Here the artist contrasts the peaceful background scene with the young woman who has experienced the loss of both arms, one leg, and other disfigurements to her body. She may well be a woman of the camp, but her terrible injuries help to recall how easily the non-combatant could become the victim of war.

must serve who used to be served, some in despair turn thief and murderer, decent girls and women through rape or otherwise are come to shame, by necessity made wanton.

In France, the chroniclers were soon followed by the social commentators in condemnation of the lack of control exercised over the soldier and his activities (in particular if he was already being paid), their vigorous language being accompanied by demands that the civilian be left in peace and tranquility.

Such expressions are a reflection of something new, a growing awareness of society as one body, and an increasing concern for that part of it which, it seemed, was suffering more than the rest from the moral and physical effects of war. Why, it was asked, was the non-combatant the war's great victim? Greed (as expressed in the line '*Radix malorum est cupiditas*'—'The desire for possessions is the root of all evils') was often accused of being the cause of the trouble: the opportunity of making a quick profit on campaign was widely seen as helping to make the recruiter's task easier. It is significant that, in the memorandum alluded to above, Fastolf, himself one of war's great beneficiaries, should have argued 'that none of the chieftains shuld in no wise raunsone, appatise [hold to collective ransom] . . . no contre nor place that thei passe thoroughe for no singuler lucre nor profite of them silfe'. With the growing recognition that effective control of troops required good leaders and strong discipline, the qualities associated with good leadership and firm discipline became regular themes in much of the literature written around 1400. In contemporary eyes, it was on discipline that the security of the civilian was largely founded. But discipline was not simply a matter of personal control of soldiers by their leaders. In turn, it depended upon such factors as the ability to pay troops well and, above all, regularly. Thus the fate of the civilian was increasingly regarded as hanging upon the resolution of other problems. It could not be isolated and dealt with on its own.

What could the law contribute? As Juvenal in antiquity had suggested, precious little. The law of arms (the *jus armorum*), although founded on wide military practice, was formulated for the needs of the soldier. Nor, in spite of the ambitions of those who wished to see its authority extended, could the secular law achieve much, particularly if the authority which exercised it was weak. The last, perhaps the only resort was the canon law which, in the tenth and eleventh centuries, had been used to protect clergy, nuns, women, and ecclesiastical property. Now, four centuries later, men turned once more to that code which came nearest to providing the non-combatant with some explicit form of legal protection. In about 1389 Honoré Bouvet, a monk trained in canon law who was prior of a Benedictine monastery in southern France, wrote his *L'Arbre des Batailles* or *Tree of Battles*. Among other things, Bouvet discussed the prevalence of violence by armed soldiers against defenceless non-combatants. Both his analysis of the problem and the solutions proposed are of interest to us. The evils of war, Bouvet argued, stemmed not from war itself, but from wrongful use and practices. Since wrong practices could be put right, it followed that something could be done for the non-combatant. This marked a change of attitude: here was a man asserting that, through the observance of canon law, the excesses of war might be prevented and the doctrine of proportionality observed. The old fatalism was dwindling. Once again, the Church and its universal law would protect the person of the non-combatant. Others too, princes and commanders who bore military responsibility, must do likewise. The common good of the community demanded that the place of the non-combatant be recognized. Let us note what Bouvet actually wrote:

> If, on both sides, war is decided upon and begun by the councils of the two kings, the soldiery may take spoils from the kingdom at will and make war freely; and if sometimes the humble and innocent suffer harm and lose their goods, it cannot be otherwise . . . Valiant men and wise, however, who follow arms should take pains, so far as they can, not to bear hard on simple and innocent folk, but only on those who make and continue war, and flee peace.

Here, then, was what looked like an important distinction. Bouvet appeared to be arguing that, in time of war, while physical possessions were liable to being looted and plundered, the individual non-combatant, provided that he did not make war and acted peacefully (that is, he did not resist), should be unmolested. Furthermore, those involved in peaceful occupations, students travelling to university or their parents going to visit them there (recall the immunity granted centuries earlier to the merchant or the pilgrim on the road) should be left to travel unmolested. Bouvet then took the example of the ploughman and his horse or oxen. Since theirs was the essentially peaceful occupation of producing food they, too, should be left untouched. Or so he argued. Yet even he realized that, in time of conflict, people must expect to suffer physical and moral consequences of war. In his anxiety to protect the rural worker, was Bouvet reluctant to admit that, in a changing society, the ploughman was now contributing to the national good and the national economy and, consequently, to the national war effort, in a way in which his predecessor of four centuries earlier had perhaps not done? Was he being realistic and up-to-date enough in his pronouncements, sufficiently tuned-in to the reality of the world outside his monastery? What should be the protection accorded to the productive non-combatant in time of war? By the late fourteenth century, men were beginning to appreciate that here was a question which needed to be faced. But answer, as yet, there came none.

Nevertheless, the increasingly difficult plight of defenceless non-combatants was attracting more and more sympathetic comment. Many of France's best writers of the period, Eustache Deschamps, Guillaume de Machaut, Christine de Pisan among them, wrote to bemoan the lack of respect shown to the civilian by the soldiery and officialdom. When, about 1416, the Norman, Alain Chartier, wrote about the effect of war upon society, he did so by describing the reactions of four women to the fate of their husbands at the recent battle of Agincourt. One was dead; another a prisoner; the third was missing; and the last had fled the field of battle. The text of *Le Livre des Quatre Dames* is a close and subtle analysis of the reactions of these women to the fate of their menfolk. From it we learn a great deal about the effects of war upon ordinary non-combatants, in this case women, who became the victims of war not through anything done to them personally, but because their husbands suffered the consequences of taking up arms and going off to war. We learn, too, of the author's sympathy for the plight in which such persons found themselves. Chartier showed himself keenly aware of the mental anguish caused by war. In so doing he added a whole dimension to the more prosaic image of physical suffering which chroniclers conveyed in their works. Even at this distance of time, his story is a moving one.

The works of the poets, the analyses of social commentators, the books of advice to kings all present important evidence of the growth of public awareness of the non-combatant's experience in wartime. Even the artists added their silent commentaries on war's effects upon the non-combatant population. Illuminated manuscripts vividly depict soldiers looting or sacking what are clearly non-military targets, or sieges of prosperous-looking towns or cities whose capture will yield a rich financial harvest and lead to the death of those who have resisted. Telling, too, are the depictions of another scene from Matthew's gospel, the massacre of the innocents, many of which survive. In such paintings as that by Giotto in the Franciscan convent at Assisi, the picture of mothers trying to save their babies from their attackers underlined, in visual form, the commonly-felt hostility of society to the soldier, horror at the unprovoked death of innocent children, and the common reaction to the terrifying experience of the women concerned. It is not surprising that the feast of Childermas was a very popular one at the end of the middle ages.

To try to deal, in the space of a short chapter, with a complex subject which merits much more is not to do it justice. A contribution of this kind can only point out where the possibilities lie. Over several centuries, the middle ages slowly developed a clearer idea of who the non-combatant was. The concept of him and her evolved because the non-combatant was directly concerned in two major developments: one, the emergence of an ordered world ruled by law; the other, the growth of a society in which war was constantly increasing in significance, not least in the way that it became an activity from which few could escape. A society was coming into existence in which the soldier and the non-combatant, the active and the passive, lived in uneasy conceptual relationship. The non-combatant's position, particularly in wartime, was both a moral and a legal issue. Ultimately lawyers would try to resolve it through international law, itself the heir of the position claimed by canon law centuries earlier. In the meantime, although the law was not always effective in

preventing violence against the non-combatant, there were always those who were touched by the innocence of war's non-combatant victims. One of the first episodes of the Hundred Years War was the destruction, largely through fire, of an area near and around Cambrai, the local population suffering terrible effects. It was in response to this tragedy that Pope Benedict XII ordered 6,000 gold florins to be sent for the relief of its victims. At its destination, the money was distributed through the practical services of churchmen, care being taken to ensure that it came into the hands of those in greatest need, the genuine victims of the war, rather than the poor of every day. Such an act has a very modern ring about it. It enables us to say one thing. If it did not prevent atrocities of this kind from happening again, the charity dispensed by the papacy showed that a humanitarian conscience, reflecting the threat which war constantly presented to the non-combatant population, existed somewhere in Christendom and, in reflection of that conscience, was ready to act when need demanded.

Normally beneath the surface, but appearing above it with increasing frequency, there existed a growing sense of hostility to the apparently senseless effects which the violence of war caused to the *petit peuple*, such a sentiment sometimes being expressed as ideas which were, in essence, pacifist. By the end of the fifteenth century strong

Facing: along with the oft-depicted 'Flight into Egypt', the 'Massacre of the Innocents' by soldiers, even those [as here] in the service of a king, underlined what could happen when quiet village life was brutally disturbed by armed men with little respect for humanity.

Above: a *Landsknecht* supervises attacks upon women and the massacre of their babies, one of whom has been impaled upon a sword in what was commonly regarded as Turkish practice. The back view of the soldier prevents us from seeing precisely what emotion, if any, the scene is causing him, but his firm, authoritative stance speaks volumes to the beholder.

opposition to this violence, sometimes likened to a people suffering the torment of crucifixion, was being expressed by highly critical social commentators. What did peace mean if the ordinary man continued to suffer at the hands of the soldier? Leaders were needed to redeem their people from the torment which too many of them were experiencing. In their different media artists denounced the atrocities of the ill-disciplined soldiery. War might appear sweet to those who had never been involved (*Dulce bellum inexpertis*, as wrote Erasmus in the early sixteenth century), but those who had experienced it at first hand knew otherwise. The voice of the great humanist was but one in a rising chorus of protest which denounced war, its effects and, in particular, the sufferings of those for whom life was already hard enough without adding the need to defend themselves against men who took advantage of their vulnerability to attack them and deprive them of their livelihoods.

13 THE CHANGING SCENE

Guns, Gunpowder, and Permanent Armies

MAURICE KEEN

IN 1471, Jean du Bueil, ageing veteran of the Hundred Years War, was present at the council of war of the French King, Louis XI, when the Burgundians invaded France. 'War has become very different,' he commented. 'In your father's days, when you had eight or ten thousand men, you reckoned that to be a very large army: today it is quite another matter. One has never seen a more numerous army than that of my lord of Burgundy, both in artillery and munitions of all kinds: yours also is the finest which has ever been mustered in the kingdom. As for me, I am not accustomed to see so many troops together.' De Bueil's shrewd remarks highlight what were probably the two most important developments which, at the end of the middle ages, were visibly changing the face of warfare. One was the capacity of governments to field military forces on an unprecedented scale, and to maintain substantial numbers of troops on a permanent basis. The other was the growing significance in war of 'artillery and munitions', of guns and gunpowder.

Two engagements of the year 1453, when Jean de Bueil was at the height of his soldiering career, seem to foreshadow the way in which, twenty years later, he thought change was taking place. One was the battle of Castillon, the final act of the Hundred Years War; when the massed English columns of John Talbot, attacking the entrenched French camp, were mown down by enfilade fire from the guns of Jean Bureau, Master of Artillery in the new French army that Charles VII had been building up since 1445. The other was the siege and ultimate capture of Constantinople by the Turks. For nearly a year before the siege, Sultan Mehmed II, with the aid of the renegade Hungarian gunfounder Urban, had been building up a massive artillery, including one great bombard with reputedly a twenty-six-foot barrel. In six weeks of bombardment his guns carved great breaches in the famous walls of Constantinople, which had so often defied onslaught. The Ottomans had an overwhelming advantage in numbers as well as in artillery, and on the night of 29 May, after bitter fighting, the city was taken by assault.

Stated succinctly, the lessons to be drawn from these two dramatic events look a good deal clearer than they really were. Castillon was in no sense a victory for field artillery. Talbot made the mistake of launching his attack on a fortified camp in such a way as to expose his advancing troops to enfilade fire from guns that Bureau had brought to batter the walls of Castillon, not for a field engagement. Nor was the Turkish capture of Constantinople a walk-over for gunnery. So stoutly was the city defended that only days before the final assault Halil Pasha, the old and trusted councillor of Mehmed's father Murad, was urging that a siege which had made no headway should be abandoned before aid should arrive for the city from the west and expose the Sultan to the risk of humiliating defeat. And when, twenty-seven years later in 1480, Mehmed's lieutenant Mesic Pasha, with a still more massive artillery and comparable superiority in numbers, subjected the Hospitaller stronghold at Rhodes to two months' bombardment and breached its walls, his final assault was repulsed, with huge losses. Gunpowder and larger armies were forcing change, but at an evolutionary rather than a revolutionary pace, neither as fast nor as sharply as the famous encounters of 1453 at first sight suggest.

By the 1450s, gunpowder artillery already had a substantial history. The basic recipe for mixing powder from charcoal, sulphur, and saltpetre was known to Roger Bacon in the thirteenth century. The first sure reference to guns is the written authorization by the Signoria of Florence of 1326 for the casting of 'cannons of metal' for the defence of the city. Very soon after that, references to the casting of cannon, the making of stone balls, and the purchase of ingredients for powder become frequent, especially in urban records. By the 1370s, guns were coming into extensive use in siege warfare.

From the first, many cannon were made of bronze. Bell founding was a well-established skill, and bell founders could easily be transformed into cannon founders. The earliest cannon we hear of were mostly relatively light pieces, but because their principal potential was seen as being for siege operations, there was a natural urge to seek to increase their size, and so their range and the force of their projectile delivery. The tendency towards massive size becomes marked in the late fourteenth century, and many of the larger pieces were now constructed of wrought iron rather than brass. Iron rods were heated and hammered together round a wooden core (to be later bored out),

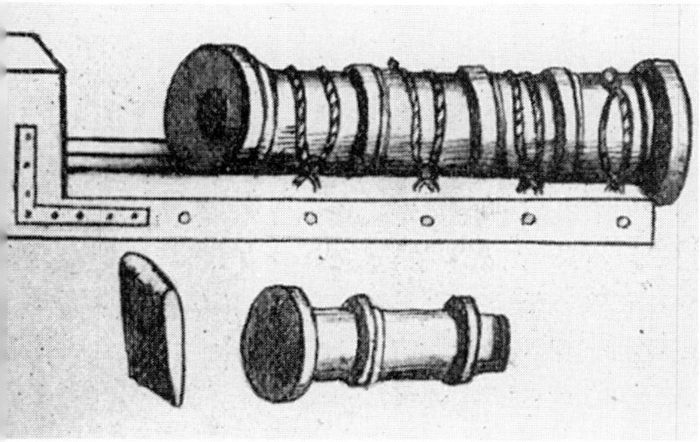

The first of these two sketches shows an early cannon mounted in a grooved wooden baulk, together with (*separately below*) the chamber and the wedge which will be hammered in to hold the chamber firmly against the breech. The second shows a similar cannon mounted in a wooden frame for firing.

and bound with iron hoops to form a barrel. They were usually breech loading. The powder charge was packed in a separate metal chamber, often as long or longer than the barrel. Plugged with a wooden plug, this chamber was wedged against the breech of the barrel, the plug resting against the ball, and wedged into position in the grooved channel of the wooden baulk in which the cannon was mounted. Then it was ready for firing through a touch hole in the chamber. By providing several chambers, which could be loaded in advance, the rate of fire could be increased. Great bombards of this type—and cannon generally—were transported by wagon, and mounted for action in a wooden frame or stall. A Nuremberg account of 1388 records that twelve horses were required to draw the wagon carrying the barrel and chambers of the great gun *Kreimhild* (great guns in this age were commonly given individual names: they were personalities in their own right on the martial scene). In addition, ten horses were needed to draw the stall, four to draw the winch (needed for mounting the gun in position), and twenty horses for the wagons loaded with stone balls (560 lbs weight each) and two hundredweight of powder. These were ponderous and expensive weapons.

There were a good many accidents with early cannon, through bursting barrels or in consequence of the chamber wedge flying out on firing: James II of Scotland, killed when the chamber of a bombard exploded at the siege of Roxburgh in 1460, was only the most distinguished casualty. But with experience, technical skill accelerated, both in the manufacture of guns and projectiles and in the preparation of powder. From around 1420, it became customary to use 'corned' gunpowder, dampened with wine or spirits, rolled into granules and dried, which much improved the force of combustion. At

'Mons Meg', a large bombard of *c.*1460, now at Edinburgh Castle, constructed from iron bars 2½ inches thick welded together, with welded over them rings of the same material. The chamber screws into the barrel, and has notches for the insertion of levers for this purpose. It is not known when it came to Scotland, but it was there in 1497, when a new 'cradill' (carriage) was made for it (the carriage illustrated is modern).

the same time, large-scale production of powder was bringing the price down sharply. By the mid-fifteenth century French gunners were commonly using iron balls, which were much more effective against masonry than stone ones. After the mid-century, the fashion for giganticism—for pieces like the great bombard founded by Urban the Hungarian for Sultan Mehmed or 'Mons Meg' (*c.*1460; calibre of 20 inches, length thirteen foot six inches, and weighing 5 tons)—began to wane; better ways were being found to achieve the same ends.

The cannon of the impressive siege train which accompanied Charles VIII's army when he invaded Italy in 1494 were lighter and of lesser calibre, but not less effective. Chambers were of reduced length in relation to the barrel: most were of bronze, and a good many were now cast in a single piece and muzzle loading. The barrels moreover were now cast with trunions (projecting gudgeons on each side) so that they could be mounted on their own carriages (two wheeled, sometimes four wheeled for heavy pieces), and pivoted to the required angle when firing. This greatly increased their mobility: Charles's artillery could keep pace with his army. 'What above all inspired terror were thirty six cannon with their carriages, drawn by horses at a speed that was incredible' wrote one astonished observer of the royal host. The number of draught animals needed to draw such an artillery was, of course, enormous.

The impact of gunpowder weapons on siege warfare took a long time to have decisive effect. There were a number of reasons for this. Heavy cannon were cumbrous instruments, and transportation (unless by water) was perforce very slow (see Chapter 8, p. 181). Furthermore, if bombardment was to be effective, guns had to be brought uncomfortably close to the walls of a town or castle. If and when they had been got into position, the rate of fire, especially of larger guns, was disappointingly low (see Chapter 8, p. 182).

In campaigns in Gascony and Maine in the 1420s, however, English artillery was proving significantly effective: and in Charles VII's campaign in 1449–50

Siege of a fifteenth-century castle: from a miniature by Loyset Liedet in an illuminated manuscript (*c.*1470) of the *Histoire de Charles Martel*. The two light cannon (one mounted with two barrels) have been brought close to the walls; the brazier in the foreground heats metal rods to apply to the touch-holes for firing.

for the reconquest of Normandy the French strength in artillery was a decisive factor. 'He had such a great number of large bombards, large cannon . . . ribaudequins and culverins that no one can remember any Christian king having such an artillery, nor one so well furnished with powder, shields and all other necessities for approaching and taking castles and towns,' wrote Berry Herald. To bring the guns up to the range where they would be effective, the Bureau brothers were already using the methods described a little later by Jean de Bueil, constructing trenches from one point of a siege to another, so as to bring guns close under cover from defender's fire and to maintain protected contact between units. At Rouen in 1449, when the Duke of Somerset in the citadel saw that 'great trenches were made there round about the said palace, as well in the fields as in the town, and bombards and cannon were laid on all sides', he lost heart and treated for surrender. In 1450 Harfleur, which in 1415 had withstood Henry V for six weeks, submitted after being bombarded for seventeen days. The English captains of a great many other places, recognizing that their walls could not face the artillery brought before them, did not wait for bombardment, but like Somerset capitulated on terms. It took a bare year to recover for France the Norman duchy that Henry V had conquered at the expense of so much 'blood and treasure', and that the English had defended so tenaciously in previous campaigns.

Artillery was comparably decisive in the Spanish campaigns in the 1480s for the reconquest of Granada, and in Charles VIII's lightning conquest of the Kingdom of Naples in 1494/5. Medieval walls were too high and too thin to resist prolonged bombardment. They could be lowered and strengthened, of course, and arrow loops could be altered to make gunports for the defenders' cannon, but as Richard Jones has written, 'no true artillery fortification can be said to have been constructed before 1450'. Soon after that, however, measures of defensive engineering began to be widely taken that would restore the balance more favourably to the besieged.

Walls were scarped with earth, so as to reduce their vulnerable height, and wall walks widened so as to carry guns. Towers along their circuit were constructed to a new design, lower, with a wide level area atop to act as a gun platform that would give heavy guns a wide angle of fire, threatening the besiegers' concentrations. Closer to ground level, they might be pierced with gunports, whence an assault could be raked with enfilade fire. These measures foreshadowed the development, from Italy, of the 'angle bastion', replacing the round tower. Its angular design greatly reduced the vulnerability of the whole structure by exposing the minimum face to frontal bombardment. By the 1520s (at latest), siege was well on its way back to the long hard slog of pre-gunpowder days. It was only for a relatively short period, from around the

The *Rocca Malatestiana*, castle at Cesena, showing an early angular tower bastion (*c.* 1466), in the walls and level with them, near the gate. Later bastions were often of considerably more complex angular construction.

middle of the fifteenth century till its end, that the attackers really held the initiative, though much always continued to depend on how far cities and princes had felt able or inclined to afford the building cost of new and more effective fortifications.

By the early sixteenth century, artillery, in consequence of its greater mobility, was coming to be of significance in the field (see below, p. 290). Much earlier, hand guns had begun to be important in battle. The earliest hand culverins were a kind of mini-cannon with a touch hole, attached to a pike staff and propped in a rest for firing. John Zizka, the Bohemian leader of the Hussite Wars, made good use of handgunners armed with culverins in his *Wagenburgen*, the laager of wagons that constituted a kind of mobile fortress (see above, Chapter 7, p. 158 and p. 159). His handgunners stood in the wagons, whose sides made an excellent rest for their weapons. The wagons could also be mounted with light cannon; while pikemen and halberdiers sheltered behind the carts, ready to make their charge when the advancing enemy had been halted and disordered by gunfire and archery. Zizka's *Wagenburgen* proved formidably successful against the German armies sent to fight him. Unlike the Hungarians, or the Russians in their wars against the Tatars, the Germans learned little from this experience.

The hand cannon was a clumsy weapon, and a thoroughly inaccurate one. The arquebus, which came into steadily extending use from the mid-fifteenth century on, had much greater possibilities. A metal tube, mounted on a wooden stock and fired from the shoulder, by means of a touch hole and a match device, it was not a difficult weapon to handle. Its ball had considerable penetrating power, and it was accurate. It took a while to reload, and that was no doubt why it only very gradually displaced the crossbow as the infantryman's favoured missile weapon. Its potential nevertheless had been appreciated early. In the 1470s Charles the Bold of Burgundy already had a good many arquebusiers in his service. His contemporary, the fighting King Matthias of Hungary, was decidedly keen on them: 'we make it a rule that one fifth of the infantry should be *arquebusiers*.' Later, in the Italian Wars, the Spanish in particular would make very effective use of them.

'As for me, I am not accustomed to see so many troops together. How do you prevent disorder and confusion among such as mass?' Thus, Jean de Bueil, quoted earlier. There was certainly something novel about the size of the armies that kings and princes brought together in the later fifteenth century, about their discipline, training, and ongoing terms of service. This was not however the consequence of any radical new perception about the political potential of military force. Development seems rather to reflect ad hoc reactions to particular circumstances and particular problems. In the matter of maintaining forces in permanent readiness for operations, the Lancastrian English system for the defence of conquered Normandy, and the growing practice among Italian city-states, in particular Venice (see above, Chapter 10, p. 221), of retaining their *condottieri* on a more long-term, settled basis may have been influential by example.

Numerically, the Turkish was the most powerful army operating in Europe in the closing middle ages. To besiege Constantinople, Sultan Mehmed brought together a force of perhaps 80,000 combatants. The Ottoman empire, which had its origin in the confederation of *ghazi* groups ('Holy Warriors') of the frontier between Christian Byzantium and Islam, was virtually a state organized for war. The *sipahis* of Anatolia and of Rumelia (the European provinces), cavalrymen settled on non-hereditary fiefs with an obligation to provide a fixed number of horsemen, were experienced fighting men rapidly mobilizable by their regional banner holders (*sancak bey*). The Sultan's elite troops were the Janissaries, reorganized by Mehmed's father Murad. They were recruited by the regular five yearly 'levy of boys' among the Christian subjects of the Ottomans, and reared to a fanatical devotion to Islam and to the calling of arms. In Mehmed's reign their numbers rose from 5,000 in the

Sultan Mehmed II (1451–1481), conqueror of Constantinople (1453). In south-eastern Europe his armies subjected the Morea, Serbia, Bosnia, and Albania to Turkish authority, and threatened Hungary. His sieges of Belgrade (1456, held by the Hungarians) and of Rhodes (1480, held by the Knights of St John) were not, however, successful.

early years to 10,000 by 1472: no Western European ruler ever attempted to maintain a personal, 'household' force on any remotely comparable scale. Cavalry was the predominant arm in the Turkish army, but as we have seen, Mehmed had a formidable artillery: he made very good use of turn coat or captive Christian gunfounders like Urban the Hungarian and George of Nuremberg.

It was in response to the Ottoman threat that King Matthias of Hungary (1458–90) set about establishing a military force on a permanent footing. It was especially strong in light cavalry ('hussars': see above, Chapter 9, p. 196): and Matthew also came to dispose of a respectable artillery, including thirty powerful bombards. This was a largely mercenary army. Outside Hungary, Moravia and Bohemia (whence came the famous 'Black Company') were with Serbia and Bosnia important recruiting grounds. Reinforced by the followings of the *voivodes* of Moldavia and Wallachia, which were strong in infantry, King Matthias could muster a very substantial field army, which was seasoned by his repeated campaigns (as often against his Christian neighbours in Bohemia, Austria, and Poland as against the Turks). The difficulty was in raising the money needed to pay his soldiers. G. Rázsó has calculated that, with an annual revenue of some 900,000 ducats, Matthias needed to set aside 400,000 ducats, given the rates of pay of the time, in order to maintain a force of 15,000 mercenaries. The fiscal burden was one that could not be borne indefinitely, and

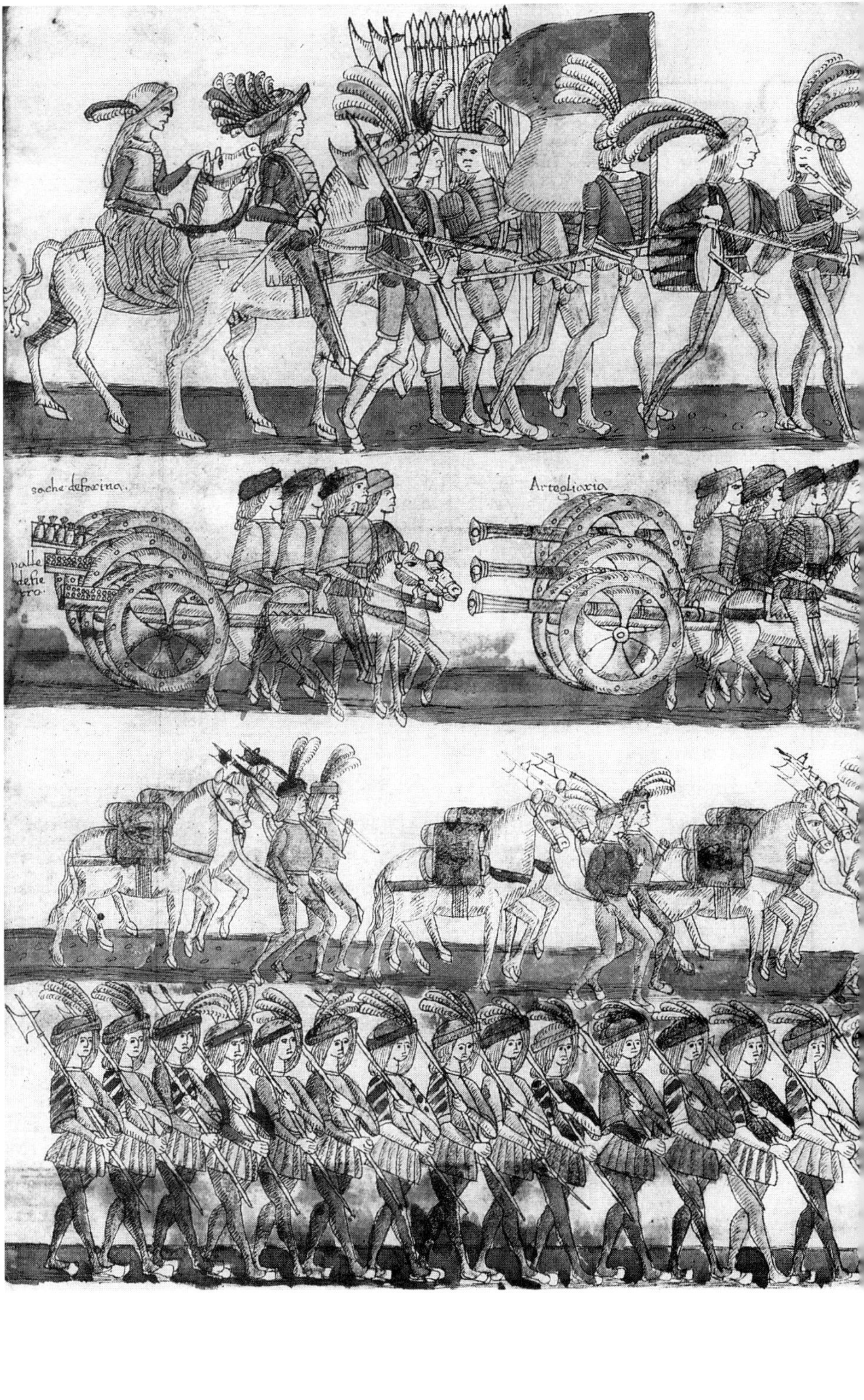
sache de farina.
palle de fie ro.
Artegliaria

his army was disbanded after his death. It was a comparatively non-professional levy, recruited in traditional medieval manner, that in 1526 went down before the Turks at Mohacs.

The real founders in the West of the permanent armies that came in due course to dominate the battlefields of Europe were the Valois Kings of France, whose success in channelling sufficient funds to pay their soldiers was the ultimate key to their achievement. The inspiration behind the measures taken in 1445 by Charles VII, the founding father of this permanent army, was not however a perceived need for a new kind of force. It was rather the opportunity which the brief truce agreed with the English the previous year seemed to offer to purge the realm of the worst of the freebooting companies who for years had lived off the land to its ruin, and to bring under effective royal control such soldiery as remained under arms against the end of the truce. A number of royal captains were appointed and commissioned to select the best troops from the existing companies, and to supervise the disbandment of the remainder. There was no general expectation in 1445 that the troops then retained would remain in service, or that the taxes (*tailles*) imposed to ensure their regular payment would continue, once the threat of military emergency had lifted. After the conclusive victories of the French over the English in Normandy in 1449–50 and in Gascony in 1451 and 1453, the troops were not disbanded, however, and the *taille* continued to be collected. A permanent French royal army thus came into being, and the French Kings, unlike the Hungarian rulers, were able to tap into sufficient fiscal resources to go on paying for it, year after year.

Charles VII's *ordonnance* of 1445, established fifteen *compaignies d'ordonnance* for Langue d'oïl, to which in 1446 were added five for Languedoc. Each company comprised notionally 100 'lances', a unit of six mounted men: a man-at-arms, a *coutillier* (armed with sword and knife), a page, two archers, and a *valet*. The company's captain, as a paid officer of the crown, was responsible for keeping up the numbers of his men and for their discipline. Outside periods of mobilization, the component lances were billeted on the community regionally in garrison towns. By an *ordonnance* of 1448, these mounted troops were reinforced by a reserve infantry of *francs archers*, recruited on the basis of one equipped archer for every fifty hearths. Later, in Louis XI's reign, this infantry was reinforced by the recruitment of pikemen rather than archers in the

Units of the French royal army, at Charles VIII's entry into Naples, 1495. The illustration shows a standard borne, a fifer and a drummer, pack horses with baggage and wheeled cannon ('drawn by horses at incredible speed'). Carts behind these carry bags of powder and balls (*palle de tiero*); infantry at the foot are in the uniform of their company.

provinces, and by bringing into royal pay a substantial and more professional body of Swiss pikemen. For the remainder of the fifteenth century and into the sixteenth, mercenary infantry, Swiss and German *Landsknechte*, always constituted an important element in the French army. The requirements of the substantial royal siege artillery meant that in wartime large numbers of carters and pioneers (to dig fortifications, siege trenches, and mines) had additionally to be mobilized.

The Burgundian army which Duke Charles the Bold (1467–77) sought to establish in a series of ordinances between 1468 and 1473 was modelled on the French one. The core element was a force of 1,250 lances 'of the ordinance', divided into companies of approximately 100 lances apiece. Each lance was supported by three infantrymen, a crossbow-man, a culverineer (or arquebusier) and a pikeman. In order to supplement the service of soldiers from his own territories, Charles recruited lances on a very large scale from Italy, and also from England and Germany: he also set about organizing a formidable artillery (he had some 400 cannon with him at the battle of Morat in 1476). Though most of Charles's native captains came of distinguished families, they were appointed, as in the French army, not on account of their fiefs and standing, but as ducal officers, and on the basis of regular pay for themselves and their men at stipulated rates (in both the French and the Burgundian armies, this made service as a man-at-arms attractive to the *noblesse*). The captains' revocable commissions were for a year at a time. Each on his appointment received a *baton* of office, and a 'paper book, bound in cramoisy, with a gilt clasp with the ducal arms on it', containing the duke's ordinances for war.

Though Charles's successive defeats suggest only mediocre talent for field command at best, in the sphere of military organization he showed real ability as well as enthusiasm. His 1473 ordinances carefully outlined the structure for his 'companies of the ordinance', each to be divided into four squadrons under a *chef d'escadre*, and subdivided into four 'chambers' of five men at arms leading their 'lances'. In order to preserve order on the march and in the field, each captain was to have his distinctive ensign; each squadron was to carry a cornet (or pennon) of the same design, embroidered with a gold letter C for the first squadron, with two Cs for the second, and so on. The leader of each chamber carried a banderole on his sallet (helmet), 'with a painted device . . . numbered I, II, III, IV respectively, inscribed beneath the C of the squadron'.

Text of Charles the Bold's military ordinance of 1473: the illuminated initial capital shows Duke Charles presenting bound copies to the captains of the newly organized companies 'of the ordinance'. The margins are decorated with arms of Burgundy and his other fiefs.

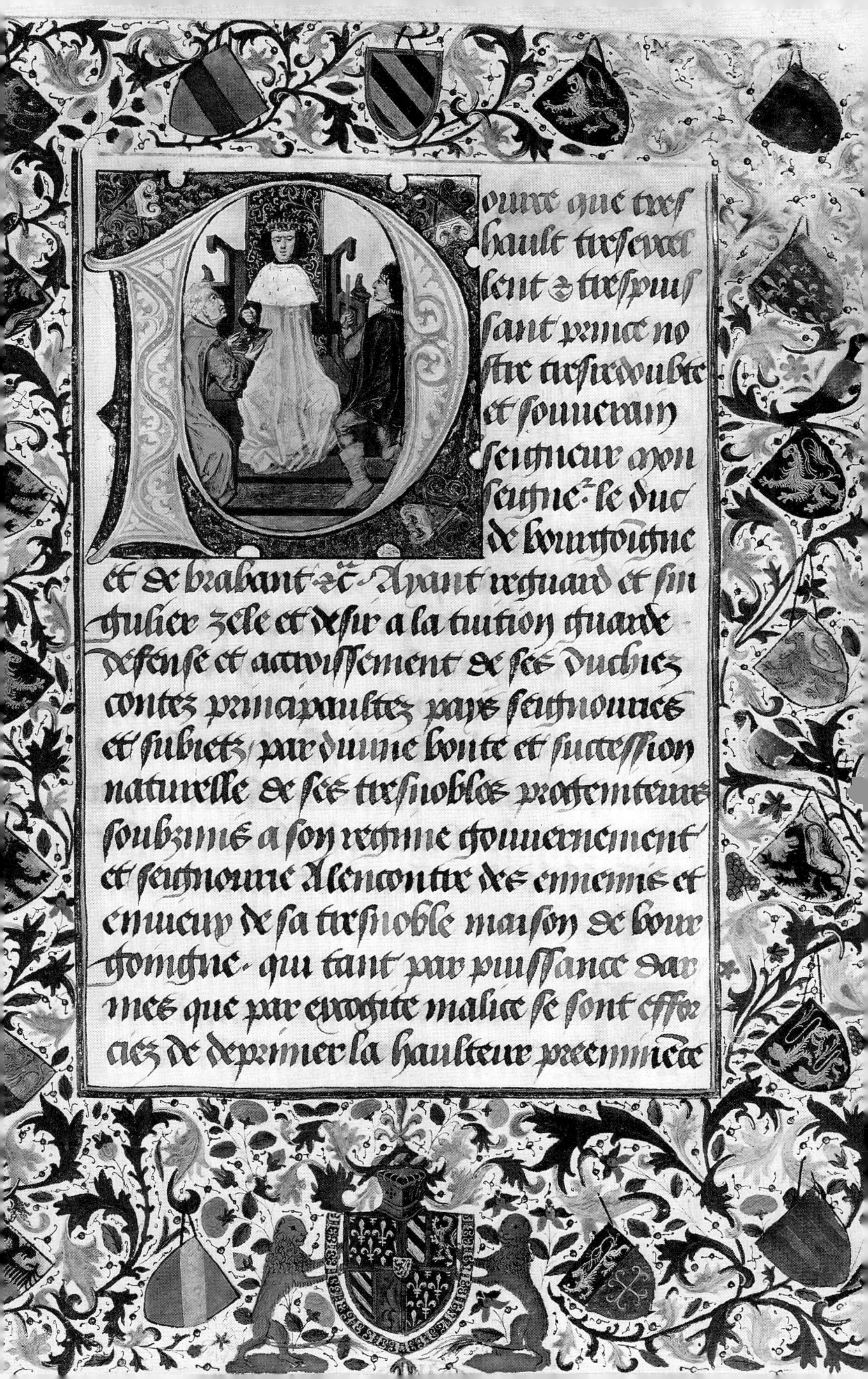
Pource que tres
hault tres excel
lent & tres puis
sant prince no
stre tres redoubte
et souverain
seigneur mon
seigneur le duc
de bourgoingne
et de brabant &c. Ayant regard et sin
gulier zele et desir a la tuition garde
defense et accroissement de ses duchez
contez principaultez pays seignouries
et subietz par divine bonte et succession
naturelle de ses tresnobles progeniteurs
soubzmis a son regime gouvernement
et seignourie alencontre des ennemis et
envieux de sa tresnoble maison de bour
goingne qui tant par puissance dar
mes que par excogite malice se sont effor
ciez de deprimer la haulteur preeminence

For this uniformed army, organized in readily recognizable units, Charles laid down strict disciplinary regulations, with heavy penalties enforceable on the spot by his captains. Most remarkable of all, however, were his provisions for martial exercises in peacetime: 'When they are in garrison, or have time and leisure to do this, the captains of the squadrons and the chambers are from time to time to take some of their men at arms out into the fields . . . to practise charging with the lance, keeping in close formation . . . (and how) to defend their ensigns, to withdraw on command, and to rally . . . and how to withstand a charge.' These detailed regulations for drilling and exercises open a genuinely fresh chapter in the story of the developing professionalism of the late medieval soldier.

Before Charles's time, his father Philip the Good of Burgundy had relied militarily on men-at-arms raised and led by the leading nobles of his territories and paid for their campaign service only, and supplemented by infantry contingents from the towns. Comparably, Ferdinand and Isabella of Spain relied principally in their first great military endeavour, the reconquest of Granada from the Moors, on contingents raised and led by their leading nobles in the traditional way, and on infantry from the town militias organized by the *hermandadas* (civic brotherhoods). But when the 'Catholic Kings' became involved in the wars in Italy after 1494, the need to establish more regular forces became apparent, and the Ordinance of Valladolid of 1496 imposed on one man in twelve, between the ages of 20 and 45, the liability to serve in the royal army. The organization of the army, as it evolved in the course of the wars, took definite shape in the form of units and sub-units comparable with those of the Burgundian army described above. The basic infantry unit was the regiment or *coronelia* (whence the word colonel) which was composed of twelve companies, notionally of 500 men each. Two of these companies were solely of pikemen; the other ten were each composed of 200 pikemen, 200 short swordsmen (the rough equivalent of the French *coutilliers*), and 100 arquebusiers. Every regiment of infantry was accompanied by a detachment of 600 cavalry, half heavy and half light. By the end of the fifteenth century, the Castilian monarchs had also acquired a substantial artillery. Among its infantry, the army of Ferdinand and Isabella was thus particularly strong in its pikemen and handgunners. On the mounted side, light cavalry (*genitors*) were always numerous, but Spanish armies were weaker in cavalry than the French or, in Charles the Bold's day, the Burgundians.

Not all rulers of this time had permanent armies. In Germany (an important European recruiting ground), the martially ambitious Emperor Maximilian was constrained by the consistent refusal of the Diets to provide the necessary funds. Nor was there in England, at the beginning of the sixteenth century, any standing force comparable with those of France or Spain. The campaigns of the Wars of the Roses had been of brief duration, and the armies that rival leaders had gathered for them did not outlast them. The hosts that Edward IV in 1475 and Henry VII in 1492 mustered for their abortive invasions of France were raised by the old-fashioned method of short-term contract. England, after the Hundred Years War, was no longer a major player in European land warfare; her kings had no need to tax their subjects in order to maintain substantial standing forces in the way that the French and Spanish monarchs did.

The later fifteenth century and the early sixteenth witnessed more major field engagements than had been the average in the wars of the middle ages. The attraction of quick results, given the enormous and spiralling cost of large-scale war (together with the temptation to believe that with large, readily mobilizable and well-armed forces such results might be achieved) was no doubt a large part of the reason for the frequency of such confrontations. In them, the martial potential of the new armies of Burgundy, France, and Spain was put to trial: they were also a testing ground for new weaponry, and for new tactical combinations of infantry (above all pikemen), cavalry, and gunners.

The fourteenth-century victories of the Swiss over the Hapsburgs at Mortgarten and Sempach had made them a name as among the most formidable soldiers of Europe (see above, Chapter 10, p. 227), and the most ferocious: they gave no quarter. The three great defeats that they inflicted on Charles the Bold's forces at Granson (1476), Morat (1476), and Nancy (1477) raised their reputation to its height. These engagements demonstrated dramatically the potential of the Swiss pike phalanx in offensive operation, closing with the enemy and charging at close quarters. Well drilled, and lightly armoured with only breastplate and helmet, the Swiss could move very swiftly, advancing to the tap of the drums which kept their pace even. Cavalry charges proved quite insufficient to halt them, let alone to throw them into disorder: it was the pikes that halted the cavalry, not vice versa. Artillery, in this Burgundian war, did not provide any better answer: it was still too cumbrous to manoeuvre in a tactical emergency. At Nancy the Swiss were onto Charles's guns before these could be trained on them.

Yet the three battles of 1476–7, Granson, Morat, and Nancy were not triumphs for the Swiss pike alone. At Granson Burgundian casualties were light, and Charles was able to re-form his defeated army: the reason for this was that the Swiss had no cavalry to follow up their success. Morat and Nancy were much more decisive. At Morat the Swiss were nominally in the service of

René, Duke of Lorraine, and he and his mounted men pursued the Burgundians fleeing along the lakeside, turning defeat into disastrous rout. At Nancy the fugitives, pursued by the cavalry of Sigismund of Austria, finally found their retreat cut off by the mounted forces of the Count of Campobasso, who had gone over from Burgundian service to the side of the confederates. The two battles effectively destroyed Charles's magnificent army; but if it had been opposed by Swiss infantry alone at them, then its history might have been longer, and different.

The engagements of the early period of the Italian wars show still more clearly how misleading it was to draw from these successes of the Swiss infantry the easy inference (as many at the time did), that the pikeman was master of the field. After Gonsalvo de Cordoba, the 'great captain' for Ferdinand and Isabella, had been roughly handled by the Swiss at Seminara in 1495, he took steps to reorganize his troops and to provide himself with substantial numbers both of pikemen and arquebusiers. When the Duke of Nemours was induced to attack him at Cerignola in 1503, his charging Swiss and French found themselves halted by the ditch that Gonsalvo had hurriedly constructed in front of his line, and subjected

The Battle of Pavia, 1525, where Charles V defeated and took prisoner Francis I of France: showing in the foreground field guns and a group of arquebusiers, with massed pikemen behind them. The heavy cavalry still carry the long lance that was the traditional arm of the mounted, chivalrous warrior.

LACITE DEPAVIE
56
ITALLIENS
LARRIEGARDE

to a hail of arquebus fire. The counter charge of the Spanish pikemen then drove them back downhill, and the Spanish light cavalry made the victory decisive in pursuit. Cerignola is often hailed as the first victory of the arquebus. Though Gonsalvo's choice of ground, the work of his pioneers on the ditch, and his capacity to pursue all contributed too, the weapon had made its mark. It did so again at Bicocca, a very similar engagement, in 1522. All agreed that at Pavia (1525), where the Spanish arquebusiers had to operate in open ground, and not from an entrenched position as in these two earlier battles, they played a significant part in the total defeat of the French.

The hard fought battle of Marignano (1515), where Francis I and the French finally triumphed over the Swiss in the pay of the Duke of Milan, illustrates other aspects of the picture. On the first day of the battle (13 September), the repeated charges of the French men-at-arms succeeded in slowing the Swiss columns sufficiently to ensure that when they closed, Francis's rival infantry of German *Landsknechte* held firm. On the second day the advancing Swiss column suffered severe losses, caused by the fire of the French artillery, and though it struggled forward it was halted by cavalry charges with the guns still playing on it. The Swiss losses were so great that they were forced to draw off, retreating in good order; the French cavalry was too tired to offer pursuit. The fighting demonstrated effectively what havoc could be wrought on a pike phalanx, if it could be halted by repeated charges in a position where it was exposed to fire from field artillery.

As the narratives of the Italian battles of the first decades of the sixteenth century make clear, black powder did not as yet rule the battlefield, though there was now a great deal more smoke. No more did Swiss or German pikemen, formidable as they were. Heavy cavalry had not lost its significance on the battlefield. The charge with the lance, in the traditional mode of chivalry, could still in the right circumstances be an effective and important manoeuvre. As ever, mounted men-at-arms formed the core of the *compaignies d'ordonnance* of the French royal army which was the model for so many others, and as Malcolm Vale has remarked, governments 'did not usually spend money, painfully gathered from taxation and loans, to underwrite forces which had outlived their usefulness'.

All the same, the signs of change, and of the passing of 'chivalry' are clear enough. Thanks in particular to the Swiss, war had become for the combatant more bloodthirsty and ferocious: casualties, among all classes, had grown in number. In battle as well as at sieges, guns had come to play a very significant role, even if not as yet a fully decisive one. Perhaps most importantly, war had become more professional for all those involved. More treatises on the art of war were written in the sixteenth century than ever before, and among their authors were some distinguished and experienced soldiers, such as Robert de Balsac, Berard Stuart, and later Gaspard de Saulx-Tavannes, who wrote with instruction in mind. Though the captains and commanders of the new armies (and indeed their elite men-at-arms) were still largely drawn from the nobility of birth, their experience and expertise were more varied than they had been traditionally. The Chevalier Bayard served for a while as captain of an infantry company; Gaspard de Saulx-Tavannes began his career as an archer: the family of Genouillac, of the old nobility of Quercy, provided a succession of Masters of Artillery to the kings of France. Old chivalry adapted itself to new ways, but there was a real difference, clearly demonstrated in a more self-conscious professionalism and in added emphasis on the honour of service to the prince as head of the common weal.

Christopher Allmand, commenting on this growing professionalism of soldiering in the new age of permanent armies, writes thus, 'The aristocratic view of war as a moment of individual opportunity was giving way to another. . . The imperative to win, indeed to survive was now taking over. The requirements to avoid the collective consequences of defeat thus led to societies choosing both soldiers and, in particular, leaders from those who had good practical experience of war.' His remarks catch aptly the changing social conception of what had once been the chivalrous calling of arms. Bayard, from whom Francis I begged knighthood on account of his reputation for prowess, was in an almost demonstrable way more of a loyal officer and less of a knight errant than had been, say, Jean de Boucicault, Marshal of France, champion of the jousting field, crusader and veteran of Nicopolis and Agincourt, a hundred years before him.

There was still a place, though, for individual adventurers in this fast altering world. If one wants to gauge whether the developments that were taking place around the end of the fifteenth century merit the fashionable title of a 'military revolution' or not, one needs to throw into the equation not only permanent armies, new gunnery, and growing professionalism, but also the new designs in shipbuilding and new advances in the art of navigation that Felipe Fernández Armesto has described in an earlier chapter in this book. These would affect significantly the pattern of warfare of the sixteenth century. They also made it possible for the early conquistadors to transport men, guns, gunpowder, and the knowledge of how to mix it, to lands of whose very existence the knights errant of the past had been unaware, with momentous consequences for the future.

FURTHER READING

1. Introduction: Warfare and the Middle Ages

P. Contamine, *War in the Middle Ages*, trans. M. Jones (Oxford, 1984).

G. Duby, *The Three Orders: Feudal Society Imagined*, trans. A. Goldhammer (Chicago, 1980).

F.-L. Ganshof, *Feudalism*, trans. P. Grierson (London, 1952).

M. Keen, *Chivalry* (New Haven, 1984).

E. McGeer, *Sowing the Dragon's Teeth: Byzantine Warfare in the Tenth Century* (Washington, DC, 1995).

M. Prestwich, *Armies and Warfare in the Middle Ages: The English Experience* (New Haven and London, 1996).

S. M. G. Reynolds, *Fiefs and Vassals* (Oxford, 1994).

F. H. Russell, *The Just War in the Middle Ages* (Cambridge, 1975).

M. Strickland, *War and Chivalry* (Cambridge, 1996).

M. Vale, *War and Chivalry* (London, 1981).

2. Carolingian and Ottonian Warfare

B. S. Bachrach, *Armies and Politics in the Early Medieval West* (Aldershot, 1993).

C. B. Bowlus, *Franks, Moravians and Magyars: The Struggle for the Middle Danube, 788–907* (Philadelphia, 1995).

F. L. Ganshof, *Frankish Institutions under Charlemagne* (Providence, RI, 1968).

P. Godman and R. Collins (eds.), *Charlemagne's Heir: New Perspectives on the Reign of Louis the Pious (814–840)* (Oxford, 1990).

G. S. Halsall, *Warfare and Society in the Barbarian West, c.450–c.900* (London, 1998).

K. Leyser, *Medieval Germany and its Neighbours, 911–1250* (London, 1982).

—— *Communications and Power in the Middle Ages: The Carolingian and Ottonian Centuries*, ed. T. Reuter (London, 1994).

J. M. Wallace-Hadrill, *Early Medieval History* (Oxford, 1975).

3. The Vikings

A. W. Brøgger and H. Shetelig, *The Viking Ships: Their Ancestry and Evolution*, trans. K. John (Oslo, 1951).

H. R. Ellis Davidson, *The Viking Road to Byzantium* (London, 1976).

P. Griffith, *The Viking Art of War* (London, 1995).

M. Harrison, *Viking Hersir 793–1066 AD* (London, 1993).

J. Haywood, *Dark Age Naval Power: A Re-assessment of Frankish and Anglo-Saxon Seafaring Activity* (London, 1991).

—— *The Penguin Historical Atlas of the Vikings* (Harmondsworth, 1995).

A. Nørgård Jørgensen and B. L. Clausen (eds.), *Military Aspects of Scandinavian Society in a European Perspective, AD 1–1300* (Copenhagen, 1997).

O. Olsen and O. Crumlin-Pedersen, *Five Viking Ships from Roskilde Fjord*, trans. B. Bluestone (Copenhagen, 1978).

P. Sawyer (ed.), *The Oxford Illustrated History of the Vikings* (Oxford, 1997).

D. G. Scragg (ed.), *The Battle of Maldon AD 991* (Oxford, 1991).

4. An Age of Expansion, *c.*1020–1204

R. Bartlett, *The Making of Europe: Conquest, Colonization and Cultural Change 950–1350* (Harmondsworth, 1993).

E. Christiansen, *The Northern Crusades: The Baltic and the Catholic Frontier 1100–1525* (London, 1980).

R. Fletcher, *The Quest for El Cid* (London, 1989).

J. France, *Western Warfare in the Age of the Crusades* (London, 1999).

N. Hooper and M. Bennett, *Cambridge Illustrated Atlas of Warfare: The Middle Ages 768–1487* (Cambridge, 1996).

H. Kennedy, *Muslim Spain and Portugal* (London, 1996).

S. Morillo, *Warfare under the Anglo-Norman Kings* (Woodbridge, 1994).

J. H. Pryor, *Geography, Technology and War: Studies in the Maritime History of the Mediterranean 649–1571* (Cambridge, 1988).

N. A. M. Rodger, *The Safeguard of the Sea: A Naval History of Britain*, i. *660–1649* (London, 1997).

R. Rogers, *Latin Siege Warfare in the Twelfth Century* (Oxford, 1992).

M. Strickland, *War and Chivalry: The Conduct and Perception of War in England and Normandy, 1066–1217* (Cambridge, 1996).

—— (ed.), *Anglo-Norman Warfare* (Woodbridge, 1992).

5. Warfare in the Latin East

GENERAL SURVEYS OF THE CRUSADES TO THE EAST

P. M. Holt, *The Age of the Crusades* (London and New York, 1986).

H. E. Mayer, *The Crusades*, trans. J. Gillingham, 2nd edn. (Oxford, 1988).

CRUSADING WARFARE

J. France, *Victory in the East: A Military History of the First Crusade* (Cambridge, 1994).

C. Marshall, *Warfare in the Latin East, 1192–1291* (Cambridge, 1992).
J. H. Pryor, *Geography, Technology and War: Studies in the Maritime History of the Mediterranean 649–1571* (Cambridge, 1988).
R. Rogers, *Latin Siege Warfare in the Twelfth Century* (Oxford, 1992).
R. C. Smail, *Crusading Warfare, 1097–1193*, 2nd edn. (Cambridge, 1995).

CASTLES

H. Kennedy, *Crusader Castles* (Cambridge, 1994).
D. Pringle, *The Red Tower* (London, 1986).

MILITARY ORDERS

M. Barber, *The New Knighthood: A History of the Order of the Temple* (Cambridge, 1994).
A. Forey, *The Military Orders from the Twelfth to the Early Fourteenth Centuries* (Basingstoke and London, 1992).
J. Riley-Smith, *The Knights of St John in Jerusalem and Cyprus c.1050–1310* (London, 1967).

MUSLIM OPPONENTS OF THE CRUSADES

M. C. Lyons and D. E. P. Jackson, *Saladin: The Politics of the Holy War* (Cambridge, 1982).
P. Thorau, *The Lion of Egypt: Sultan Baybars I and the Near East in the Thirteenth Century*, trans. P. M. Holt (London and New York, 1992).

6. European Warfare, *c.*1200–1320

E. Christiansen, *The Northern Crusades: The Baltic and the Catholic Frontier 1100–1525* (London and Basingstoke, 1980).
P. Contamine, *War in the Middle Ages*, trans. M. Jones (Oxford, 1984).
—— (ed.), *Histoire militaire de la France*, i. *Des origines à 1715* (Paris, 1992).
D. Crouch, *William Marshal: Court, Career and Chivalry in the Angevin Empire 1147–1219* (London and New York, 1990).
G. Duby, *The Legend of Bouvines: War, Religion and Culture in the Middle Ages*, trans. C. Tihanyi (Berkeley and Los Angeles, 1990).
W. C. Jordan, *Louis IX and the Challenge of the Crusade: A Study in Rulership* (Princeton, 1979).
E. Lalou, 'Les Questions militaires sous le règne de Philippe le Bel', in P. Contamine and others (eds.), *Guerre et société en France, en Angleterre et en Bourgogne XIVe–XVe siècles* (Villeneuve d'Ascq Cedex, 1991), 37–62.
M. Prestwich, *Armies and Warfare in the Middle Ages: The English Experience* (New Haven and London, 1996).
F. H. Russell, *The Just War in the Middle Ages* (Cambridge, 1975).
J. Sumption, *The Albigensian Crusade* (London and Boston, 1978).
J. F. Verbruggen, *The Art of Warfare in Western Europe during the Middle Ages*, trans. S. Willard and S. C. M. Southern (Woodbridge, 1997).
D. P. Waley, 'The Army of the Florentine Republic from the Twelfth to the Fourteenth Century', in N. Rubinstein (ed.), *Florentine Studies: Politics and Society in Renais-*

sance Florence (London, 1968), 70–108.
—— '*Condotte* and *Condottieri* in the Thirteenth Century', *Proceedings of the British Academy*, 61 (1975), 337–71.

7. The Age of the Hundred Years War

P. Contamine, *War in the Middle Ages*, trans. M. Jones (Oxford, 1984).
Kenneth Fowler, *The Age of Plantagenet and Valois* (New York, 1967).
—— (ed.), *The Hundred Years War* (London, 1971).
H. J. Hewitt, *The Organization of War under Edward III 1338–62* (Manchester, 1966).
Richard W. Kaeuper, *War, Justice and Public Order: England and France in the Later Middle Ages* (Oxford, 1988).
Maurice H. Keen, *The Laws of War in the Late Middle Ages* (London, 1965).
R. A. Newhall, *Muster and Review* (Cambridge, Mass., 1940).
Michael Prestwich, *The Three Edwards: War and the State in England 1272–1377* (London, 1980).
—— *Armies and Warfare in the Middle Ages: The English Experience* (New Haven and London, 1996).
Malcolm Vale, *War and Chivalry* (London, 1981).
J. F. Verbruggen, *The Art of Warfare in Western Europe during the Middle Ages: From the Eighth Century to 1340*, trans. S. Willard and S. C. M. Southern (Woodbridge, 1997).

8. Fortifications and Sieges in Western Europe, 800–1450

J. Bradbury, *The Medieval Siege* (Woodbridge, 1992).
P. Contamine, *War in the Middle Ages*, trans. M. Jones (Oxford, 1984).
A. Corfis and M. Wolfe (eds.), *The Medieval City under Siege* (Woodbridge, 1995).
R. Higham and P. Barker, *Timber Castles* (London, 1992).
D. Hill and A. Rumble (eds.), *The Defence of Wessex: The Burghal Hidage and Anglo-Saxon Fortifications* (Manchester, 1996).
S. Morillo, *Warfare under the Anglo-Norman Kings, 1066–1135* (Woodbridge, 1994).
M. Prestwich, *Armies and Warfare in the Middle Ages: The English Experience* (New Haven and London, 1996).

9. Arms, armour, and horses

Andrew Ayton, *Knights and Warhorses: Military Service and the English Aristocracy under Edward III* (Woodbridge, 1994).
Claude Blair, *European Armour circa 1066 to circa 1700* (London, repr. 1979).
Jim Bradbury, *The Medieval Archer* (Woodbridge, 1985).
John Clark, *The Medieval Horse and its Equipment, c.1150–c.1450* (London, 1995).
R. H. C. Davis, *The Medieval Warhorse: Origin, Development and Redevelopment* (London, 1989).
Charles Gladitz, *Horse Breeding in the Medieval World* (Dublin, 1997).
Ann Hyland, *The Medieval Warhorse from Byzantium to the Crusades* (Stroud, 1994).

The Warhorse, 1250–1600 (Stroud, 1998).
Miklós Jankovich, *They Rode into Europe* (London, 1971).
David C. Nicolle, *Arms and Armour of the Crusading Era, 1050–1350* (2 vols.; White Plains, NY, 1988).
R. E. Oakeshott, *The Sword in the Age of Chivalry* (London, 1964).
Bengt Thordeman, *Armour from the Battle of Visby, 1361* (2 vols.; Stockholm, 1939).
Malcolm Vale, *War and Chivalry* (London, 1981).

10. Mercenaries

GENERAL

P. Contamine, *War in the Middle Ages*, trans. M. Jones (Oxford, 1984), Chs. 3, 4.
M. Prestwich, *Armies and Warfare in the Middle Ages: The English Experience* (New Haven and London, 1996), Ch. 6.
J. F. Verbruggen, *The Art of Warfare in Western Europe during the Middle Ages* (Amsterdam, 1977), Ch. 3.

THE EARLIER MEDIEVAL PERIOD

J. H. Beeler, *Warfare in Feudal Europe* (Ithaca, NY, 1971).
S. Brown, 'The Mercenary and his Master: Military Service and Monetary Rewards in the 11th and 12th Centuries', *History*, 74 (1989).
M. Chibnall, 'Mercenaries and the *familia regis* under Henry I', *History*, 62 (1977).
J. O. Prestwich, 'The Military Household of the Norman Kings', *English Historical Review*, 96 (1981).

THE LATER MEDIEVAL PERIOD

C. C. Bayley, *War and Society in Renaissance Florence* (Toronto, 1961).
F. Gilbert, 'Machiavelli and the Renaissance of the Art of War', in E. M. Earle (ed.), *Makers of Modern Strategy* (Princeton, 1952).
M. E. Mallett, *Mercenaries and their Masters: Warfare in Renaissance Italy* (London, 1974).
F. Redlich, *The German Military Enterpriser and his Work Force*, i (Wiesbaden, 1964–5).
D. Waley, 'The Army of the Florentine Republic from the 12th to the 14th Century', in N. Rubinstein (ed.), *Florentine Studies* (London, 1968).

11. Naval Warfare in Europe after the Viking Age, *c.*1100–1500

P. Adam, 'Conclusions sur les développements des techniques nautiques médiévales', *Revue d'histoire économique et sociale*, 54 (1976), 560–7.
H. Ahrweiler, *Byzance et la mer: La Marine de la guerre, la politique et les institutions maritimes de Byzance au VIIe–XVe siècles* (Paris, 1966).
D. Ayalon, 'The Mamluks and Naval Power: A Phase of the Struggle between Islam and Christian Europe', *Proceedings of the Israel Academy of Sciences and Humanities*, 1 (1965), 1–12.
P. Charanis, 'Piracy in the Aegean during the Reign of Michael VIII Palaeologus', *Annuaire de l'Institut de Philologie et d'Histoire Orientales et Slaves*, 10 (1950), 127–36.
E. Christianen, *The Northern Crusades: The Baltic and the Catholic Frontier, 1100–1525*

(London, 1980).
A. Ehrenkreutz, 'The Place of Saladin in the Naval History of the Mediterranean Sea in the Middle Ages', *Journal of the American Oriental Society*, 75 (1955), 100–16.
F. Fernández-Armesto, *Before Columbus: Exploration and Colonisation from the Mediterranean to the Atlantic, 1229–1492* (London, 1987).
—— 'The Sea and Chivalry in Late Medieval Spain', in J. B. Hattendorff (ed.), *Maritime History*, i. *The Age of Discovery* (Malabar, Fla., 1996), 123–36.
I. Friel, *The Good Ship* (Baltimore, 1995).
G. Hutchinson, *Medieval Ships and Shipping* (London, 1994).
F. C. Lane, 'Naval Actions and Fleet Organization, 1499–1502', in J. R. Hale (ed.), *Renaissance Venice* (London, 1973), 146–73.
—— *Venice: A Maritime Republic* (Baltimore, 1973).
A. Luttrell, 'Late Medieval Galley Oarsmen', in R. Ragosta (ed.), *Le Genti del mare mediterraneo* (Naples, 1981), i. 87–101.
M. Mollat, 'Philippe-Auguste et la mer', in *Actes du colloque Philippe-Auguste* (Paris, 1980).
—— *Europe and the Sea* (Oxford, 1993).
J. H. Pryor, *Geography, Technology and War: Studies in the Maritime History of the Mediterranean, 649–1571* (Cambridge, 1988).
W. S. Reid, 'Sea Power in the Anglo-Scottish War, 1296–1328', *The Mariner's Mirror*, 46 (1960), 7–23.
N. A. M. Rodger, *The Safeguard of the Sea: A Naval History of Britain*, i. *660–1649* (New York, 1998).
W. L. Rodgers, *Naval Warfare under Oars: Fourth to Sixteenth Centuries* (Annapolis, Md., 1939).
J. P. C. Sumption, *The Hundred Years' War*, i. *Trial by battle* (London, 1990).
E. G. R. Taylor, *The Haven-Finding Art: A History of Navigation from Odysseus to Captain Cook* (London, 1956).
J. T. Tinniswood, 'English Galleys, 1272–1377', *The Mariner's Mirror*, 35 (1949), 276–315.
R. W. Unger, *The Art of Medieval Technology: Images of Noah the Shipbuilder* (New Brunswick, 1991).
C. Villain-Gandossi, S. Busuttil, and P. Adam (eds.), *Medieval Ships and the Birth of Technological Societies* (2 vols.; Valleta, 1989–91).

12. War and the Non-Combatant in the Middle Ages

C. T. Allmand, 'The War and the Non-Combatant', in K. A. Fowler (ed.), *The Hundred Years War* (London, 1971), 163–83.
P. Contamine, *War in the Middle Ages*, trans. M. Jones (Oxford, 1984).
H. E. J. Cowdrey, 'The Peace and the Truce of God in the Eleventh Century', *Past & Present*, 46 (1970), 42–67.
J. R. Hale, *Artists and Warfare in the Renaissance* (New Haven and London, 1990).
T. Head and R. Landes (eds.), *The Peace of God: Social Violence and Religious Response in France around the Year 1000* (Cornell, NY, 1992).

H. J. Hewitt, *The Organization of War under Edward III, 1338–62* (Manchester and New York, 1966).

C. J. Holdsworth, 'Ideas and Reality: Some Attempts to Control and Defuse War in the Twelfth Century', in W. J. Sheils (ed.), *The Church and War* (Oxford, 1983), 59–78.

J. T. Johnson, *Ideology, Reason and the Limitation of War: Religious and Secular Concepts, 1200–1740* (Princeton, 1975).

B. Lowe, *Imagining Peace. A History of Early English Pacifist Ideas, 1340–1560* (University Park, PA, 1997).

T. Meron, *Henry's Wars and Shakespeare's Laws: Perspectives on the Law of War in the Later Middle Ages* (Oxford, 1993).

F. H. Russell, *The Just War in the Middle Ages* (Cambridge, 1975).

N. A. R. Wright, 'The *Tree of Battles* of Honoré Bouvet and the Laws of War', in C. T. Allmand (ed.), *War, Literature and Politics in the Late Middle Ages* (Liverpool, 1976), 12–31.

—— *Knights and Peasants: The Hundred Years War in the French Countryside* (Woodbridge, 1998).

13. The Changing Scene: Guns, Gunpowder, and Permanent Armies

C. T. Allmand (ed.), *New Cambridge Medieval History*, vii (Cambridge, 1998), ch. 8, 'War'.

F. Babinger, *Mehmed the Conqueror and his Time* (Princeton, 1978).

C. M. Cipolla, *Guns and Sails in the Early Phase of European Expansion (1400–1700)* (London, 1965).

R. C. Clephan, 'The Ordnance of the Fourteenth and Fifteenth Centuries', *Archaeological Journal*, 68 (1911).

P. Contamine, *Guerre, état et société à la fin du moyen age* (Paris, 1972).

A. E. Goodman, *The Wars of the Roses: Military Activity and English Society* (London, 1981).

J. R. Hale, 'The Early Development of the Bastion: An Italian Chronology 1450–*c.*1534', in J. R. Hale, J. R. L. Highfield, and B. Smalley (eds.), *Europe in the Late Middle Ages* (London, 1965), 466–94.

F. G. Heymann, *John Zizka and the Hussite Revolution* (Princeton, 1955).

R. B. Merriman, *The Rise of the Spanish Empire*, ii (New York, 1918).

Sir Charles Oman, *The Art of War in the Middle Ages*, ii (London, 1924).

—— *The Art of War in the Sixteenth Century* (London, 1937).

G. Rázsó, 'The Mercenary Army of King Matthias Corvinus', in J. M. Bak and B. K. Király (eds.), *From Hunyadi to Rakocki: War and Society in Late Medieval and Early Modern Hungary* (Brooklyn, NY, 1982), 125–40.

R. Sablonier, 'États et structures militaires dans la confédération [suisse] autour des années 1480', in *Cinq-centième anniversaire de la bataille de Nancy* (1979), 429–77.

M. G. A. Vale, *War and Chivalry: Warfare and Aristocratic Culture in England, France and Burgundy at the End of the Middle Ages* (London, 1981).

R. Vaughan, *Charles the Bold: The Last Valois Duke of Burgundy* (London, 1973).

CHRONOLOGICAL TABLE OF IMPORTANT DATES AND EVENTS

714	Charles Martel becomes ruler of Francia
717	Victory of Charles Martel over Neustrian Frankish opponents at Vinchy (21 March)
732	Charles Martel defeats Islamic invading forces near Poitiers (17 October): effective end of Moorish threats to penetrate beyond Pyrenees
733–48	Frankish campaigns against Frisia, Burgundy, Provence (733–41); Aleman nia and Bavaria (743–8)
751	Pippin III, father of Charlemagne, becomes King of the Franks
768	Charlemagne becomes King of the Franks
771	Completion of the Frankish conquest of Aquitaine
772–85	Charlemagne's first Saxon war
774	Frankish conquest of Lombardy
778	Frankish campaign in Spain, rearguard of the army ambushed and defeated at Roncevaux (engagement remembered in the *Song of Roland*)
787–8	Frankish conquest of Bavaria
792–803	Charlemagne's second Saxon war
793	Viking sack of Lindisfarne, Northumberland (8 June), marking conventional beginning of the 'Viking Age'
794–5	Numerous Viking raids on islands off the coasts of Scotland and Ireland
795	Charlemagne's army captures the Avar ring, and their treasure: collapse of Avar power follows
799	First recorded Viking raid on Francia, on the monastery of St Philibert on the island of Noirmoutier
800	Charlemagne crowned Emperor in Rome
800–1	Siege of Barcelona by Spanish Muslims

808	Godfred, King of the Danes, reinforces the defensive line of the Danevirke, in Southern Jutland
810	Danish attack on Frisia, large tribute taken
814	Death of Charlemagne: succeeded as Emperor by his son Louis the Pious (814–40)
830–5	Civil wars between Louis the Pious and his sons
834–7	Successive Danish attacks on the major Frankish trading settlement at Dorestad
835	First recorded Danish raid on England, on the Isle of Sheppey (Thames estuary)
837	Two large Norwegian fleets appear on the Boyne and the Liffey: more intensive phase of Viking warfare in Ireland commences
840–3	Following the death of Louis the Pious, civil war reopens between his sons in Francia
841	Battle of Fontenoy (25 June): Lothar (eldest son of Louis) defeated by Charles the Bald and Louis the German (younger sons)
843	Treaty of Verdun: partition of the Frankish empire between Charles the Bald (to be King of West Francia), Louis (King of the Germans), and Lothar (titular Emperor and ruler of the 'Middle Kingdom')
858–9	East Frankish invasion of West Francia
860	Scandinavian 'Rus' attack Constantinople
864	Charles the Bald, at assembly of Pîtres, orders the fortification of strategic bridges in West Francia
865	Landing of the Danish 'Great Army' in East Anglia; inaugurating more intensive 'Viking' warfare in England
869–88	Prolonged internal fighting in Francia over the division of territories, with Italy, Lotharingia, and Burgundy all establishing separate identities
*c.*870	King Harald Fairhair wins naval victory at Hafrsfjord, near Stavanger, and extends his power in Norway
875	Charles the Bald invades Italy
876	Charles the Bald attempts to conquer East Francia, but is defeated at Andernach (8 October)
877	Charles the Bald invades Italy again
878	West Saxons under King Alfred defeat the Danes under Guthrum at Edington (May)
879	Scandinavian forces establish an encampment at Asselt, inaugurating more intensive Viking warfare in the Frankish region (879–91)
881	Franks under King Louis III defeat a Viking army at Saucourt-en-Vimeu (3 August); remembered in the celebratory poem *Ludwigslied*
	Magyar raids on East Francia
882	Charles III the Fat unsuccessfully besieges Asselt

885–6 Long-drawn-out but unsuccessful siege of Paris by Danes under King Sigfred

888 Charles the Fat deposed: Arnulf becomes King of the Franks

891 Vikings engaged in constructing a winter camp on the River Dyle near Louvain are defeated by a Frankish army under Arnulf

895–6 Magyar conquest of the Carpathian basin

895–900 The 'classic' Viking warship, later buried at Gokstad, is built in southern Norway

896 Disbandment of the remnants of the Danish army in England; it returns to Francia

899 Italians under King Berengar defeated by the Magyars at Brenta (24 September)

907 The Russian Prince Oleg attacks Constantinople

910 Danish raiders defeated by King Edward the Elder at Tettenhall (6 August), presaging West Saxon conquest of north-eastern England

911 Treaty of Claire-sur-Epte: the Viking leader Rollo established in the region of future Normandy, by agreement with the West Frankish King Charles the Simple

914 A great Viking fleet arrives at Waterford, inaugurating a second intensive phase of Viking warfare in Ireland

919 Henry I the Fowler, duke of Saxony, becomes King of the East Franks (Germans)

Dublin Vikings annihilate a major Irish army at Islandbridge (14 September): zenith of Scandinavian power in Ireland

923 Battle of Soissons (15 June): Carolingian Charles the Simple of West Francia defeated by Robert, Capetian Count of Paris (killed in the battle): Raoul of Burgundy becomes King of the West Franks

Battle of Fiorenzuola (17 July): Berengar I of Italy defeated by Rudolf II of Burgundy

933 Henry the Fowler, King of East Franks, defeats the Magyars at Riade (15 March)

936(73) Otto I becomes King of East Francia

937 West Saxons under King Æthelstan defeat a coalition led by Olaf Guthfrithsson, King of Dublin, at *Brunanburh*

939 Otto I defeats East Frankish rebels under Henry of Bavaria, Eberhard of Franconia and Giselbert of Lotharingia in two battles, at Birten and at Andernach

941 Varangian naval attack on Constantinople under the leadership of Igor, Prince of Kiev, repulsed by Greek fire

950–1 Otto I's first expedition to Italy

955 Battle of the Lechfeld (10 August): great victory of Otto I over the Magyars

958–67	Ottonian campaigns against Slavs on German eastern borders
962–5	Otto I's second expedition to Italy
962	Otto I crowned Emperor in Rome
967–72	Otto I's third expedition to Italy
973	Death of Otto I, succeeded by Otto II
975	Council of Le Puy: Bishop Guy calls on all good churchmen to respect the property of the church and the poor: and involves Counts of Brioude and Gévaudan in enforcing the council's canons
980	Vikings resume raids on England, marking beginning of the 'second Viking Age'
	Dubliners and their allies from the Scottish Isles defeated at Tara by King Mael Sechnaill of Mide (Meath)
982	Otto II defeated by the Saracens near Stilo in south Italy (July)
983	Death of Otto II: major rising of the Slavs against the Germans on the Elbe frontier
989	Church Council at Charroux imposes penalties on those who attack churches, clerks, peasants, and their beasts
991	A local English force under Ealdorman Byrtnoth is defeated by Danish Vikings at Maldon, Essex (10? August); commemorated in the poem *The Battle of Maldon*
1000	Olaf Tryggvason, King of Norway, defeated and killed in battle against Sven Forkbeard, King of Denmark, at Svold
1003–18	Campaigns of Emperor Henry II, King of East Franks, against the Poles.
1008	Death of Abd al Malik; break up of the Muslim Caliphate of Córdoba (Spain)
1014	A Leinster and Dublin Viking coalition, along with Viking allies from the Isle of Man and the Scottish Isles, is defeated by Brian Bórama (Brian Boru), King of Munster, at Clontarf (23 April)
1015	Pisans and Genoese commence attacks on Muslims of Corsica and Sardinia
1016	Danish defeat of King Edmund Ironside at Ashingdon (18 October) leads to the temporary partition of England
	Cnut of Denmark becomes King of England, following the death (30 November) of Edmund Ironside
1018	Byzantine Greeks defeat Lombards and Norman mercenaries at Cannae (S. Italy, early October)
1023	Peace Council at Beauvais, which imposes an 'oath of peace'
1026	Danes win naval victory over Swedes at Stangebjerg
1027	Church Council at Toulouges proclaims Truce of God, limiting fighting to certain days of the week (Mon.–Wed.), and banning it in Advent and Lent

1028	Danes win naval victory over Swedes and Norwegians at Helgeå
1030	Norman leader Rainulf becomes lord of Aversa (S. Italy)
	Olaf Haraldsson, exiled King of Norway, is defeated and killed at Stiklestad (30 June)
1038–41	Last Greek Byzantine expedition to Sicily, under George Maniaces
1041	Norman victory over the Greeks at Cannae
1046	Arrival in Italy of Robert Guiscard, future Norman leader, in Southern Italy
1047	William Duke of Normandy defeats Norman rebels at Val-ès-Dunes (January)
1051	Norman victory over forces assembled by Pope Leo IX at Civitate, S. Italy (23 June)
1054	Church Council of Narbonne forbids the shedding of Christian blood by Christians
1059	Pope Nicholas II at Melfi recognizes Robert Guiscard as Duke of Apulia
1061	Normans under Roger de Hauteville first invade Sicily
1064	Capture of Coimbra (Spain) from the Moors
1066	Battles of Fulford (20 September), Stamford Bridge (25 September), and Hastings (14 October); Harald Hardrada, King of Norway, defeated and killed at Stamford Bridge, Harold of England at Hastings. William of Normandy becomes King of England
1071	Robert Guiscard takes Bari (S. Italy). Seljuk Turks under Alp Arslan defeat the Byzantines under Emperor Romanus Diogenes at Mantzikert (26 August)
1072	Palermo (Sicily) taken by the Normans
1073	Revolt of the Saxons against Henry IV of Germany
	Amalfi taken by the Normans
1075	Henry IV defeats the Saxons on the Unstrut (9 June)
1077–1122	Wars of Investiture in Germany and Italy, between Emperors Henry IV and V and supporters of the papacy
1078	Henry IV defeated by the Saxons at Mellrichstadt (7 August)
1080	Henry IV defeated by the Saxons at Flarchheim (27 January) and again on the Elster (15 October)
1085	Capture of Toledo (Spain) from the Moors
	Capture of Syracuse (Sicily) by the Normans
1085–6	Threatened Danish invasion of England precipitates mobilization of troops, followed by the Domesday survey of the country
1086	Henry IV defeated by the Saxons and others at Pleichfeld (11 August)
	Alfonso VI of Castile defeated by the Almoravids at Sagrajas (23 October)
1088	Baronial rebellion against William II of England, quashed after William's

	successful siege of Rochester
1091	Completion of the Norman Conquest of Sicily
1094	Capture of Valencia by the Cid from the Moors (recaptured 1102)
1095	Pope Urban II preaches the First Crusade at the Council of Clermont. At the same council, the Pope endorses the principles of the Peace of God
1096	First Crusade armies reach Constantinople, and confer with Greek Emperor Alexius I Comnenus.
	Church Council at Rouen affirms the Peace of God, on the basis of the Clermont decree
1097–8	Crusaders besiege and finally take Antioch (October 1097–June 1098)
1099	Crusaders capture Jerusalem (15 July) and found the crusader Kingdom of Jerusalem
1104	Foundation of the Arsenal of Venice
1106	Henry I of England defeats Duke Robert of Normandy at Tinchebrai (28 September) and reunites England and Normandy
1109	Crusaders capture Tripoli (12 July)
1115	Henry V of Germany defeated by the Saxons at Welfesholz (11 February); end of the Saxon wars
1119	Roger, crusader Prince of Antioch, defeated and killed at the Battle of Blood (Darb Sarmada: 28 June)
	Henry I of England defeats forces of Louis VI of France at the Battle of Brémule (20 August)
1124	Battle of Bourgthéroulde (26 March); Anglo-Norman victory over the French.
	Crusaders, aided by Venetian fleet, capture Tyre (7 July)
1127	Roger II of Sicily seizes Apulia after the death of William of Apulia
	Zengi becomes governor of Mosul; beginnings of Muslim recovery in Syria and Mesopotamia
1130	Roger II proclaimed King of Sicily
1135	Stephen succeeds Henry I as King of England and Duke of Normandy, despite claims of Henry's daughter Matilda, wife of Geoffrey of Anjou
1136–44	Geoffrey of Anjou overruns Normandy
1138	David I of Scotland defeated by the English at the Battle of the Standard (22 August)
1139–53	Civil war in England between followers of Stephen and Matilda
1141	King Stephen captured at the Battle of Lincoln (2 February)
1144–6	County of Edessa conquered from the crusaders by Zengi
1146	Death of Zengi; succeeded by his sons
1147–8	Second Crusade to Syria; ends with the failure of the crusaders before Damascus (July 1148)

1147	Henry the Lion of Saxony, aided by Albrecht the Bear and Adolf of Holstein, leads a German crusade against the Slavs east of the Elbe
	Alfonso VII of Castile takes Almeria from the Moors (7 October), and the Portuguese take Lisbon (24 October)
1148	Raymond Berengar of Barcelona and the Aragonese take Tortosa
1153	Christians under King Baldwin III of Jerusalem capture Ascalon
1154	Nur al-Din, son of Zengi, becomes ruler of Damascus (until his death in 1174)
1155	Emperor Frederick Barbarossa's first expedition to Italy
1160–2	Frederick Barbarossa besieges and finally takes Milan
1163–9	Crusaders under King Amaury of Jerusalem compete with Nur al-Din Din's lieutenants, Shirkuh and Saladin, for control of Fatimed Egypt
1167–77	Renewed wars of Frederick Barbarossa with the cities of the Lombard League
1169	Saladin becomes Vizir of Egypt
1171–2	Henry II of England's expedition to Ireland
1173	French and Scots support rebellion against Henry II
1174	King William of Scotland captured at Alnwick; end of the rebellion against Henry II
	Saladin establishes control over both Egypt and Damascus, following death of Nur al-Din
1176	Frederick Barbarossa defeated by the Milanese at Legnano (29 May)
1177	Saladin defeated at Montgisard (25 November) by the forces of the 'leper king', Baldwin IV of Jerusalem
1187	Battle of Hattin (4 July): Saladin defeats the crusaders under King Guy de Lusignan and overruns most of the Kingdom of Jerusalem, including the Holy City
1188–92	The Third Crusade
1189–91	Crusaders besiege and finally, under leadership of Philip Augustus of France and Richard I of England, take Acre (July 1191)
1191–2	Richard the Lionheart of England, on crusade, campaigns in Southern Palestine
1191	Battle of Arsur (6 September); victory of Richard the Lionheart over Saladin
1192	Richard the Lionheart leaves Holy Land from Acre: end of Third Crusade
1193	Death of Saladin
1194–1204	Wars of Philip II Augustus of France against Richard and John of England, in Normandy and the Loire Valley
1194	Richard I defeats Philip of France at Fréteval (4 July)
	Emperor Henry VI, son of Frederick Barbarossa, conquers Kingdom of

Sicily

1195 Alfonso VIII of Castile defeated by the Almohads at Alarcos (19 July)

1197 Richard I builds a new castle, Château Gaillard, to dominate the Seine at Les Andelys

1204 Latin Forces of the Fourth Crusade capture Constantinople from the Greeks

Conquest of Normandy by the French, from King John of England

1209–29 Albigensian Crusade against the heretics of Languedoc: northern French crusading hosts led initially by Simon de Montfort (d. 1218) and later under royal leadership

1212 Battle of Las Navas de Tolosa (16 July): victory of King Peter of Aragon over the Moorish Almohads

1213 Battle of Muret (12 September): victory of the northern French crusaders led by Simon de Montfort over the confederation of King Peter of Aragon, Count Raymond VI of Toulouse and the lords of Languedoc

1214 Battle of Bouvines (27 July): victory of Philip II Augustus of France over the allies of John of England, who included Otto IV of Germany, the Count of Flanders, and Rainald of Dammartin

1215–17 Civil war in England, rebel barons, backed by Prince Louis of France, oppose first King John, and after his death supporters of his son Henry III

1217–21 Fifth Crusade

1217 Battle of Lincoln (20 May); William Marshal, for Henry III, defeats rebel barons and French led by Prince Louis

Battle of Sandwich (24 August); English naval victory over French fleet of Eustace the Monk

1217–18 Unsuccessful siege of Toulouse by Albigensian crusaders; Simon de Montfort killed in its course

1219 Christian forces of Fifth Crusade capture Damietta (5 November) on the Nile delta

1221 Fifth Crusade surrounded in the Nile delta and surrenders (30 August); Damietta evacuated

1228–9 Crusade of the Emperor Frederick II: Jerusalem reoccupied by the Christians after negotiations with Sultan of Egypt

1229 Teutonic Order begins the conquest of Prussia

Conquest of Majorca by Jaume I of Aragon

1237 Battle of Cortenuova (27 November): victory of Frederick II over the forces of the second Lombard League

1241 Mongol invasion of eastern Europe: they defeat the Poles at Leignitz and the Hungarians at Mohi (April)

1244 Khorasmians storm and take Jerusalem (23 August): subsequently combined Khorasmian and Egyptian forces defeat the Syrian crusader army

	at La Forbie (17 October)
1248	Frederick II defeated by his Italian enemies at Parma (19 February)
	Conquest of Seville by Ferdinand III of Castile
1248–54	First crusade of King Louis IX of France
1250	Louis IX overwhelmed and captured (6 April) at Mansourah (Egypt): on release withdraws to Syria (Acre)
1254	Foundation of Königsberg (Prussia) by the Teutonic Knights
	Louis IX returns to France
1260	Mamluks of Egypt defeat the Mongols at 'Ain Jalut' (3 September)
	Victory of the Italian Ghibellines over the Guelfs at Montaperti (4 September)
1260–77	Reign of Sultan Baybars of Egypt and Syria
1261	Byzantine recapture of Constantinople
1264	Battle of Lewes (14 May): victory of Simon de Montfort the Younger and rebel English barons over King Henry III
1265	Battle of Evesham (4 August): Simon de Montfort defeated and killed by Lord Edward, son of Henry III
1265–8	Charles Count of Anjou invades Italy, as champion of the Church and the Guelfs against Manfred of Sicily and the Ghibellines
1266	Charles of Anjou defeats Manfred at Benevento (26 February), and makes good his title as King of Sicily
	Baybars captures Saphet (Syria) from the crusaders
1268	Charles of Anjou defeats the German and Ghibelline forces of Conradin at Tagliacozzo (23 August): Conradin executed
	Baybars captures Beaufort, Jaffa, and Antioch
1270	Second crusade of Louis IX, to Tunis: death of Louis IX (25 August)
1271	Baybars captures Crac des Chevaliers
1277–83	Edward I of England conquers Wales
1278	Battle of Durnkrut/Marchfield (26 August): German Emperor, Rudolf of Habsburg, with Hungarian support, defeats Ottokar of Bohemia
1282–1302	War of the Sicilian Vespers; following rising of the Sicilians against Charles of Anjou and Aragonese intervention in their support
1283	Catalans under Roger Loria win naval victory over the Angevin fleet off Malta (8 June)
1284	Battle of Meloria (6 August): Genoese naval victory over the Pisans
1285	Unsuccessful French invasion of Aragon
	Catalan victory over French fleet off Palamos (4 September)
	Muslim capture of Marqab
1289	Muslim capture of Tripoli

1291	Muslim capture of Acre (18 May): end of the Frankish states in Syria and Palestine
1294	French establish the *Clos des Galées* (naval arsenal) at Rouen
1294–7	Anglo-French war, chief field of operations in Gascony
1296	Commencement of Edward I's Scottish wars
1297	Victory of the Scots under William Wallace over the English at Stirling Bridge (11 September)
1298	Victory of Edward I over the Scots at Falkirk (22 July)
1302	Battle of Courtrai (11 July): Flemings defeat King Philip IV and the French
	Treaty of Caltabellotta: end of the war of the Sicilian Vespers
1303–12	Following the Treaty of Caltabellotta, Catalan companies engaged on the Sicilian side first take service with the Byzantine Emperor (1303), subsequently with the Duke of Athens; and after turning against both, establish the Catalan Duchy of Athens
1311	Battle of Kephissos (15 March): mercenaries of the Catalan Company defeat the Frankish Duke of Athens
1314	Battle of Bannockburn (23–4 June): Robert Bruce defeats the English royal army of Edward II
1315	Battle of Mortgarten (15 November): Swiss victory over the Austrians
1324–5	War of St Sardos between French and English in Aquitaine
1328	Battle of Cassell (28 August): French under Philip VI defeat the Flemings
1330	Battle of Posada (November): Wallachians defeat the Hungarians
1332	English troops defeat a larger Scottish army at Dupplin Moor (8 August)
1333	Battle of Halidon Hill (19 July): Edward III victorious over the Scots
1337	Opening of the Hundred Years War between England and France
1339	Battle of Laupen (21 June): victory of the Swiss (of Berne) over a coalition of Fribourg, the Bishop of Basle, and local nobles
1340	Battle of Sluys (24 June): major English naval victory over the French
	Iberian powers defeat a Moorish fleet at Tarifa (30 October)
1342	Werner of Urslingen's mercenary company established in Italy
1346	Battle of Crécy (26 August): English under Edward III defeat the French under Philip VI
	Battle of Neville's Cross (17 October): Scottish invaders defeated by the English
1346–7	Edward III besieges Calais and starves it into surrender (September 1346–August 1347)
1347	Hungarian troops enter Italy in support of Queen Joanna I of Naples
1347–50	First outbreak of plague (the Black Death) in Europe
1349	Battle of Meleto: mercenaries under Fra Moriale, Werner of Urslingen, and Conrad of Landau, fighting for Joanna I, defeat army of the

	Neapolitan barons
1354	Execution in Rome of the mercenary captain, Fra Moriale
1356	Battle of Poitiers (19 September): Edward the Black Prince defeats and captures King John II of France
1360	Peace of Brétigny between England and France: Aquitaine ceded to the English as an independent principality
1366–70	War of Succession in Castile; King Pedro the Cruel (formally allied with England) challenged for the throne by his bastard brother, Henry of Trastamare, with French support. Pedro driven out 1366
1367	Battle of Nájera (3 April): Franco Castilian army of Henry of Trastamare defeated by Edward the Black Prince, in alliance with Pedro the Cruel, who is restored to Castilian throne
1369	Reopening of the Anglo-French war
1370	Battle of Montiel (14 March): French mercenaries under Du Guesclin defeat Pedro the Cruel who is afterwards killed: Henry of Trastamare becomes King of Castile
1377	Franco-Castilian fleet raids the English south coast (summer): Rye and Portsmouth damaged
1378	Outbreak of the Great Schism in the Papacy, between Roman and Avignonese Popes
1379	Battle of Marino (30 April): Alberigo da Barbiano, in service of Pope Urban VI, defeats the Breton mercenary companies supporting the Avignonese Pope Clement VII
1382	Battle of Westrozebeke (27 November): French troops crush Flemish rebels
1385	Battle of Aljubarotta (14 August): Anglo-Portuguese army of James of Aviz defeats the Castilians
1386	Battle of Sempach (9 July): Swiss victory over the Austrians
1387	Battle of Castagnaro (11 March): Sir John Hawkwood, in service of Padua, defeats the Veronese
1394	Death of Sir John Hawkwood
1396	Battle of Nicopolis (25 September): the Ottoman Sultan Bayazid I defeats the combined army of the Hungarians and French crusaders
1402	Death of Gian Galeazzo Visconti, Duke of Milan
	Ottoman Sultan Bayazid defeated and taken prisoner in battle near Ankara (20 July) by Timur the Tartar
1410	Battle of Tannenburg (15 July): Teutonic Knights defeated by the Poles and Lithuanians
1415	Battle of Agincourt (25 October): Henry V's great victory over the French
1416	Battle of San Egidio: Braccio de Montone, *condottiere* captain, defeats the Perugians

1417	Henry V invades Normandy, and takes Caen and Alençon
1418–19	Henry V besieges Rouen and starves it into surrender (August 1418–January 1419)
1420	Treaty of Troyes: Henry V recognized by Charles VI and the Burgundians as heir of France
	First German crusade against the Bohemian Hussites: repulsed by Zizka at the Vitkov (14 July)
1421	Battle of Baugé (22 March): Franco-Scottish army defeats the English under the Duke of Clarence
1422	Battle of Arbedo (30 June): Milanese defeat the Swiss
	Death of King Henry V (31 August)
1424	Zizka triumphs in the civil war of the Hussites at Malesor (7 June)
	Battle of Verneuil, the 'second Agincourt' (17 August): Franco-Scottish army defeated by John Duke of Bedford, Regent of France
1428–9	English siege of Orléans (October 1428–May 1429): broken up by Joan of Arc
1429	Battle of Patay (18 June): English defeated by Joan of Arc
1431	Frederick of Brandenberg, leading Imperial forces, defeated by the Hussites at Taus (14 August)
1434	Battle of Lipany (30 May): Catholic and moderate Hussite nobles defeat the radical Hussite Taborites and Orphans led by Zizka's successor, Prokop the Bald: effective end of the Hussite wars
1435	Peace Congress of Arras; Philip Duke of Burgundy leaves the English alliance and renews loyalty to Charles VII of France
1442	Alfonso V of Aragon seizes the throne of Naples
1444	French defeat a small Swiss army at St Jacob-en-Birs (24 August)
	Battle of Varna (10 November): Hungarian and Polish crusading army de feated by the Ottomans
1448	Battle of Caravaggio (15 September): Milanese defeat the Venetians on land
	Battle of Kossovo Polje (18–19 October): Ottomans defeat Hungarians under John Hunyadi
1449	French recover Rouen from the English with little fighting (October)
1450	Battle of Formigny (15 April): English field army under Sir Thomas Kyriell defeated by the French: followed by final collapse of English in Normandy (August)
1453	Sultan Mehmet II the Conqueror besieges Constantinople (April–May) and captures the city for the Ottomans
	Battle of Castillon (17 July): English field army in Gascony led by John Talbot Earl of Shrewsbury defeated by the French
1454	Peace of Lodi, between the major Italian states (Florence, Venice, Milan,

	the Papacy, and later including Naples)
1455	Battle of St Albans (22 May): victory of the Yorkist lords in the first engagement of the Wars of the Roses in England
1456	John Hunyadi successfully defends Belgrade against the Turks
1459–67	Turkish conquest of most of the southern Balkans: Serbia (1459); the Morea (1460); Bosnia (1464); Herzegovina (1467)
1460	Yorkists defeat and capture Henry VI of Lancaster at Northampton (10 July); but are defeated by his Queen Margaret at Wakefield (30 December)
1461	Battle of Towton (29 March): Yorkist victory clinches Edward IV's position as King of England
1465	War of the Public Weal in France: indecisive engagement at Monthléry (16 July) between the forces of Louis XI and those of the League, under Charles of Charolais, future Charles the Bold of Burgundy
1471	Edward IV returns to England from Flanders, and defeats Lancastrians at Barnet (14 April) and Tewkesbury (4 May)
1472	Hostilities between France and Burgundy
1475	Charles the Bold of Burgundy unsuccessfully besieges Neuss
	Edward IV invades France, but comes to terms with Louis XI at Picquigny
1476	Charles the Bold of Burgundy defeated by the Swiss at Grandson (2 March) and Morat (22 June)
1477	Charles the Bold defeated and killed at the battle of Nancy (5 January)
	Maximilian of Austria marries Mary, heiress of Burgundy; leading to further hostilities with Louis XI
1479	Louis XI's forces defeated by Maximilian at Guinegate (7 August)
	Union of Aragon and Castile under Ferdinand and Isabella
1480	First, unsuccessful, siege of Rhodes by the Turks
1481	Commencement under Ferdinand and Isabella, of new war of reconquest from the Moors in southern Spain
1485	Battle of Bosworth (22 August): victory of Henry Tudor over Richard III of England
1492	Fall of Granada (2 January) to the Spaniards: final completion of the wars of reconquest from the Moors
1494	Charles VIII invades Italy, in pursuit of French claims in Naples
1495	Charles VIII enters Naples: at Fornovo (14 July) defeats the forces of the League of Venice, formed to oppose him
1499	Accession of Louis XII of France; preparations for a renewed Italian offensive
	Beginning of Turkish-Venetian war
1500	Louis XII takes Milan

1502	French and Spaniards at war in Italy over the Kingship of Naples
1503	Gonsalvo de Córdoba, 'the Great Captain' for Spain, defeats the French at Cerignola (April) and at Garigliano (28 December)
1515	Battle of Marj Dabiq (24 August): Ottomans defeat the Egyptian Mamluks
	Battle of Marignano (14–15 September): Swiss in the pay of Milan defeated by the French
1516	Battle of Raydaniya (23 January): Ottomans again defeat the Mamluks
1525	Battle of Pavia (25 February): victory of the Emperor Charles V over the French under Francis I, who is taken prisoner
1526	Battle of Mohács (28 August): Ottomans under Süleyman the Magnificent defeat the Hungarians

ILLUSTRATION SOURCES

The editor and publishers wish to thank the following for their kind permission to reproduce the illustrations on the following pages:

Key: BL=British Library BN=Bibliothèque Nationale de France

Chapter and part-title openings are of the Courtrai chest by kind permission of the Warden and Fellows of New College, Oxford

11, 13 Warden and Fellows of New College, Oxford

15, 16 Nicholas Hooper & Matthew Bennett *The Cambridge Illustrated Atlas of Warfare: The Middle Ages, 768–1487* (Cambridge University Press 1996)

20 Bibliotheek der Rijksuniversiteit, Leiden (Periz F 17 fol 22r)

21 Glasgow Museums: Art Gallery & Museum, Kelvingrove

22, 23 Württembergische Landesbibliothek / Bildarchiv Foto Marburg (Cod. bibl. fol 3, 12v, 21v)

29 Stiftsbibliothek St Gallen (Cod.Sang.22 s.141 Nr 17)

32 Bibliotheek der Rijksuniversiteit, Leiden (Periz F 17 fol 9r)

37, 39 Antikvarisk-topografiska arkivet, Stockholm

40 English Heritage Photo Library

43 University Museum of National Antiquities Oslo, Norway, photo by E Schwitters

46 Donald Scragg 'The Battle of Maldon' Blackwell, 1991

48 Antikvarisk-topografiska arkivet, Stockholm

50 Andromeda Oxford Ltd

52 University Museum of National Antiquities Oslo, Norway

53 Antikvarisk-topografisca arkivet, Stockholm

56 University Museum of National Antiquities Oslo, Norway, photo by Ove Holst

60 Master and Fellows of Trinity College, Cambridge (Ms o.9.34 f.24r)

67 The Pierpont Morgan Library / Art Resource, NY (M 638 f 24v)

68–9 A. F. Kersting

72 Jean Dieuzaide, Toulouse

77 The Pierpont Morgan Library / Art Resource, NY (M 736 f 7v)

79 BN (Ms fr 9083 f 142)

82 Staatsbibliothek zu Berlin—Preussischer Kulturbesitz (Ms.germ. fol. 282, fol. 46r)

84 Public Record Office Image Library (E36 / 274)

86 Fitzwilliam Museum, Cambridge (Ms Marlay Add 1 f86r)

96–7 A. F. Kersting

101 BN (Ms fr 2630 f 22v)

102 Sonia Halliday Photographs, photo by Jane Taylor

104 **top**, Denys Pringle

104 **bottom**, Denys Pringle 'The Red Tower', drawing by Peter E. Leach, British School of Archaeology in Jerusalem

105 M. Benvenisti 'Crusaders in the Holy Land' Israel Universities Press, Jerusalem 1970

106 Sonia Halliday Photographs, photo by Jane Taylor

108 BN (Ms fr 9084 f 64v)

110 Biblioteca Medicea Laurenziana, Florence (Ms Plut 61.10 c 33)

111 BN (Ms fr 2630 f 111v)

114–15 Warden and Fellows of New College, Oxford

116 BL (Ms Roy 2AXII f 220)
119 Musée Atger (Ms 49 f 206r) / le service photographique de la Bibliothèque Interuniversitaire de Montpellier
121 Giraudon
124 BL (Ms Stowe 553 f 61v)
127 Institut Amatller d'Art Hispanic (Palacio Real Mayor, Barcelona)
128 The Pierpont Morgan Library / Art Resource, NY (M 638 f 27v)
130 © CNMHS
132 BL (Ms Lansdowne f 23v)
138 © Stadsarchief, Ghent, photo by C. Hourez
140 Based on J. F. Verbruggen 'De Krijgskunst in West Europa in de Middelenwen' 1954 Verhandelungen van de Koninklijke Vlaamse Academie voor Wetenschappen, Letteren en Schone Kunsten van Belgie; Klasse der Letteren, Verhandeling 20
143 BN (Ms fr 2643 f 207)
145 BL (Ms Roy 20 CVII f 137)
147 BL (Ms Add 15269 f 178v)
152 BN (Ms fr 2644 f 135)
155 Giraudon (Archives Nationales Inv. Vitr. 41N)
156 **top** The Governing Body of Christ Church, Oxford (Ms 92 f 70v)
156 **centre** © Stadsarchief, Ghent, photo by C. Hourez
156 **bottom** Bildarchiv der Österreichischen Nationalbibliothek, Vienna
159 BL (AC 801 / 9 Jab IV) H Toman Husitske 'Valecnictvi . . .' 1898
167 The Bodleian Library, Oxford (Ms Junius 11 f 81)
169 V&A Picture Library
173 Giraudon
174 BN (Ms Latin 11015 f 47)
177 © CNMHS photo by Lonchampt
178 **top** Aerofilms
178 **bottom** A. F. Kersting
181 The Board of Trustees of the Armouries (I.34)
184 BN (Ms Latin 6067 f 55v)
187 Archivi Alinari
189 Universitätsbibliothek Heidelberg (Cod.Pal. Germ.848 f 237r)
194 BL (Ms Add 47682 f 40)
196 Országos Széchényi Könyvtár, Budapest
200 **left** BL (Ms Cotton XI f53)
200 **right** Primási Levéltár, Archivum Primatiale, Esztergom
201 Syndics of Cambridge University Library (E. M. Beloe 'Monumental Brasses of Nofolk' 1890)
203 Országos Széchényi Könyvtár, Budapest
204 BL (Ms Cotton Julius EIV f 4)
206 Trustees of the Wallace Collection
212 V&A Picture Library
216 Giraudon (Bibliothèque de l'Arsenal, Paris)
220 Archivi Alinari
221 Archivio di Stato, Siena, photo by Lensini
224 © photo RMN
226 BL (Ms Roy 16 GIX f 76v)
227 Burgerbibliothek, Bern (Mss. h.h. I 1–3)
233 BN (Atlas by Petrus Vesconte 1313 GE DD 687, f5)
234–5 Biblioteca Marciana, Venice (Cod. marc. Gr.Z.479(=881) f 23r), photo by Toso
237 Burgerbibliothek, Bern (Cod 120 II f 119r)
238 Institut Amatller d'Art Hispanic (Biblioteca Nacional, Madrid; Sinopsis Historiarum Juan Skylitzes)
240–1 BL
243 Olaus Magnus 'Description of the Northern Peoples' Hakluyt Society, reprinted by permission of David Higham Associates, photo by The Warburg Institute
246 BN (Ms Ars 5187 f59)
248 Institut Amatller d'Art Hispanic
256–7 Oeffentliche Kunstsammlung Basel, Kupferstichkabinett (Einblattholzschnitt 'Die Schlacht bei Dornach') photo by Oeffentliche Kunstsammlung Basel, Martin Bühler
262 BL (Ms Roy 20 C VII f 41v)
266 Oeffentliche Kunstsammlung Basel, Kupferstichkabinett (Urs Graf 'Armloses Mädchen mit Stelzfuss') photo by Oeffentliche Kunstsammlung Basel, Martin Bühler
270 The J. Paul Getty Museum, Los Angeles (Ms Ludwig IX.7 f 96v 'Llangattock Hours' 1450–1460 tempera, gold paint and gold leaf on vellum bound between wood boards covered with original brown calf 26.4 x 18.4 cm)
271 © British Museum
275 Syndics of Cambridge University Library ('Archaeological Journal', Volume LXVIII 1911 p75)
276 Crown copyright: reproduced by permission of Historic Scotland
277 Copyright Bibliothèque royale Albert 1er, Brussels (Ms 8 f 65v)
279 Archivi Alinari
281 BN
282 The Pierpont Morgan Library / Art Resource, NY (M. 801, f 109v)
285 BN (Ms Fr 23963 f2)
288–9 Ashmolean Museum, Oxford 'The Battle of Pavia' detail

Picture research by Sandra Assersohn

INDEX

Page numbers in bold type refer to illustrations and maps; further textual reference is indicated in bold italics